702

MONKEY FOOD

The Complete

"I WAS SEVEN iN '75"

Collection

by *ellen forney*

D1504913

FANTAGRAPHiCS BOOKS, iNC.
SEATTLE

2

 FOR MOM & DAD & MATT.

SEATTLE CARTOONIST/ILLUSTRATOR ELLEN FORNEY'S WEEKLY COMIC STRIP "I WAS SEVEN IN '75" HAS APPEARED IN NEWSPAPERS THE STRANGER (SEATTLE), THE ROCKET (SEATTLE), CITY PAGES (MINNEAPOLIS), AND THE AUSTIN CHRONICLE, & IN PULSE! MAGAZINE. HER WORK HAS APPEARED IN NUMEROUS MAGAZINES, NEWSPAPERS, BOOKS, AND WEB SITES, AND HAS BEEN INKED ONTO AT LEAST ONE HUMAN BEING. SHE DRIVES A MERCURY COUGAR (V8, 302) THAT, LIKE SHE, WAS INTRODUCED INTO THE WORLD IN 1968.

ellenforney @ halcyon.com
www.ellenforney.com

EXCERPTS FROM Forever... © 1957 BY JUDY BLUME (POCKET BOOKS, A DIVISION OF SIMON AND SCHUSTER, NEW YORK).

FANTAGRAPHICS BOOKS: 7563 LAKE CITY WAY NE, SEATTLE, WA 98115

WRITTEN, DRAWN & DESIGNED BY ellen forney
PUBLISHED BY GARY GROTH & KIM THOMPSON

ISBN: 1-56097-362-5   PRINTED IN CANADA

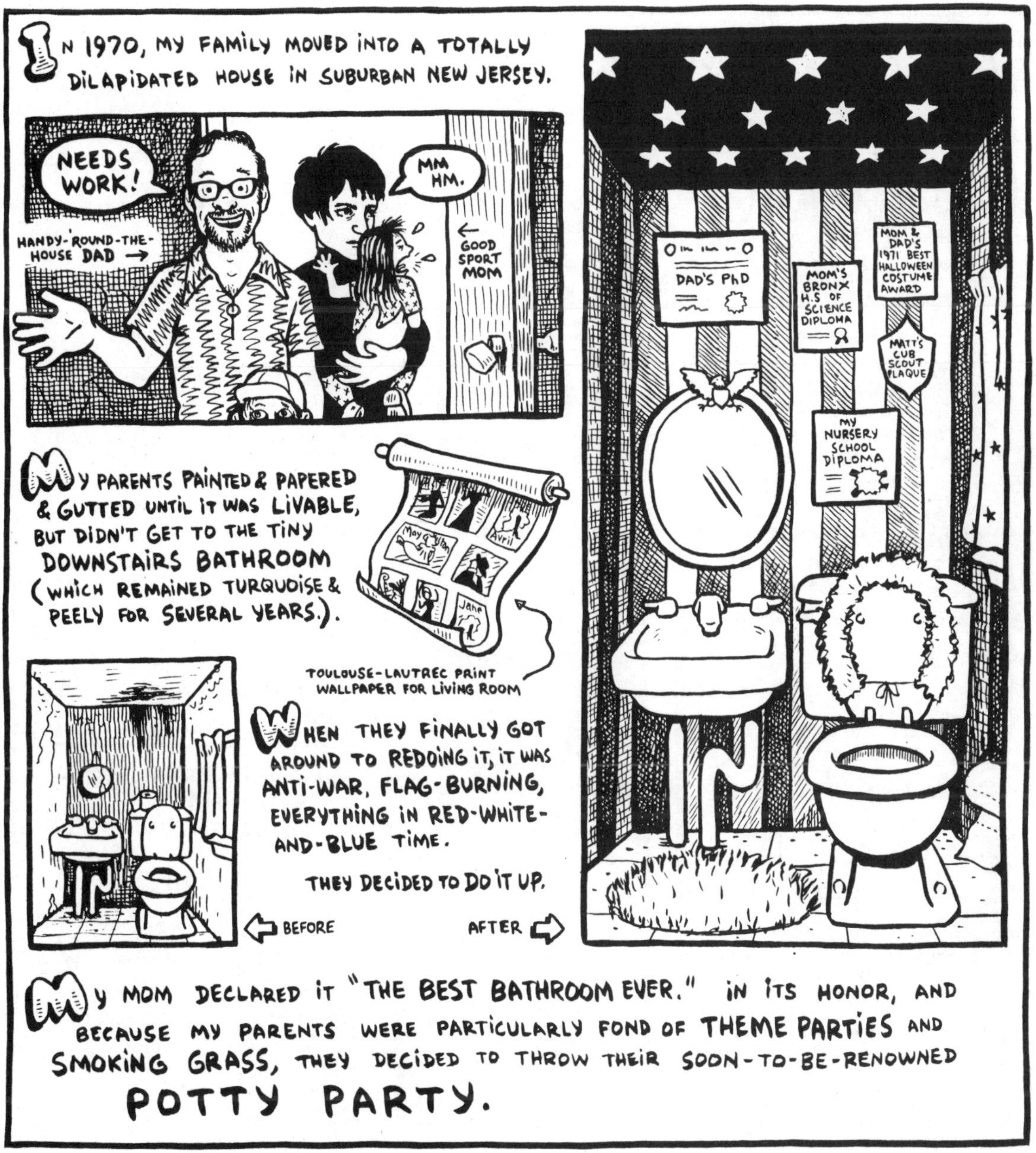
IN 1970, MY FAMILY MOVED INTO A TOTALLY DILAPIDATED HOUSE IN SUBURBAN NEW JERSEY.
NEEDS WORK!
HANDY-'ROUND-THE-HOUSE DAD →
MM HM.
← GOOD SPORT MOM
MY PARENTS PAINTED & PAPERED & GUTTED UNTIL IT WAS LIVABLE, BUT DIDN'T GET TO THE TINY DOWNSTAIRS BATHROOM (WHICH REMAINED TURQUOISE & PEELY FOR SEVERAL YEARS.).
Avril
Jane
TOULOUSE-LAUTREC PRINT WALLPAPER FOR LIVING ROOM
WHEN THEY FINALLY GOT AROUND TO REDOING IT, IT WAS ANTI-WAR, FLAG-BURNING, EVERYTHING IN RED-WHITE-AND-BLUE TIME.
THEY DECIDED TO DO IT UP.
BEFORE
AFTER
DAD'S PhD
MOM'S BRONX H.S OF SCIENCE DIPLOMA
MOM & DAD'S 1971 BEST HALLOWEEN COSTUME AWARD
MATT'S CUB SCOUT PLAQUE
MY NURSERY SCHOOL DIPLOMA
MY MOM DECLARED IT "THE BEST BATHROOM EVER." IN ITS HONOR, AND BECAUSE MY PARENTS WERE PARTICULARLY FOND OF THEME PARTIES AND SMOKING GRASS, THEY DECIDED TO THROW THEIR SOON-TO-BE-RENOWNED POTTY PARTY.

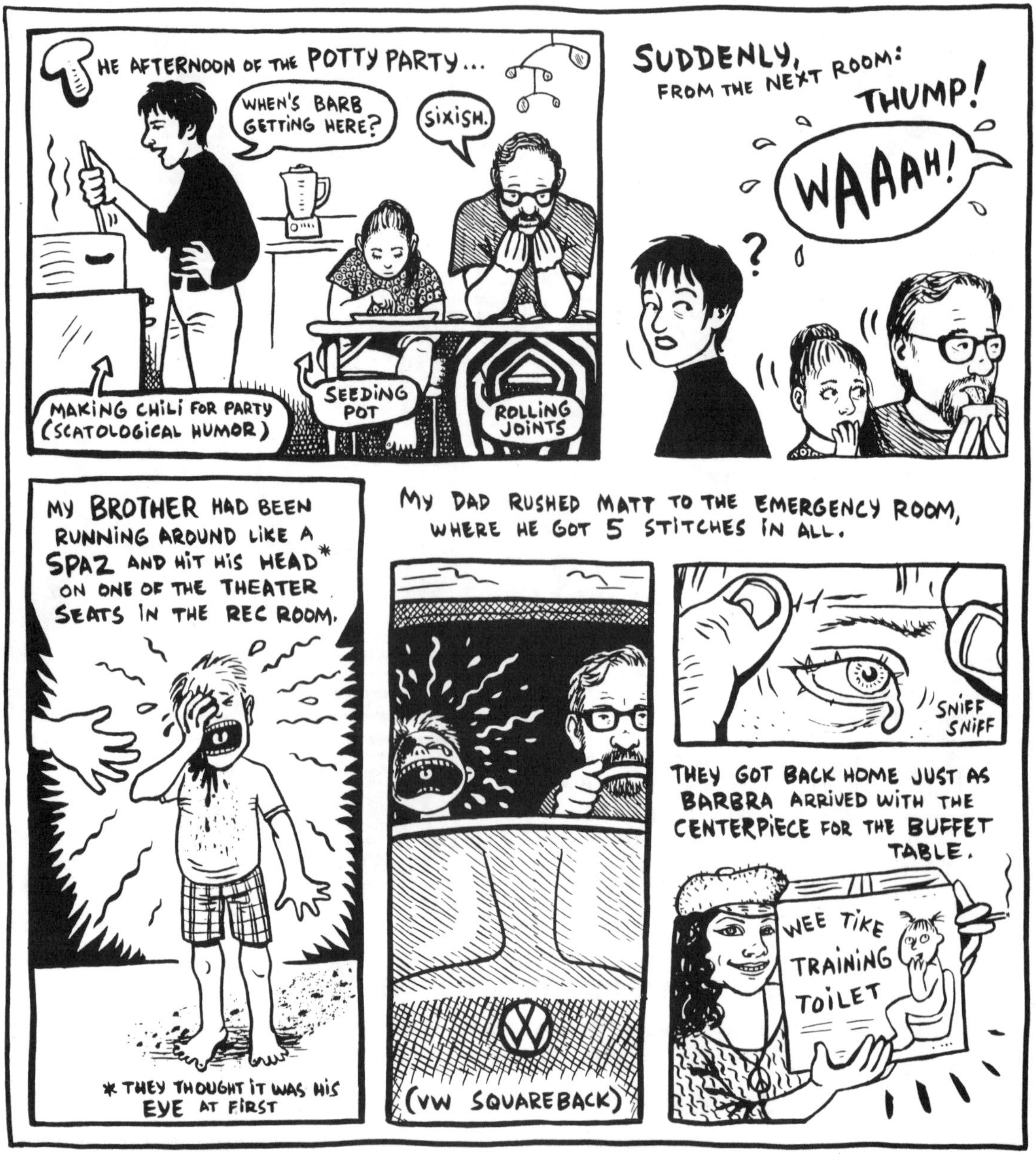
THE AFTERNOON OF THE POTTY PARTY...
WHEN'S BARB GETTING HERE?
SIXISH.
MAKING CHILI FOR PARTY (SCATOLOGICAL HUMOR)
SEEDING POT
ROLLING JOINTS
SUDDENLY, FROM THE NEXT ROOM:
THUMP!
WAAAH!
?
MY BROTHER HAD BEEN RUNNING AROUND LIKE A SPAZ AND HIT HIS HEAD* ON ONE OF THE THEATER SEATS IN THE REC ROOM.
* THEY THOUGHT IT WAS HIS EYE AT FIRST
MY DAD RUSHED MATT TO THE EMERGENCY ROOM, WHERE HE GOT 5 STITCHES IN ALL.
(VW SQUAREBACK)
SNIFF SNIFF
THEY GOT BACK HOME JUST AS BARBRA ARRIVED WITH THE CENTERPIECE FOR THE BUFFET TABLE.
WEE TIKE TRAINING TOILET

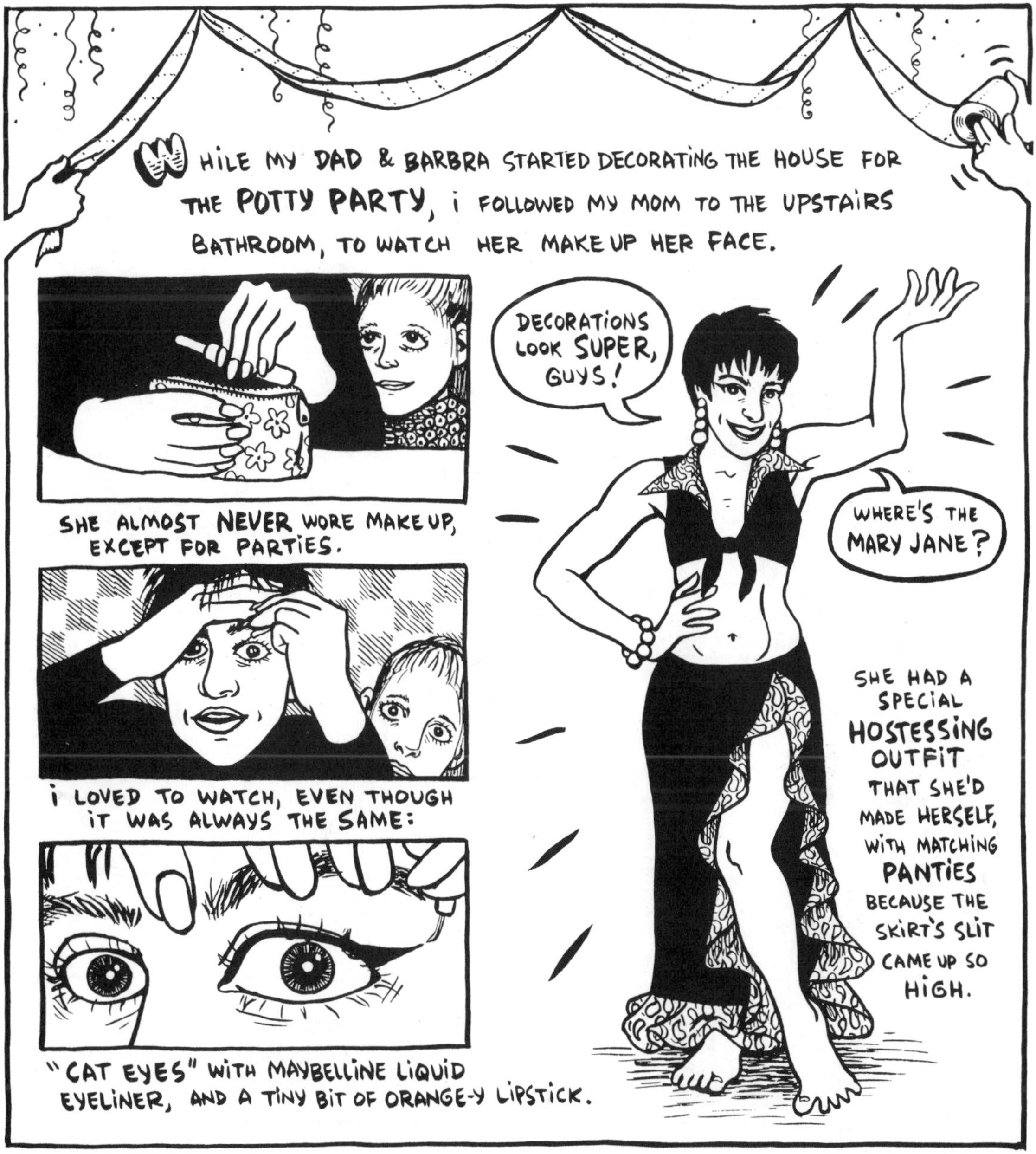
WHILE MY DAD & BARBRA STARTED DECORATING THE HOUSE FOR THE POTTY PARTY, I FOLLOWED MY MOM TO THE UPSTAIRS BATHROOM, TO WATCH HER MAKE UP HER FACE.
SHE ALMOST NEVER WORE MAKE UP, EXCEPT FOR PARTIES.
I LOVED TO WATCH, EVEN THOUGH IT WAS ALWAYS THE SAME:
"CAT EYES" WITH MAYBELLINE LIQUID EYELINER, AND A TINY BIT OF ORANGE-Y LIPSTICK.
DECORATIONS LOOK SUPER, GUYS!
WHERE'S THE MARY JANE?
SHE HAD A SPECIAL HOSTESSING OUTFIT THAT SHE'D MADE HERSELF, WITH MATCHING PANTIES BECAUSE THE SKIRT'S SLIT CAME UP SO HIGH.

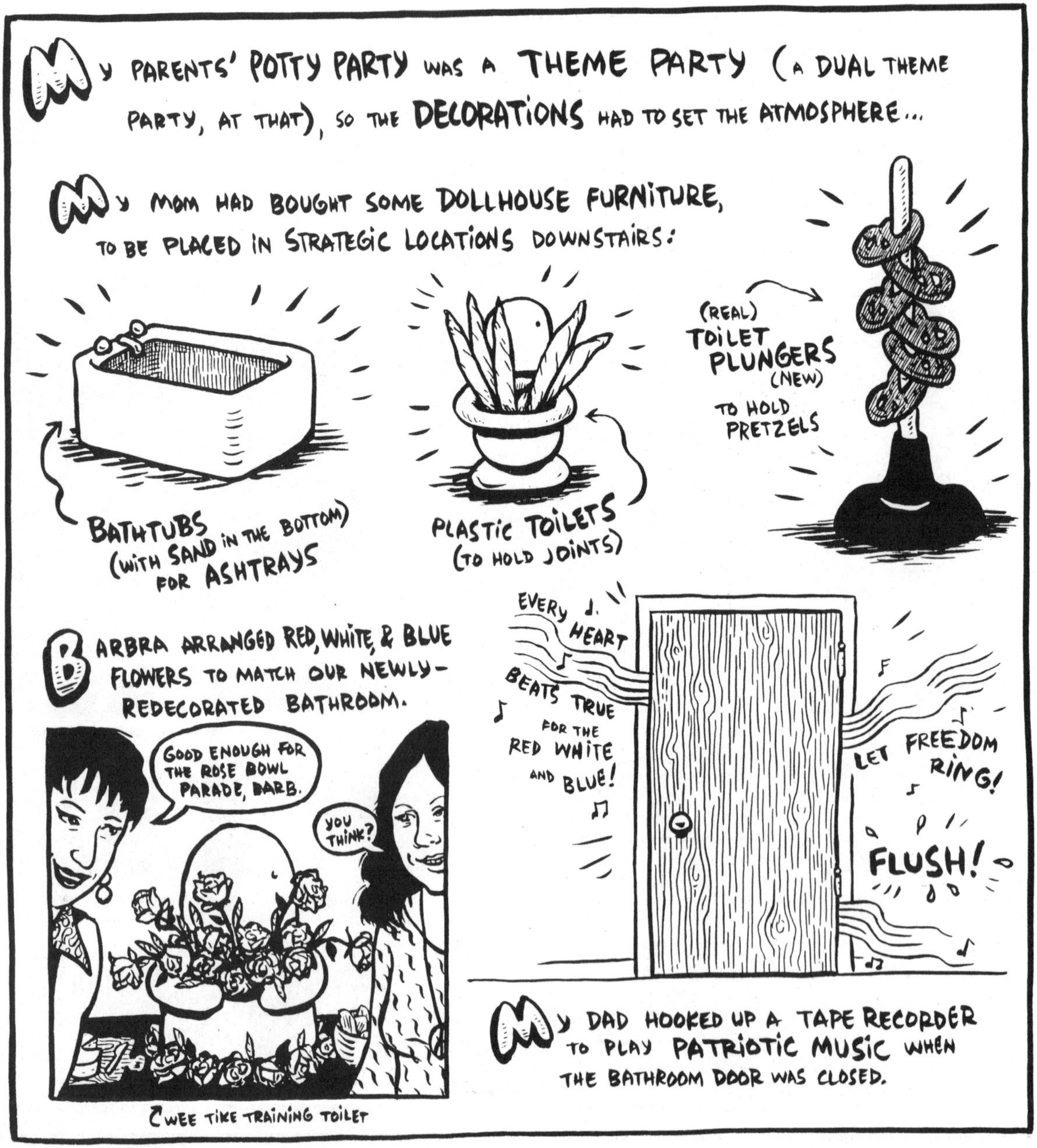
My parents' POTTY PARTY was a THEME PARTY (a dual theme party, at that), so the DECORATIONS had to set the ATMOSPHERE...
My mom had bought some DOLLHOUSE FURNITURE, to be placed in STRATEGIC LOCATIONS downstairs:
BATHTUBS (with SAND in the bottom) for ASHTRAYS
PLASTIC TOILETS (to hold joints)
(REAL) TOILET PLUNGERS (NEW) TO HOLD PRETZELS
Barbra arranged RED, WHITE, & BLUE FLOWERS to match our newly-redecorated bathroom.
GOOD ENOUGH FOR THE ROSE BOWL PARADE, BARB.
YOU THINK?
WEE TIKE TRAINING TOILET
EVERY HEART BEATS TRUE FOR THE RED WHITE AND BLUE!
LET FREEDOM RING!
FLUSH!
My dad hooked up a TAPE RECORDER to play PATRIOTIC MUSIC when the BATHROOM DOOR was closed.

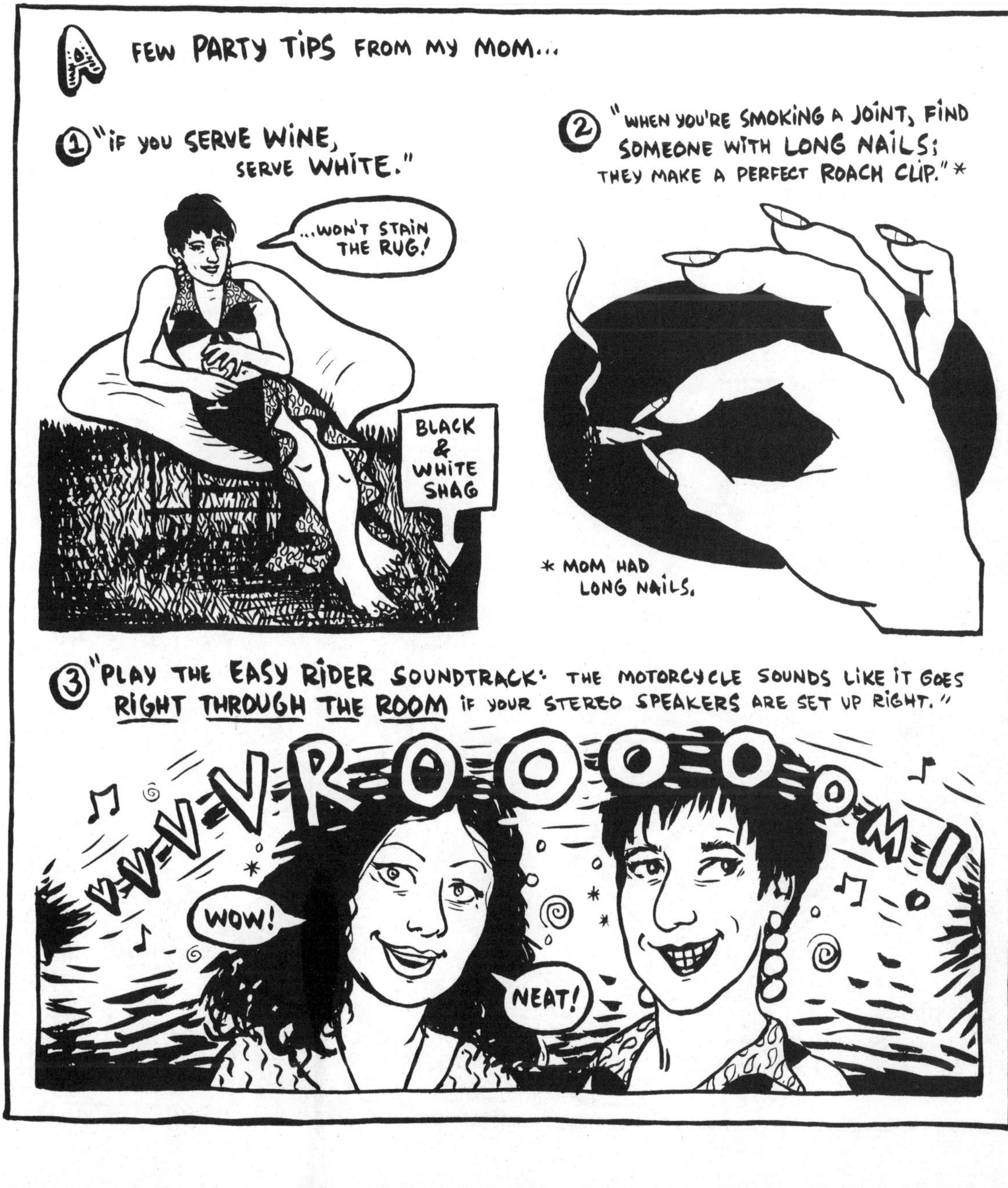
A FEW PARTY TIPS FROM MY MOM...
1 "IF YOU SERVE WINE, SERVE WHITE."
...WON'T STAIN THE RUG!
BLACK & WHITE SHAG
2 "WHEN YOU'RE SMOKING A JOINT, FIND SOMEONE WITH LONG NAILS; THEY MAKE A PERFECT ROACH CLIP." *
* MOM HAD LONG NAILS.
3 "PLAY THE EASY RIDER SOUNDTRACK: THE MOTORCYCLE SOUNDS LIKE IT GOES RIGHT THROUGH THE ROOM IF YOUR STEREO SPEAKERS ARE SET UP RIGHT."
VVVVROOOOOM!
WOW!
NEAT!

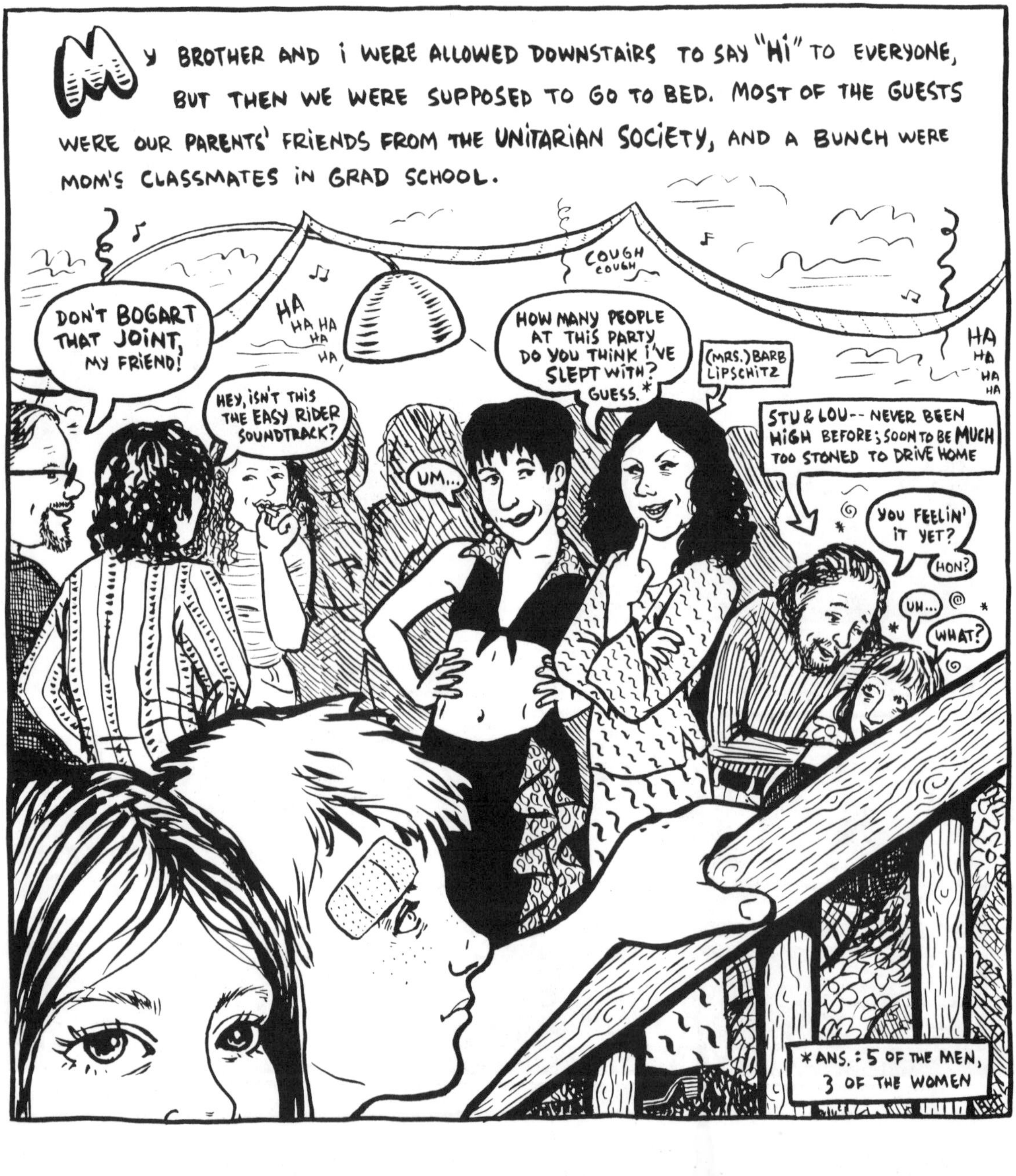
MY BROTHER AND I WERE ALLOWED DOWNSTAIRS TO SAY "HI" TO EVERYONE, BUT THEN WE WERE SUPPOSED TO GO TO BED. MOST OF THE GUESTS WERE OUR PARENTS' FRIENDS FROM THE UNITARIAN SOCIETY, AND A BUNCH WERE MOM'S CLASSMATES IN GRAD SCHOOL.
COUGH COUGH
DON'T BOGART THAT JOINT, MY FRIEND!
HA HA HA HA HA HA
HEY, ISN'T THIS THE EASY RIDER SOUNDTRACK?
UM...
HOW MANY PEOPLE AT THIS PARTY DO YOU THINK I'VE SLEPT WITH? GUESS.*
(MRS.) BARB LIPSCHITZ
HA HA HA HA
STU & LOU-- NEVER BEEN HIGH BEFORE; SOON TO BE MUCH TOO STONED TO DRIVE HOME
YOU FEELIN' IT YET? HON?
UH...
WHAT?
*ANS.: 5 OF THE MEN, 3 OF THE WOMEN

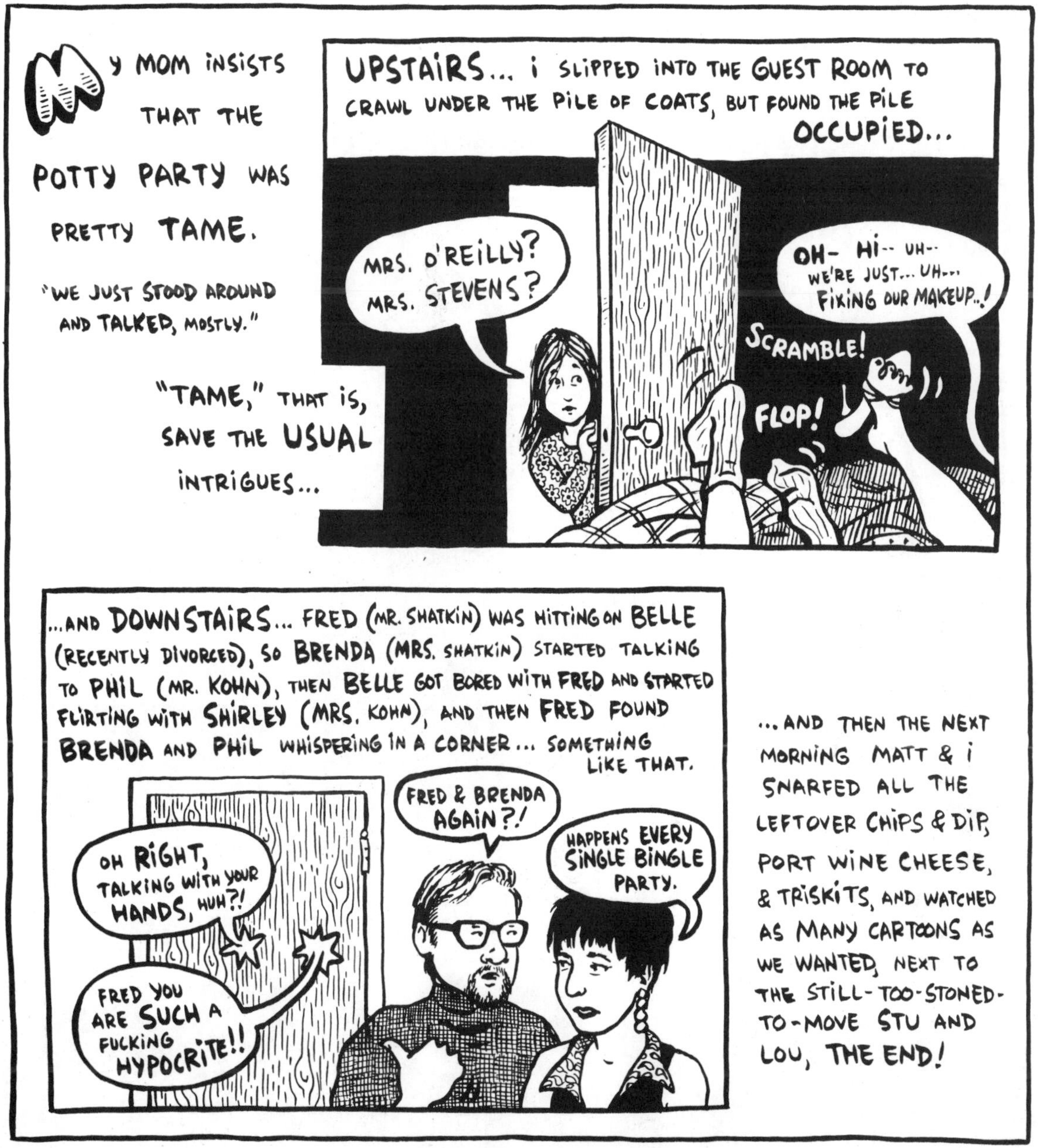
My mom insists that the potty party was pretty TAME.
"We just stood around and talked, mostly."
"TAME," that is, save the USUAL intrigues...
UPSTAIRS... i slipped into the guest room to crawl under the pile of coats, but found the pile OCCUPIED...
MRS. O'REILLY? MRS. STEVENS?
OH- HI-- UH-- WE'RE JUST... UH... FIXING OUR MAKEUP..!
SCRAMBLE!
FLOP!
...AND DOWNSTAIRS... FRED (MR. SHATKIN) WAS HITTING ON BELLE (RECENTLY DIVORCED), SO BRENDA (MRS. SHATKIN) STARTED TALKING TO PHIL (MR. KOHN), THEN BELLE GOT BORED WITH FRED AND STARTED FLIRTING WITH SHIRLEY (MRS. KOHN), AND THEN FRED FOUND BRENDA AND PHIL WHISPERING IN A CORNER... SOMETHING LIKE THAT.
OH RIGHT, TALKING WITH YOUR HANDS, HUH?!
FRED YOU ARE SUCH A FUCKING HYPOCRITE!!
FRED & BRENDA AGAIN?!
HAPPENS EVERY SINGLE BINGLE PARTY.
...AND THEN THE NEXT MORNING MATT & i SNARFED ALL THE LEFTOVER CHIPS & DIP, PORT WINE CHEESE, & TRISKITS, AND WATCHED AS MANY CARTOONS AS WE WANTED, NEXT TO THE STILL-TOO-STONED-TO-MOVE STU AND LOU, THE END!

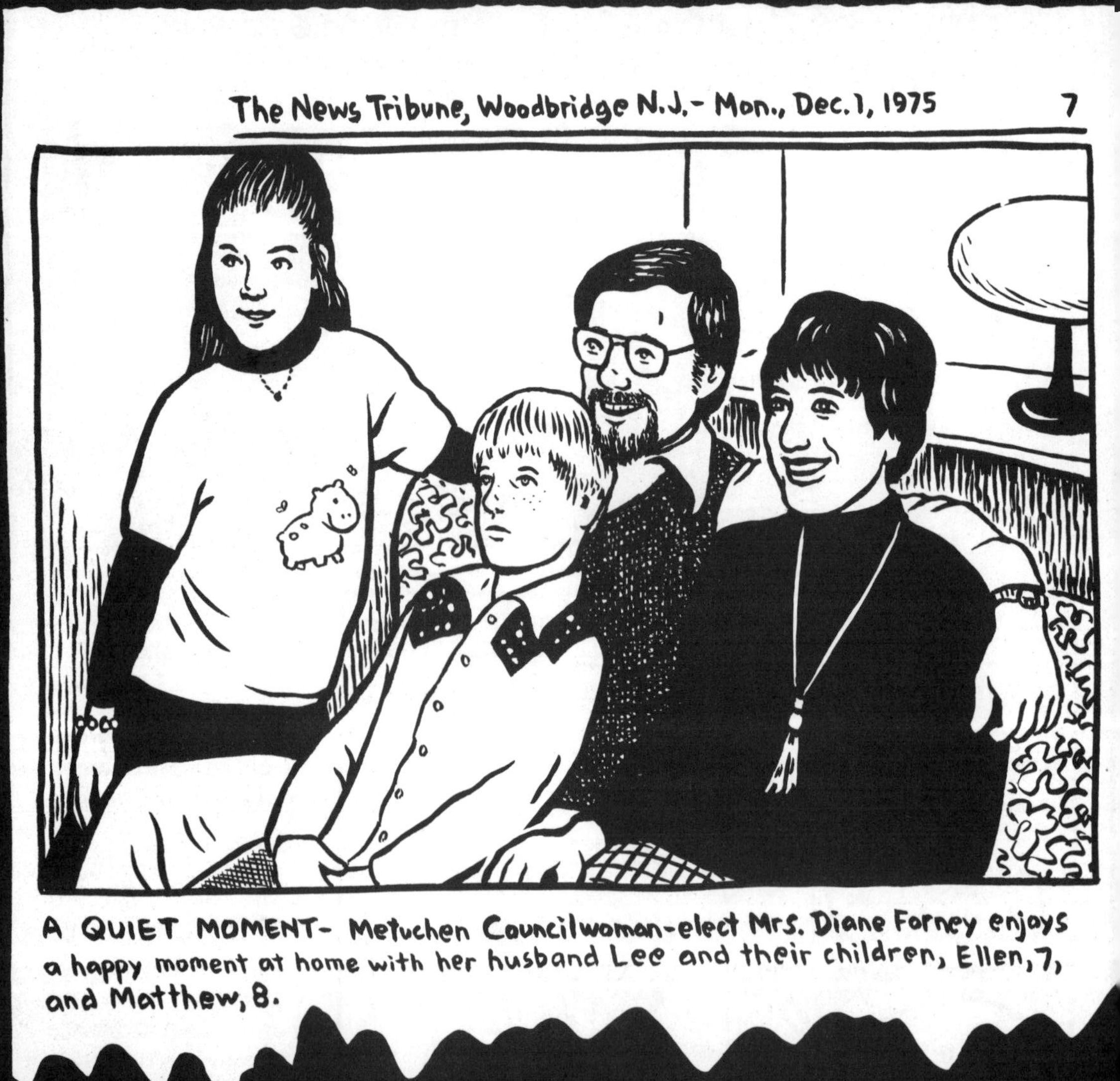
The News Tribune, Woodbridge N.J.- Mon., Dec. 1, 1975
7
A QUIET MOMENT- Metuchen Councilwoman-elect Mrs. Diane Forney enjoys a happy moment at home with her husband Lee and their children, Ellen, 7, and Matthew, 8.

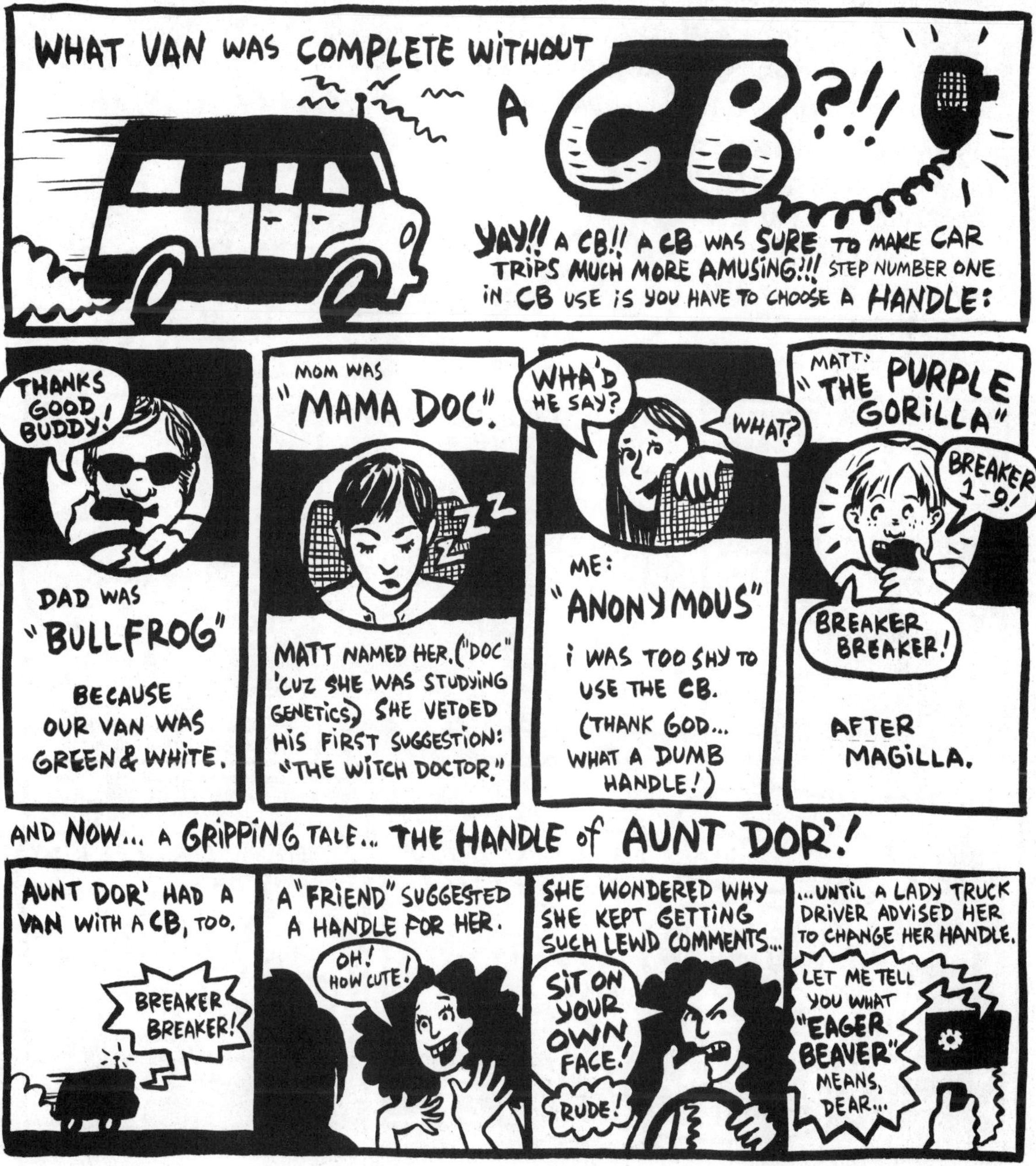
WHAT VAN WAS COMPLETE WITHOUT
A CB?!!
YAY!! A CB!! A CB WAS SURE TO MAKE CAR TRIPS MUCH MORE AMUSING!!! STEP NUMBER ONE IN CB USE IS YOU HAVE TO CHOOSE A HANDLE:
THANKS GOOD BUDDY!
DAD WAS "BULLFROG"
BECAUSE OUR VAN WAS GREEN & WHITE.
MOM WAS "MAMA DOC".
ZZZ
MATT NAMED HER. ("DOC" 'CUZ SHE WAS STUDYING GENETICS.) SHE VETOED HIS FIRST SUGGESTION: "THE WITCH DOCTOR."
WHA'D HE SAY?
WHAT?
ME: "ANONYMOUS"
I WAS TOO SHY TO USE THE CB.
(THANK GOD... WHAT A DUMB HANDLE!)
MATT: "THE PURPLE GORILLA"
BREAKER 1-9!
BREAKER BREAKER!
AFTER MAGILLA.
AND NOW... A GRIPPING TALE... THE HANDLE OF AUNT DOR'!
AUNT DOR' HAD A VAN WITH A CB, TOO.
BREAKER BREAKER!
A "FRIEND" SUGGESTED A HANDLE FOR HER.
OH! HOW CUTE!
SHE WONDERED WHY SHE KEPT GETTING SUCH LEWD COMMENTS...
SIT ON YOUR OWN FACE!
RUDE!
...UNTIL A LADY TRUCK DRIVER ADVISED HER TO CHANGE HER HANDLE.
LET ME TELL YOU WHAT "EAGER BEAVER" MEANS, DEAR...

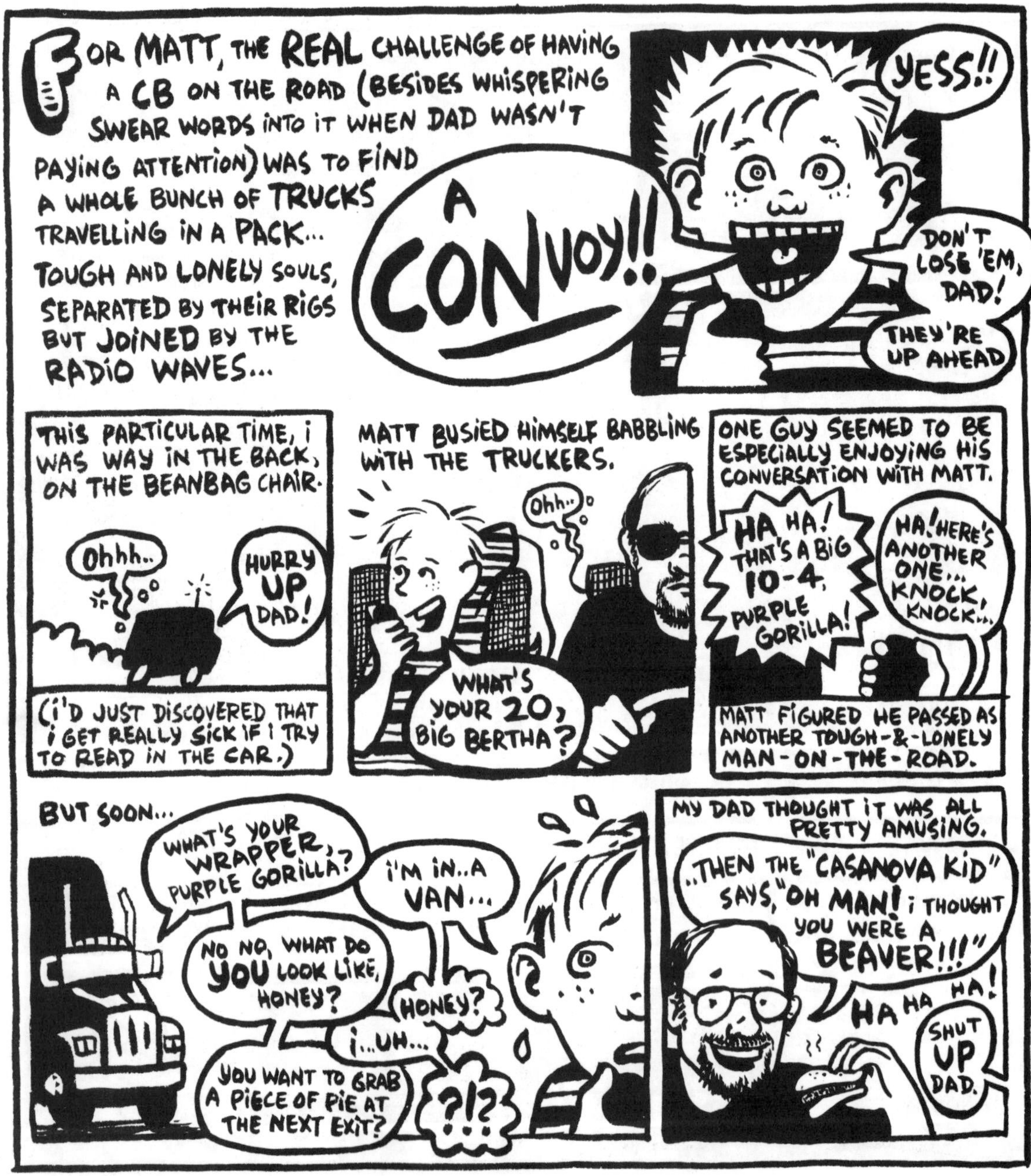
FOR MATT, THE REAL CHALLENGE OF HAVING A CB ON THE ROAD (BESIDES WHISPERING SWEAR WORDS INTO IT WHEN DAD WASN'T PAYING ATTENTION) WAS TO FIND A WHOLE BUNCH OF TRUCKS TRAVELLING IN A PACK...
TOUGH AND LONELY SOULS, SEPARATED BY THEIR RIGS BUT JOINED BY THE RADIO WAVES...
A CONVOY!!
YESS!!
DON'T LOSE 'EM, DAD!
THEY'RE UP AHEAD
THIS PARTICULAR TIME, I WAS WAY IN THE BACK, ON THE BEANBAG CHAIR.
Ohhh..
HURRY UP DAD!
(I'D JUST DISCOVERED THAT I GET REALLY SICK IF I TRY TO READ IN THE CAR.)
MATT BUSIED HIMSELF BABBLING WITH THE TRUCKERS.
Ohh..
WHAT'S YOUR 20, BIG BERTHA?
ONE GUY SEEMED TO BE ESPECIALLY ENJOYING HIS CONVERSATION WITH MATT.
HA HA! THAT'S A BIG 10-4, PURPLE GORILLA!
HA! HERE'S ANOTHER ONE... KNOCK, KNOCK...
MATT FIGURED HE PASSED AS ANOTHER TOUGH-&-LONELY MAN-ON-THE-ROAD.
BUT SOON...
WHAT'S YOUR WRAPPER, PURPLE GORILLA?
I'M IN..A VAN...
NO NO, WHAT DO YOU LOOK LIKE, HONEY?
HONEY?
I...UH...
YOU WANT TO GRAB A PIECE OF PIE AT THE NEXT EXIT?
?!?
MY DAD THOUGHT IT WAS ALL PRETTY AMUSING.
..THEN THE "CASANOVA KID" SAYS, "OH MAN! I THOUGHT YOU WERE A BEAVER!!!"
HA HA HA!
SHUT UP DAD.

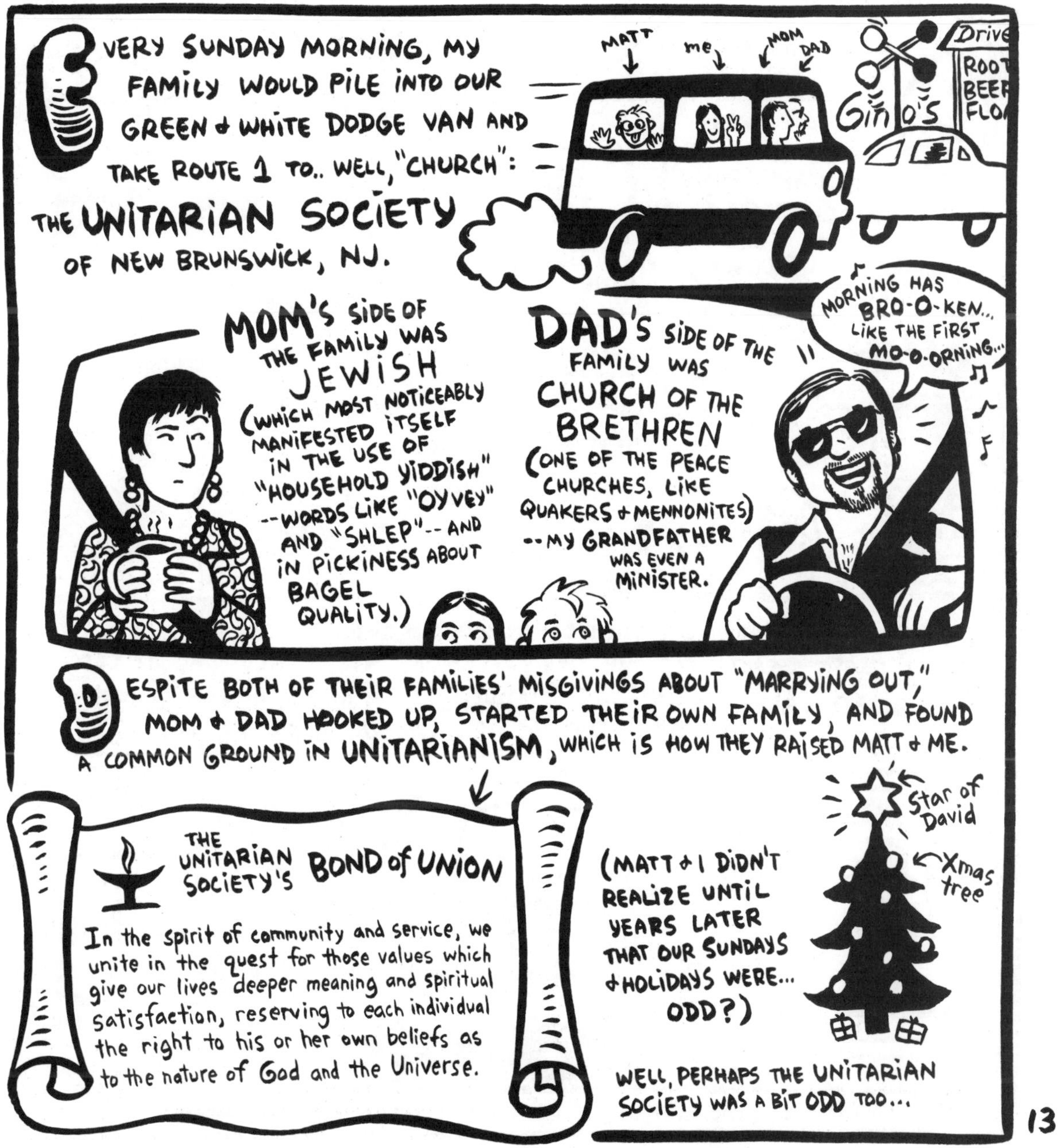
EVERY SUNDAY MORNING, MY FAMILY WOULD PILE INTO OUR GREEN & WHITE DODGE VAN AND TAKE ROUTE 1 TO.. WELL, "CHURCH":
THE UNITARIAN SOCIETY OF NEW BRUNSWICK, NJ.
MATT
me
MOM
DAD
Drive
ROOT BEER FLO
Gino's
MOM'S SIDE OF THE FAMILY WAS JEWISH (WHICH MOST NOTICEABLY MANIFESTED ITSELF IN THE USE OF "HOUSEHOLD YIDDISH" --WORDS LIKE "OY VEY" AND "SHLEP"-- AND IN PICKINESS ABOUT BAGEL QUALITY.)
DAD'S SIDE OF THE FAMILY WAS CHURCH OF THE BRETHREN (ONE OF THE PEACE CHURCHES, LIKE QUAKERS & MENNONITES) --MY GRANDFATHER WAS EVEN A MINISTER.
MORNING HAS BRO-O-KEN... LIKE THE FIRST MO-O-ORNING...
DESPITE BOTH OF THEIR FAMILIES' MISGIVINGS ABOUT "MARRYING OUT," MOM & DAD HOOKED UP, STARTED THEIR OWN FAMILY, AND FOUND A COMMON GROUND IN UNITARIANISM, WHICH IS HOW THEY RAISED MATT & ME.
THE UNITARIAN SOCIETY'S BOND of UNION
In the spirit of community and service, we unite in the quest for those values which give our lives deeper meaning and spiritual satisfaction, reserving to each individual the right to his or her own beliefs as to the nature of God and the Universe.
(MATT & I DIDN'T REALIZE UNTIL YEARS LATER THAT OUR SUNDAYS & HOLIDAYS WERE... ODD?)
Star of David
Xmas tree
WELL, PERHAPS THE UNITARIAN SOCIETY WAS A BIT ODD TOO...

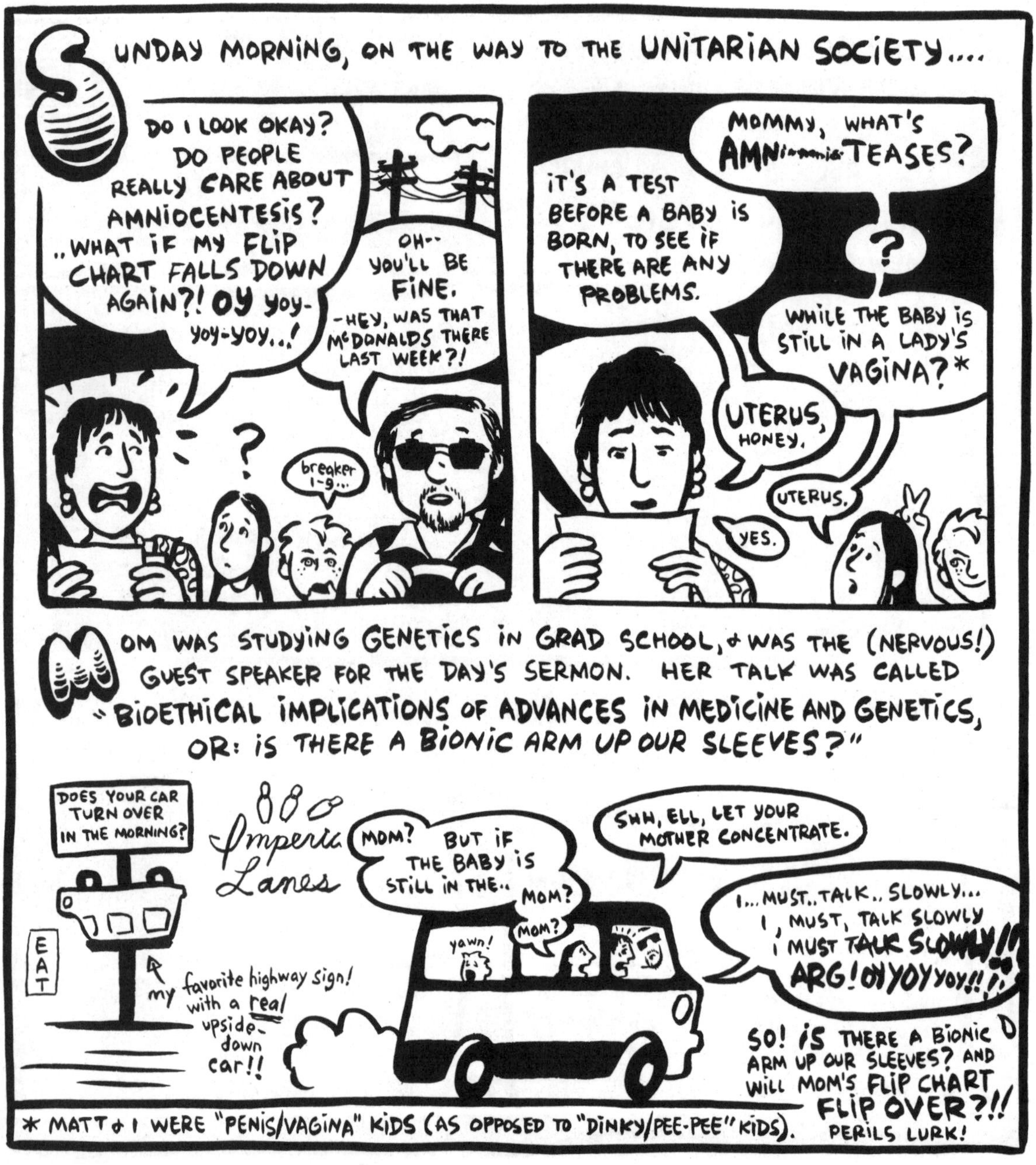
SUNDAY MORNING, ON THE WAY TO THE UNITARIAN SOCIETY....
DO I LOOK OKAY? DO PEOPLE REALLY CARE ABOUT AMNIOCENTESIS? ..WHAT IF MY FLIP CHART FALLS DOWN AGAIN?! OY yoy-yoy-yoy..!
?
breaker 1-9...
OH-- YOU'LL BE FINE. -HEY, WAS THAT McDONALDS THERE LAST WEEK?!
MOMMY, WHAT'S AMN TEASES?
IT'S A TEST BEFORE A BABY IS BORN, TO SEE IF THERE ARE ANY PROBLEMS.
?
WHILE THE BABY IS STILL IN A LADY'S VAGINA?*
UTERUS, HONEY.
UTERUS.
YES.
MOM WAS STUDYING GENETICS IN GRAD SCHOOL, & WAS THE (NERVOUS!) GUEST SPEAKER FOR THE DAY'S SERMON. HER TALK WAS CALLED "BIOETHICAL IMPLICATIONS OF ADVANCES IN MEDICINE AND GENETICS, OR: IS THERE A BIONIC ARM UP OUR SLEEVES?"
DOES YOUR CAR TURN OVER IN THE MORNING?
EAT
my favorite highway sign! with a real upside-down car!!
Imperia Lanes
MOM? BUT IF THE BABY IS STILL IN THE..
MOM?
MOM?
yawn!
SHH, ELL, LET YOUR MOTHER CONCENTRATE.
I... MUST.. TALK.. SLOWLY... I, MUST, TALK SLOWLY I MUST TALK SLOWLY!! ARG! OY YOY yoy!!
SO! IS THERE A BIONIC ARM UP OUR SLEEVES? AND WILL MOM'S FLIP CHART FLIP OVER?!! PERILS LURK!
* MATT & I WERE "PENIS/VAGINA" KIDS (AS OPPOSED TO "DINKY/PEE-PEE" KIDS).

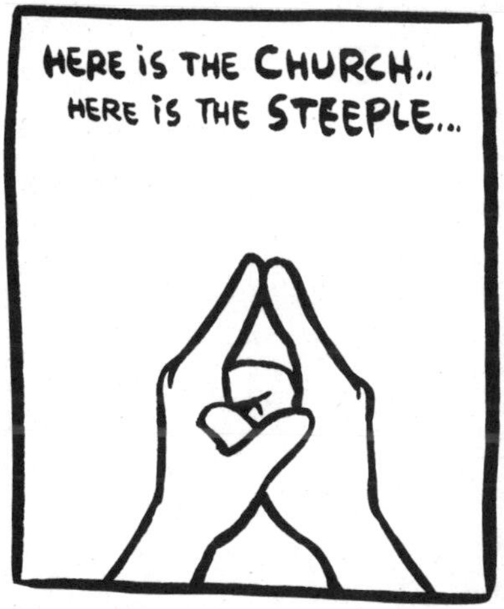
HERE iS THE CHURCH..
HERE iS THE STEEPLE...

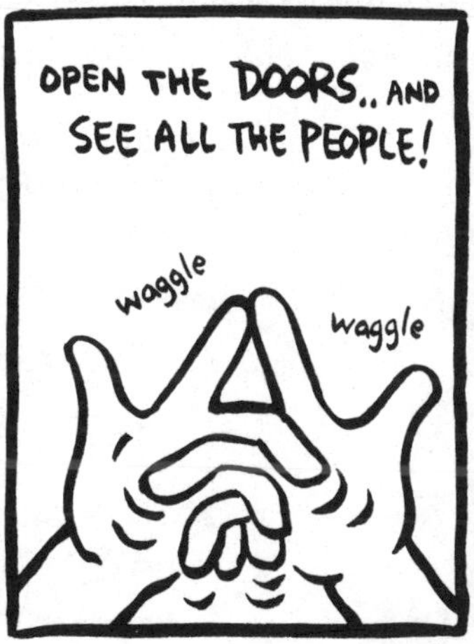
OPEN THE DOORS.. AND
SEE ALL THE PEOPLE!
waggle
waggle

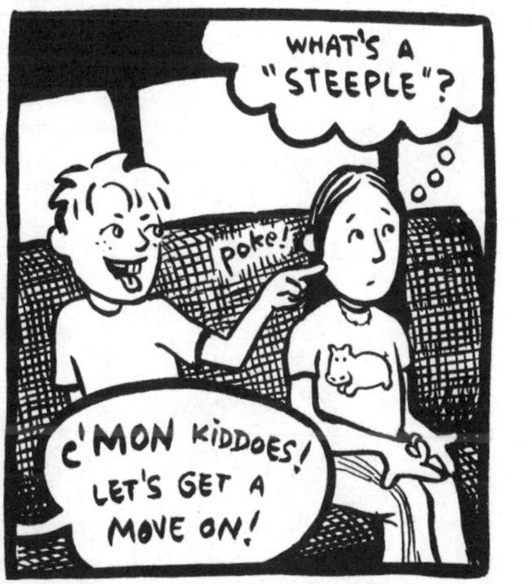
WHAT'S A "STEEPLE"?
poke!
C'MON KIDDOES! LET'S GET A MOVE ON!

THE UNITARIAN SOCIETY (DESIGNED BY SOME UNITARIAN ARCHITECT IN 1967) DIDN'T EVEN VAGUELY RESEMBLE A REGULAR CHURCH. A FEW OF THE MORE "CONSERVATIVE" CONGREGATION MEMBERS CALLED IT "THE CATERPILLAR ON THE HILL" BUT THE REST OF US THOUGHT IT WAS NEAT.

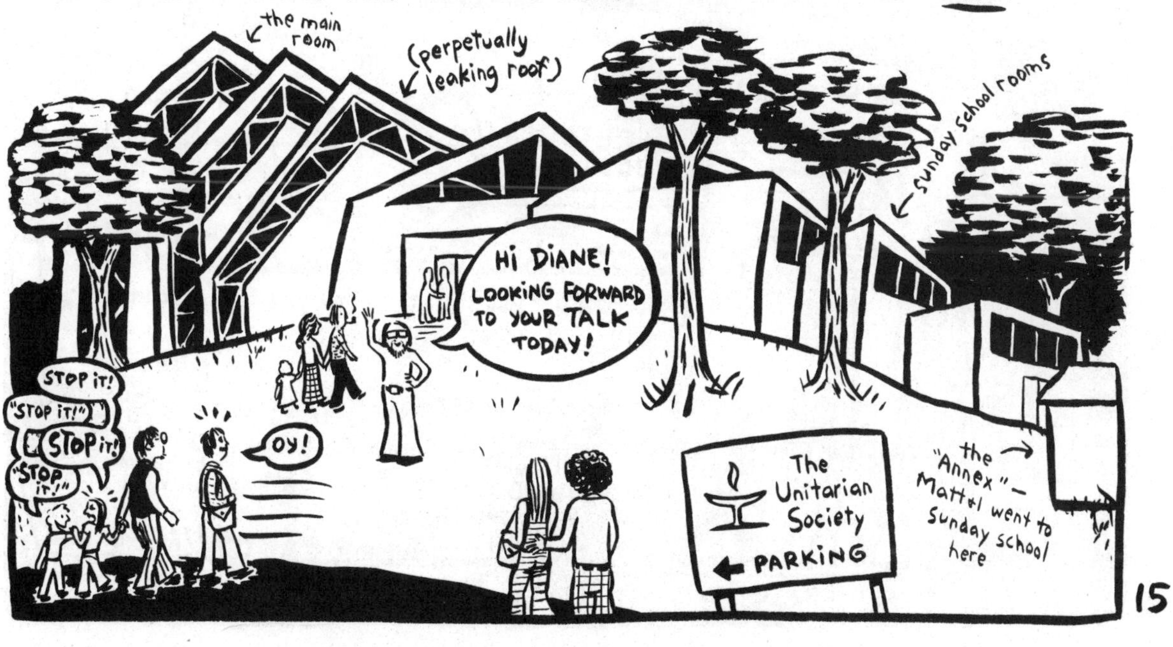
the main room
(perpetually leaking roof)
Sunday school rooms
Hi DIANE! LOOKING FORWARD TO YOUR TALK TODAY!
STOP iT!
"STOP iT!"
STOP iT!
"STOP iT!"
OY!
The Unitarian Society
PARKING
the "Annex"— Matt+I went to Sunday school here

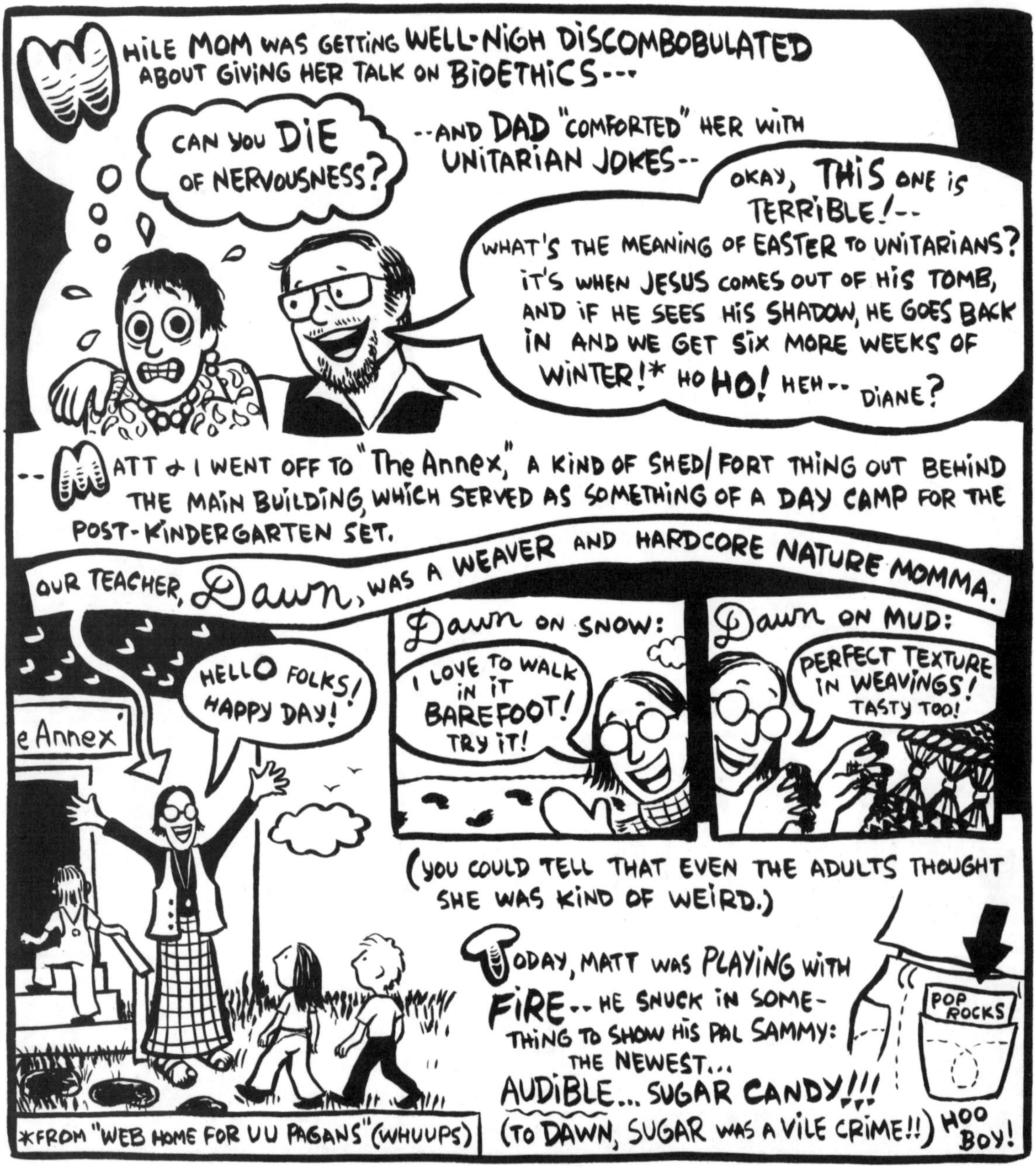
WHILE MOM WAS GETTING WELL-NIGH DISCOMBOBULATED ABOUT GIVING HER TALK ON BIOETHICS---
CAN YOU DIE OF NERVOUSNESS?
--AND DAD "COMFORTED" HER WITH UNITARIAN JOKES--
OKAY, THIS ONE IS TERRIBLE!--
WHAT'S THE MEANING OF EASTER TO UNITARIANS? IT'S WHEN JESUS COMES OUT OF HIS TOMB, AND IF HE SEES HIS SHADOW, HE GOES BACK IN AND WE GET SIX MORE WEEKS OF WINTER!* HO HO! HEH-- DIANE?
--MATT & I WENT OFF TO "The Annex," A KIND OF SHED/FORT THING OUT BEHIND THE MAIN BUILDING, WHICH SERVED AS SOMETHING OF A DAY CAMP FOR THE POST-KINDERGARTEN SET.
OUR TEACHER, Dawn, WAS A WEAVER AND HARDCORE NATURE MOMMA.
e Annex
HELLO FOLKS! HAPPY DAY!
Dawn ON SNOW:
I LOVE TO WALK IN IT BAREFOOT! TRY IT!
Dawn ON MUD:
PERFECT TEXTURE IN WEAVINGS! TASTY TOO!
(YOU COULD TELL THAT EVEN THE ADULTS THOUGHT SHE WAS KIND OF WEIRD.)
TODAY, MATT WAS PLAYING WITH FIRE-- HE SNUCK IN SOMETHING TO SHOW HIS PAL SAMMY: THE NEWEST... AUDIBLE... SUGAR CANDY!!!
POP ROCKS
(TO DAWN, SUGAR WAS A VILE CRIME!!) HOO BOY!
*FROM "WEB HOME FOR UU PAGANS" (WHUUPS)

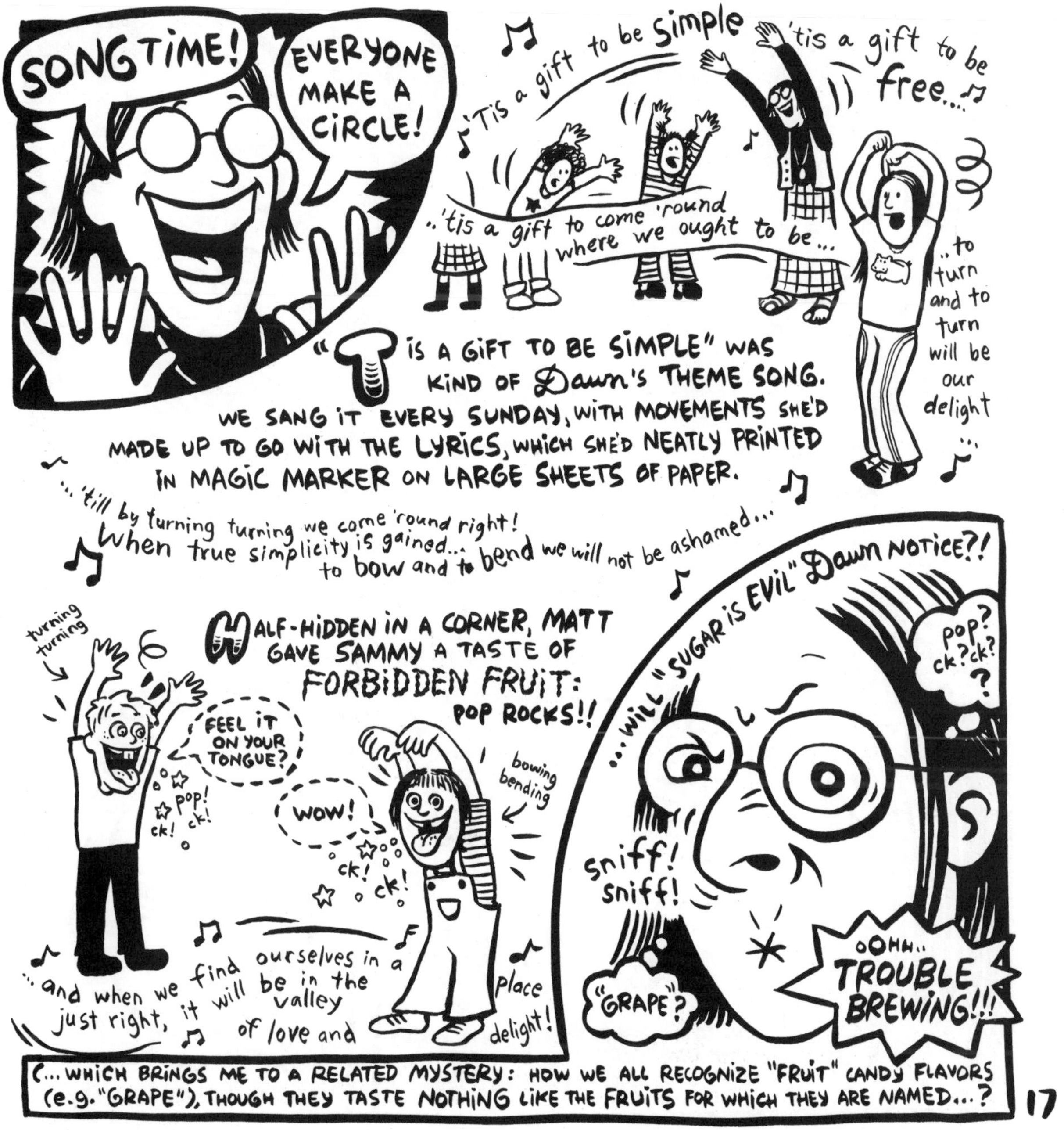
SONG TIME!
EVERYONE MAKE A CIRCLE!
'Tis a gift to be simple 'tis a gift to be free...
..'tis a gift to come 'round where we ought to be...
..to turn and to turn will be our delight
"TIS A GIFT TO BE SIMPLE" WAS KIND OF DAWN'S THEME SONG. WE SANG IT EVERY SUNDAY, WITH MOVEMENTS SHE'D MADE UP TO GO WITH THE LYRICS, WHICH SHE'D NEATLY PRINTED IN MAGIC MARKER ON LARGE SHEETS OF PAPER.
...'till by turning turning we come 'round right!
When true simplicity is gained... to bow and to bend we will not be ashamed...
HALF-HIDDEN IN A CORNER, MATT GAVE SAMMY A TASTE OF FORBIDDEN FRUIT: POP ROCKS!!
turning turning
FEEL IT ON YOUR TONGUE?
pop! ck! ck!
WOW!
ck! ck!
bowing bending
...and when we find ourselves in a place just right, it will be in the valley of love and delight!
...WILL "SUGAR IS EVIL" DAWN NOTICE?!
pop? ck? ck? ?
sniff! sniff!
"GRAPE"?
OOHH.. TROUBLE BREWING!!!
(...WHICH BRINGS ME TO A RELATED MYSTERY: HOW WE ALL RECOGNIZE "FRUIT" CANDY FLAVORS (e.g. "GRAPE"), THOUGH THEY TASTE NOTHING LIKE THE FRUITS FOR WHICH THEY ARE NAMED...?

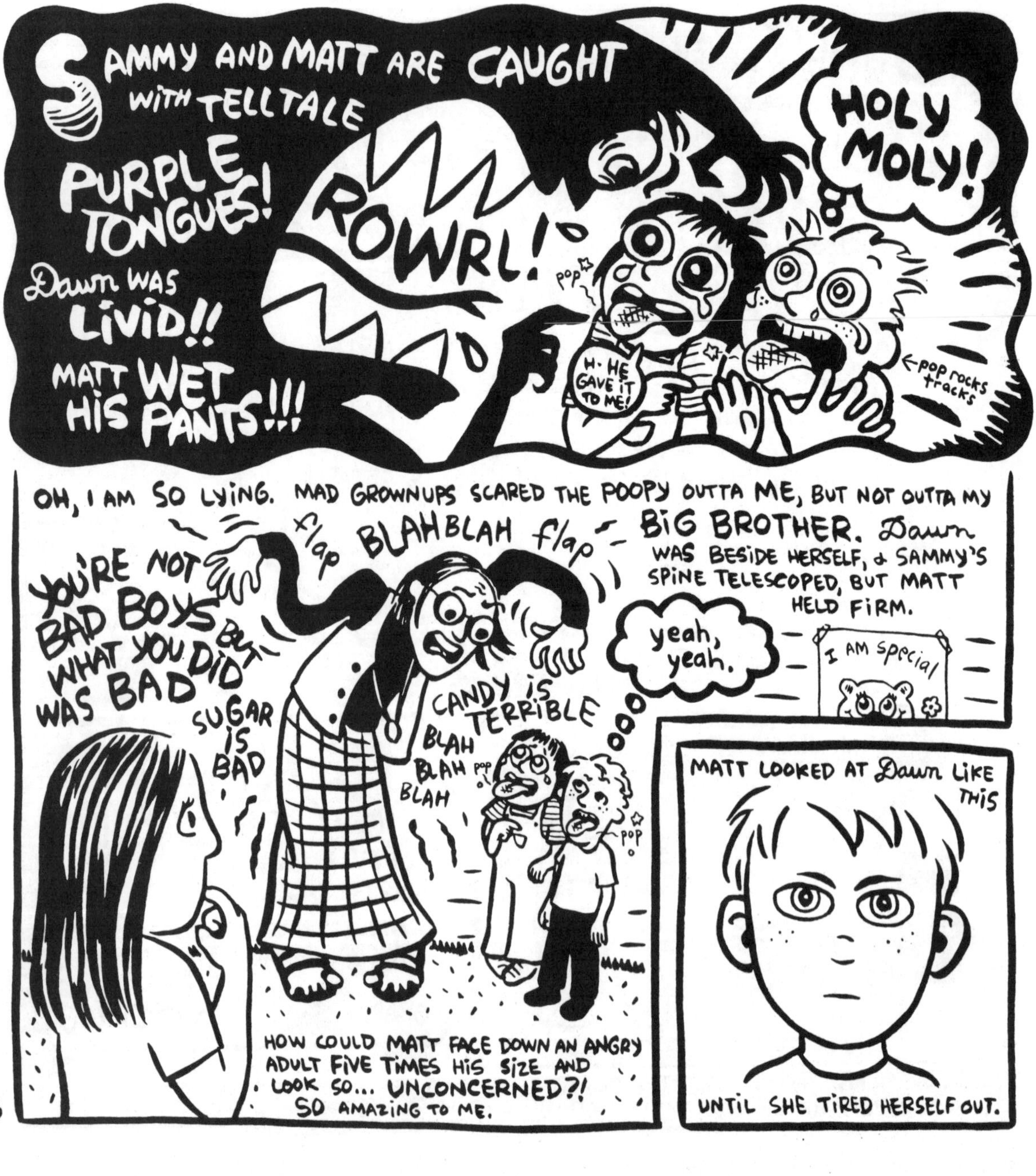
SAMMY AND MATT ARE CAUGHT WITH TELLTALE PURPLE TONGUES!
Dawn WAS LIVID!!
MATT WET HIS PANTS!!!
ROWRL!
pop
H-HE GAVE IT TO ME!
HOLY MOLY!
pop rocks tracks
OH, I AM SO LYING. MAD GROWNUPS SCARED THE POOPY OUTTA ME, BUT NOT OUTTA MY BIG BROTHER. Dawn WAS BESIDE HERSELF, & SAMMY'S SPINE TELESCOPED, BUT MATT HELD FIRM.
flap BLAHBLAH flap
YOU'RE NOT BAD BOYS BUT WHAT YOU DID WAS BAD
SUGAR IS BAD
CANDY IS TERRIBLE
BLAH BLAH BLAH
pop
pop
yeah, yeah.
I AM Special
HOW COULD MATT FACE DOWN AN ANGRY ADULT FIVE TIMES HIS SIZE AND LOOK SO... UNCONCERNED?! SO AMAZING TO ME.
MATT LOOKED AT Dawn LIKE THIS
UNTIL SHE TIRED HERSELF OUT.

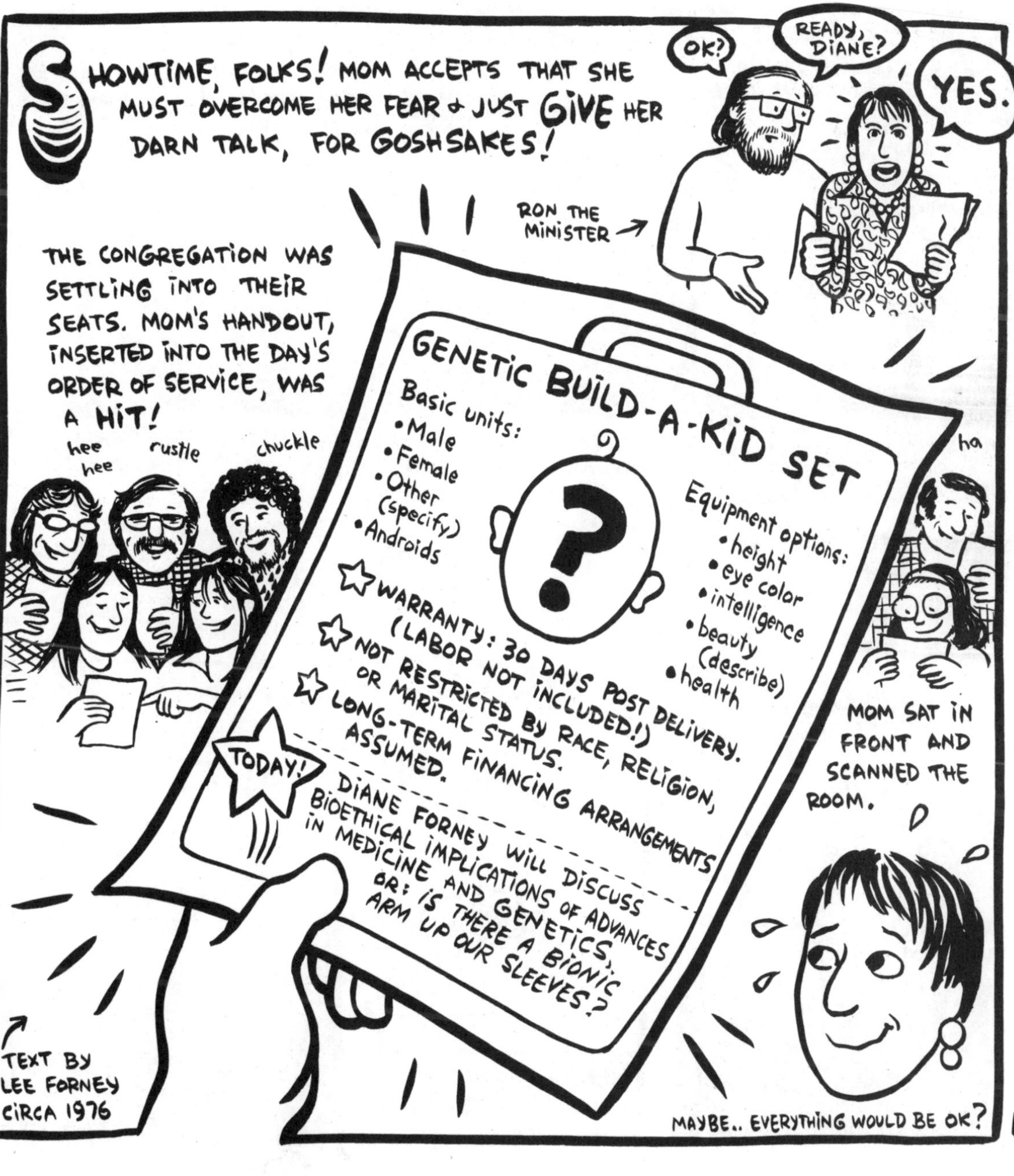
SHOWTIME, FOLKS! MOM ACCEPTS THAT SHE MUST OVERCOME HER FEAR & JUST GIVE HER DARN TALK, FOR GOSHSAKES!
OK?
READY, DIANE?
YES.
RON THE MINISTER
THE CONGREGATION WAS SETTLING INTO THEIR SEATS. MOM'S HANDOUT, INSERTED INTO THE DAY'S ORDER OF SERVICE, WAS A HIT!
hee hee
rustle
chuckle
ha
GENETIC BUILD-A-KID SET
Basic units:
•Male
•Female
•Other (specify)
•Androids
?
Equipment options:
•height
•eye color
•intelligence
•beauty (describe)
•health
WARRANTY: 30 DAYS POST DELIVERY. (LABOR NOT INCLUDED!)
NOT RESTRICTED BY RACE, RELIGION, OR MARITAL STATUS.
LONG-TERM FINANCING ARRANGEMENTS ASSUMED.
TODAY!
DIANE FORNEY WILL DISCUSS BIOETHICAL IMPLICATIONS OF ADVANCES IN MEDICINE AND GENETICS, OR: IS THERE A BIONIC ARM UP OUR SLEEVES?
MOM SAT IN FRONT AND SCANNED THE ROOM.
TEXT BY LEE FORNEY CIRCA 1976
MAYBE.. EVERYTHING WOULD BE OK?

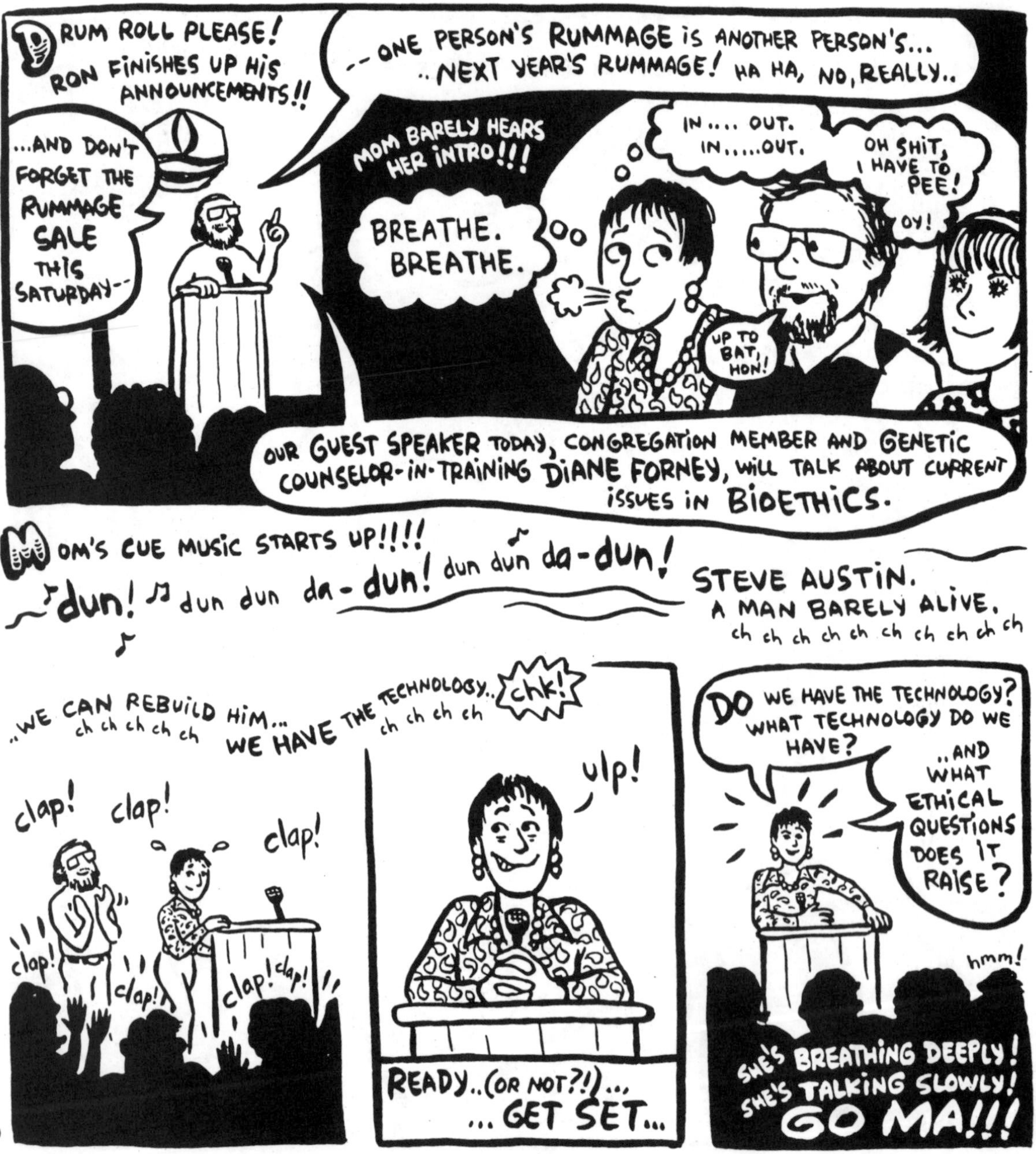
DRUM ROLL PLEASE! RON FINISHES UP HIS ANNOUNCEMENTS!!
--ONE PERSON'S RUMMAGE IS ANOTHER PERSON'S... ..NEXT YEAR'S RUMMAGE! HA HA, NO, REALLY..
...AND DON'T FORGET THE RUMMAGE SALE THIS SATURDAY--
MOM BARELY HEARS HER INTRO!!!
BREATHE. BREATHE.
IN.... OUT. IN.....OUT.
OH SHIT, I HAVE TO PEE!
OY!
UP TO BAT, HON!
OUR GUEST SPEAKER TODAY, CONGREGATION MEMBER AND GENETIC COUNSELOR-IN-TRAINING DIANE FORNEY, WILL TALK ABOUT CURRENT ISSUES IN BIOETHICS.
MOM'S CUE MUSIC STARTS UP!!!!
dun! dun dun da-dun! dun dun da-dun!
STEVE AUSTIN. A MAN BARELY ALIVE.
ch ch ch ch ch ch ch ch ch ch
..WE CAN REBUILD HIM... ch ch ch ch ch WE HAVE THE TECHNOLOGY.. ch ch ch ch
WE HAVE
chk!
clap! clap! clap! clap! clap! clap! clap!
ulp!
READY..(OR NOT?!)..., ...GET SET...
DO WE HAVE THE TECHNOLOGY? WHAT TECHNOLOGY DO WE HAVE?
..AND WHAT ETHICAL QUESTIONS DOES IT RAISE?
hmm!
SHE'S BREATHING DEEPLY! SHE'S TALKING SLOWLY! GO MA!!!

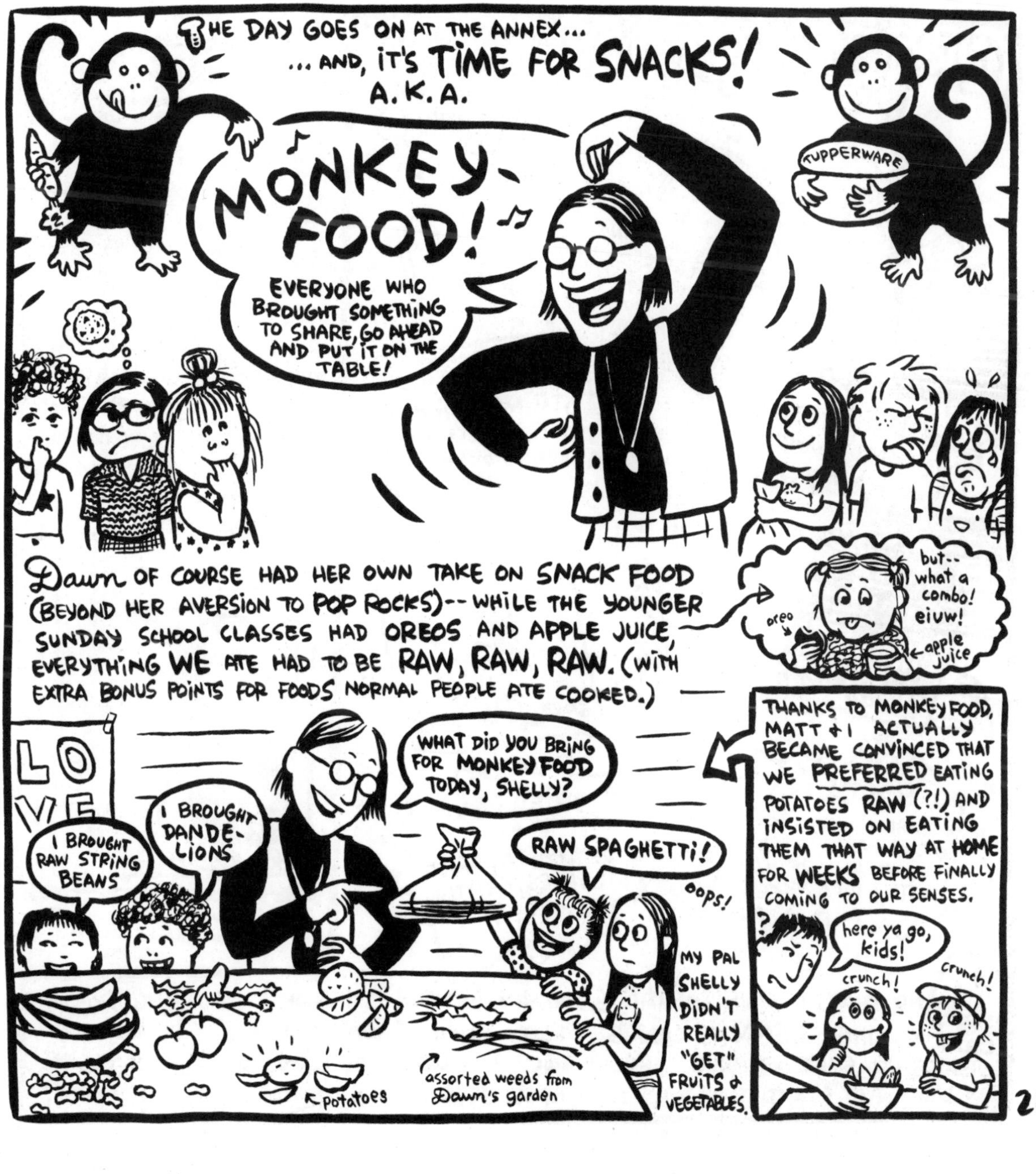
THE DAY GOES ON AT THE ANNEX...
... AND, IT'S TIME FOR SNACKS!
A.K.A.
MONKEY-FOOD!
EVERYONE WHO BROUGHT SOMETHING TO SHARE, GO AHEAD AND PUT IT ON THE TABLE!
TUPPERWARE
DAWN OF COURSE HAD HER OWN TAKE ON SNACK FOOD (BEYOND HER AVERSION TO POP ROCKS)-- WHILE THE YOUNGER SUNDAY SCHOOL CLASSES HAD OREOS AND APPLE JUICE, EVERYTHING WE ATE HAD TO BE RAW, RAW, RAW. (WITH EXTRA BONUS POINTS FOR FOODS NORMAL PEOPLE ATE COOKED.)
but-- what a combo! eiuw!
oreo
apple juice
WHAT DID YOU BRING FOR MONKEY FOOD TODAY, SHELLY?
I BROUGHT RAW STRING BEANS
I BROUGHT DANDE-LIONS
RAW SPAGHETTI!
oops!
LOVE
potatoes
assorted weeds from Dawn's garden
MY PAL SHELLY DIDN'T REALLY "GET" FRUITS & VEGETABLES.
THANKS TO MONKEY FOOD, MATT & I ACTUALLY BECAME CONVINCED THAT WE PREFERRED EATING POTATOES RAW (?!) AND INSISTED ON EATING THEM THAT WAY AT HOME FOR WEEKS BEFORE FINALLY COMING TO OUR SENSES.
?
here ya go, kids!
crunch!
crunch!

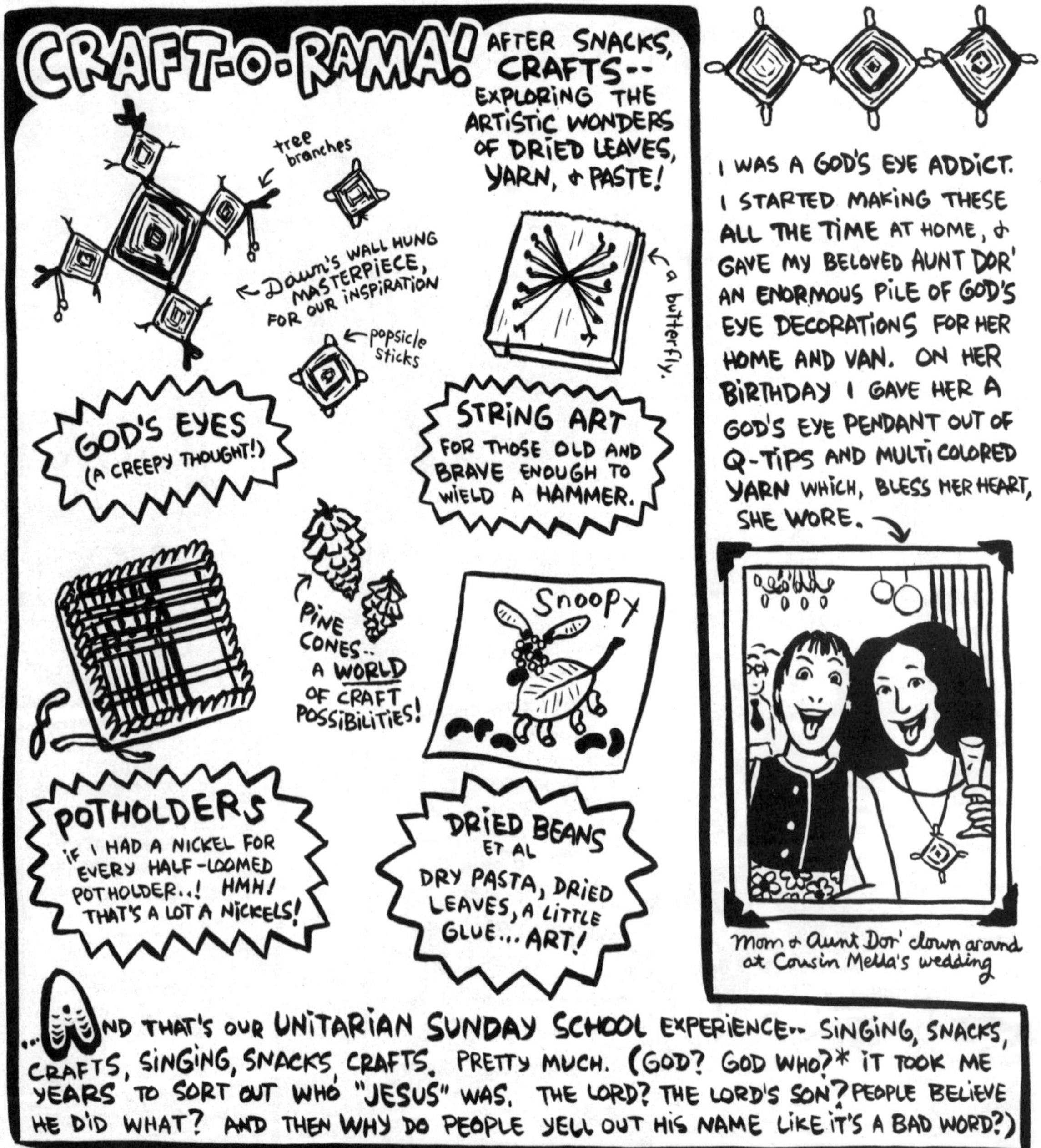

CRAFT-O-RAMA!
AFTER SNACKS, CRAFTS-- EXPLORING THE ARTISTIC WONDERS OF DRIED LEAVES, YARN, & PASTE!
tree branches
Dawn's WALL HUNG MASTERPIECE, FOR OUR INSPIRATION
popsicle sticks
a butterfly.
GOD'S EYES (A CREEPY THOUGHT!)
STRING ART FOR THOSE OLD AND BRAVE ENOUGH TO WIELD A HAMMER.
PINE CONES-- A WORLD OF CRAFT POSSIBILITIES!
Snoopy
POTHOLDERS IF I HAD A NICKEL FOR EVERY HALF-LOOMED POTHOLDER..! HMM! THAT'S A LOT A NICKELS!
DRIED BEANS ET AL DRY PASTA, DRIED LEAVES, A LITTLE GLUE... ART!
I WAS A GOD'S EYE ADDICT. I STARTED MAKING THESE ALL THE TIME AT HOME, & GAVE MY BELOVED AUNT DOR' AN ENORMOUS PILE OF GOD'S EYE DECORATIONS FOR HER HOME AND VAN. ON HER BIRTHDAY I GAVE HER A GOD'S EYE PENDANT OUT OF Q-TIPS AND MULTI COLORED YARN WHICH, BLESS HER HEART, SHE WORE.
Mom & Aunt Dor' clown around at Cousin Mella's wedding
...AND THAT'S OUR UNITARIAN SUNDAY SCHOOL EXPERIENCE-- SINGING, SNACKS, CRAFTS, SINGING, SNACKS, CRAFTS. PRETTY MUCH. (GOD? GOD WHO?* IT TOOK ME YEARS TO SORT OUT WHO "JESUS" WAS. THE LORD? THE LORD'S SON? PEOPLE BELIEVE HE DID WHAT? AND THEN WHY DO PEOPLE YELL OUT HIS NAME LIKE IT'S A BAD WORD?)

*I MEAN, EXCEPT FOR THE YARN EYE THING.

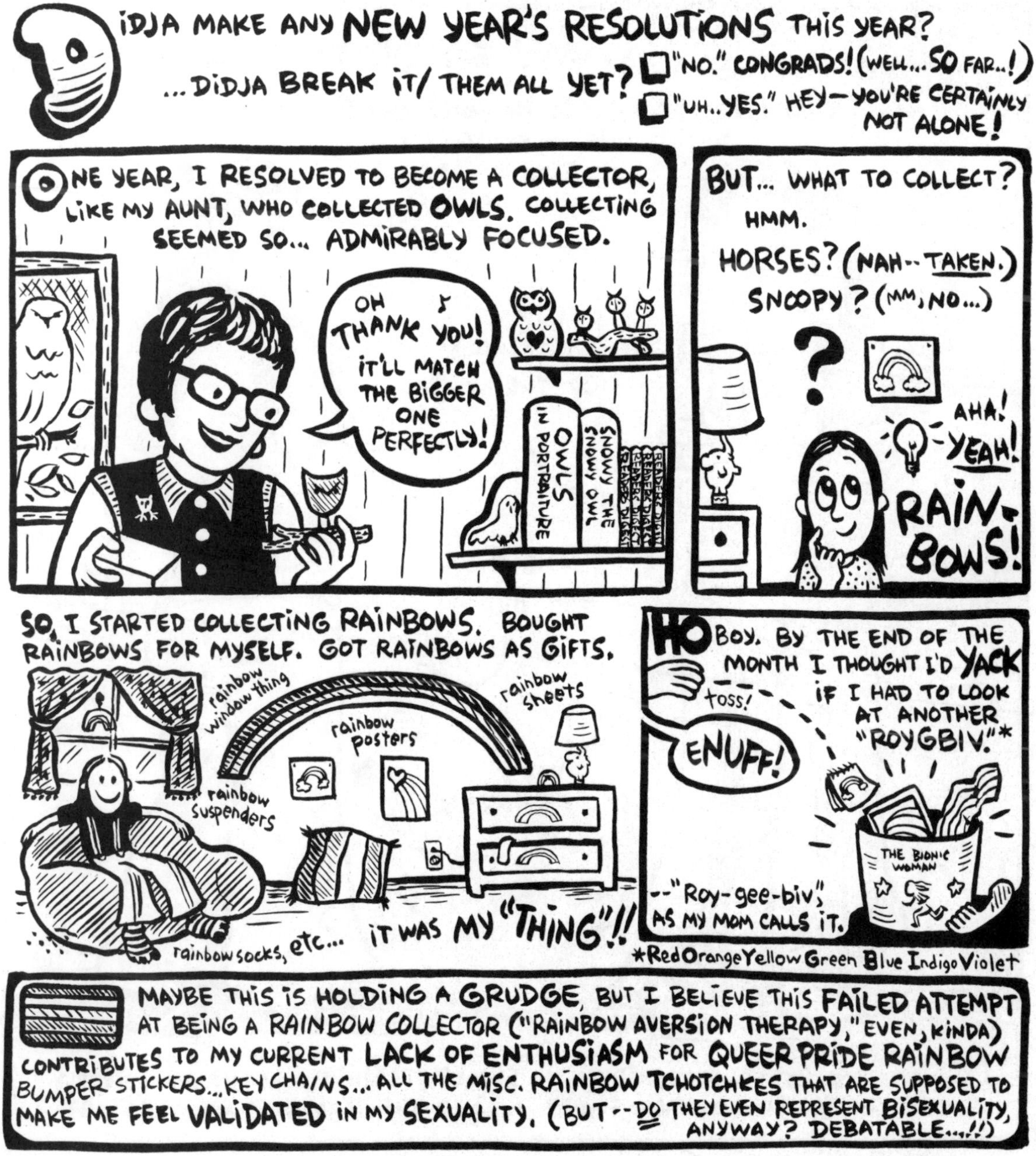
DIDJA MAKE ANY NEW YEAR'S RESOLUTIONS THIS YEAR?
... DIDJA BREAK IT/ THEM ALL YET?
"NO." CONGRADS! (WELL... SO FAR..!)
"UH.. YES." HEY— YOU'RE CERTAINLY NOT ALONE!
ONE YEAR, I RESOLVED TO BECOME A COLLECTOR, LIKE MY AUNT, WHO COLLECTED OWLS. COLLECTING SEEMED SO... ADMIRABLY FOCUSED.
OH THANK YOU! IT'LL MATCH THE BIGGER ONE PERFECTLY!
OWLS IN PORTRAITURE
SNOWY THE SNOWY OWL
READER'S DIGEST
BUT... WHAT TO COLLECT?
HMM.
HORSES? (NAH -- TAKEN.)
SNOOPY? (MM, NO...)
?
AHA!
YEAH!
RAINBOWS!
SO, I STARTED COLLECTING RAINBOWS. BOUGHT RAINBOWS FOR MYSELF. GOT RAINBOWS AS GIFTS.
rainbow window thing
rainbow posters
rainbow sheets
rainbow suspenders
rainbow socks, etc...
IT WAS MY "THING"!!
HO BOY. BY THE END OF THE MONTH I THOUGHT I'D YACK IF I HAD TO LOOK AT ANOTHER "ROYGBIV."*
toss!
ENUFF!
THE BIONIC WOMAN
--"Roy-gee-biv," AS MY MOM CALLS IT.
*RedOrangeYellowGreenBlueIndigoViolet
MAYBE THIS IS HOLDING A GRUDGE, BUT I BELIEVE THIS FAILED ATTEMPT AT BEING A RAINBOW COLLECTOR ("RAINBOW AVERSION THERAPY," EVEN, KINDA) CONTRIBUTES TO MY CURRENT LACK OF ENTHUSIASM FOR QUEER PRIDE RAINBOW BUMPER STICKERS... KEY CHAINS... ALL THE MISC. RAINBOW TCHOTCHKES THAT ARE SUPPOSED TO MAKE ME FEEL VALIDATED IN MY SEXUALITY. (BUT -- DO THEY EVEN REPRESENT BISEXUALITY, ANYWAY? DEBATABLE...!!)

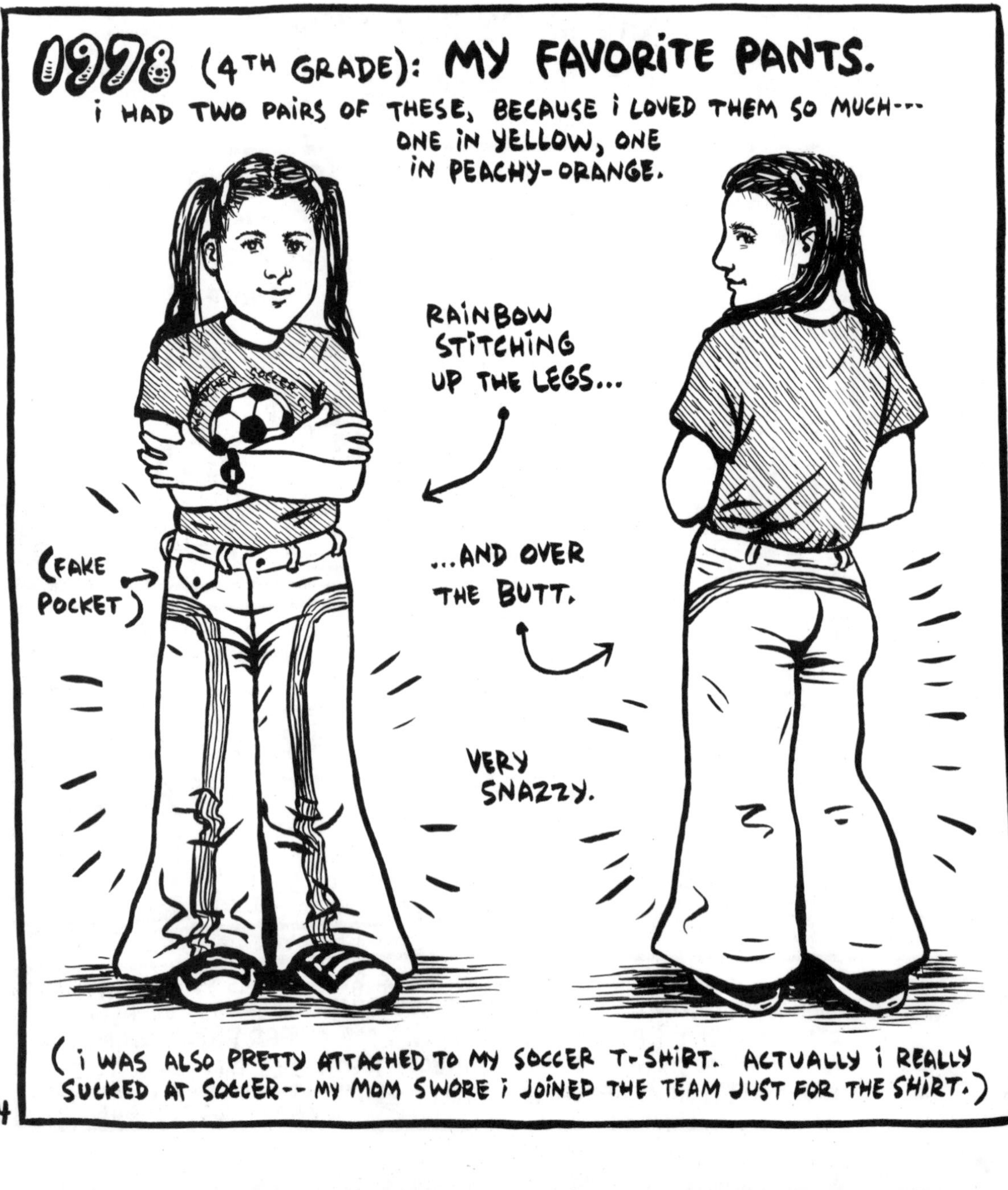

1978 (4TH GRADE): MY FAVORITE PANTS.
I HAD TWO PAIRS OF THESE, BECAUSE I LOVED THEM SO MUCH--- ONE IN YELLOW, ONE IN PEACHY-ORANGE.
RAINBOW STITCHING UP THE LEGS...
(FAKE POCKET)
...AND OVER THE BUTT.
VERY SNAZZY.
(I WAS ALSO PRETTY ATTACHED TO MY SOCCER T-SHIRT. ACTUALLY I REALLY SUCKED AT SOCCER-- MY MOM SWORE I JOINED THE TEAM JUST FOR THE SHIRT.)

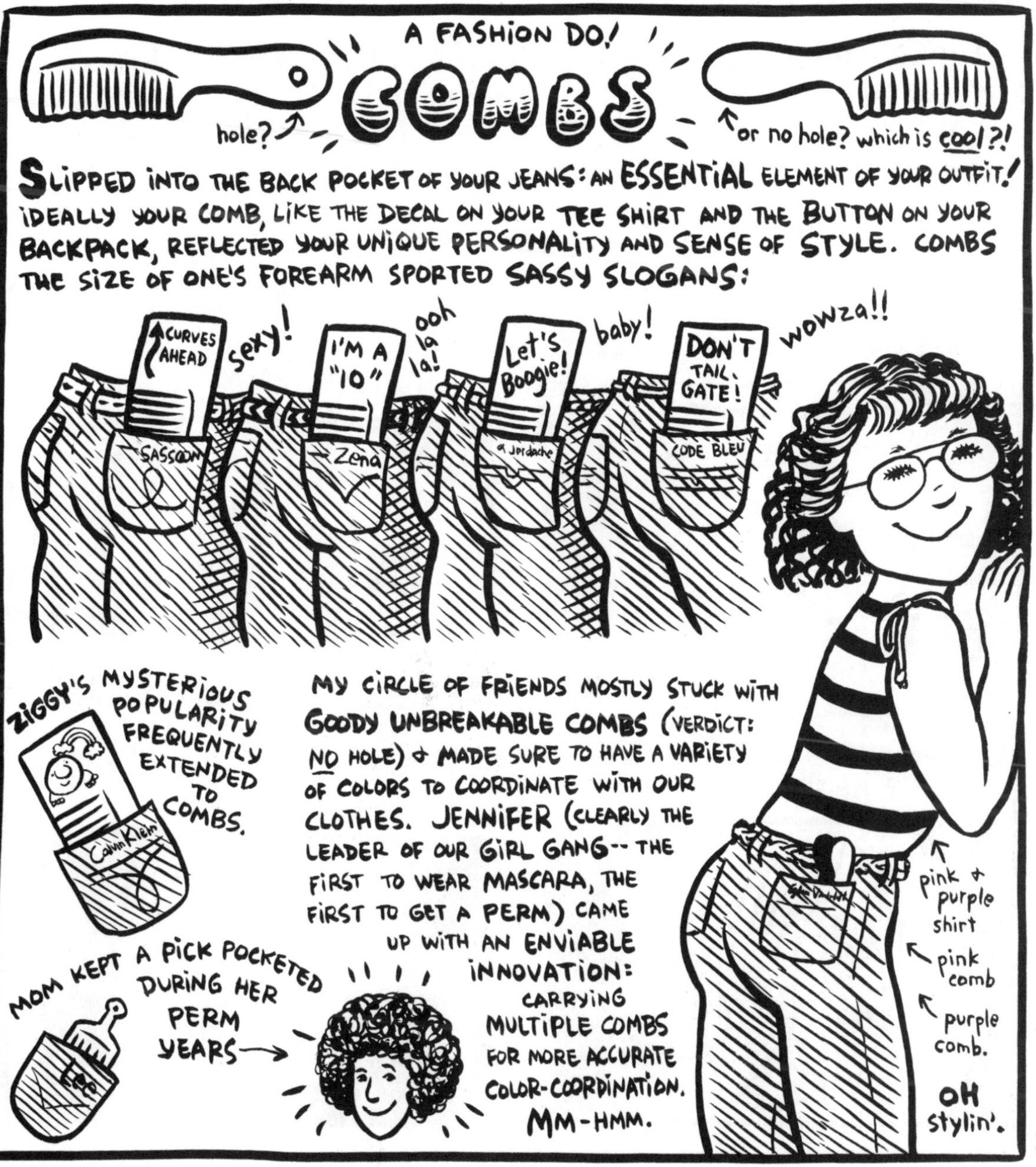
A FASHION DO!
COMBS
hole?
or no hole? which is cool?!
SLIPPED INTO THE BACK POCKET OF YOUR JEANS: AN ESSENTIAL ELEMENT OF YOUR OUTFIT! IDEALLY YOUR COMB, LIKE THE DECAL ON YOUR TEE SHIRT AND THE BUTTON ON YOUR BACKPACK, REFLECTED YOUR UNIQUE PERSONALITY AND SENSE OF STYLE. COMBS THE SIZE OF ONE'S FOREARM SPORTED SASSY SLOGANS:
CURVES AHEAD
sexy!
SASSOON
I'M A "10"
ooh la la!
Zena
Let's Boogie!
baby!
Jordache
DON'T TAIL-GATE!
wowza!!
CODE BLEU
ZIGGY'S MYSTERIOUS POPULARITY FREQUENTLY EXTENDED TO COMBS.
Calvin Klein
MY CIRCLE OF FRIENDS MOSTLY STUCK WITH GOODY UNBREAKABLE COMBS (VERDICT: NO HOLE) & MADE SURE TO HAVE A VARIETY OF COLORS TO COORDINATE WITH OUR CLOTHES. JENNIFER (CLEARLY THE LEADER OF OUR GIRL GANG -- THE FIRST TO WEAR MASCARA, THE FIRST TO GET A PERM) CAME UP WITH AN ENVIABLE INNOVATION: CARRYING MULTIPLE COMBS FOR MORE ACCURATE COLOR-COORDINATION. MM-HMM.
MOM KEPT A PICK POCKETED DURING HER PERM YEARS
Lee
pink & purple shirt
pink comb
purple comb.
OH stylin'.

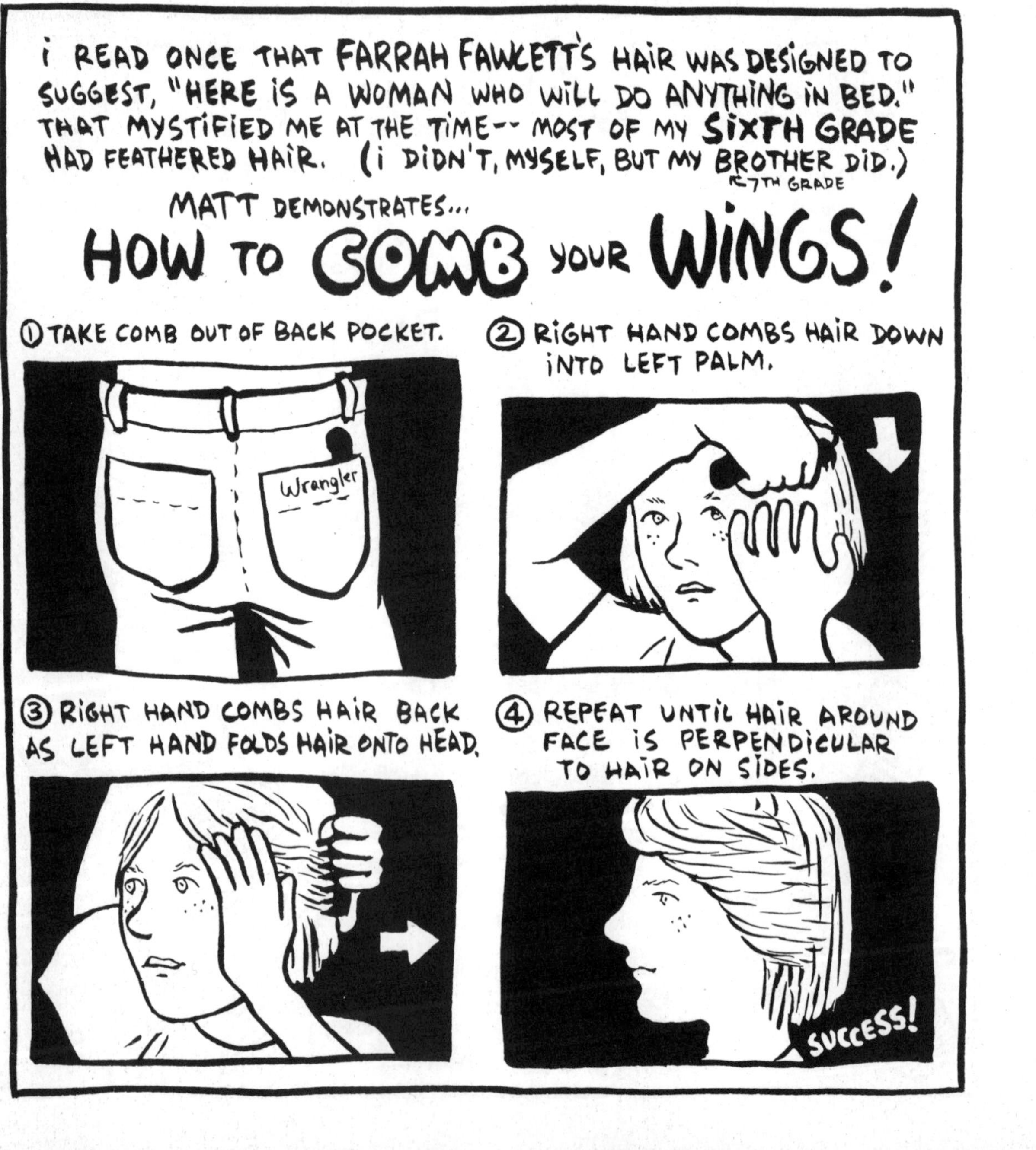
i READ ONCE THAT FARRAH FAWCETT'S HAiR WAS DESiGNED TO SUGGEST, "HERE iS A WOMAN WHO WiLL DO ANYTHiNG iN BED." THAT MYSTiFiED ME AT THE TiME-- MOST OF MY SiXTH GRADE HAD FEATHERED HAiR. (i DiDN'T, MYSELF, BUT MY BROTHER DiD.)
7TH GRADE
MATT DEMONSTRATES...
HOW TO COMB YOUR WiNGS!
① TAKE COMB OUT OF BACK POCKET.
Wrangler
② RiGHT HAND COMBS HAiR DOWN iNTO LEFT PALM.
③ RiGHT HAND COMBS HAiR BACK AS LEFT HAND FOLDS HAiR ONTO HEAD.
④ REPEAT UNTiL HAiR AROUND FACE iS PERPENDiCULAR TO HAiR ON SiDES.
SUCCESS!

Overhead view of me on rec room rug
(with Dad standing on chair), 1975

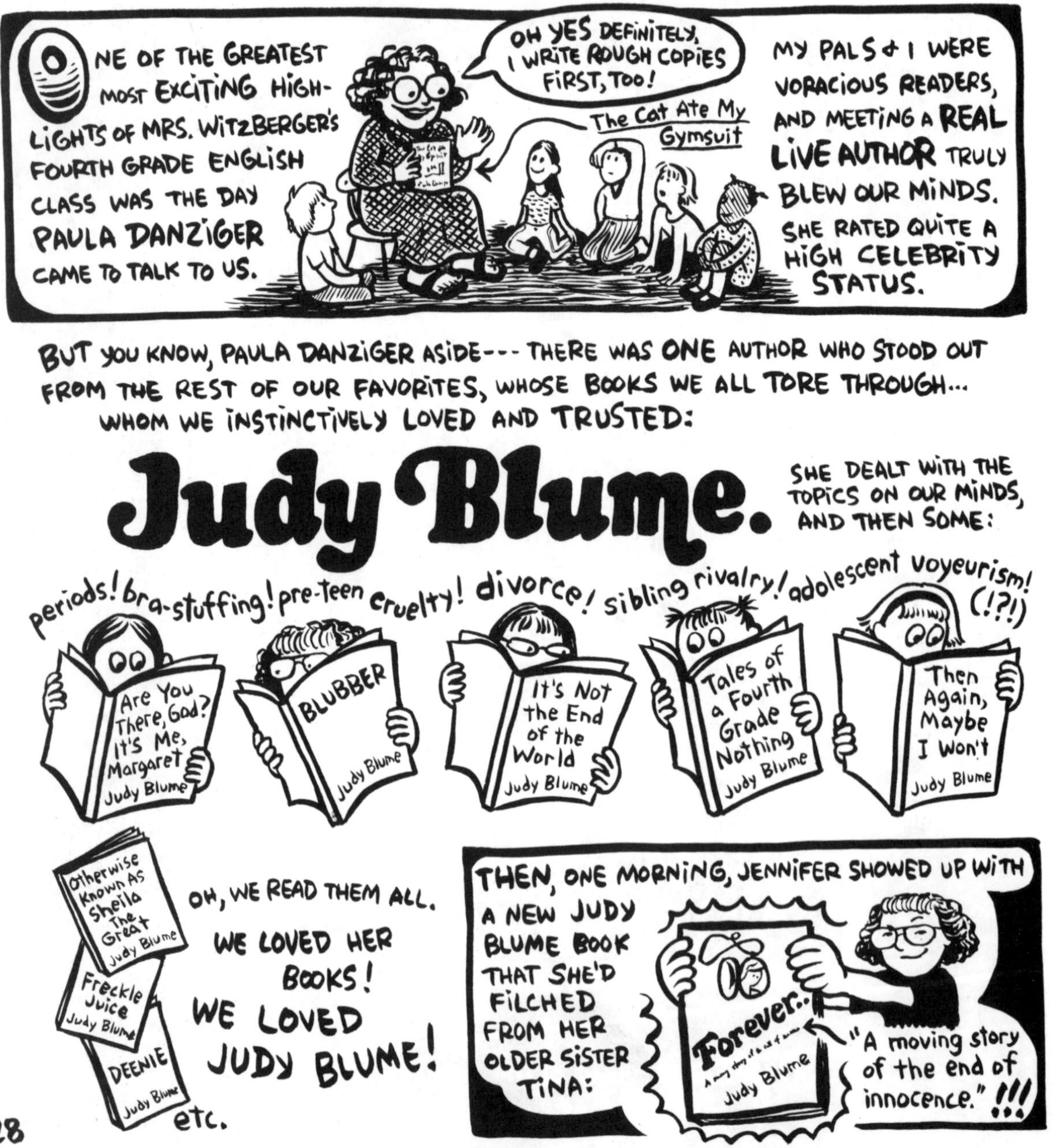
ONE OF THE GREATEST MOST EXCITING HIGH-LIGHTS OF MRS. WITZBERGER'S FOURTH GRADE ENGLISH CLASS WAS THE DAY PAULA DANZIGER CAME TO TALK TO US.
OH YES DEFINITELY, I WRITE ROUGH COPIES FIRST, TOO!
The Cat Ate My Gymsuit
MY PALS & I WERE VORACIOUS READERS, AND MEETING A REAL LIVE AUTHOR TRULY BLEW OUR MINDS.
SHE RATED QUITE A HIGH CELEBRITY STATUS.
BUT YOU KNOW, PAULA DANZIGER ASIDE--- THERE WAS ONE AUTHOR WHO STOOD OUT FROM THE REST OF OUR FAVORITES, WHOSE BOOKS WE ALL TORE THROUGH... WHOM WE INSTINCTIVELY LOVED AND TRUSTED:
Judy Blume.
SHE DEALT WITH THE TOPICS ON OUR MINDS, AND THEN SOME:
periods! bra-stuffing! pre-teen cruelty! divorce! sibling rivalry! adolescent voyeurism! (!?!)
Are You There, God? It's Me, Margaret Judy Blume
BLUBBER Judy Blume
It's Not the End of the World Judy Blume
Tales of a Fourth Grade Nothing Judy Blume
Then Again, Maybe I Won't Judy Blume
Otherwise Known As Sheila The Great Judy Blume
Freckle Juice Judy Blume
DEENIE Judy Blume
OH, WE READ THEM ALL.
WE LOVED HER BOOKS!
WE LOVED JUDY BLUME!
etc.
THEN, ONE MORNING, JENNIFER SHOWED UP WITH A NEW JUDY BLUME BOOK THAT SHE'D FILCHED FROM HER OLDER SISTER TINA:
Forever.. Judy Blume
"A moving story of the end of innocence." !!!

FOREVER SOON MADE ITS COVERT WAY AROUND MY LI'L CIRCLE OF FRIENDS. GRACIOUS! THERE WAS *ACTUAL SEX* IN IT! WE WERE JUDY BLUME AFICIONADAS, BUT <u>FOREVER</u> WAS LIKE, A WHOLE 'NOTHER THING!!*

WE VERY QUICKLY LEARNED WHERE TO FIND THE BOOK'S HIGHLIGHTS. AND~ WE GOT A **NEW CODE WORD** FOR (penis)!!

PAGE 85: He led my hand to his penis. "Katherine... I'd like you to meet Ralph."

THIS WAS GOOD, BECAUSE SHELLY HAD REALLY BEEN DRIVING ME CRAZY WITH HER NOTES, IN WHICH SHE'D FIGURE OUT WAYS TO DISGUISE THE WORD "PENIS!"

A pen is not a pencil! write back!

Forever... Judy Blume

PAGE 116: "I'm sorry," he said, "I couldn't hold off." ... "I'm not disappointed." But I was. I'd wanted it to be perfect. "Maybe it was the rubber," Michael said. "I should have bought the more expensive kind."

HOO HOO!

*MAY I DIGRESS A MOMENT? I'D LIKE TO POINT OUT

"a whole 'nother" dilemma.

"A WHOLE 'NOTHER THING." "A WHOLE 'NOTHER WORLD." OBVIOUSLY THE GRAMMAR IS **WRONG.** BUT, WHAT ARE THE ALTERNATIVES TO THIS CURIOUS CONSTRUCTION? "ANOTHER WHOLE THING." UH... *NOT.* "A WHOLE OTHER THING." GRAMMATICALLY CORRECT, YES, BUT DOESN'T PACK NEARLY THE "OTHERNESS" PUNCH THAT EVEN THE <u>SPLIT</u> "ANOTHER" DOES. "A WHOLE 'NOTHER"--IT'S A WHOLE 'NOTHER THING.

BROUGHT TO YOU BY THE A WHOLE 'NOTHER COUNCIL.

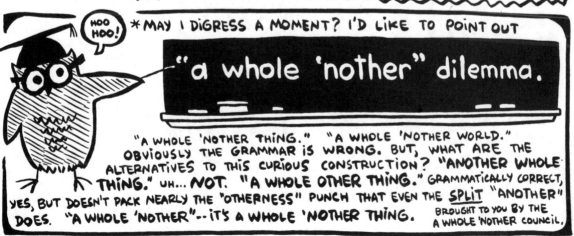

29

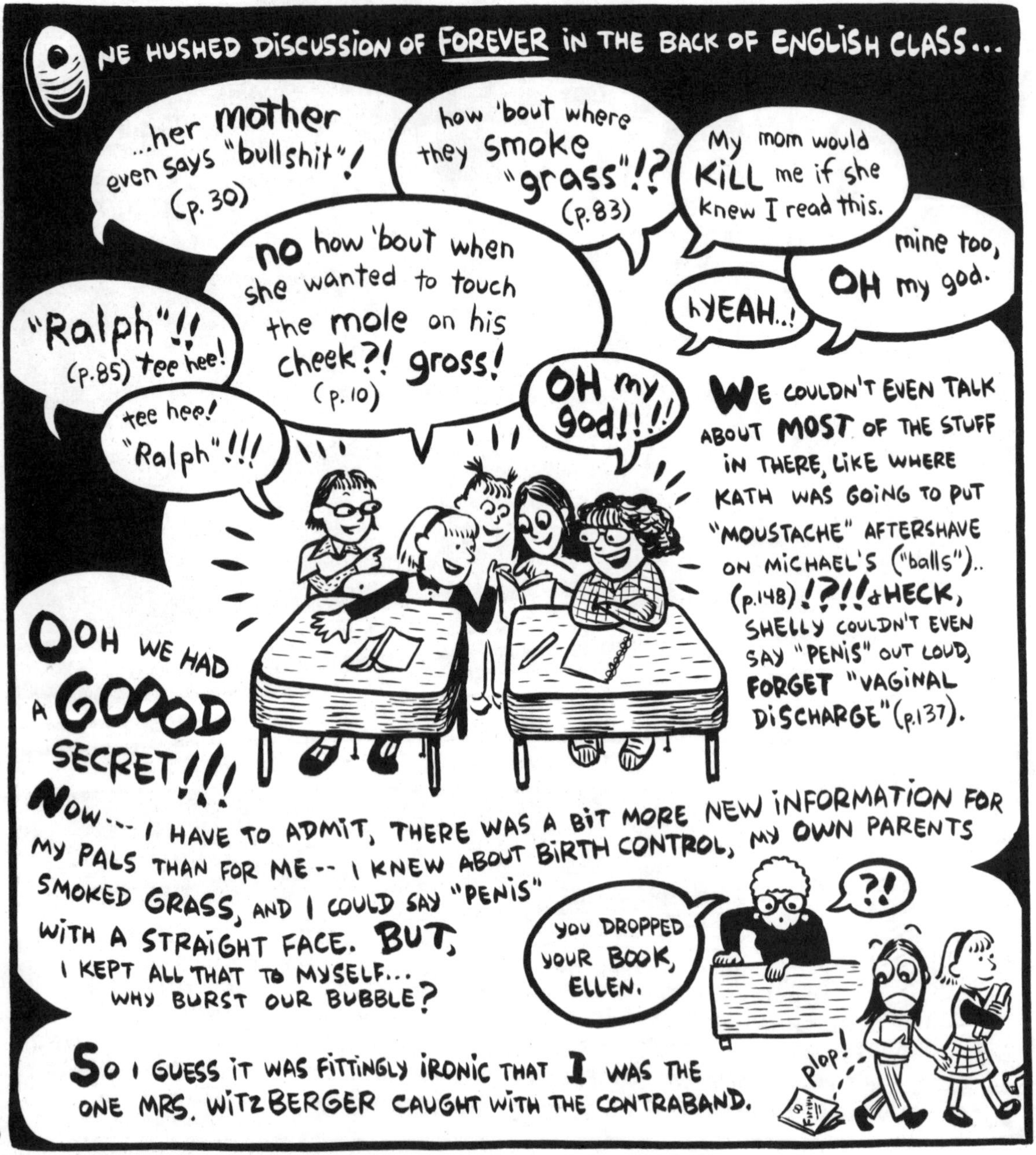
ONE HUSHED DISCUSSION OF FOREVER IN THE BACK OF ENGLISH CLASS...
...her mother even says "bullshit"! (p. 30)
how 'bout where they smoke "grass"!? (p. 83)
My mom would KILL me if she knew I read this.
mine too, OH my god.
hYEAH..!
no how 'bout when she wanted to touch the mole on his cheek?! gross! (p. 10)
"Ralph"!! (p. 85) tee hee!
tee hee! "Ralph"!!!
OH my god!!!!
WE COULDN'T EVEN TALK ABOUT MOST OF THE STUFF IN THERE, LIKE WHERE KATH WAS GOING TO PUT "MOUSTACHE" AFTERSHAVE ON MICHAEL'S ("balls").. (p.148) !?!! & HECK, SHELLY COULDN'T EVEN SAY "PENIS" OUT LOUD, FORGET "VAGINAL DISCHARGE" (p.137).
OOH WE HAD A GOOOOD SECRET!!!
NOW... I HAVE TO ADMIT, THERE WAS A BIT MORE NEW INFORMATION FOR MY PALS THAN FOR ME -- I KNEW ABOUT BIRTH CONTROL, MY OWN PARENTS SMOKED GRASS, AND I COULD SAY "PENIS" WITH A STRAIGHT FACE. BUT, I KEPT ALL THAT TO MYSELF... WHY BURST OUR BUBBLE?
YOU DROPPED YOUR BOOK, ELLEN.
?!
plop!
SO I GUESS IT WAS FITTINGLY IRONIC THAT I WAS THE ONE MRS. WITZBERGER CAUGHT WITH THE CONTRABAND.

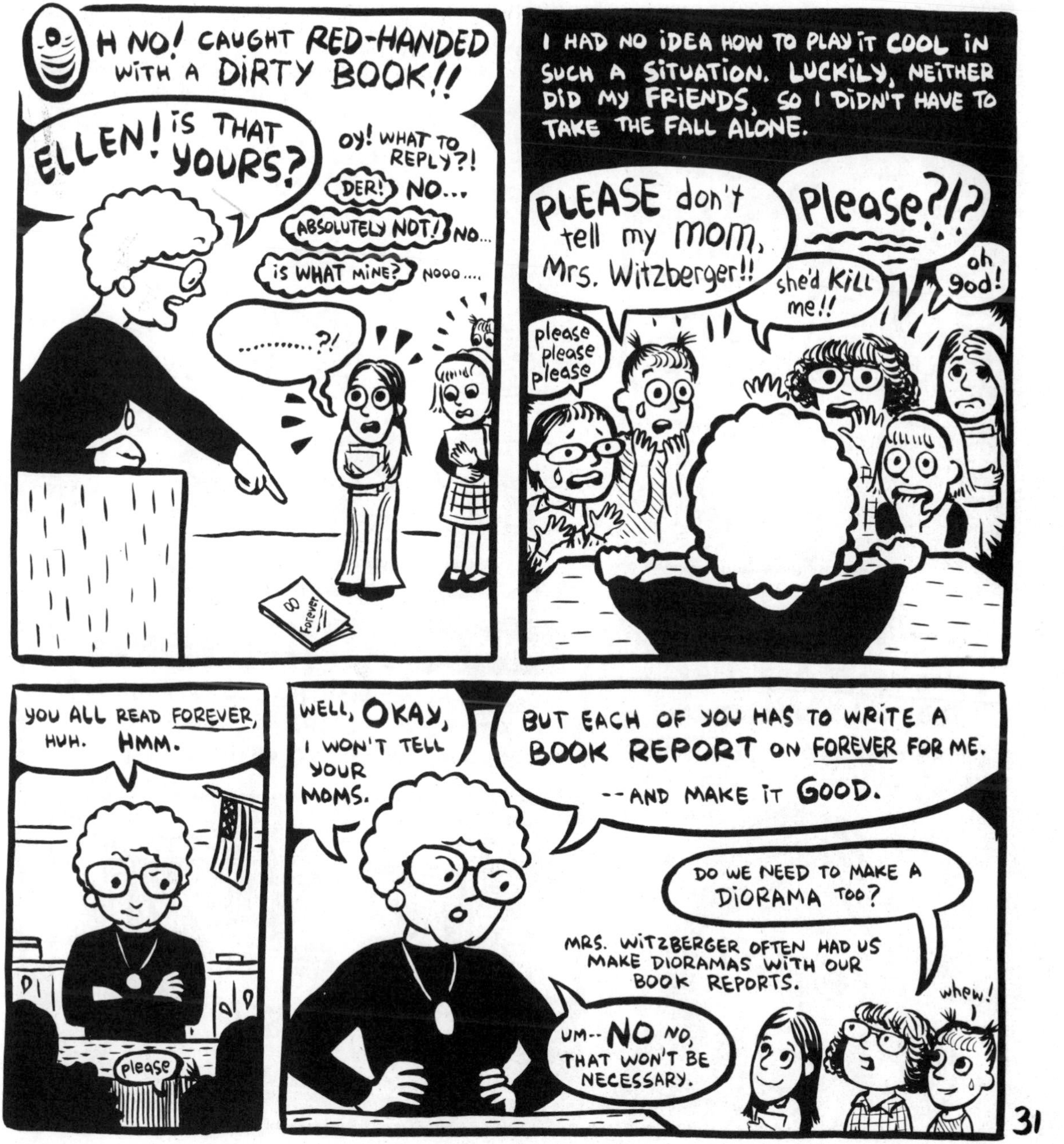
OH NO! CAUGHT RED-HANDED WITH A DIRTY BOOK!!
ELLEN! IS THAT YOURS?
OY! WHAT TO REPLY?!
DER! NO...
ABSOLUTELY NOT! NO...
IS WHAT MINE? NOOO....
..........?!
Forever
I HAD NO IDEA HOW TO PLAY IT COOL IN SUCH A SITUATION. LUCKILY, NEITHER DID MY FRIENDS, SO I DIDN'T HAVE TO TAKE THE FALL ALONE.
PLEASE don't tell my mom, Mrs. Witzberger!!
Please?!?
she'd KILL me!!
oh god!
please please please
YOU ALL READ FOREVER, HUH. HMM.
please
WELL, OKAY, I WON'T TELL YOUR MOMS.
BUT EACH OF YOU HAS TO WRITE A BOOK REPORT ON FOREVER FOR ME.
--AND MAKE IT GOOD.
DO WE NEED TO MAKE A DIORAMA TOO?
MRS. WITZBERGER OFTEN HAD US MAKE DIORAMAS WITH OUR BOOK REPORTS.
UM-- NO NO, THAT WON'T BE NECESSARY.
whew!

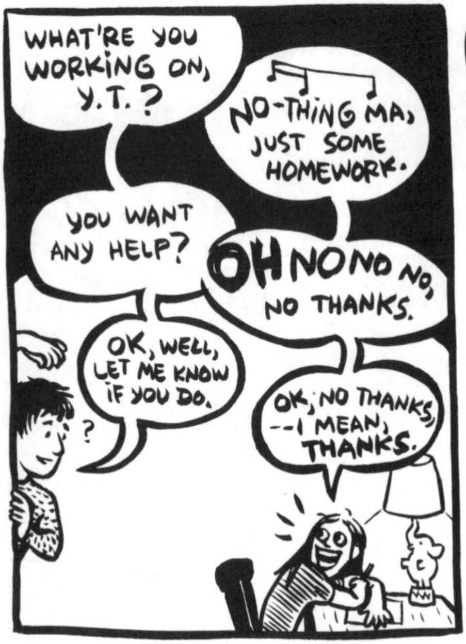
WHAT'RE YOU WORKING ON, Y.T.?
NO-THING MA, JUST SOME HOMEWORK.
YOU WANT ANY HELP?
OH NO NO NO, NO THANKS.
OK, WELL, LET ME KNOW IF YOU DO.
?
OK, NO THANKS, --I MEAN, THANKS.

MOM USUALLY HELPED EDIT MY WRITING FOR ENGLISH CLASS. THOUGH I KNEW SHE WOULDN'T CARE THAT I'D READ FOREVER, I ALSO KNEW SHE WOULD CARE (MAYBE A LOT) THAT I'D KEPT IT A SECRET. (WHAT WAS I ASHAMED OF, ETC.) BETTER TO AVOID THE NEEDLESSLY EMBARRASSING HEART-TO-HEART, IF POSSIBLE.

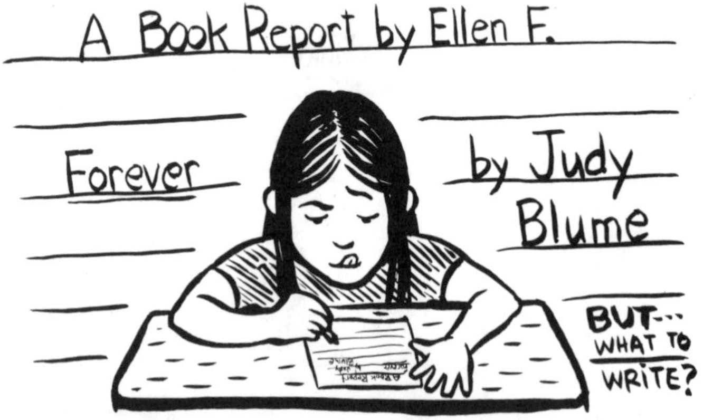
A Book Report by Ellen F.
Forever
by Judy Blume
BUT--- WHAT TO WRITE?

WHAT DID MRS. WITZBERGER WANT FROM US? SHOULD I WRITE ABOUT STUFF LIKE... "RALPH"?!! SUDDENLY I WISHED WE HAD TO DO A DIORAMA AFTER ALL (THOSE WERE EASY TO ACE).

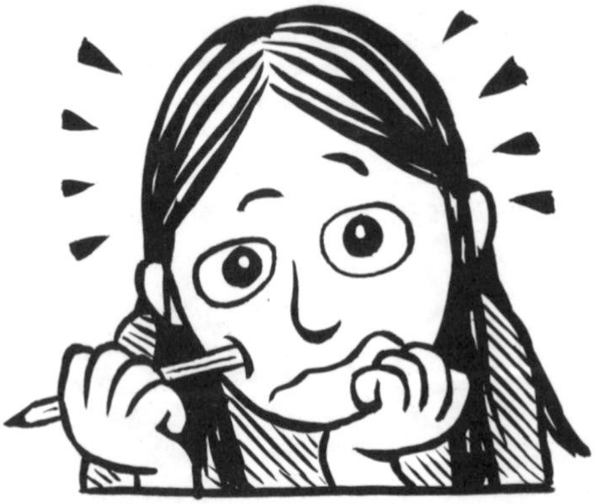

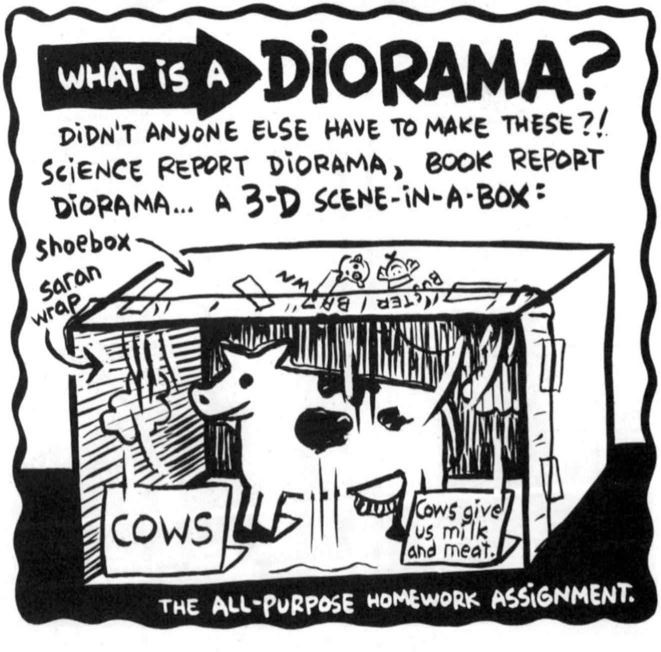
WHAT IS A DIORAMA?
DIDN'T ANYONE ELSE HAVE TO MAKE THESE?! SCIENCE REPORT DIORAMA, BOOK REPORT DIORAMA... A 3-D SCENE-IN-A-BOX:
shoebox
saran wrap
COWS
Cows give us milk and meat.
THE ALL-PURPOSE HOMEWORK ASSIGNMENT.

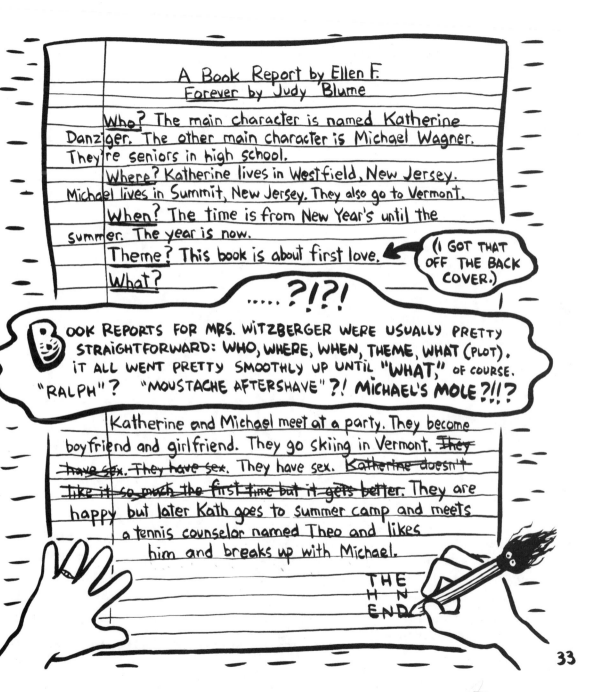

A Book Report by Ellen F.
Forever by Judy Blume

Who? The main character is named Katherine Danziger. The other main character is Michael Wagner. They're seniors in high school.

Where? Katherine lives in Westfield, New Jersey. Michael lives in Summit, New Jersey. They also go to Vermont.

When? The time is from New Year's until the summer. The year is now.

Theme? This book is about first love.

(I GOT THAT OFF THE BACK COVER.)

What?

..... ?!?!

BOOK REPORTS FOR MRS. WITZBERGER WERE USUALLY PRETTY STRAIGHTFORWARD: WHO, WHERE, WHEN, THEME, WHAT (PLOT). IT ALL WENT PRETTY SMOOTHLY UP UNTIL "WHAT," OF COURSE. "RALPH"? "MOUSTACHE AFTERSHAVE"?! MICHAEL'S MOLE?!!?

Katherine and Michael meet at a party. They become boyfriend and girlfriend. They go skiing in Vermont. ~~They have sex. They have sex.~~ They have sex. ~~Katherine doesn't like it so much the first time but it gets better.~~ They are happy but later Kath goes to summer camp and meets a tennis counselor named Theo and likes him and breaks up with Michael.

THE
H N
END

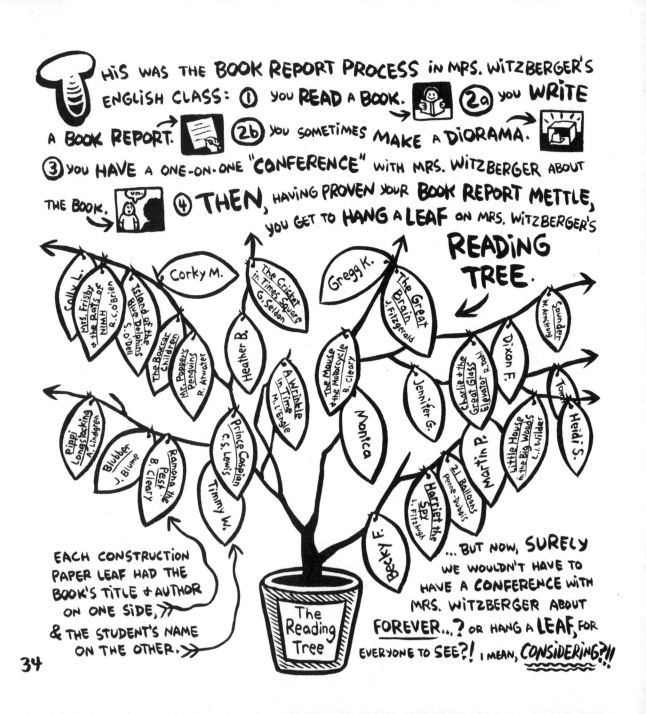

THIS WAS THE BOOK REPORT PROCESS IN MRS. WITZBERGER'S ENGLISH CLASS: ① YOU READ A BOOK. ②a YOU WRITE A BOOK REPORT. ②b YOU SOMETIMES MAKE A DIORAMA. ③ YOU HAVE A ONE-ON-ONE "CONFERENCE" WITH MRS. WITZBERGER ABOUT THE BOOK. ④ THEN, HAVING PROVEN YOUR BOOK REPORT METTLE, YOU GET TO HANG A LEAF ON MRS. WITZBERGER'S

READING TREE.

The Reading Tree

EACH CONSTRUCTION PAPER LEAF HAD THE BOOK'S TITLE & AUTHOR ON ONE SIDE, & THE STUDENT'S NAME ON THE OTHER.

... BUT NOW, SURELY WE WOULDN'T HAVE TO HAVE A CONFERENCE WITH MRS. WITZBERGER ABOUT FOREVER...? OR HANG A LEAF, FOR EVERYONE TO SEE?! I MEAN, CONSIDERING?!!

Leaf names and titles:
- Sally L.
- Mrs. Frisby & the Rats of NIMH — R.C. O'Brien
- Island of the Blue Dolphins — S. O'Dell
- Corky M.
- The Boxcar Children
- Mr. Popper's Penguins — R. Atwater
- The Cricket in Times Square — G. Selden
- Heather B.
- A Wrinkle in Time — M. L'Engle
- Gregg K.
- The Mouse & the Motorcycle — B. Cleary
- The Great Brain — J. Fitzgerald
- Sounder — W. Armstrong
- Dixon F.
- Charlie & the Great Glass Elevator — R. Dahl
- Jennifer G.
- Tom T.
- Monica
- Little House in the Big Woods — L.I. Wilder
- Heidi S.
- Pippi Longstocking — A. Lindgren
- Blubber — J. Blume
- Ramona the Pest — B. Cleary
- Prince Caspian — C.S. Lewis
- Timmy W.
- Martin P.
- 21 Balloons — Pène Dubois
- Harriet the Spy — L. Fitzhugh
- Becky F.

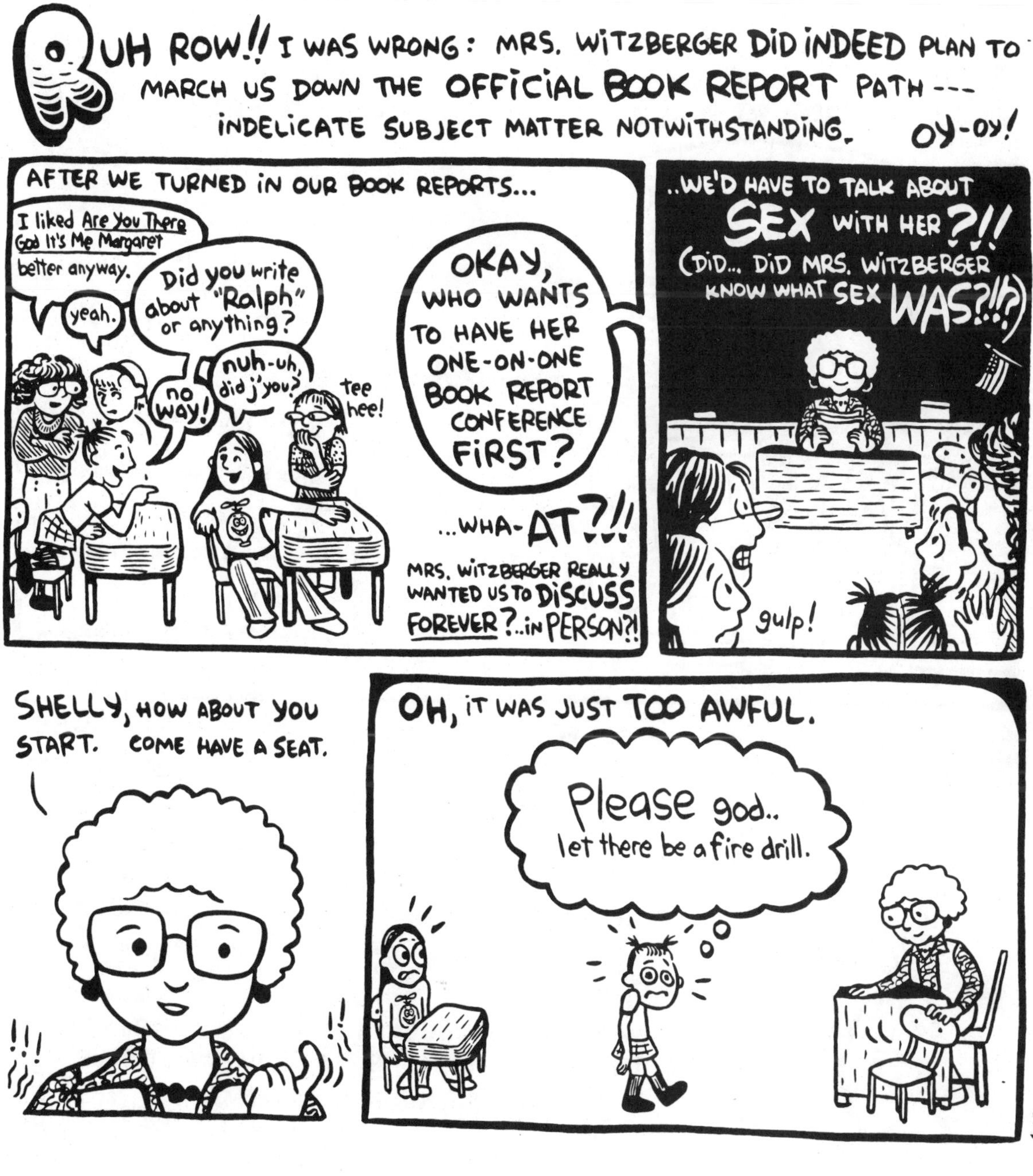
RUH ROW!! I WAS WRONG: MRS. WITZBERGER DID INDEED PLAN TO MARCH US DOWN THE OFFICIAL BOOK REPORT PATH --- INDELICATE SUBJECT MATTER NOTWITHSTANDING.
OY-OY!
AFTER WE TURNED IN OUR BOOK REPORTS...
I liked Are You There God It's Me Margaret better anyway.
yeah.
Did you write about "Ralph" or anything?
no way!
nuh-uh, did j'you?
tee hee!
OKAY, WHO WANTS TO HAVE HER ONE-ON-ONE BOOK REPORT CONFERENCE FIRST?
...WHA-AT?!!
MRS. WITZBERGER REALLY WANTED US TO DISCUSS FOREVER?..IN PERSON?!
..WE'D HAVE TO TALK ABOUT SEX WITH HER?!!
(DID... DID MRS. WITZBERGER KNOW WHAT SEX WAS?!!?)
gulp!
SHELLY, HOW ABOUT YOU START. COME HAVE A SEAT.
OH, IT WAS JUST TOO AWFUL.
Please god.. let there be a fire drill.

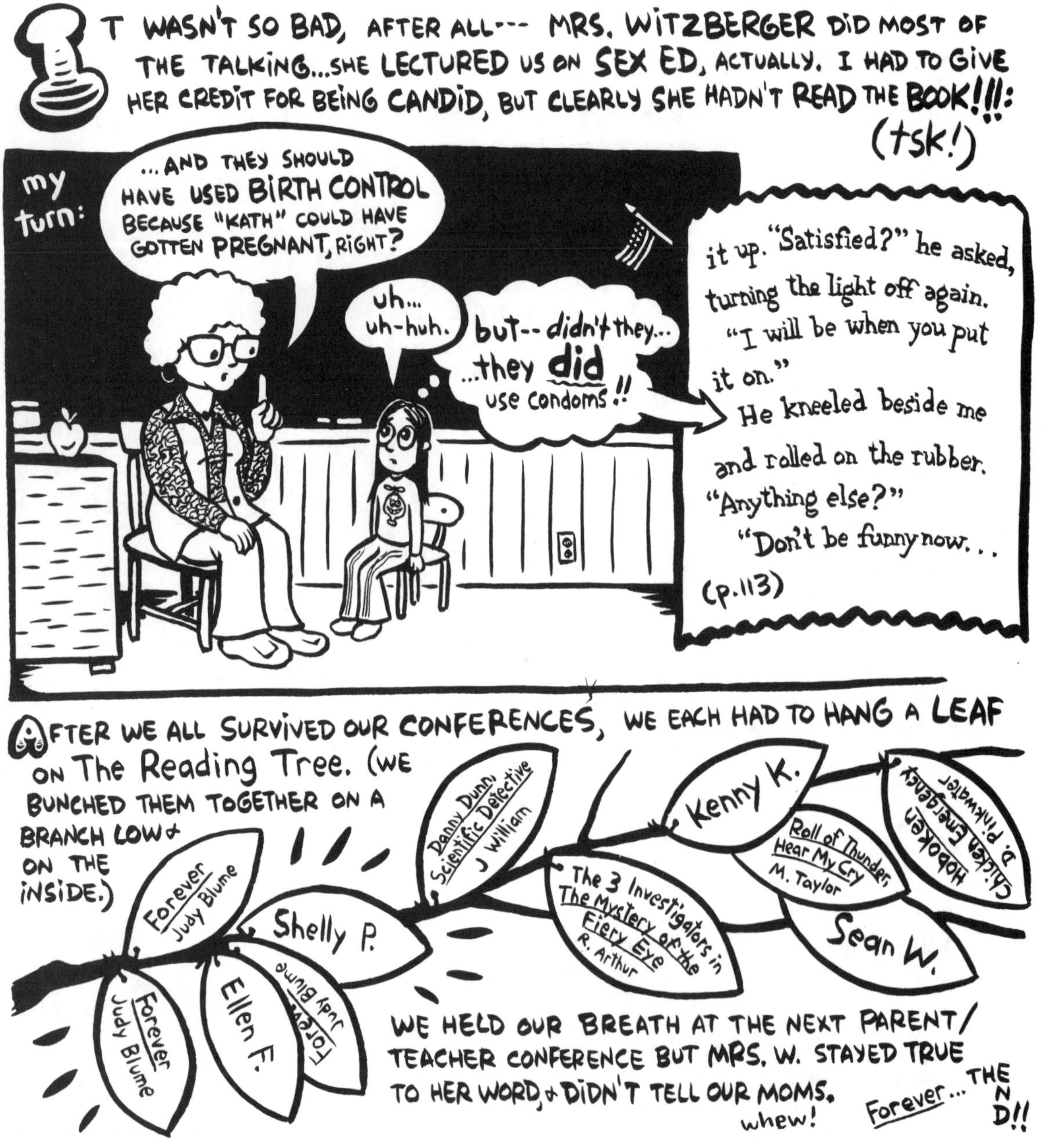
IT WASN'T SO BAD, AFTER ALL--- MRS. WITZBERGER DID MOST OF THE TALKING...SHE LECTURED US ON SEX ED, ACTUALLY. I HAD TO GIVE HER CREDIT FOR BEING CANDID, BUT CLEARLY SHE HADN'T READ THE BOOK!!!:
(tsk!)
my turn:
...AND THEY SHOULD HAVE USED BIRTH CONTROL BECAUSE "KATH" COULD HAVE GOTTEN PREGNANT, RIGHT?
uh... uh-huh.
but-- didn't they... ...they did use condoms!!
it up. "Satisfied?" he asked, turning the light off again. "I will be when you put it on." He kneeled beside me and rolled on the rubber. "Anything else?" "Don't be funny now...
(p.113)
AFTER WE ALL SURVIVED OUR CONFERENCES, WE EACH HAD TO HANG A LEAF ON The Reading Tree. (WE BUNCHED THEM TOGETHER ON A BRANCH LOW & ON THE INSIDE.)
Forever Judy Blume
Shelly P.
Danny Dunn, Scientific Detective J William
The 3 Investigators in The Mystery of the Fiery Eye R. Arthur
Kenny K.
Roll of Thunder, Hear My Cry M. Taylor
Hoboken Chicken Emergency D. Pinkwater
Sean W.
Forever Judy Blume
Ellen F.
Forever Judy Blume
WE HELD OUR BREATH AT THE NEXT PARENT/TEACHER CONFERENCE BUT MRS. W. STAYED TRUE TO HER WORD, & DIDN'T TELL OUR MOMS.
whew!
Forever... THE END!!

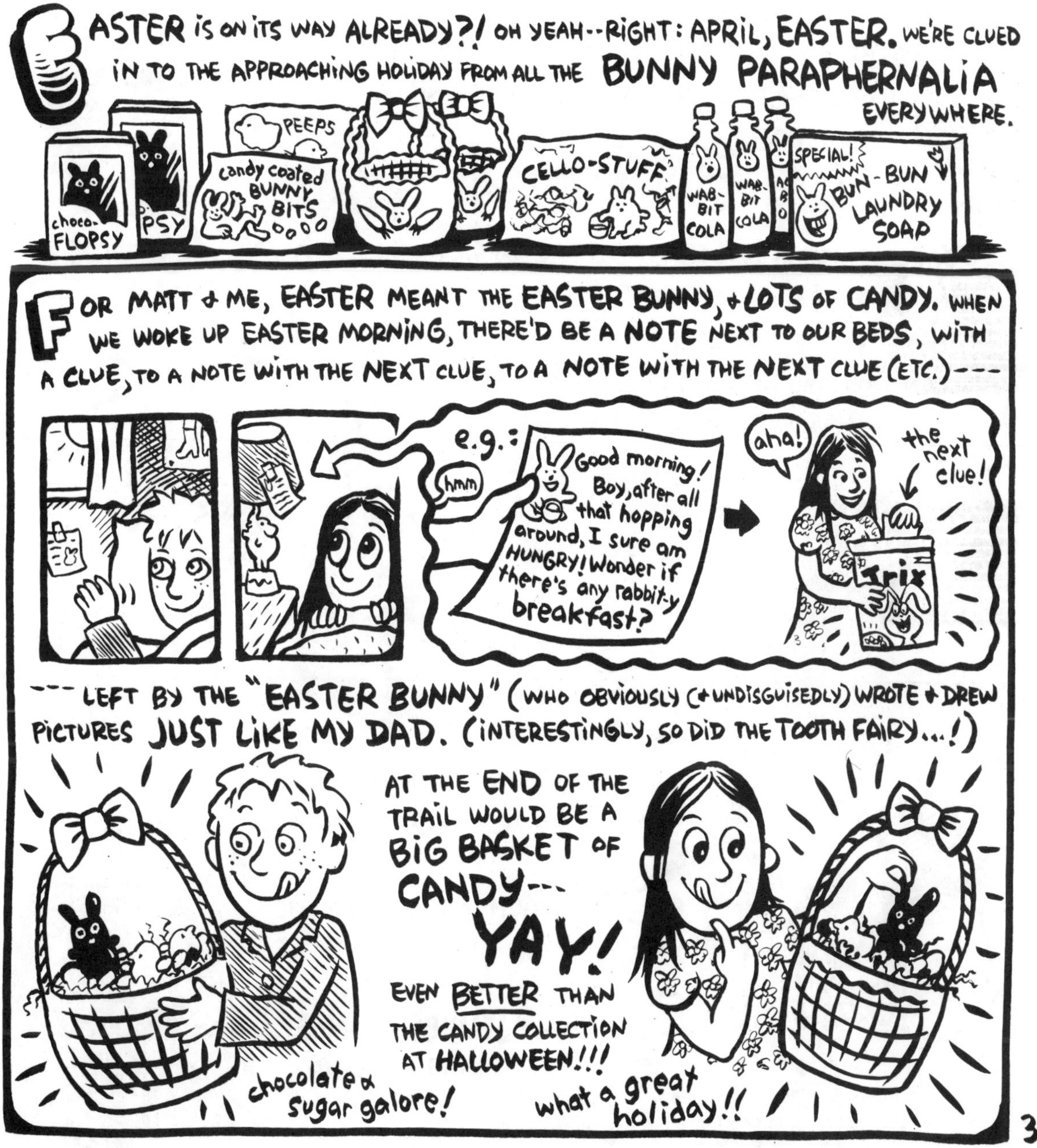
EASTER IS ON ITS WAY ALREADY?! OH YEAH--RIGHT: APRIL, EASTER. WE'RE CLUED IN TO THE APPROACHING HOLIDAY FROM ALL THE BUNNY PARAPHERNALIA EVERYWHERE.
choco-FLOPSY
PSY
PEEPS
candy coated BUNNY BITS
CELLO-STUFF
WAB-BIT COLA
WAB-BIT COLA
SPECIAL!
BUN-BUN LAUNDRY SOAP
FOR MATT & ME, EASTER MEANT THE EASTER BUNNY, & LOTS OF CANDY. WHEN WE WOKE UP EASTER MORNING, THERE'D BE A NOTE NEXT TO OUR BEDS, WITH A CLUE, TO A NOTE WITH THE NEXT CLUE, TO A NOTE WITH THE NEXT CLUE (ETC.)---
hmm
e.g.:
Good morning! Boy, after all that hopping around, I sure am HUNGRY! Wonder if there's any rabbit-y breakfast?
aha!
the next clue!
Trix
---LEFT BY THE "EASTER BUNNY" (WHO OBVIOUSLY (& UNDISGUISEDLY) WROTE & DREW PICTURES JUST LIKE MY DAD. (INTERESTINGLY, SO DID THE TOOTH FAIRY...!)
AT THE END OF THE TRAIL WOULD BE A BIG BASKET OF CANDY---
YAY!
EVEN BETTER THAN THE CANDY COLLECTION AT HALLOWEEN!!!
chocolate & sugar galore!
what a great holiday!!

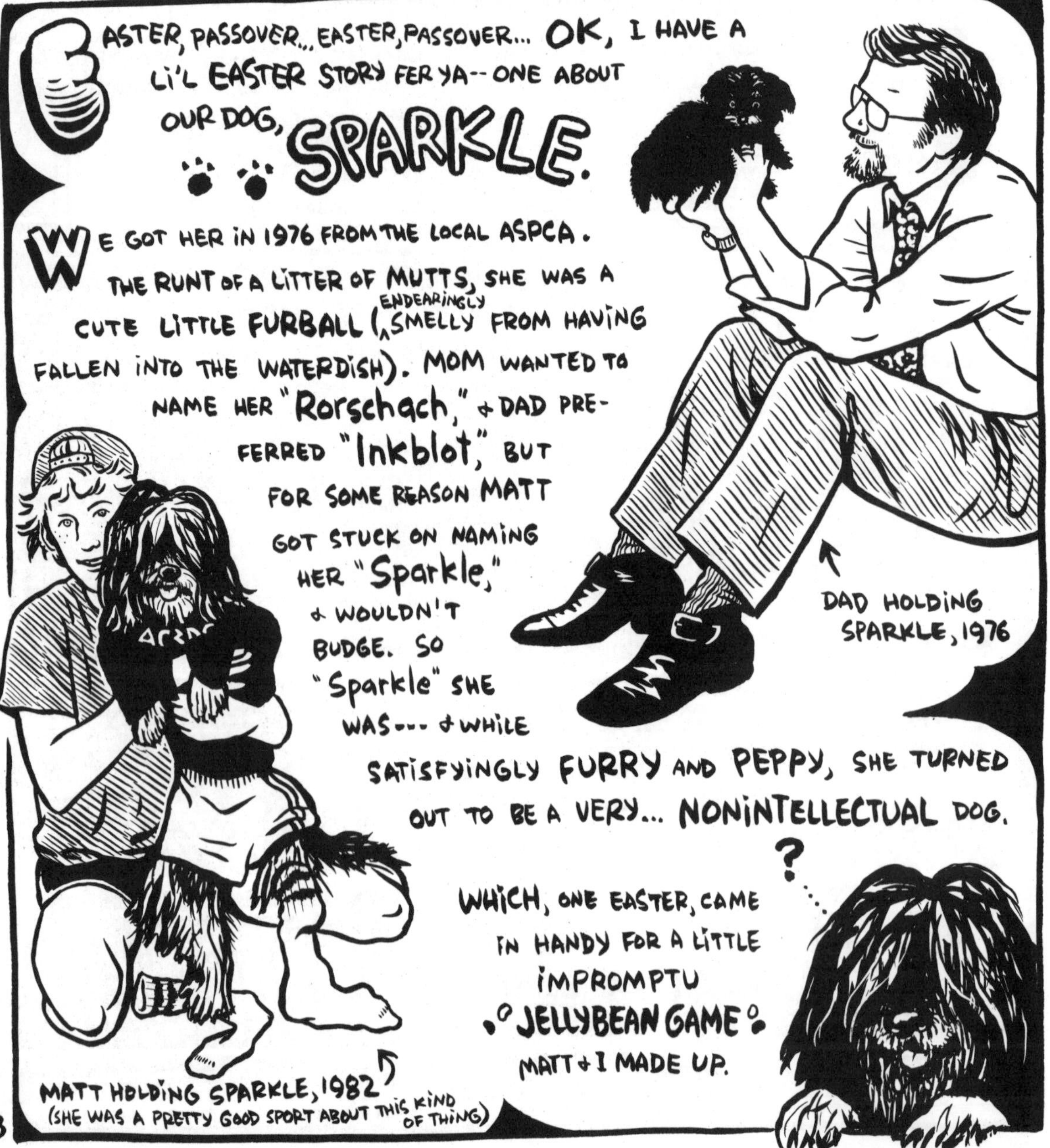
EASTER, PASSOVER... EASTER, PASSOVER... OK, I HAVE A LI'L EASTER STORY FER YA-- ONE ABOUT OUR DOG, SPARKLE.
WE GOT HER IN 1976 FROM THE LOCAL ASPCA. THE RUNT OF A LITTER OF MUTTS, SHE WAS A CUTE LITTLE FURBALL (ENDEARINGLY SMELLY FROM HAVING FALLEN INTO THE WATERDISH). MOM WANTED TO NAME HER "Rorschach," & DAD PREFERRED "Inkblot," BUT FOR SOME REASON MATT GOT STUCK ON NAMING HER "Sparkle," & WOULDN'T BUDGE. SO "Sparkle" SHE WAS--- & WHILE SATISFYINGLY FURRY AND PEPPY, SHE TURNED OUT TO BE A VERY... NONINTELLECTUAL DOG.
DAD HOLDING SPARKLE, 1976
?
WHICH, ONE EASTER, CAME IN HANDY FOR A LITTLE IMPROMPTU JELLYBEAN GAME MATT & I MADE UP.
MATT HOLDING SPARKLE, 1982
(SHE WAS A PRETTY GOOD SPORT ABOUT THIS KIND OF THING)

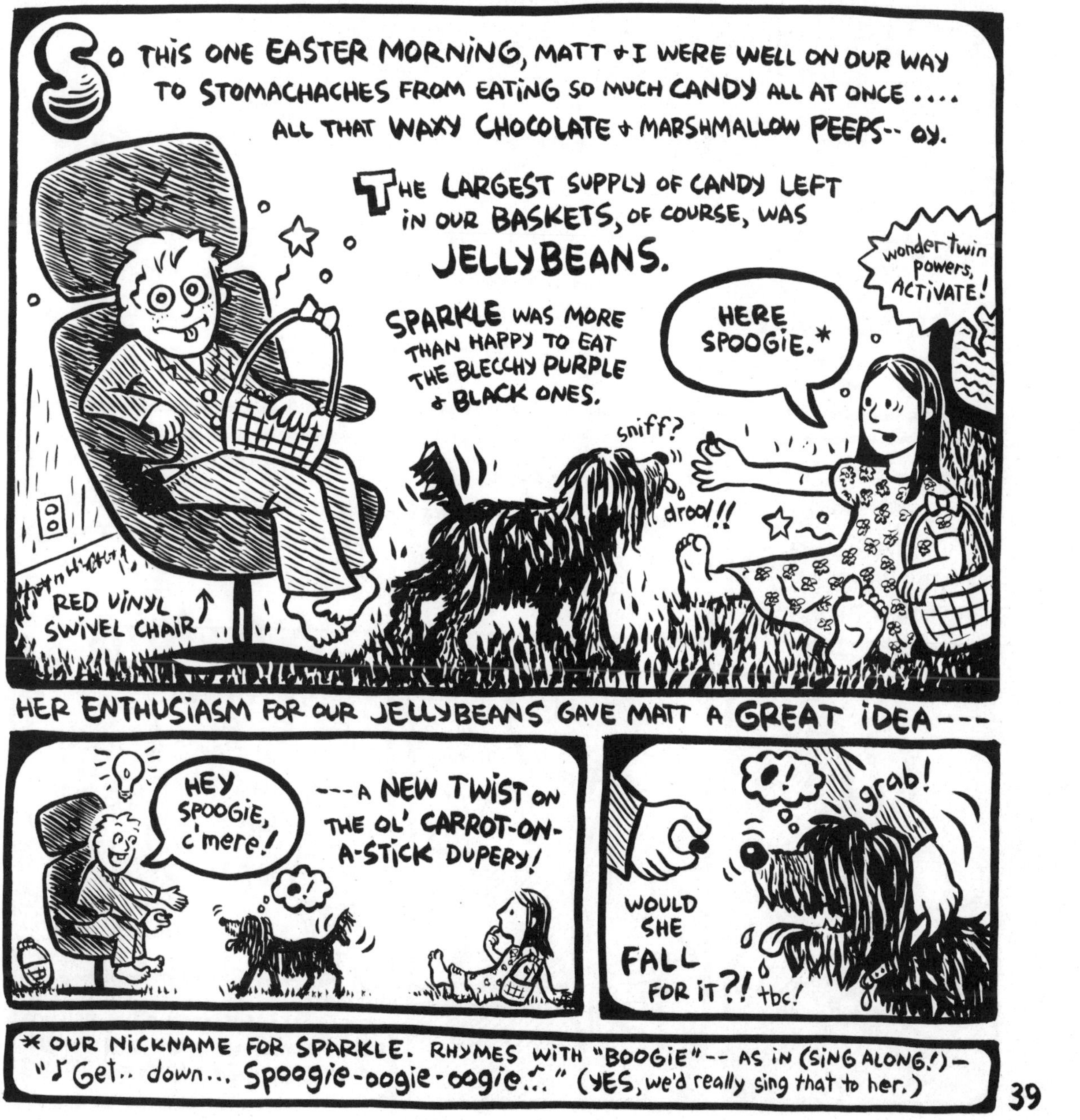
So this one EASTER MORNING, MATT & I WERE WELL ON OUR WAY TO STOMACHACHES FROM EATING SO MUCH CANDY ALL AT ONCE.... ALL THAT WAXY CHOCOLATE & MARSHMALLOW PEEPS-- OY.
THE LARGEST SUPPLY OF CANDY LEFT IN OUR BASKETS, OF COURSE, WAS JELLYBEANS.
SPARKLE WAS MORE THAN HAPPY TO EAT THE BLECCHY PURPLE & BLACK ONES.
wonder twin powers, ACTIVATE!
HERE SPOOGIE.*
sniff?
drool!!
RED VINYL SWIVEL CHAIR
HER ENTHUSIASM FOR OUR JELLYBEANS GAVE MATT A GREAT IDEA---
HEY SPOOGIE, c'mere!
---A NEW TWIST ON THE OL' CARROT-ON-A-STICK DUPERY!
grab!
WOULD SHE FALL FOR IT?!
tbc!
* OUR NICKNAME FOR SPARKLE. RHYMES WITH "BOOGIE"-- AS IN (SING ALONG!)— "♪ Get.. down... Spoogie-oogie-oogie♪." (YES, we'd really sing that to her.)

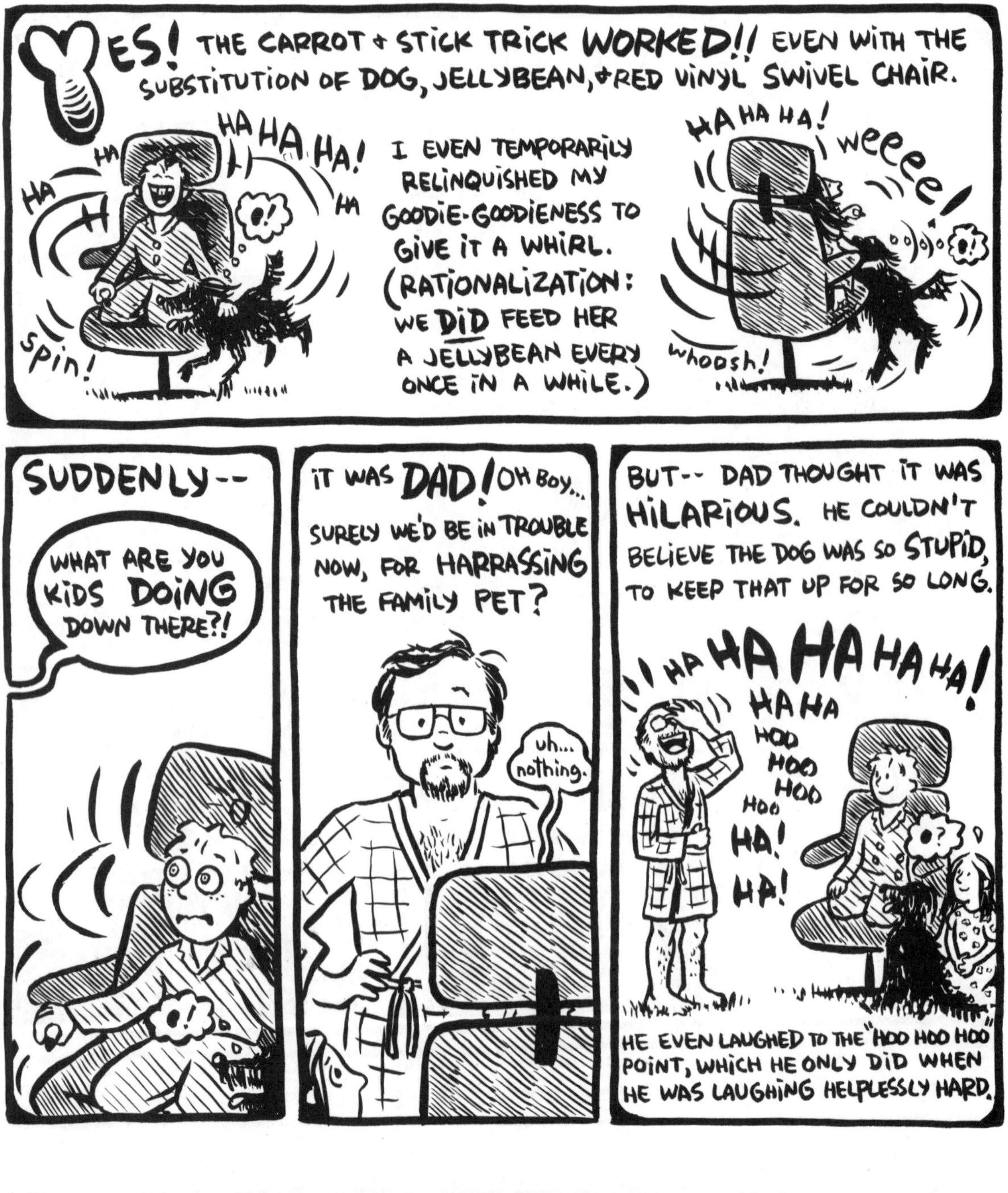
YES! THE CARROT & STICK TRICK WORKED!! EVEN WITH THE SUBSTITUTION OF DOG, JELLYBEAN, & RED VINYL SWIVEL CHAIR.
HA HA HA!
HA
HA
HA
spin!
I EVEN TEMPORARILY RELINQUISHED MY GOODIE-GOODIENESS TO GIVE IT A WHIRL. (RATIONALIZATION: WE DID FEED HER A JELLYBEAN EVERY ONCE IN A WHILE.)
HA HA HA!
weeee!
whoosh!
SUDDENLY--
WHAT ARE YOU KIDS DOING DOWN THERE?!
IT WAS DAD! OH Boy...
SURELY WE'D BE IN TROUBLE NOW, FOR HARRASSING THE FAMILY PET?
uh... nothing.
BUT-- DAD THOUGHT IT WAS HILARIOUS. HE COULDN'T BELIEVE THE DOG WAS SO STUPID, TO KEEP THAT UP FOR SO LONG.
HA HA HA HA HA HA!
HA HA
HOO HOO HOO
HOO
HA!
HA!
HE EVEN LAUGHED TO THE "HOO HOO HOO" POINT, WHICH HE ONLY DID WHEN HE WAS LAUGHING HELPLESSLY HARD.

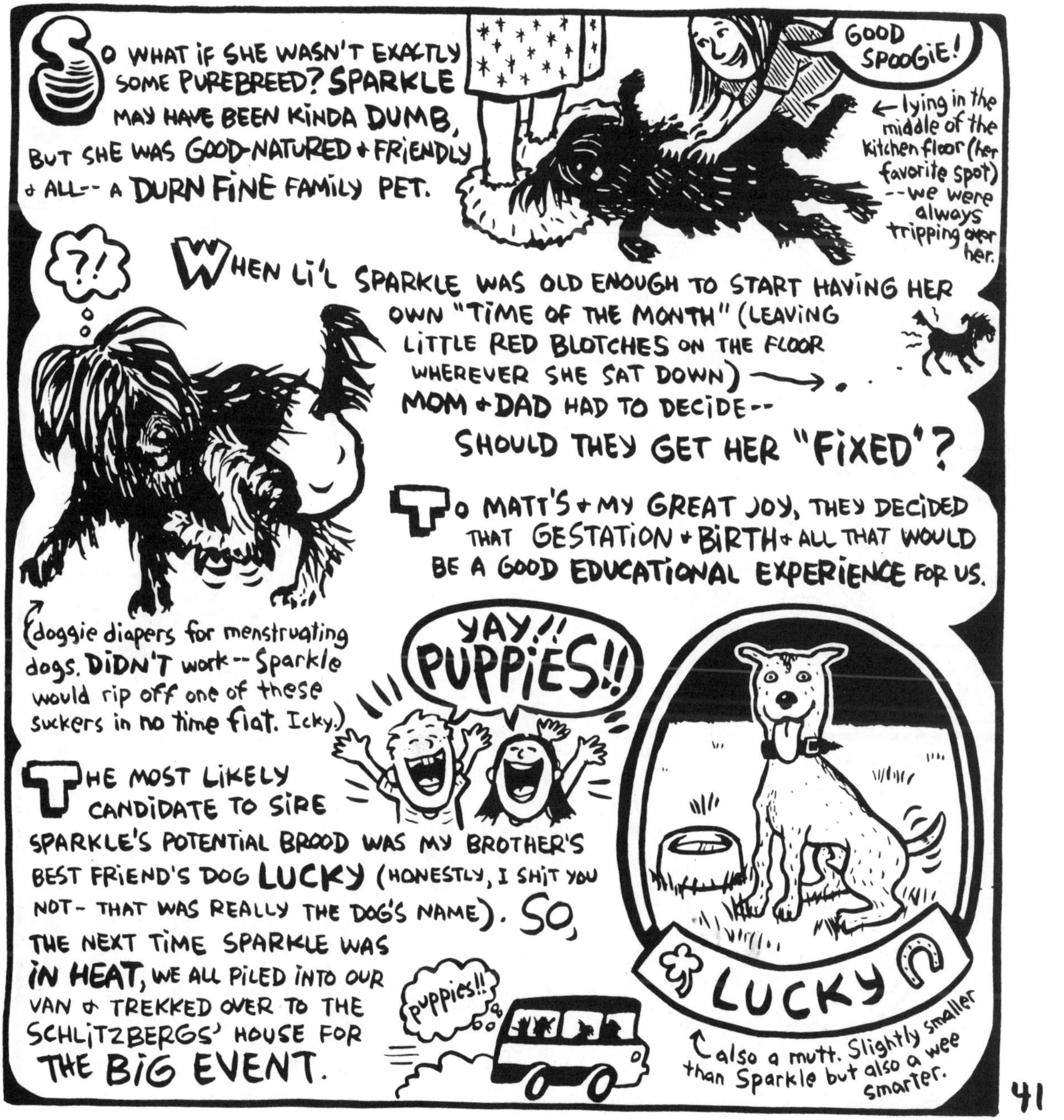
SO WHAT IF SHE WASN'T EXACTLY SOME PUREBREED? SPARKLE MAY HAVE BEEN KINDA DUMB, BUT SHE WAS GOOD-NATURED & FRIENDLY & ALL-- A DURN FINE FAMILY PET.
GOOD SPOOGIE!
← lying in the middle of the kitchen floor (her favorite spot) --we were always tripping over her.
?!
WHEN LI'L SPARKLE WAS OLD ENOUGH TO START HAVING HER OWN "TIME OF THE MONTH" (LEAVING LITTLE RED BLOTCHES ON THE FLOOR WHEREVER SHE SAT DOWN) → . . MOM & DAD HAD TO DECIDE--
SHOULD THEY GET HER "FIXED"?
TO MATT'S & MY GREAT JOY, THEY DECIDED THAT GESTATION & BIRTH & ALL THAT WOULD BE A GOOD EDUCATIONAL EXPERIENCE FOR US.
(doggie diapers for menstruating dogs. DIDN'T work-- Sparkle would rip off one of these suckers in no time flat. Icky.)
YAY!! PUPPIES!!
THE MOST LIKELY CANDIDATE TO SIRE SPARKLE'S POTENTIAL BROOD WAS MY BROTHER'S BEST FRIEND'S DOG LUCKY (HONESTLY, I SHIT YOU NOT- THAT WAS REALLY THE DOG'S NAME). SO, THE NEXT TIME SPARKLE WAS IN HEAT, WE ALL PILED INTO OUR VAN & TREKKED OVER TO THE SCHLITZBERGS' HOUSE FOR THE BIG EVENT.
puppies!!
LUCKY
↑ also a mutt. Slightly smaller than Sparkle but also a wee smarter.

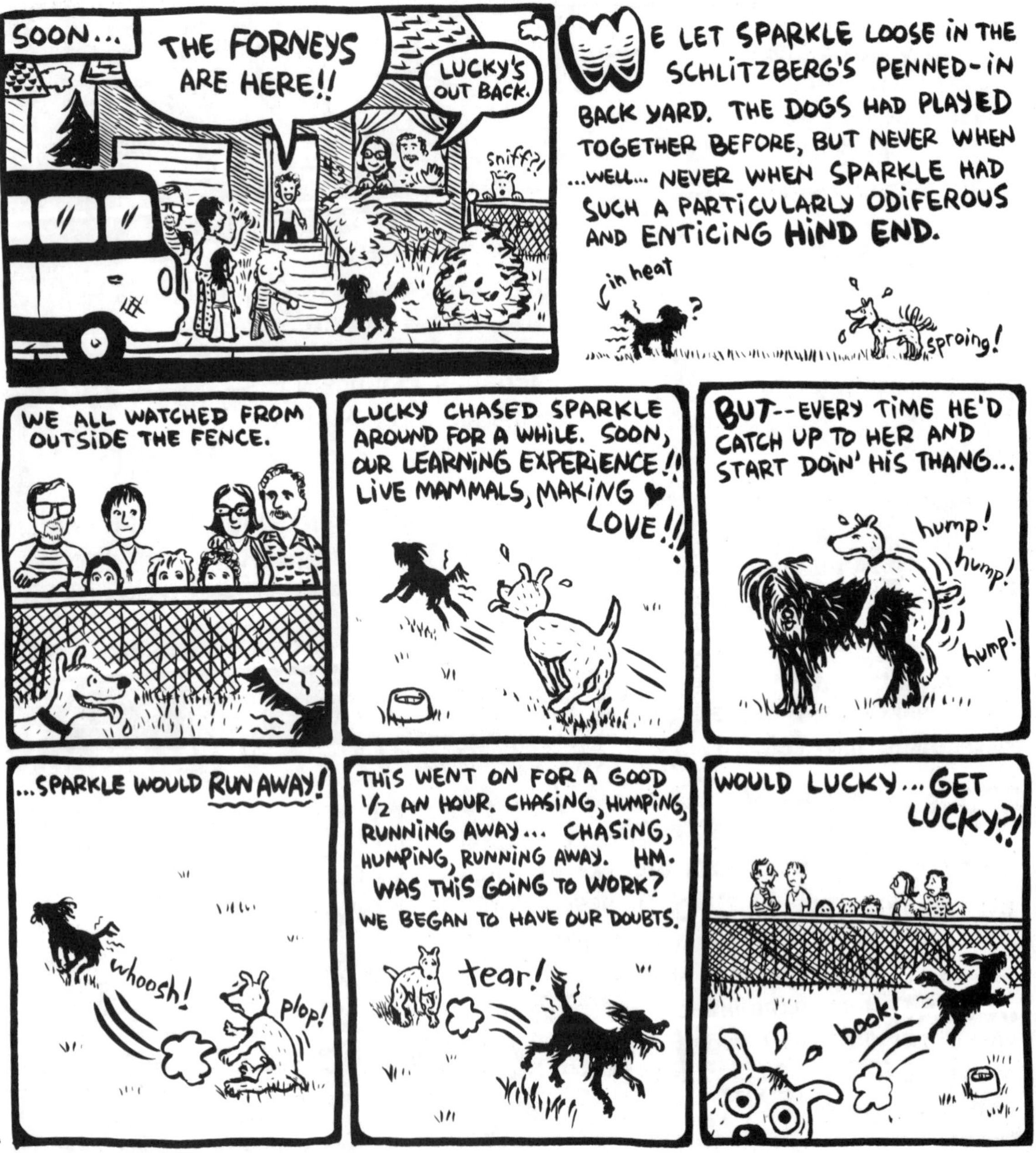
SOON...
THE FORNEYS ARE HERE!!
LUCKY'S OUT BACK.
sniff?!
WE LET SPARKLE LOOSE IN THE SCHLITZBERG'S PENNED-IN BACK YARD. THE DOGS HAD PLAYED TOGETHER BEFORE, BUT NEVER WHEN ...WELL... NEVER WHEN SPARKLE HAD SUCH A PARTICULARLY ODIFEROUS AND ENTICING HIND END.
in heat
sproing!
WE ALL WATCHED FROM OUTSIDE THE FENCE.
LUCKY CHASED SPARKLE AROUND FOR A WHILE. SOON, OUR LEARNING EXPERIENCE!! LIVE MAMMALS, MAKING ♥ LOVE!!!
BUT--EVERY TIME HE'D CATCH UP TO HER AND START DOIN' HIS THANG...
hump!
hump!
hump!
...SPARKLE WOULD RUN AWAY!
whoosh!
plop!
THIS WENT ON FOR A GOOD 1/2 AN HOUR. CHASING, HUMPING, RUNNING AWAY... CHASING, HUMPING, RUNNING AWAY. HM. WAS THIS GOING TO WORK?
WE BEGAN TO HAVE OUR DOUBTS.
tear!
WOULD LUCKY...GET LUCKY?!
book!

FINALLY, SPARKLE STOOD STILL LONG ENOUGH FOR LUCKY TO SEAL THE DEAL...

pork!!

...BUT APPARENTLY SHE'D HAD ENOUGH SOON THEREAFTER, & TRIED TO RUN AWAY AGAIN.

OH NO!

WHAT THE..?

NOW, ANYONE KNOWLEDGEABLE ABOUT CANINE REPRODUCTION WILL TELL YOU THIS IS NORMAL, BUT, WELL, WE DIDN'T KNOW TO EXPECT THIS:

WHEN DOGS MATE, THE MALE DOG EJACULATES ALMOST IMMEDIATELY, AND THE BASE OF HIS PENIS SWELLS SO HE CAN'T PULL OUT. THIS IS KNOWN AS THE "COITAL LOCK."

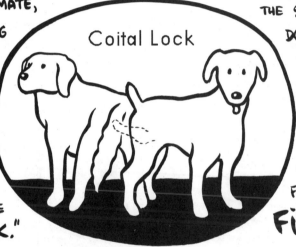

Coital Lock

THE STUCK-TOGETHER DOGS THEN ROTATE RUMP-TO-RUMP (ONE THEORY IS IN THIS POSITION THEY CAN BETTER FIGHT OFF INTRUDERS--- AN ODD IMAGE, NO?) FOR UP TO FORTY-FIVE MINUTES!!!

SO, WHEN SPARKLE TOOK OFF... OOOGH. WE DIDN'T KNOW WHO TO FEEL SORRIER FOR, SPARKLE OR LUCKY.

dragging Lucky around yard

yelp!

YOW!

yipe!

OY. QUITE SOME SEX ED.

they look like a pushmepullyou.*

MAN THAT HURTS.

*FROM DR. DOOLITTLE

43

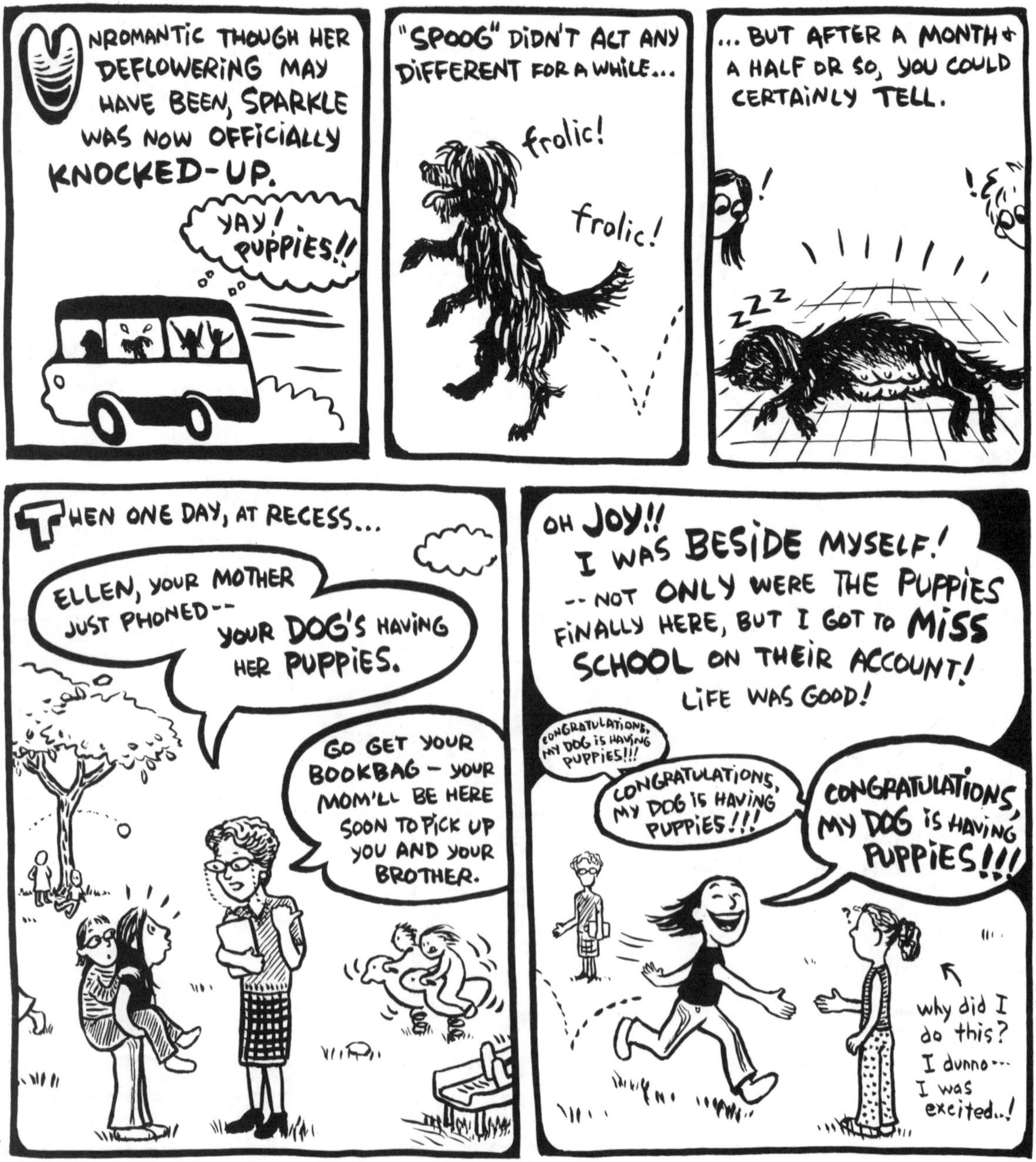
UNROMANTIC THOUGH HER DEFLOWERING MAY HAVE BEEN, SPARKLE WAS NOW OFFICIALLY KNOCKED-UP.
YAY! PUPPIES!!
"SPOOG" DIDN'T ACT ANY DIFFERENT FOR A WHILE...
frolic!
frolic!
... BUT AFTER A MONTH & A HALF OR SO, YOU COULD CERTAINLY TELL.
!
!
ZZZ
THEN ONE DAY, AT RECESS...
ELLEN, YOUR MOTHER JUST PHONED-- YOUR DOG'S HAVING HER PUPPIES.
GO GET YOUR BOOKBAG - YOUR MOM'LL BE HERE SOON TO PICK UP YOU AND YOUR BROTHER.
OH JOY!! I WAS BESIDE MYSELF! -- NOT ONLY WERE THE PUPPIES FINALLY HERE, BUT I GOT TO MISS SCHOOL ON THEIR ACCOUNT! LIFE WAS GOOD!
CONGRATULATIONS, MY DOG IS HAVING PUPPIES!!!
CONGRATULATIONS, MY DOG IS HAVING PUPPIES!!!
CONGRATULATIONS, MY DOG IS HAVING PUPPIES!!!
why did I do this? I dunno--- I was excited..!

BY THE TIME WE GOT HOME, SPARKLE HAD DELIVERED FOUR TINY PUPPIES!! AND-- AS MOM TOLD US IN THE CAR, SPEEDING HOME -- THEY WERE IN THE LITTLE CORNER/FORT/THING IN MY ROOM!!! WHAT AN HONOR!

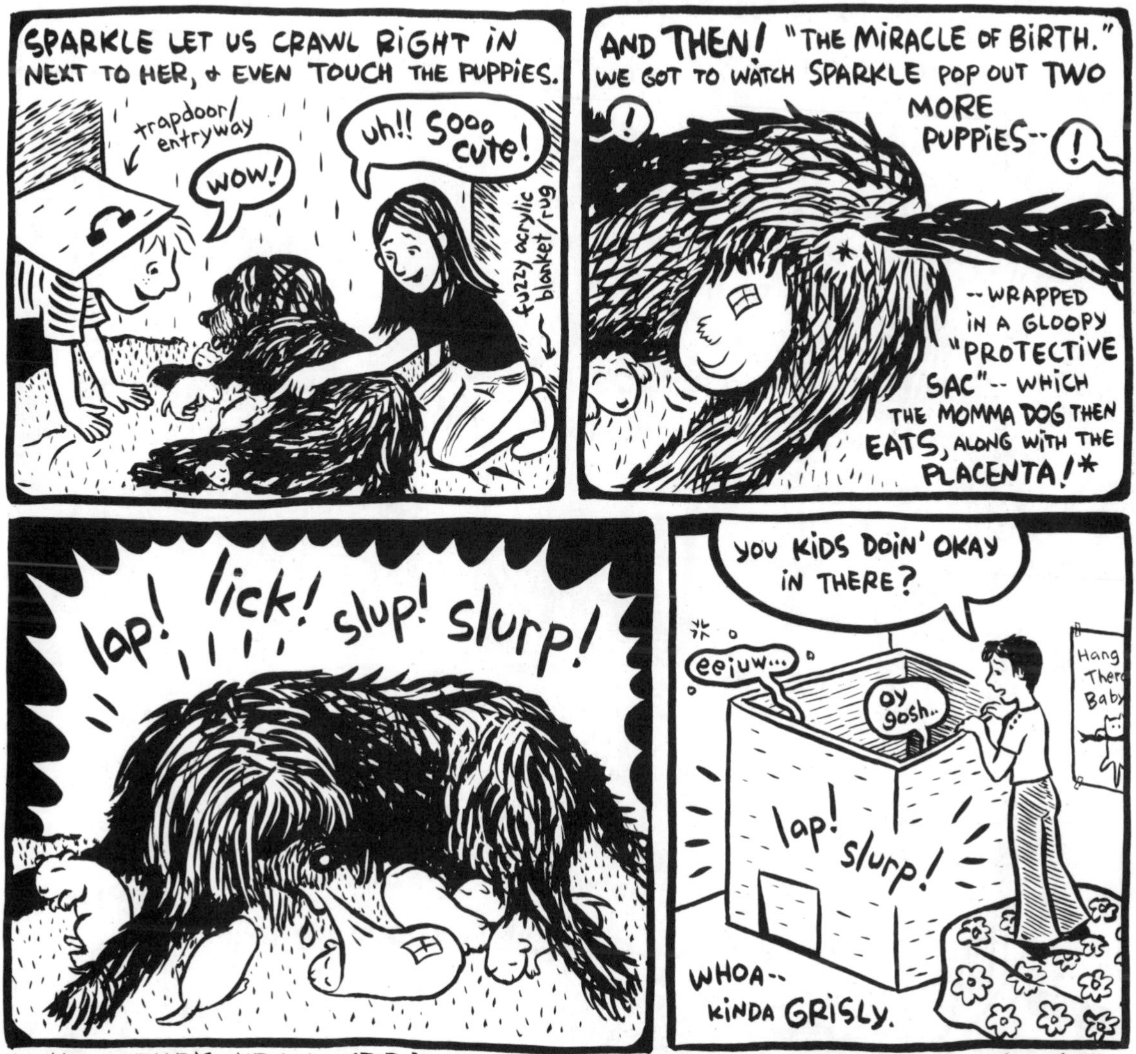

SPARKLE LET US CRAWL RIGHT IN NEXT TO HER, & EVEN TOUCH THE PUPPIES.
trapdoor/ entryway
WOW!
uh!! Sooo cute!
fuzzy acrylic blanket/rug
AND THEN! "THE MIRACLE OF BIRTH." WE GOT TO WATCH SPARKLE POP OUT TWO MORE PUPPIES--
!
!
--WRAPPED IN A GLOOPY "PROTECTIVE SAC"-- WHICH THE MOMMA DOG THEN EATS, ALONG WITH THE PLACENTA!*
lap! lick! slup! slurp!
YOU KIDS DOIN' OKAY IN THERE?
eeiuw...
oy gosh..
Hang There Baby
lap! slurp!
WHOA-- KINDA GRISLY.

*OH BUT THAT'S NOT ALL-- STOP IF YOU KNOW THIS ALREADY BUT THE MOMMA DOG HAS TO LICK THE PUPPIES' "ANOGENITAL REGIONS" TO MAKE THEM "GO"-- & SHE EATS ALL THAT TOO. mm, mmm.

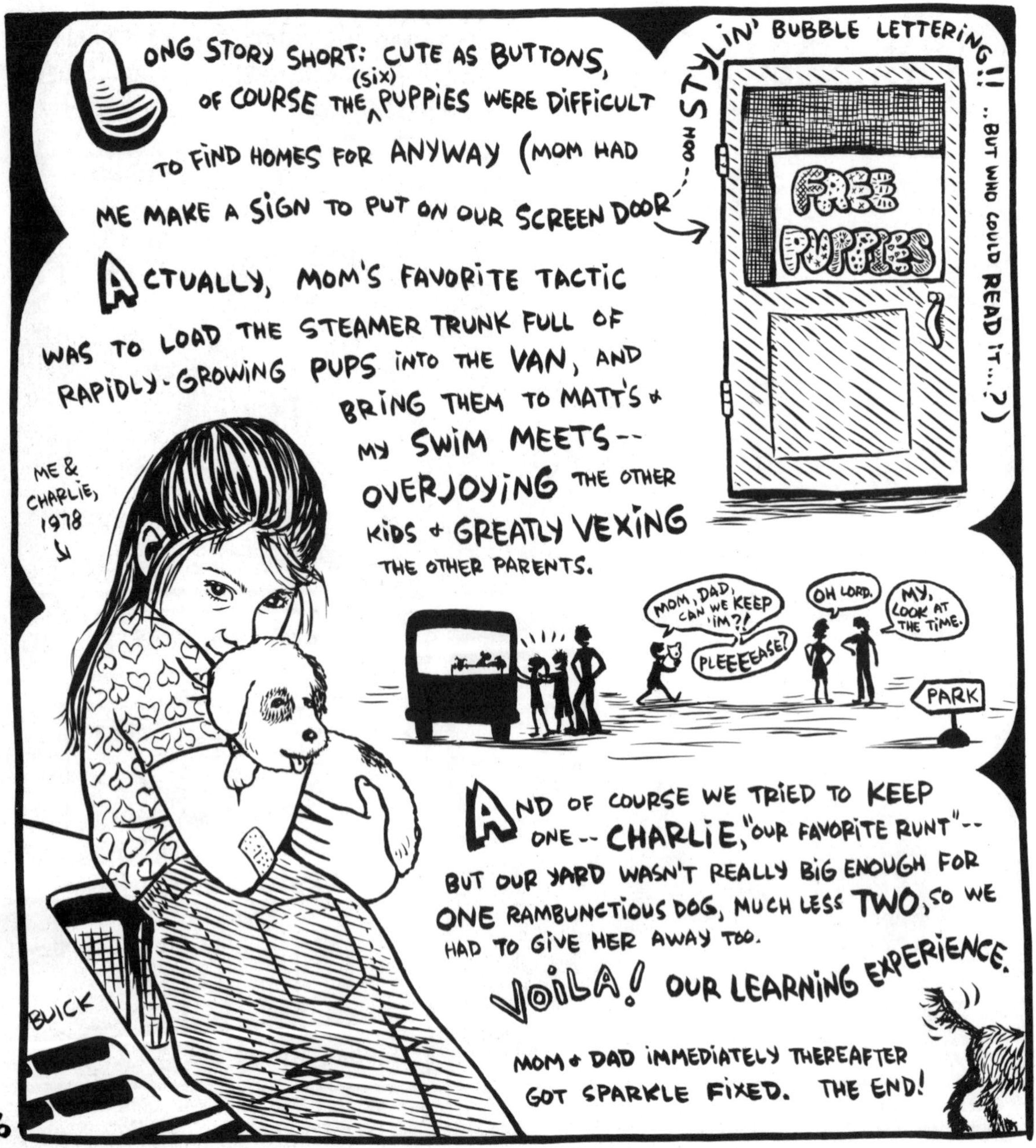

LONG STORY SHORT: CUTE AS BUTTONS, OF COURSE THE (SIX) PUPPIES WERE DIFFICULT TO FIND HOMES FOR ANYWAY (MOM HAD ME MAKE A SIGN TO PUT ON OUR SCREEN DOOR
OOO STYLIN' BUBBLE LETTERING!! ..BUT WHO COULD READ IT...?)
FREE PUPPIES
ACTUALLY, MOM'S FAVORITE TACTIC WAS TO LOAD THE STEAMER TRUNK FULL OF RAPIDLY-GROWING PUPS INTO THE VAN, AND BRING THEM TO MATT'S & MY SWIM MEETS-- OVERJOYING THE OTHER KIDS & GREATLY VEXING THE OTHER PARENTS.
ME & CHARLIE, 1978
MOM, DAD, CAN WE KEEP 'IM?!
PLEEEEASE?
OH LORD.
MY, LOOK AT THE TIME.
PARK
AND OF COURSE WE TRIED TO KEEP ONE -- CHARLIE, "OUR FAVORITE RUNT" -- BUT OUR YARD WASN'T REALLY BIG ENOUGH FOR ONE RAMBUNCTIOUS DOG, MUCH LESS TWO, SO WE HAD TO GIVE HER AWAY TOO.
VOILA! OUR LEARNING EXPERIENCE.
BUICK
MOM & DAD IMMEDIATELY THEREAFTER GOT SPARKLE FIXED. THE END!

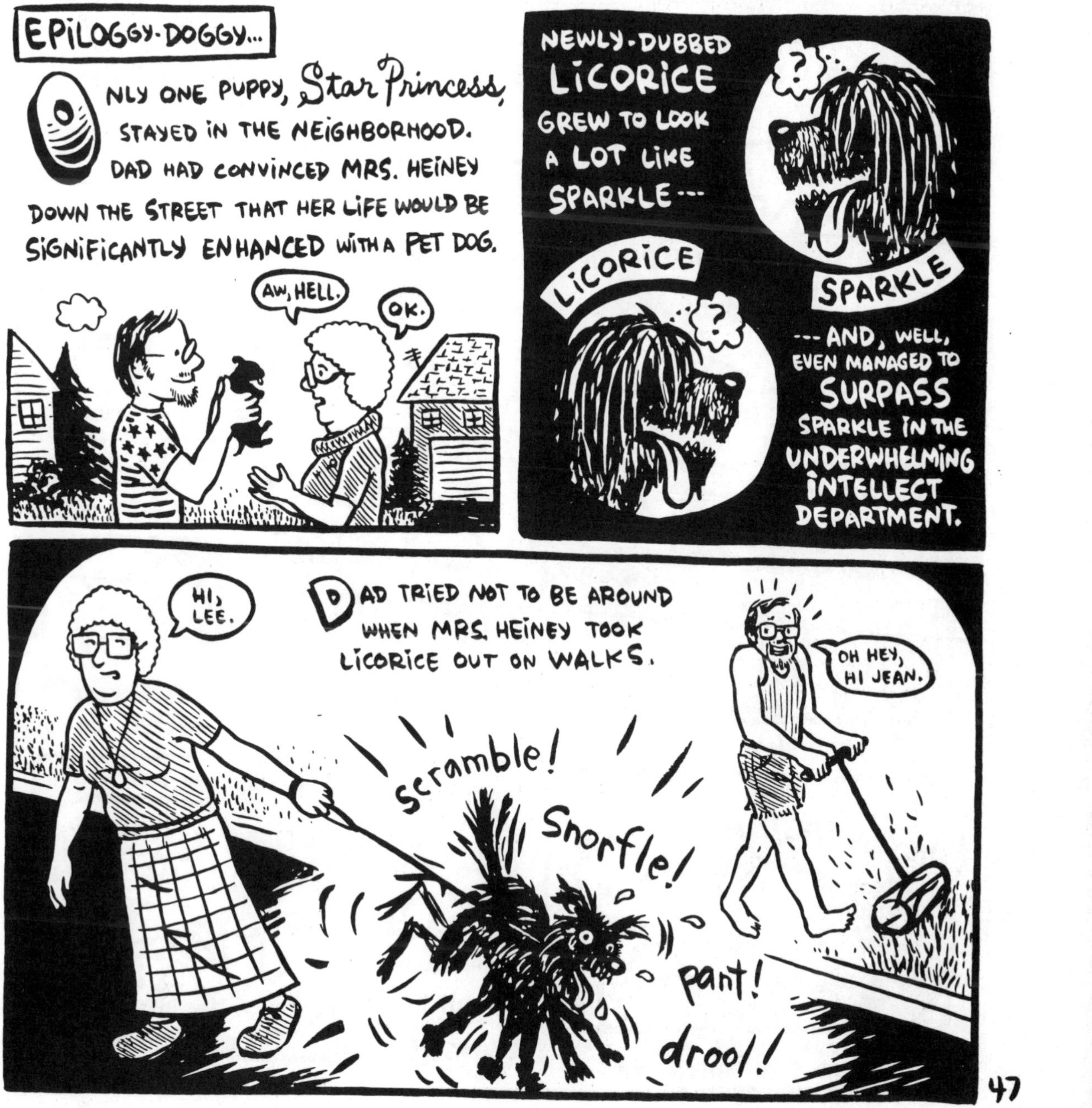
EPILOGGY-DOGGY...
ONLY ONE PUPPY, Star Princess, STAYED IN THE NEIGHBORHOOD. DAD HAD CONVINCED MRS. HEINEY DOWN THE STREET THAT HER LIFE WOULD BE SIGNIFICANTLY ENHANCED WITH A PET DOG.
AW, HELL.
OK.
NEWLY-DUBBED LICORICE GREW TO LOOK A LOT LIKE SPARKLE---
?
SPARKLE
LICORICE
?
---AND, WELL, EVEN MANAGED TO SURPASS SPARKLE IN THE UNDERWHELMING INTELLECT DEPARTMENT.
HI, LEE.
DAD TRIED NOT TO BE AROUND WHEN MRS. HEINEY TOOK LICORICE OUT ON WALKS.
OH HEY, HI JEAN.
scramble!
Snorfle!
pant!
drool!

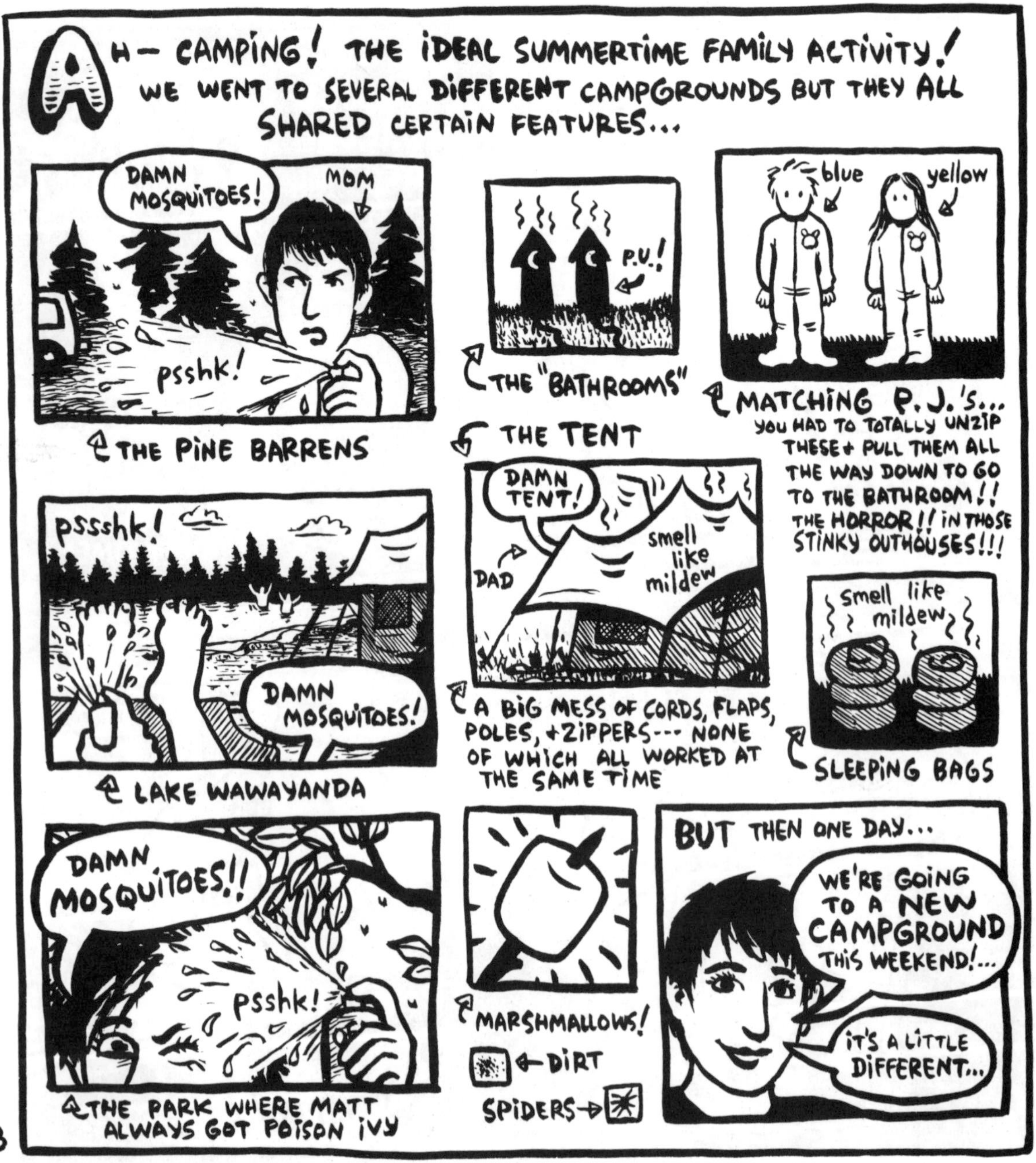
AH — CAMPING! THE IDEAL SUMMERTIME FAMILY ACTIVITY!
WE WENT TO SEVERAL DIFFERENT CAMPGROUNDS BUT THEY ALL SHARED CERTAIN FEATURES...
DAMN MOSQUITOES!
MOM
psshk!
THE PINE BARRENS
P.U.!
THE "BATHROOMS"
blue
yellow
MATCHING P.J.'s... YOU HAD TO TOTALLY UNZIP THESE + PULL THEM ALL THE WAY DOWN TO GO TO THE BATHROOM!! THE HORROR!! IN THOSE STINKY OUTHOUSES!!!
THE TENT
DAMN TENT!
DAD
smell like mildew
A BIG MESS OF CORDS, FLAPS, POLES, + ZIPPERS--- NONE OF WHICH ALL WORKED AT THE SAME TIME
pssshk!
DAMN MOSQUITOES!
LAKE WAWAYANDA
smell like mildew
SLEEPING BAGS
DAMN MOSQUITOES!!
psshk!
THE PARK WHERE MATT ALWAYS GOT POISON IVY
MARSHMALLOWS!
DIRT
SPIDERS
BUT THEN ONE DAY...
WE'RE GOING TO A NEW CAMPGROUND THIS WEEKEND!...
IT'S A LITTLE DIFFERENT...

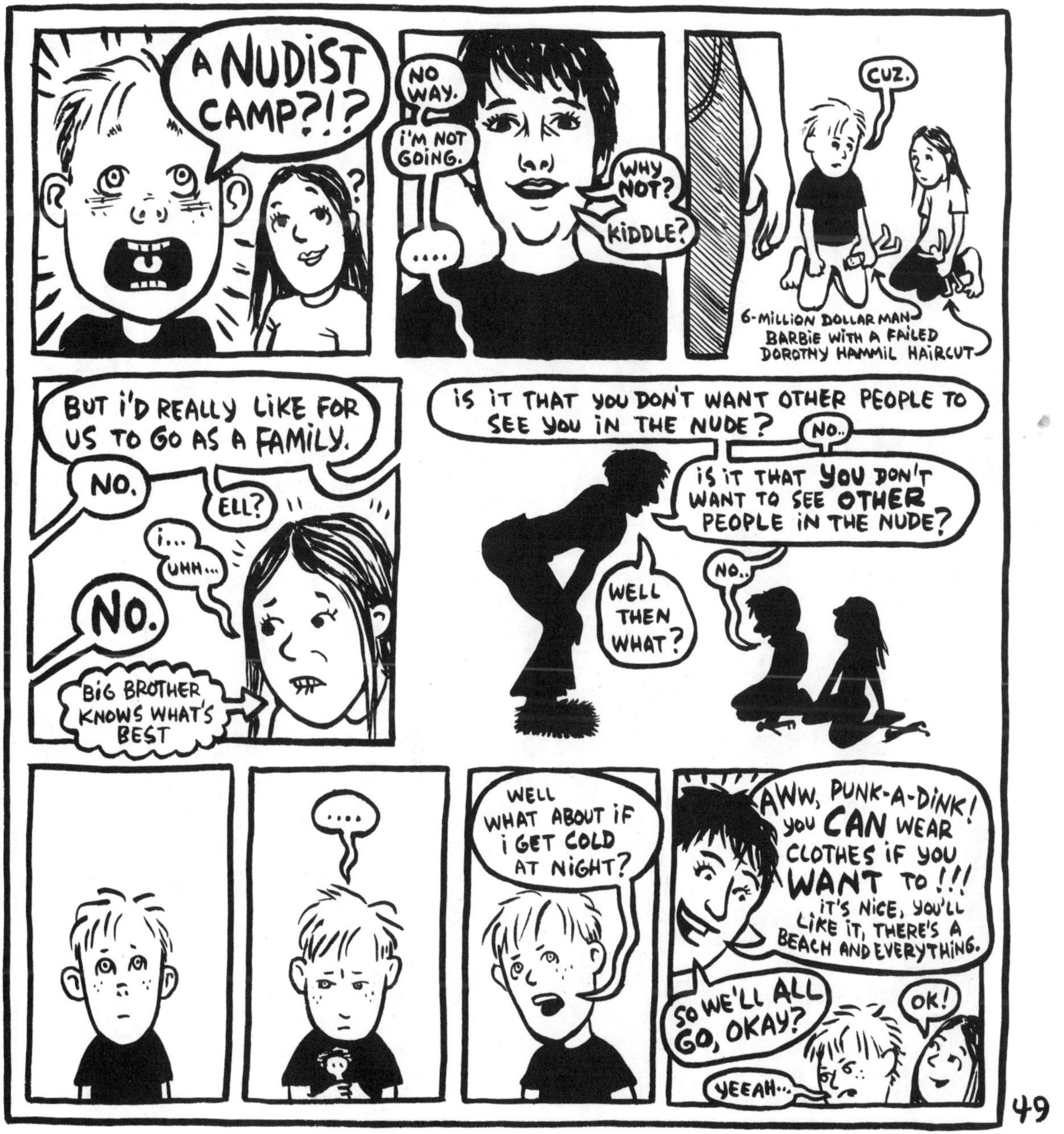
A NUDIST CAMP?!?
?
NO WAY.
I'M NOT GOING.
WHY NOT?
KIDDLE?
....
CUZ.
6-MILLION DOLLAR MAN
BARBIE WITH A FAILED DOROTHY HAMMIL HAIRCUT
BUT I'D REALLY LIKE FOR US TO GO AS A FAMILY.
NO.
ELL?
I... UHH...
NO.
BIG BROTHER KNOWS WHAT'S BEST
IS IT THAT YOU DON'T WANT OTHER PEOPLE TO SEE YOU IN THE NUDE?
NO..
IS IT THAT YOU DON'T WANT TO SEE OTHER PEOPLE IN THE NUDE?
NO..
WELL THEN WHAT?
....
WELL WHAT ABOUT IF I GET COLD AT NIGHT?
AWW, PUNK-A-DINK! YOU CAN WEAR CLOTHES IF YOU WANT TO!!!
IT'S NICE, YOU'LL LIKE IT, THERE'S A BEACH AND EVERYTHING.
SO WE'LL ALL GO, OKAY?
OK!
YEEAH...

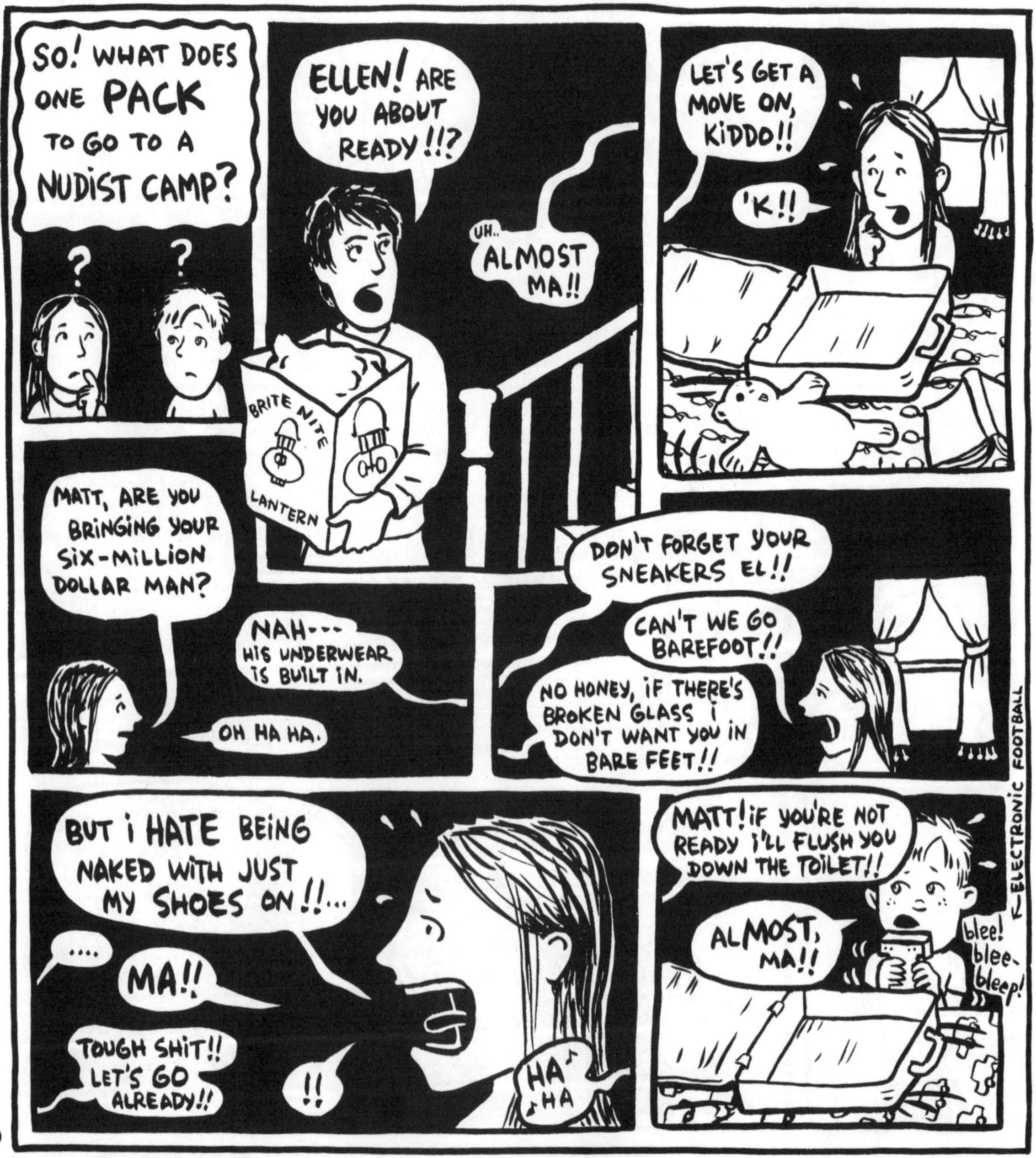
SO! WHAT DOES ONE PACK TO GO TO A NUDIST CAMP?
?
?
ELLEN! ARE YOU ABOUT READY!!?
UH.. ALMOST MA!!
BRITE NITE LANTERN
LET'S GET A MOVE ON, KiDDO!!
'K!!
MATT, ARE YOU BRINGING YOUR SIX-MILLION DOLLAR MAN?
NAH--- HIS UNDERWEAR IS BUILT IN.
OH HA HA.
DON'T FORGET YOUR SNEAKERS EL!!
CAN'T WE GO BAREFOOT!!
NO HONEY, iF THERE'S BROKEN GLASS i DON'T WANT YOU IN BARE FEET!!
BUT i HATE BEING NAKED WITH JUST MY SHOES ON!!...
....
MA!!
TOUGH SHIT!! LET'S GO ALREADY!!
!!
HA HA
MATT! iF YOU'RE NOT READY i'LL FLUSH YOU DOWN THE TOILET!!
ALMOST, MA!!
blee! blee-bleep!
ELECTRONIC FOOTBALL

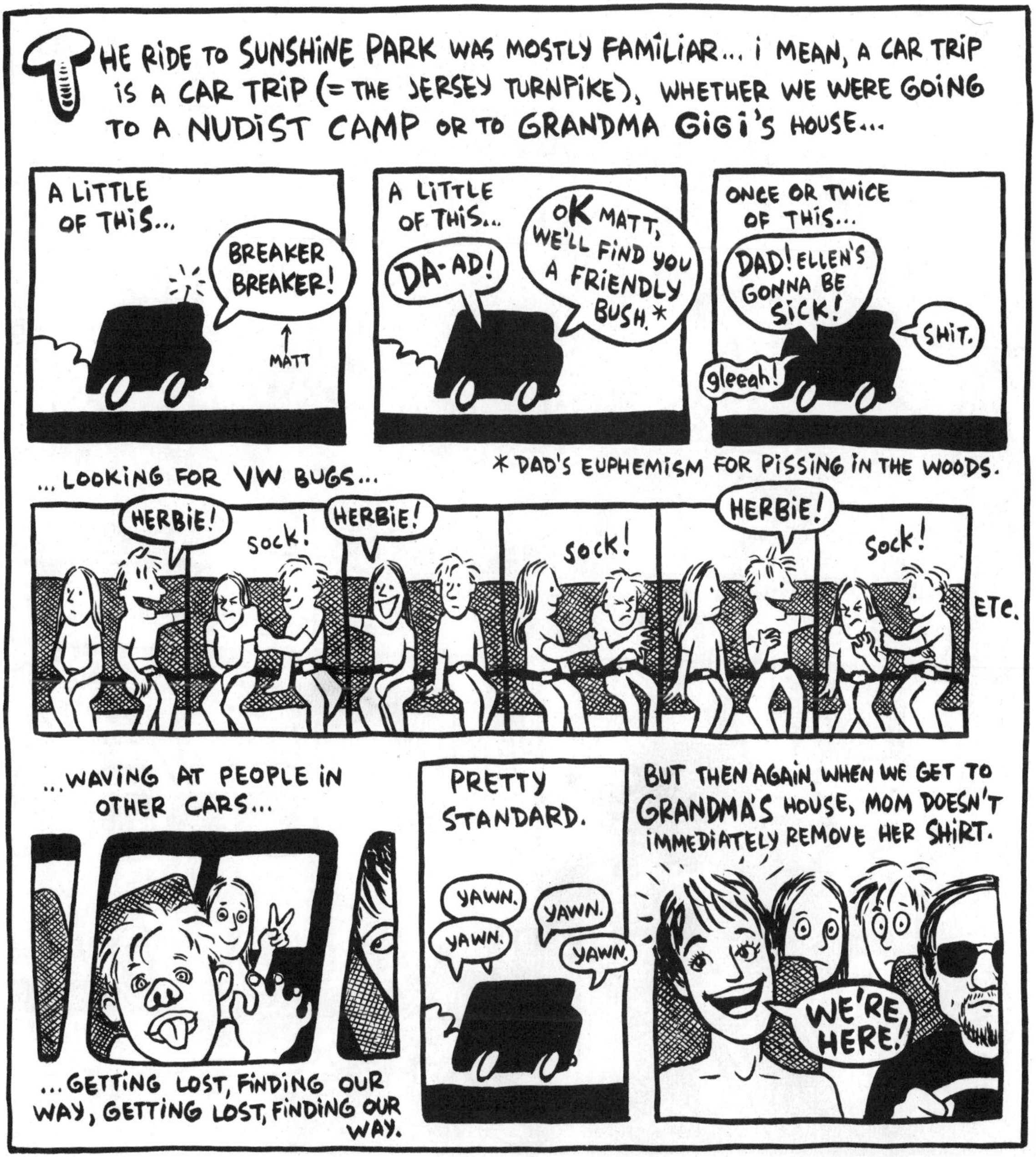
THE RIDE TO SUNSHINE PARK WAS MOSTLY FAMILIAR... I MEAN, A CAR TRIP IS A CAR TRIP (= THE JERSEY TURNPIKE), WHETHER WE WERE GOING TO A NUDIST CAMP OR TO GRANDMA GIGI'S HOUSE...
A LITTLE OF THIS...
BREAKER BREAKER!
MATT
A LITTLE OF THIS...
DA-AD!
OK MATT, WE'LL FIND YOU A FRIENDLY BUSH.*
ONCE OR TWICE OF THIS...
DAD! ELLEN'S GONNA BE SICK!
SHIT.
gleeah!
* DAD'S EUPHEMISM FOR PISSING IN THE WOODS.
... LOOKING FOR VW BUGS...
HERBIE!
sock!
HERBIE!
sock!
HERBIE!
sock!
ETC.
... WAVING AT PEOPLE IN OTHER CARS...
... GETTING LOST, FINDING OUR WAY, GETTING LOST, FINDING OUR WAY.
PRETTY STANDARD.
YAWN.
YAWN.
YAWN.
YAWN.
BUT THEN AGAIN, WHEN WE GET TO GRANDMA'S HOUSE, MOM DOESN'T IMMEDIATELY REMOVE HER SHIRT.
WE'RE HERE!

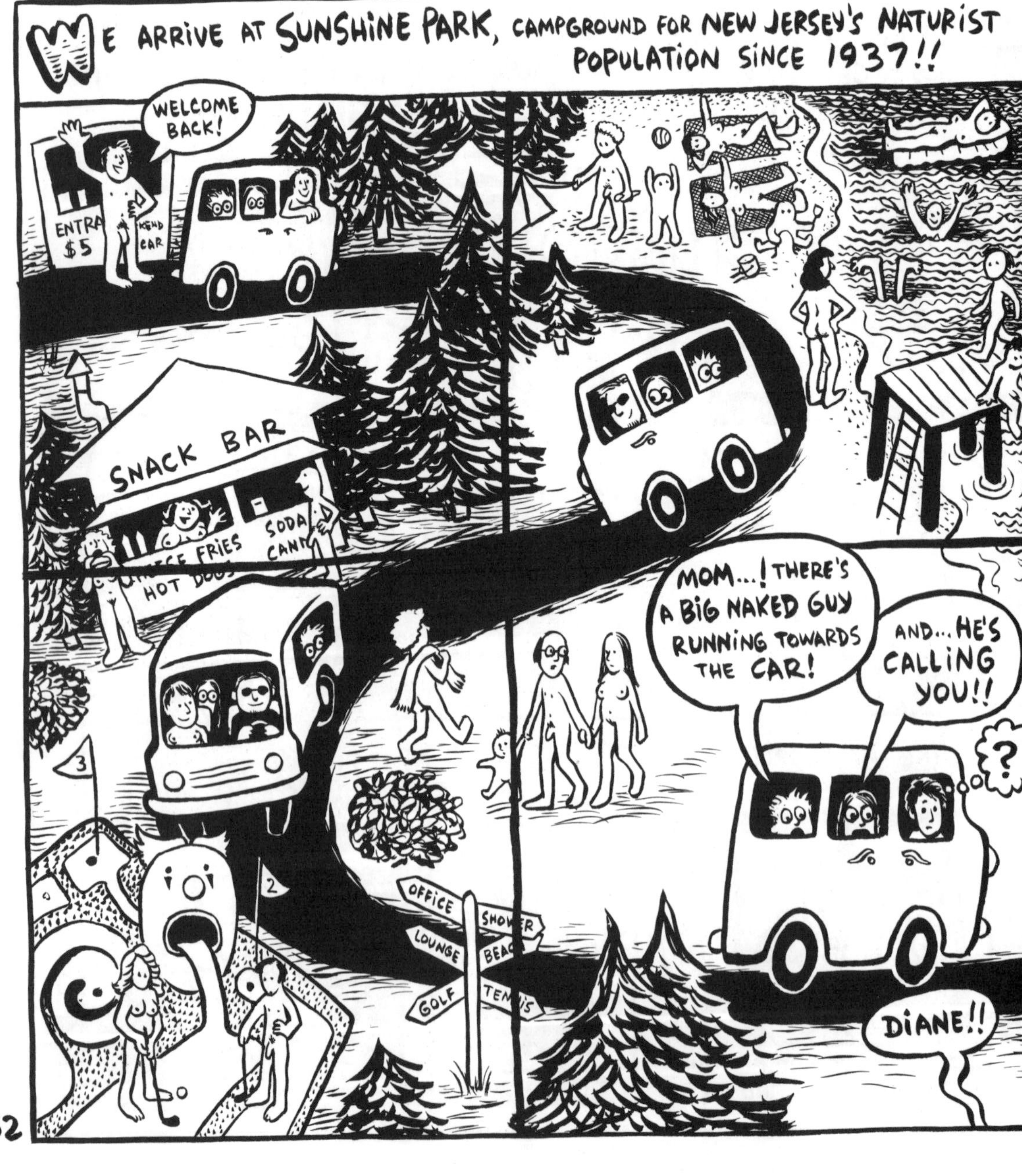
WE ARRIVE AT SUNSHINE PARK, CAMPGROUND FOR NEW JERSEY'S NATURIST POPULATION SINCE 1937!!
WELCOME BACK!
$5
SNACK BAR
FRIES
SODA
OFFICE
LOUNGE
GOLF
MOM...! THERE'S A BIG NAKED GUY RUNNING TOWARDS THE CAR!
AND... HE'S CALLING YOU!!
?
DIANE!!

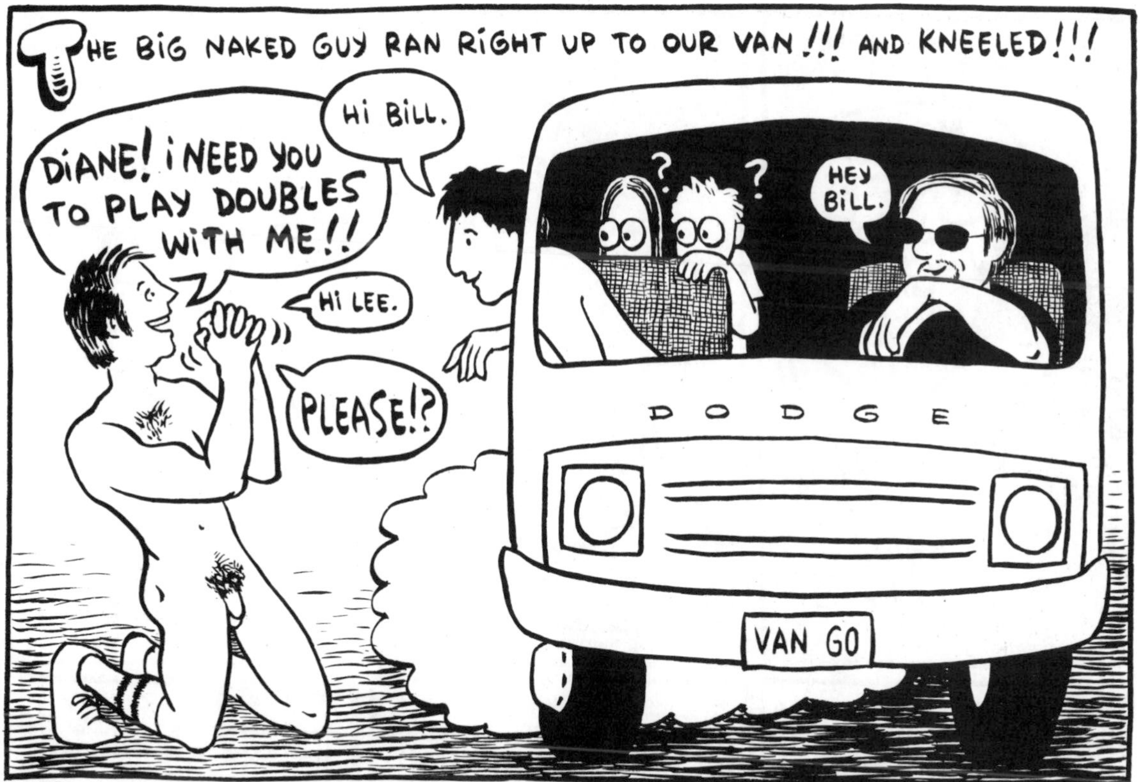
THE BIG NAKED GUY RAN RIGHT UP TO OUR VAN!!! AND KNEELED!!!
DIANE! I NEED YOU TO PLAY DOUBLES WITH ME!!
HI BILL.
HI LEE.
PLEASE!?
??
HEY BILL.
DODGE
VAN GO

MY MOM HAD BEATEN BILL IN A TENNIS GAME THE PREVIOUS WEEKEND. THIS TIME SOME GUY HAD BROUGHT A TENNIS PRO (A REAL PRO!) TO SUNSHINE PARK, AND THEY HAD CHALLENGED BILL TO A MATCH.

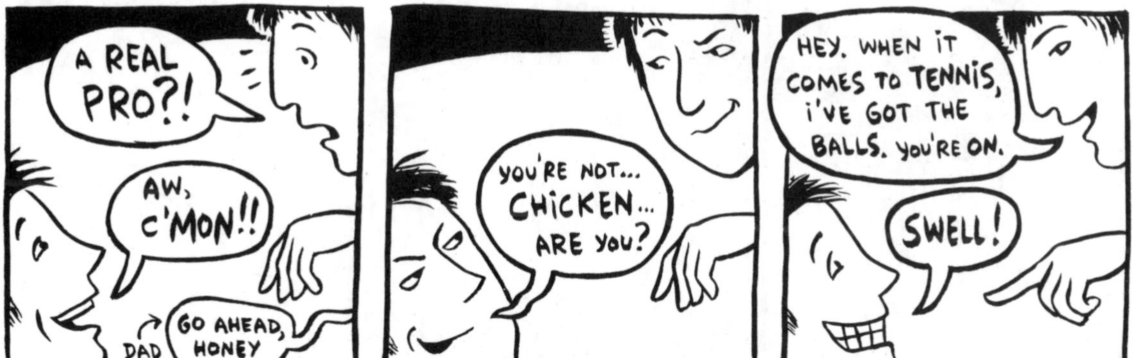
A REAL PRO?!
AW, C'MON!!
DAD
GO AHEAD, HONEY
YOU'RE NOT... CHICKEN... ARE YOU?
HEY. WHEN IT COMES TO TENNIS, I'VE GOT THE BALLS. YOU'RE ON.
SWELL!

MOM TROTTED OFF WITH BILL TO CONQUER THE "TENNIS PRO."
HE'S NATIONALLY RANKED!
OY! YOU GUYS COME CHEER ME ON LATER, OK?
BYE MA
DAD WRESTLED WITH THE TENT FOR A BIT WHILE MATT & I HUNTED MARSHMALLOW STICKS.
(SIGH.) NOW THEN.*
STINK!
FLAPS!
PEGS!
POLES!
CORDS!
*SAYING "NOW THEN" ALL THE TIME WAS MY DAD'S NASTIEST HABIT. MATT WAS ALLOWED ONE NOSE-PICK FOR EACH "NOW THEN."
SOON...
OH, LET'S HIT THE BEACH FIRST. WHAT DO YOU SAY?
'K.
'K.
EVERYONE ON THE BEACH HAD A PAINTING ON THEIR ABDOMEN.
LEE! YOU BROUGHT THE KIDS!
BODY PAINTS
LEW, ONE OF SUNSHINE PARK'S FOUNDERS, WOULD PAINT ANYTHING YOU REQUESTED, SO LONG AS IT WASN'T TOO COMPLICATED.
HI THERE MISSY! WOULD YOU LIKE YOUR TUMMY PAINTED?
A RAIN-BOW?
A DAISY?
MATT HAD ALREADY ABANDONED ME TO JUMP OFF THE DOCK WITH THE REST OF THE BOYS.
A KITTY CAT?
A BUTTER-FLY?
HM?

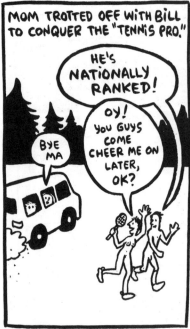

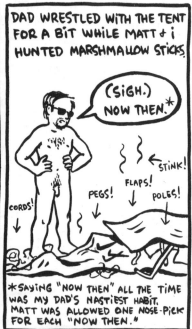

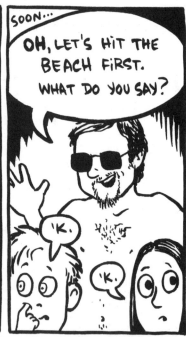

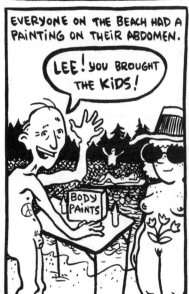

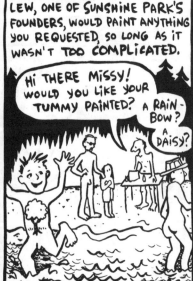

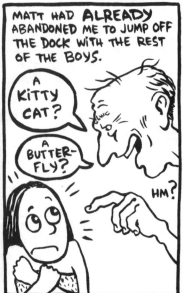

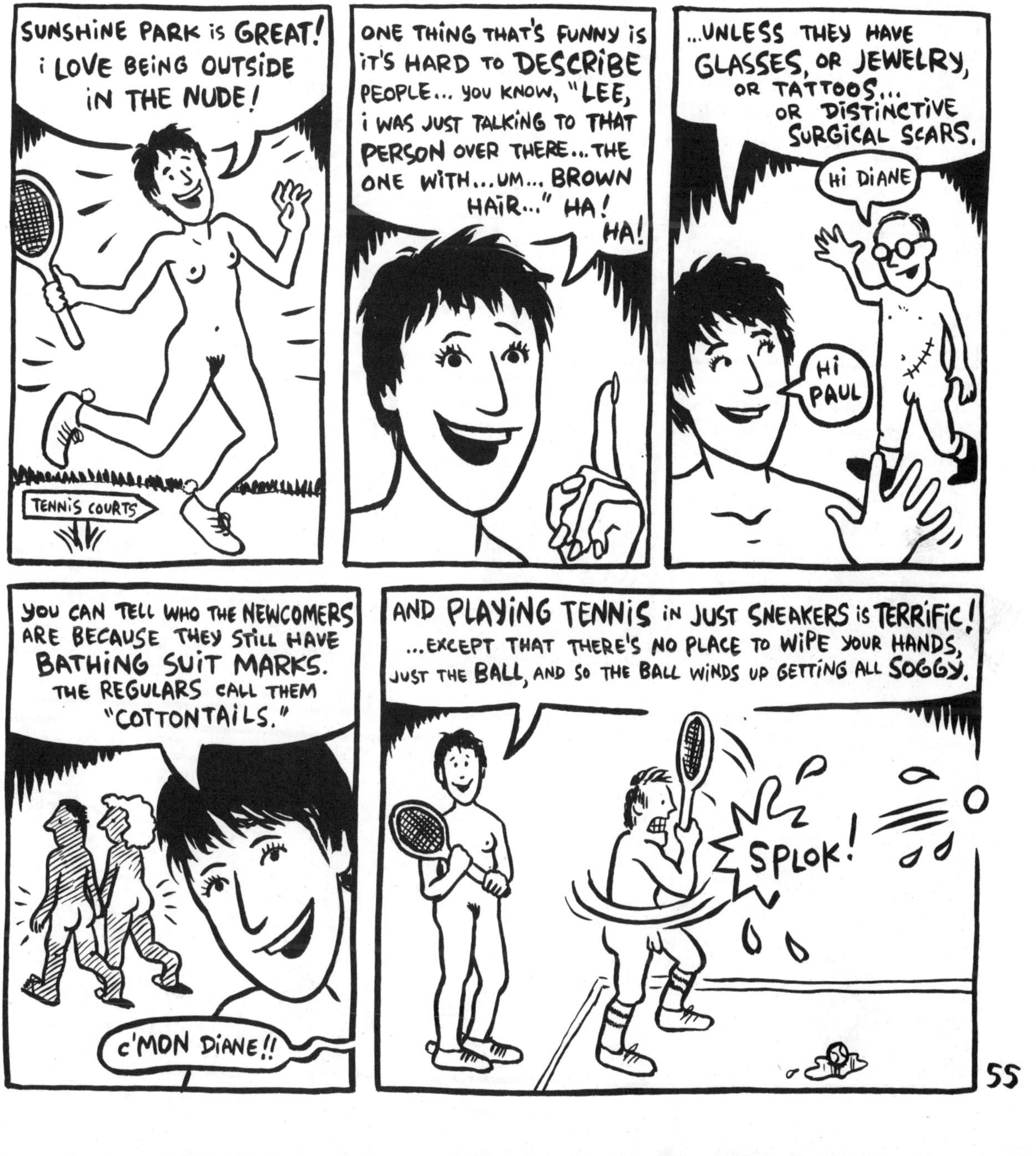
SUNSHINE PARK IS GREAT! I LOVE BEING OUTSIDE IN THE NUDE!
TENNIS COURTS
ONE THING THAT'S FUNNY IS IT'S HARD TO DESCRIBE PEOPLE... YOU KNOW, "LEE, I WAS JUST TALKING TO THAT PERSON OVER THERE... THE ONE WITH... UM... BROWN HAIR..." HA! HA!
...UNLESS THEY HAVE GLASSES, OR JEWELRY, OR TATTOOS... OR DISTINCTIVE SURGICAL SCARS.
HI DIANE
HI PAUL
YOU CAN TELL WHO THE NEWCOMERS ARE BECAUSE THEY STILL HAVE BATHING SUIT MARKS. THE REGULARS CALL THEM "COTTONTAILS."
C'MON DIANE!!
AND PLAYING TENNIS IN JUST SNEAKERS IS TERRIFIC! ...EXCEPT THAT THERE'S NO PLACE TO WIPE YOUR HANDS, JUST THE BALL, AND SO THE BALL WINDS UP GETTING ALL SOGGY.
SPLOK!

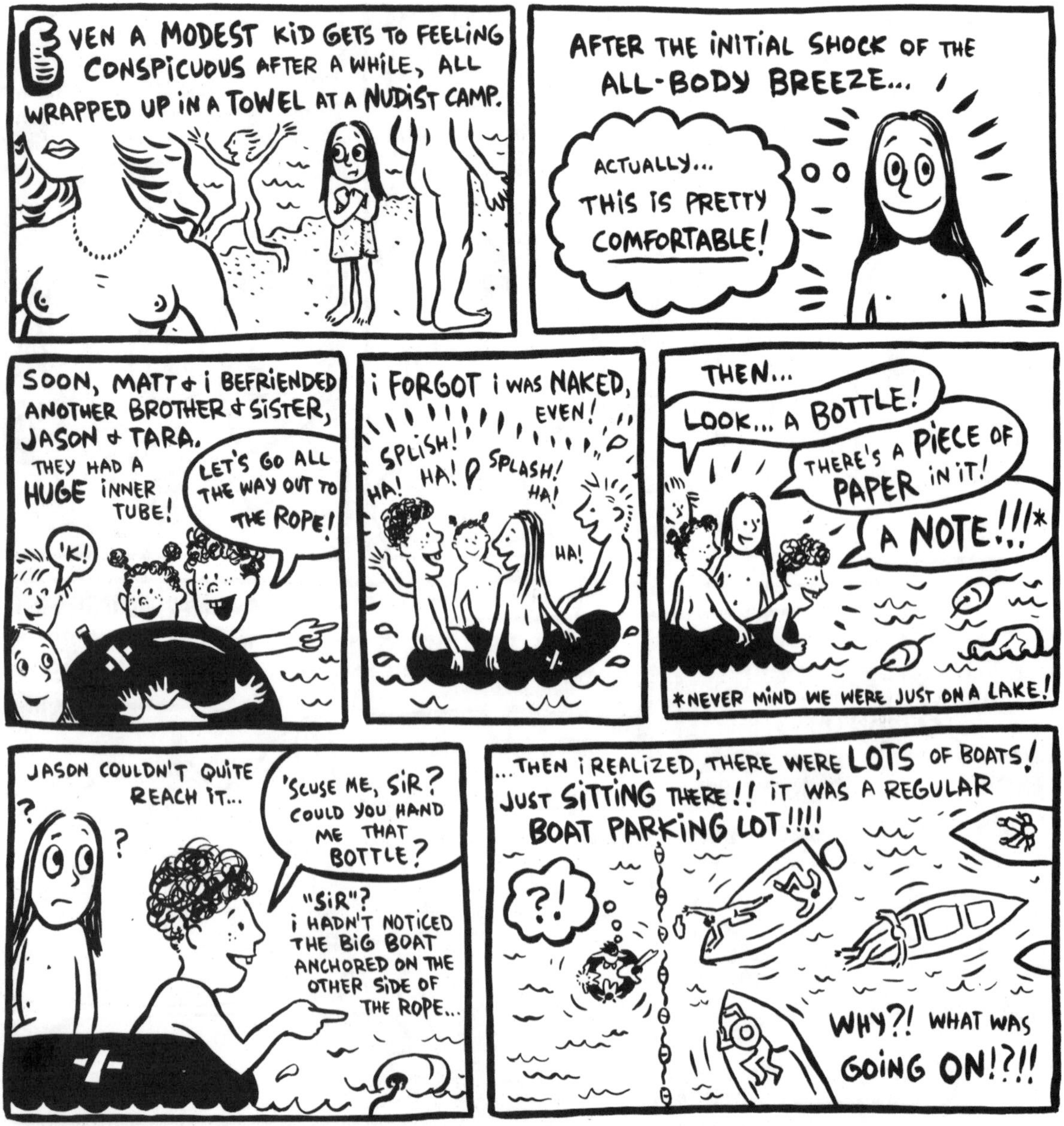
EVEN A MODEST KID GETS TO FEELING CONSPICUOUS AFTER A WHILE, ALL WRAPPED UP IN A TOWEL AT A NUDIST CAMP.
AFTER THE INITIAL SHOCK OF THE ALL-BODY BREEZE...
ACTUALLY... THIS IS PRETTY COMFORTABLE!
SOON, MATT & I BEFRIENDED ANOTHER BROTHER & SISTER, JASON & TARA.
THEY HAD A HUGE INNER TUBE!
LET'S GO ALL THE WAY OUT TO THE ROPE!
'K!
I FORGOT I WAS NAKED, EVEN!
SPLISH!
HA! HA!
SPLASH!
HA!
HA!
THEN...
LOOK... A BOTTLE!
THERE'S A PIECE OF PAPER IN IT!
A NOTE!!!*
*NEVER MIND WE WERE JUST ON A LAKE!
JASON COULDN'T QUITE REACH IT...
?
?
'SCUSE ME, SIR? COULD YOU HAND ME THAT BOTTLE?
"SIR"? I HADN'T NOTICED THE BIG BOAT ANCHORED ON THE OTHER SIDE OF THE ROPE...
...THEN I REALIZED, THERE WERE LOTS OF BOATS! JUST SITTING THERE!! IT WAS A REGULAR BOAT PARKING LOT!!!!
?!
WHY?! WHAT WAS GOING ON!?!!

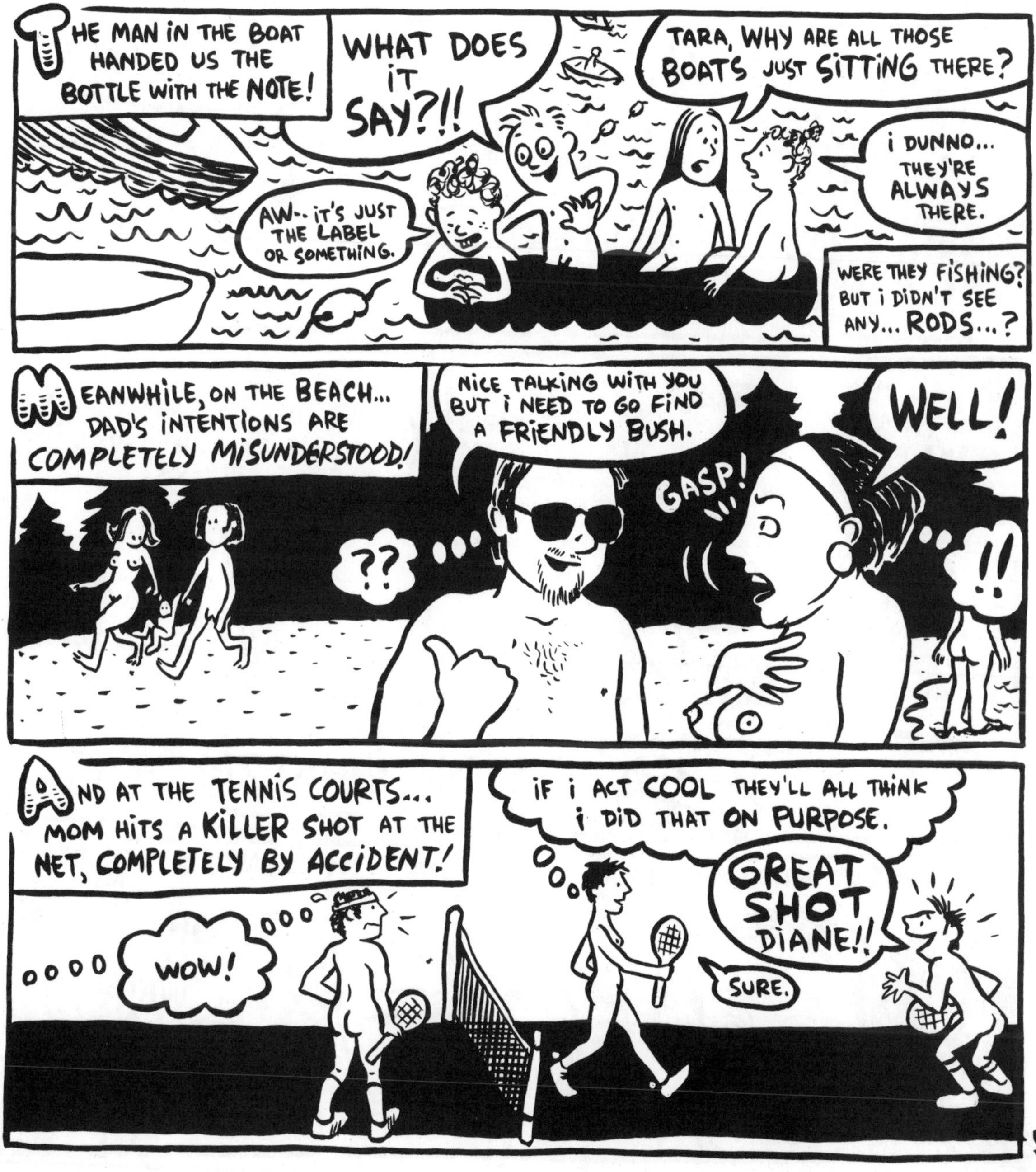
THE MAN IN THE BOAT HANDED US THE BOTTLE WITH THE NOTE!
WHAT DOES IT SAY?!!
TARA, WHY ARE ALL THOSE BOATS JUST SITTING THERE?
I DUNNO... THEY'RE ALWAYS THERE.
AW.. IT'S JUST THE LABEL OR SOMETHING.
WERE THEY FISHING? BUT I DIDN'T SEE ANY... RODS...?
MEANWHILE, ON THE BEACH... DAD'S INTENTIONS ARE COMPLETELY MISUNDERSTOOD!
NICE TALKING WITH YOU BUT I NEED TO GO FIND A FRIENDLY BUSH.
WELL!
GASP!
??
!!
AND AT THE TENNIS COURTS... MOM HITS A KILLER SHOT AT THE NET, COMPLETELY BY ACCIDENT!
IF I ACT COOL THEY'LL ALL THINK I DID THAT ON PURPOSE.
GREAT SHOT DIANE!!
WOW!
SURE.

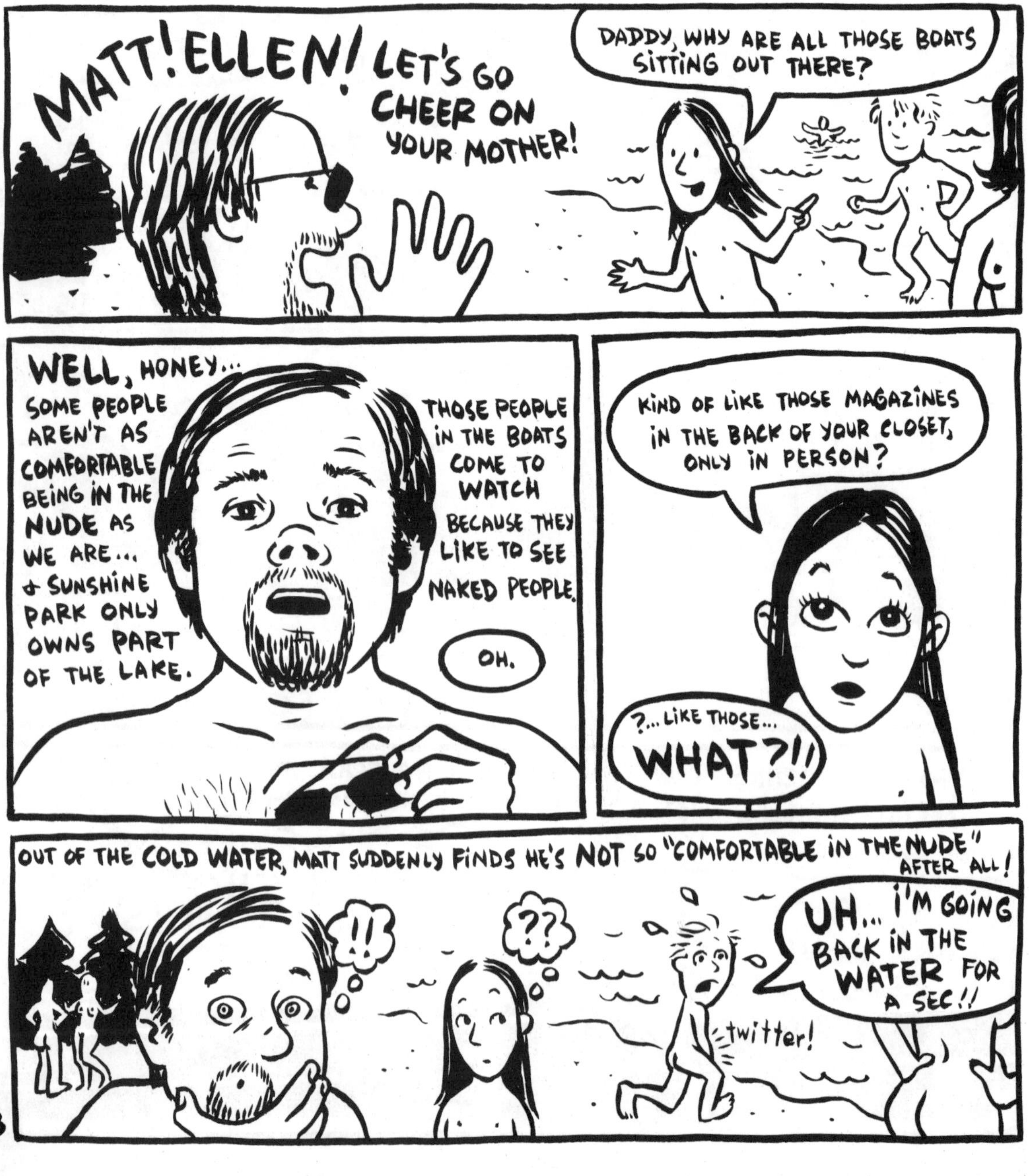
MATT! ELLEN! LET'S GO CHEER ON YOUR MOTHER!
DADDY, WHY ARE ALL THOSE BOATS SITTING OUT THERE?
WELL, HONEY...
SOME PEOPLE AREN'T AS COMFORTABLE BEING IN THE NUDE AS WE ARE... & SUNSHINE PARK ONLY OWNS PART OF THE LAKE.
THOSE PEOPLE IN THE BOATS COME TO WATCH BECAUSE THEY LIKE TO SEE NAKED PEOPLE.
OH.
KIND OF LIKE THOSE MAGAZINES IN THE BACK OF YOUR CLOSET, ONLY IN PERSON?
?... LIKE THOSE... WHAT?!!
OUT OF THE COLD WATER, MATT SUDDENLY FINDS HE'S NOT SO "COMFORTABLE IN THE NUDE" AFTER ALL!
!!
??
UH... I'M GOING BACK IN THE WATER FOR A SEC!!
twitter!

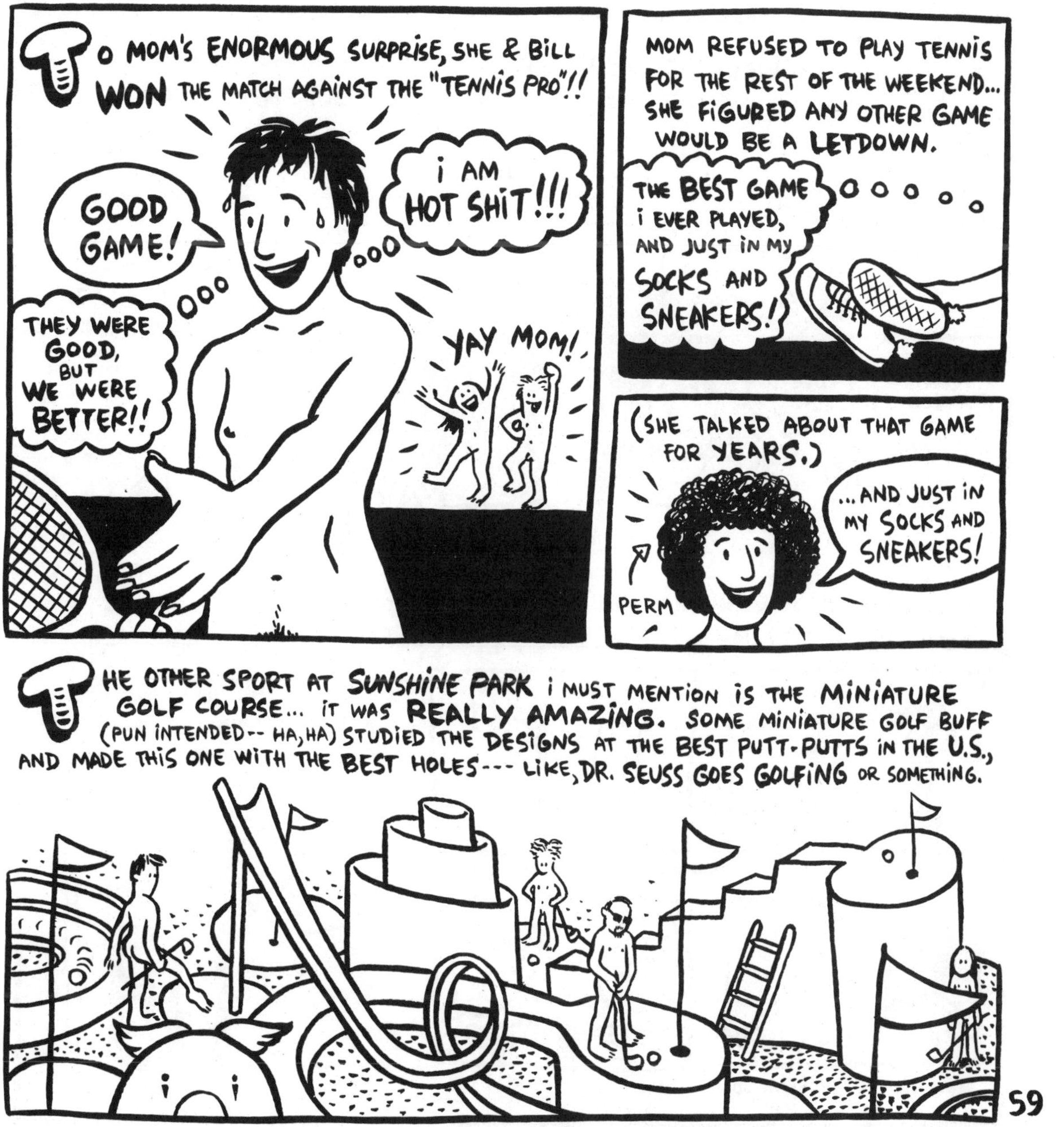
TO MOM'S ENORMOUS SURPRISE, SHE & BILL WON THE MATCH AGAINST THE "TENNIS PRO"!!
GOOD GAME!
I AM HOT SHIT!!!
THEY WERE GOOD, BUT WE WERE BETTER!!
YAY MOM!
MOM REFUSED TO PLAY TENNIS FOR THE REST OF THE WEEKEND... SHE FIGURED ANY OTHER GAME WOULD BE A LETDOWN.
THE BEST GAME I EVER PLAYED, AND JUST IN MY SOCKS AND SNEAKERS!
(SHE TALKED ABOUT THAT GAME FOR YEARS.)
...AND JUST IN MY SOCKS AND SNEAKERS!
PERM
THE OTHER SPORT AT SUNSHINE PARK I MUST MENTION IS THE MINIATURE GOLF COURSE... IT WAS REALLY AMAZING. SOME MINIATURE GOLF BUFF (PUN INTENDED-- HA, HA) STUDIED THE DESIGNS AT THE BEST PUTT-PUTTS IN THE U.S., AND MADE THIS ONE WITH THE BEST HOLES--- LIKE, DR. SEUSS GOES GOLFING OR SOMETHING.

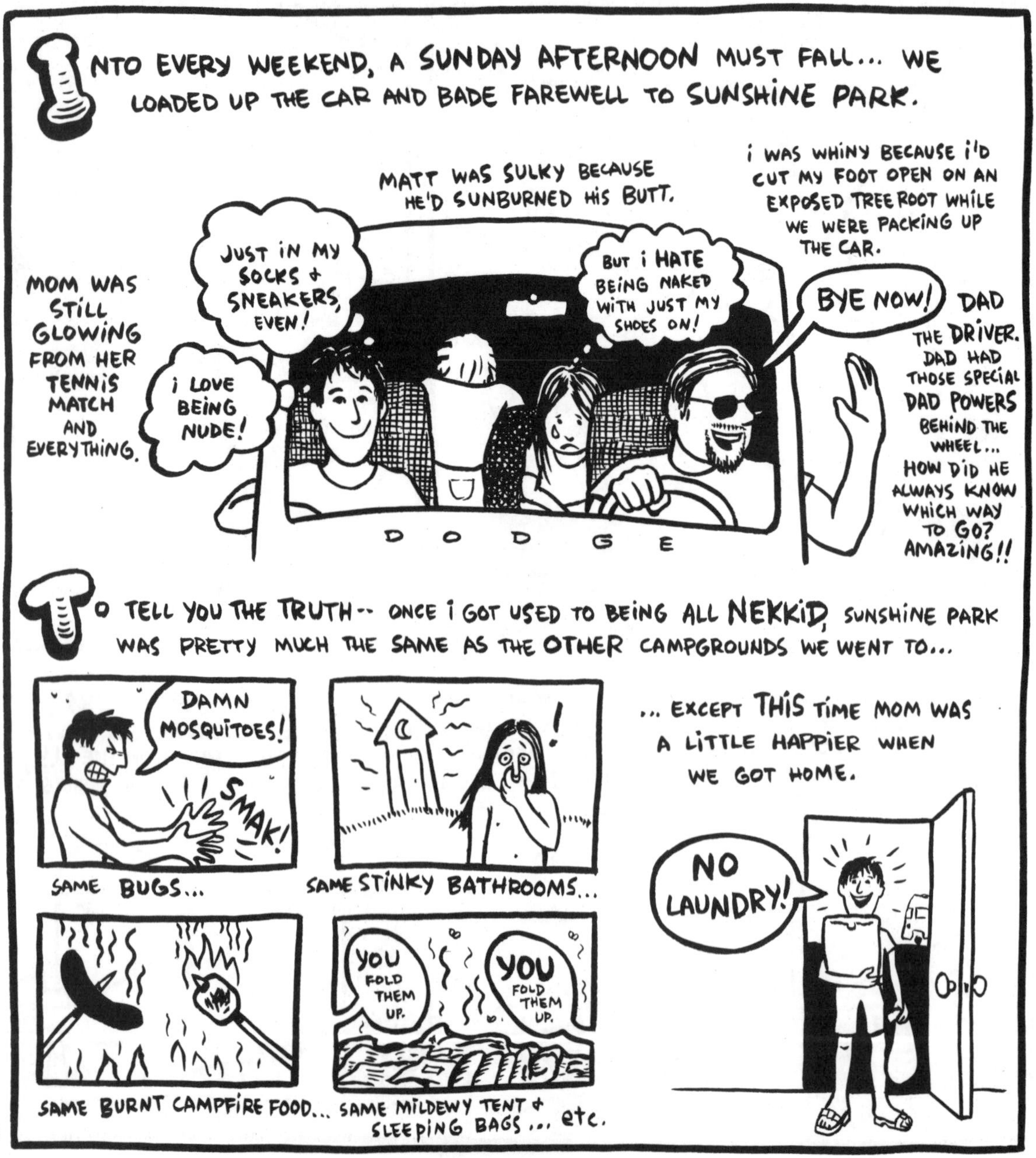
INTO EVERY WEEKEND, A SUNDAY AFTERNOON MUST FALL... WE LOADED UP THE CAR AND BADE FAREWELL TO SUNSHINE PARK.
MOM WAS STILL GLOWING FROM HER TENNIS MATCH AND EVERYTHING.
I LOVE BEING NUDE!
JUST IN MY SOCKS & SNEAKERS, EVEN!
MATT WAS SULKY BECAUSE HE'D SUNBURNED HIS BUTT.
BUT I HATE BEING NAKED WITH JUST MY SHOES ON!
I WAS WHINY BECAUSE I'D CUT MY FOOT OPEN ON AN EXPOSED TREE ROOT WHILE WE WERE PACKING UP THE CAR.
BYE NOW!
DAD THE DRIVER. DAD HAD THOSE SPECIAL DAD POWERS BEHIND THE WHEEL... HOW DID HE ALWAYS KNOW WHICH WAY TO GO? AMAZING!!
D O D G E
TO TELL YOU THE TRUTH -- ONCE I GOT USED TO BEING ALL NEKKID, SUNSHINE PARK WAS PRETTY MUCH THE SAME AS THE OTHER CAMPGROUNDS WE WENT TO...
DAMN MOSQUITOES!
SMAK!
SAME BUGS...
!
SAME STINKY BATHROOMS...
SAME BURNT CAMPFIRE FOOD...
YOU FOLD THEM UP.
YOU FOLD THEM UP.
SAME MILDEWY TENT & SLEEPING BAGS... etc.
... EXCEPT THIS TIME MOM WAS A LITTLE HAPPIER WHEN WE GOT HOME.
NO LAUNDRY!

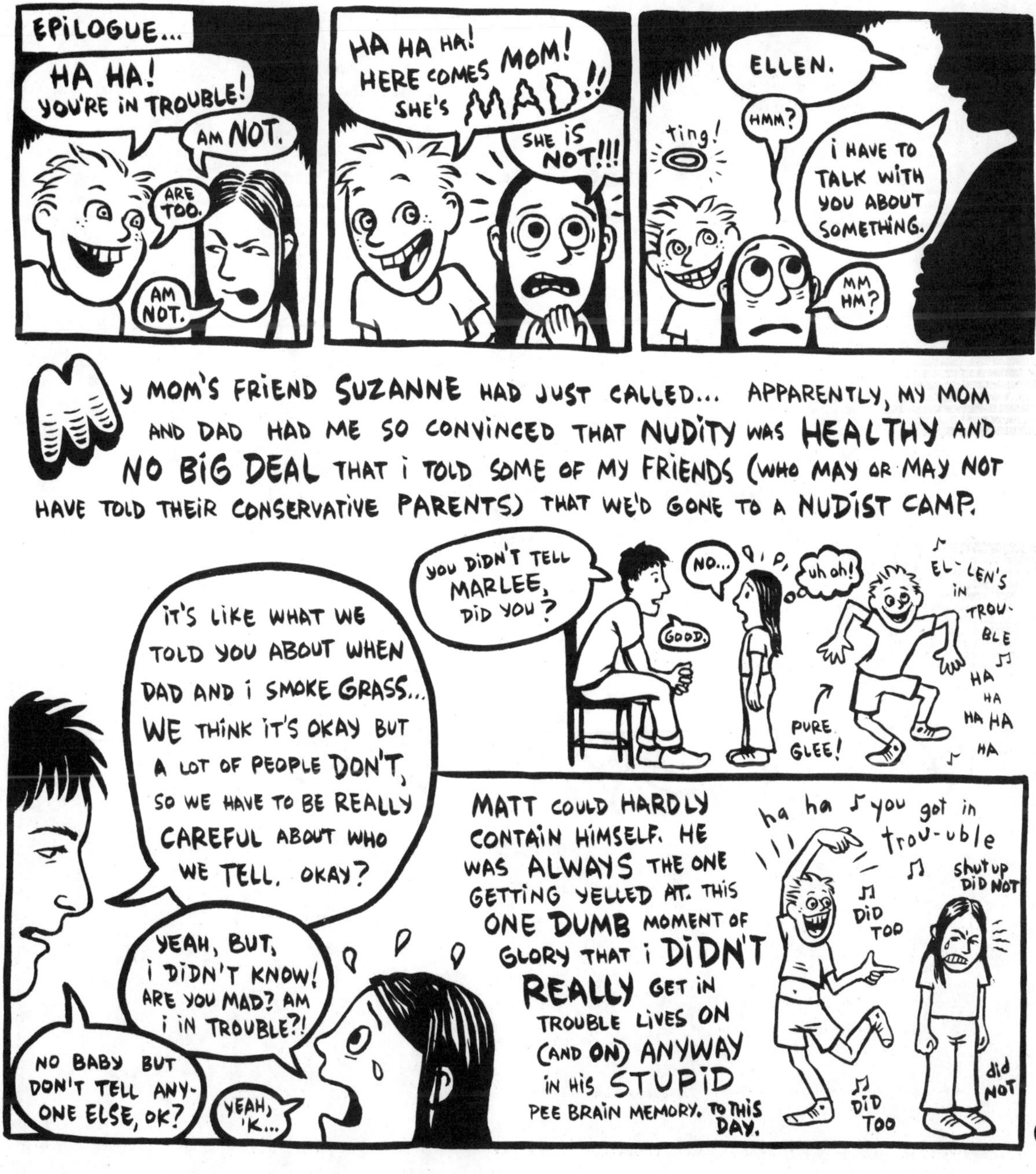
EPILOGUE...
HA HA! YOU'RE IN TROUBLE!
AM NOT.
ARE TOO.
AM NOT.
HA HA HA! HERE COMES MOM! SHE'S MAD!!
SHE IS NOT!!!
ELLEN.
ting!
HMM?
I HAVE TO TALK WITH YOU ABOUT SOMETHING.
MM HM?
MY MOM'S FRIEND SUZANNE HAD JUST CALLED... APPARENTLY, MY MOM AND DAD HAD ME SO CONVINCED THAT NUDITY WAS HEALTHY AND NO BIG DEAL THAT I TOLD SOME OF MY FRIENDS (WHO MAY OR MAY NOT HAVE TOLD THEIR CONSERVATIVE PARENTS) THAT WE'D GONE TO A NUDIST CAMP.
YOU DIDN'T TELL MARLEE, DID YOU?
NO...
GOOD.
uh oh!
EL-LEN'S IN TROU-BLE HA HA HA HA HA
PURE GLEE!
IT'S LIKE WHAT WE TOLD YOU ABOUT WHEN DAD AND I SMOKE GRASS... WE THINK IT'S OKAY BUT A LOT OF PEOPLE DON'T, SO WE HAVE TO BE REALLY CAREFUL ABOUT WHO WE TELL. OKAY?
YEAH, BUT, I DIDN'T KNOW! ARE YOU MAD? AM I IN TROUBLE?!
NO BABY BUT DON'T TELL ANYONE ELSE, OK?
YEAH, 'K...
MATT COULD HARDLY CONTAIN HIMSELF. HE WAS ALWAYS THE ONE GETTING YELLED AT. THIS ONE DUMB MOMENT OF GLORY THAT I DIDN'T REALLY GET IN TROUBLE LIVES ON (AND ON) ANYWAY IN HIS STUPID PEE BRAIN MEMORY. TO THIS DAY.
ha ha you got in trou-uble
shut up DID NOT
DID TOO
did NOT
DID TOO

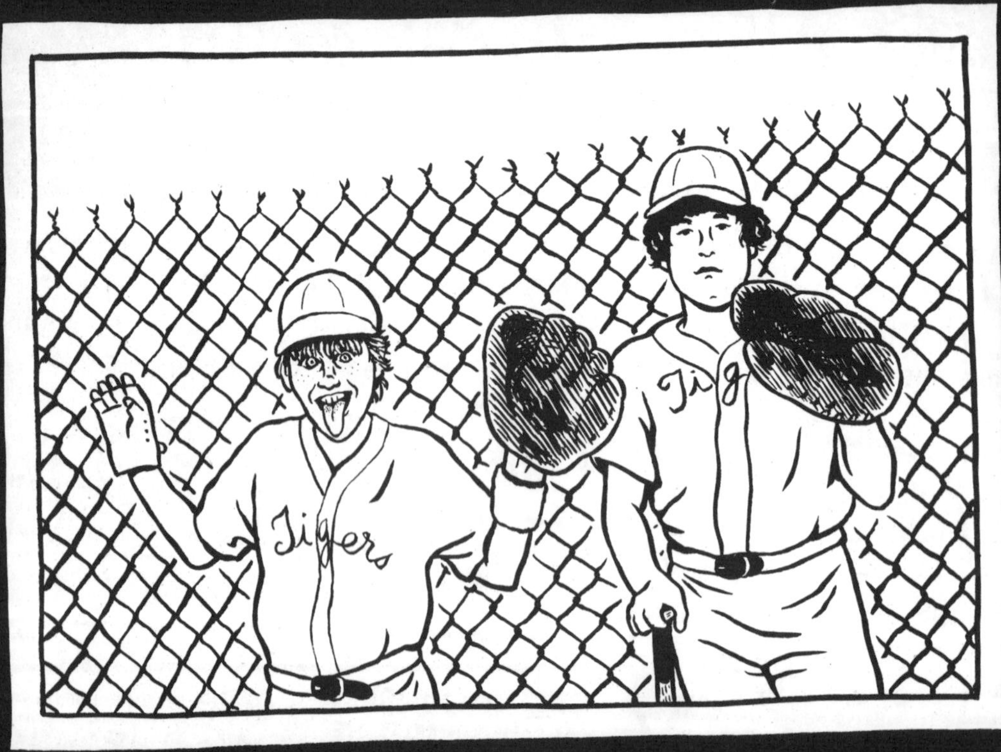
Tigers
Tig

Matt (catcher) & Charlie (pitcher) prepare for the Little League All-Star game, 1976.

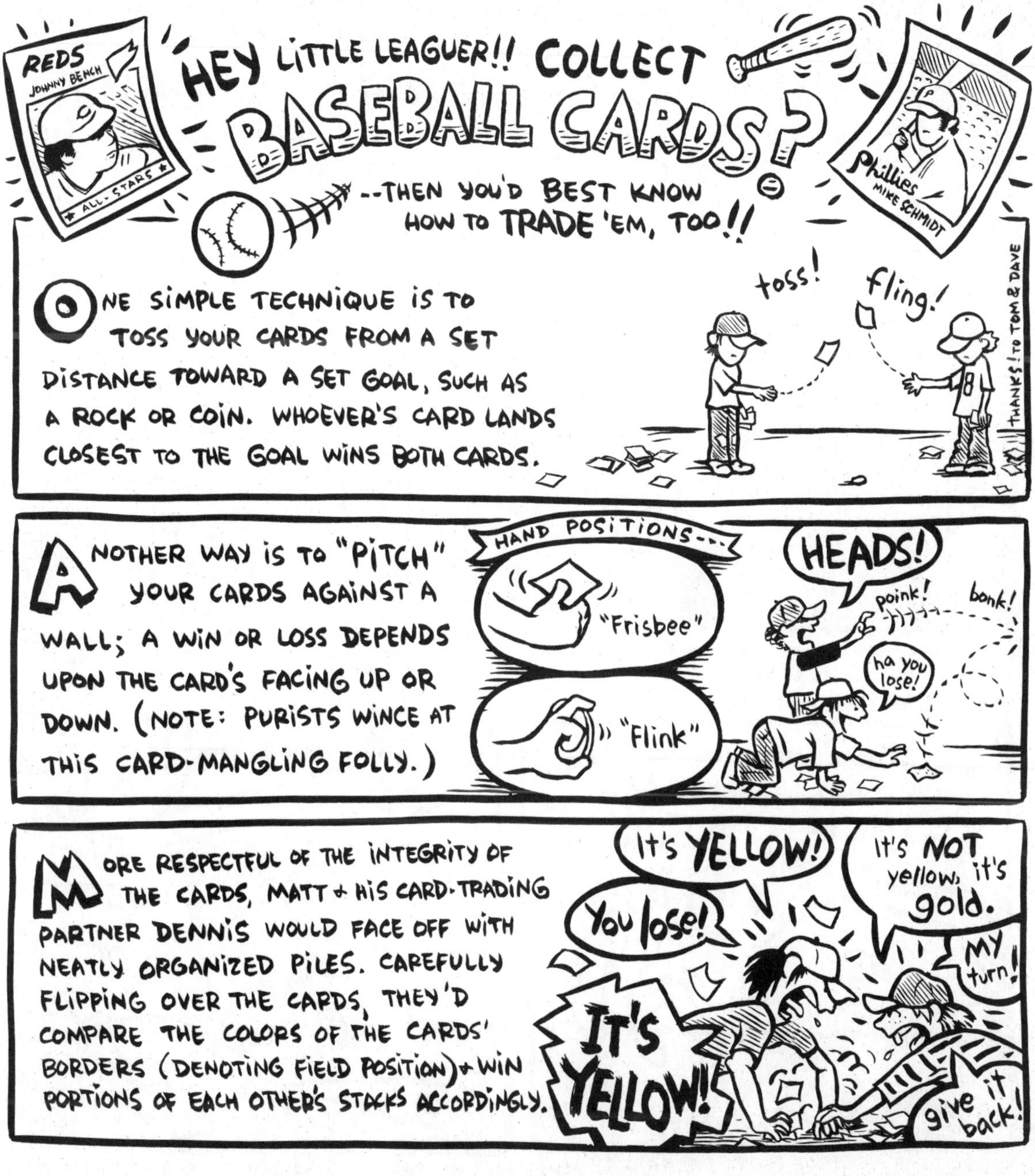

REDS
JOHNNY BENCH
ALL-STARS
HEY LITTLE LEAGUER!! COLLECT
BASEBALL CARDS?
--THEN YOU'D BEST KNOW HOW TO TRADE 'EM, TOO!!
Phillies
MIKE SCHMIDT
ONE SIMPLE TECHNIQUE IS TO TOSS YOUR CARDS FROM A SET DISTANCE TOWARD A SET GOAL, SUCH AS A ROCK OR COIN. WHOEVER'S CARD LANDS CLOSEST TO THE GOAL WINS BOTH CARDS.
toss!
fling!
THANKS! TO TOM & DAVE
ANOTHER WAY IS TO "PITCH" YOUR CARDS AGAINST A WALL; A WIN OR LOSS DEPENDS UPON THE CARD'S FACING UP OR DOWN. (NOTE: PURISTS WINCE AT THIS CARD-MANGLING FOLLY.)
HAND POSITIONS...
"Frisbee"
"Flink"
HEADS!
poink!
bonk!
ha you lose!
MORE RESPECTFUL OF THE INTEGRITY OF THE CARDS, MATT & HIS CARD-TRADING PARTNER DENNIS WOULD FACE OFF WITH NEATLY ORGANIZED PILES. CAREFULLY FLIPPING OVER THE CARDS, THEY'D COMPARE THE COLORS OF THE CARDS' BORDERS (DENOTING FIELD POSITION) & WIN PORTIONS OF EACH OTHER'S STACKS ACCORDINGLY.
It's YELLOW!
You lose!
It's NOT yellow, it's gold.
MY turn!
IT'S YELLOW!
give it back!

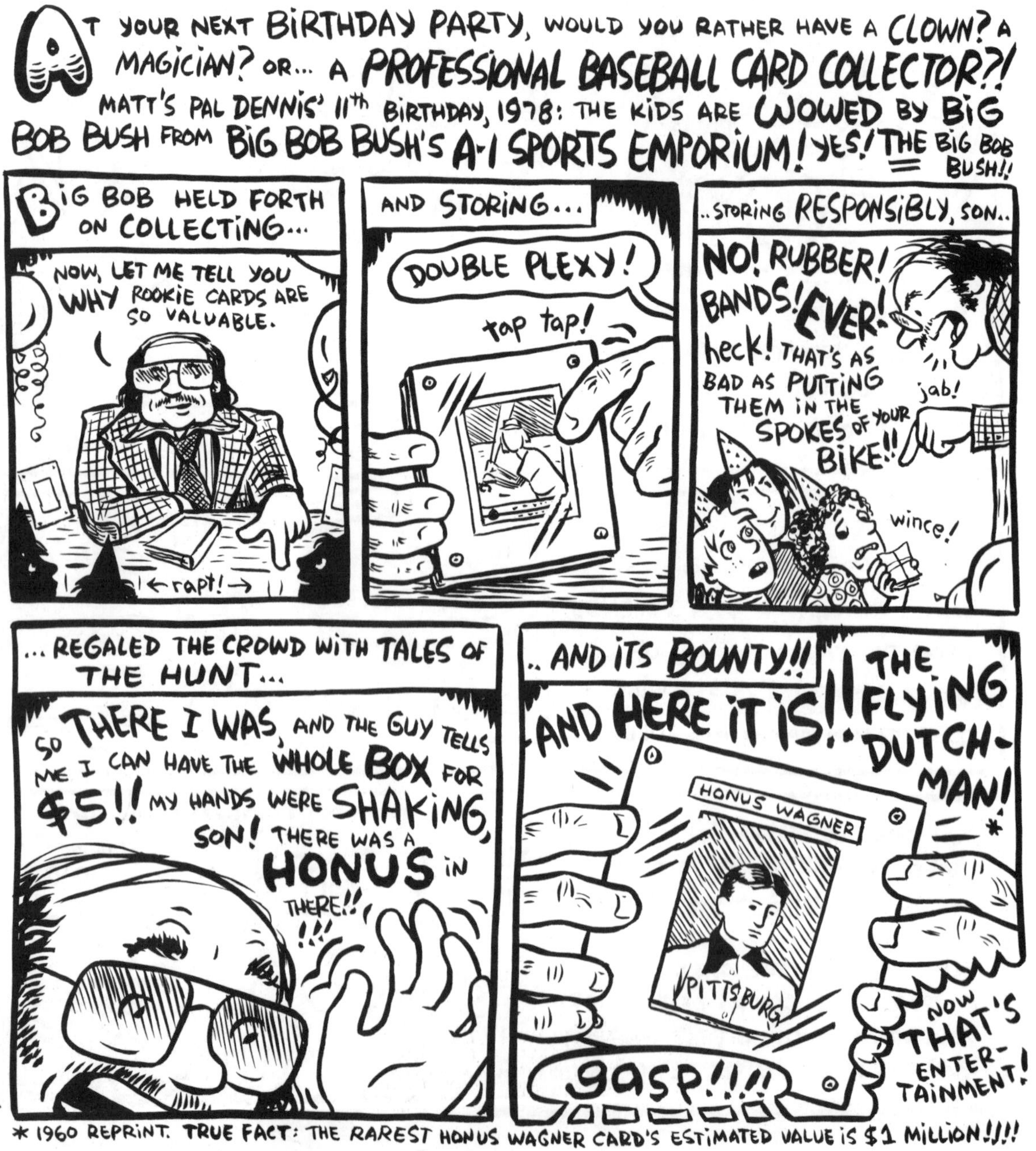
At your next BIRTHDAY PARTY, would you rather have a CLOWN? A MAGICIAN? or... a PROFESSIONAL BASEBALL CARD COLLECTOR?!
MATT'S PAL DENNIS' 11th BIRTHDAY, 1978: THE KIDS ARE WOWED BY BIG BOB BUSH FROM BIG BOB BUSH'S A-1 SPORTS EMPORIUM! YES! THE BIG BOB BUSH!!
BIG BOB HELD FORTH ON COLLECTING...
NOW, LET ME TELL YOU WHY ROOKIE CARDS ARE SO VALUABLE.
←rapt!→
AND STORING...
DOUBLE PLEXY!
tap tap!
..STORING RESPONSIBLY, SON..
NO! RUBBER! BANDS! EVER! heck! THAT'S AS BAD AS PUTTING THEM IN THE SPOKES OF YOUR BIKE!!
jab!
wince!
... REGALED THE CROWD WITH TALES OF THE HUNT...
SO THERE I WAS, AND THE GUY TELLS ME I CAN HAVE THE WHOLE BOX FOR $5!! MY HANDS WERE SHAKING, SON! THERE WAS A HONUS IN THERE!!
!!!
.. AND ITS BOUNTY!!
AND HERE IT IS!!
THE FLYING DUTCH-MAN!*
HONUS WAGNER
PITTSBURG
gasp!!!!
NOW THAT'S ENTER-TAINMENT!

* 1960 REPRINT. TRUE FACT: THE RAREST HONUS WAGNER CARD'S ESTIMATED VALUE IS $1 MILLION!!!!

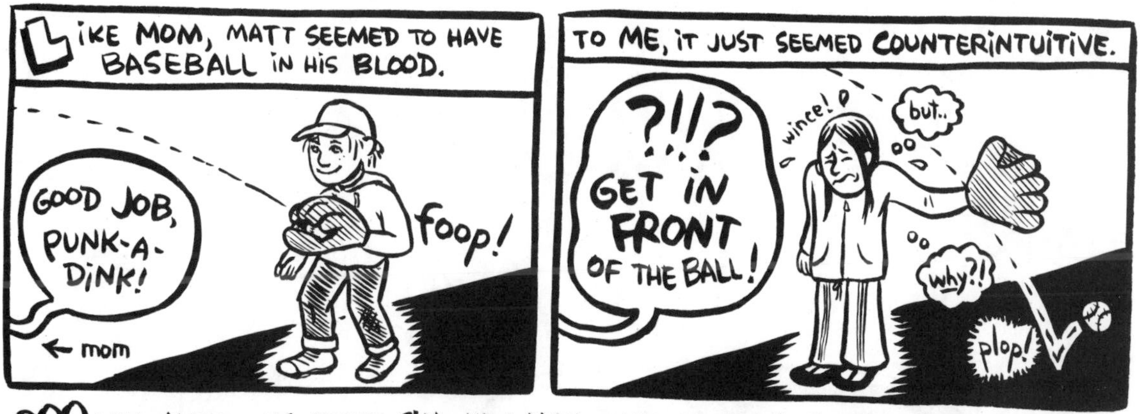
LIKE MOM, MATT SEEMED TO HAVE BASEBALL IN HIS BLOOD.
GOOD JOB, PUNK-A-DINK!
← mom
foop!
TO ME, IT JUST SEEMED COUNTERINTUITIVE.
?!!? GET IN FRONT OF THE BALL!
wince!
but..
why?!
plop!

WHEN MATT WAS ABOUT SIX, HE & MOM TOOK TO PLAYING CATCH BEFORE DINNER. OUR FRONT YARD WASN'T QUITE BIG ENOUGH & THE BACK HAD TOO MANY TREES, SO THEY'D PLAY ON WOODWILD STREET IN FRONT OF OUR HOUSE.

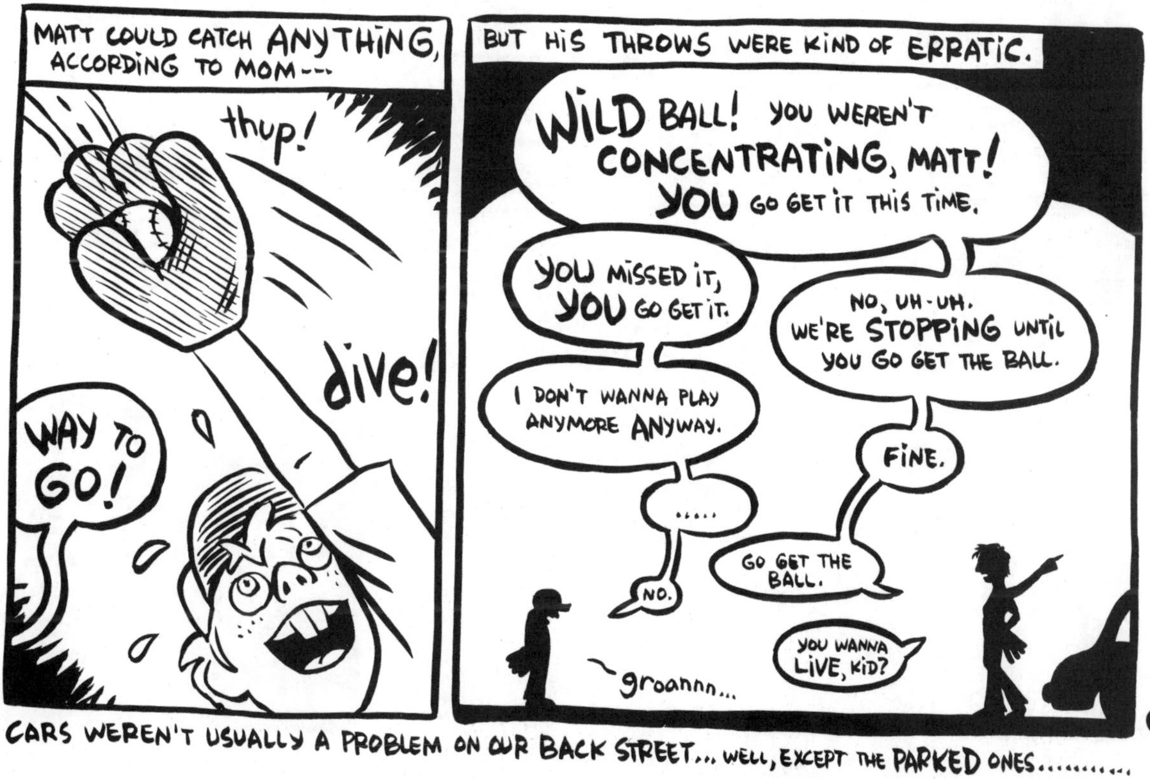
MATT COULD CATCH ANYTHING, ACCORDING TO MOM---
thup!
dive!
WAY TO GO!
BUT HIS THROWS WERE KIND OF ERRATIC.
WILD BALL! YOU WEREN'T CONCENTRATING, MATT! YOU GO GET IT THIS TIME.
YOU MISSED IT, YOU GO GET IT.
NO, UH-UH. WE'RE STOPPING UNTIL YOU GO GET THE BALL.
I DON'T WANNA PLAY ANYMORE ANYWAY.
FINE.
.....
GO GET THE BALL.
NO.
YOU WANNA LIVE, KID?
groannn...

CARS WEREN'T USUALLY A PROBLEM ON OUR BACK STREET... WELL, EXCEPT THE PARKED ONES..........

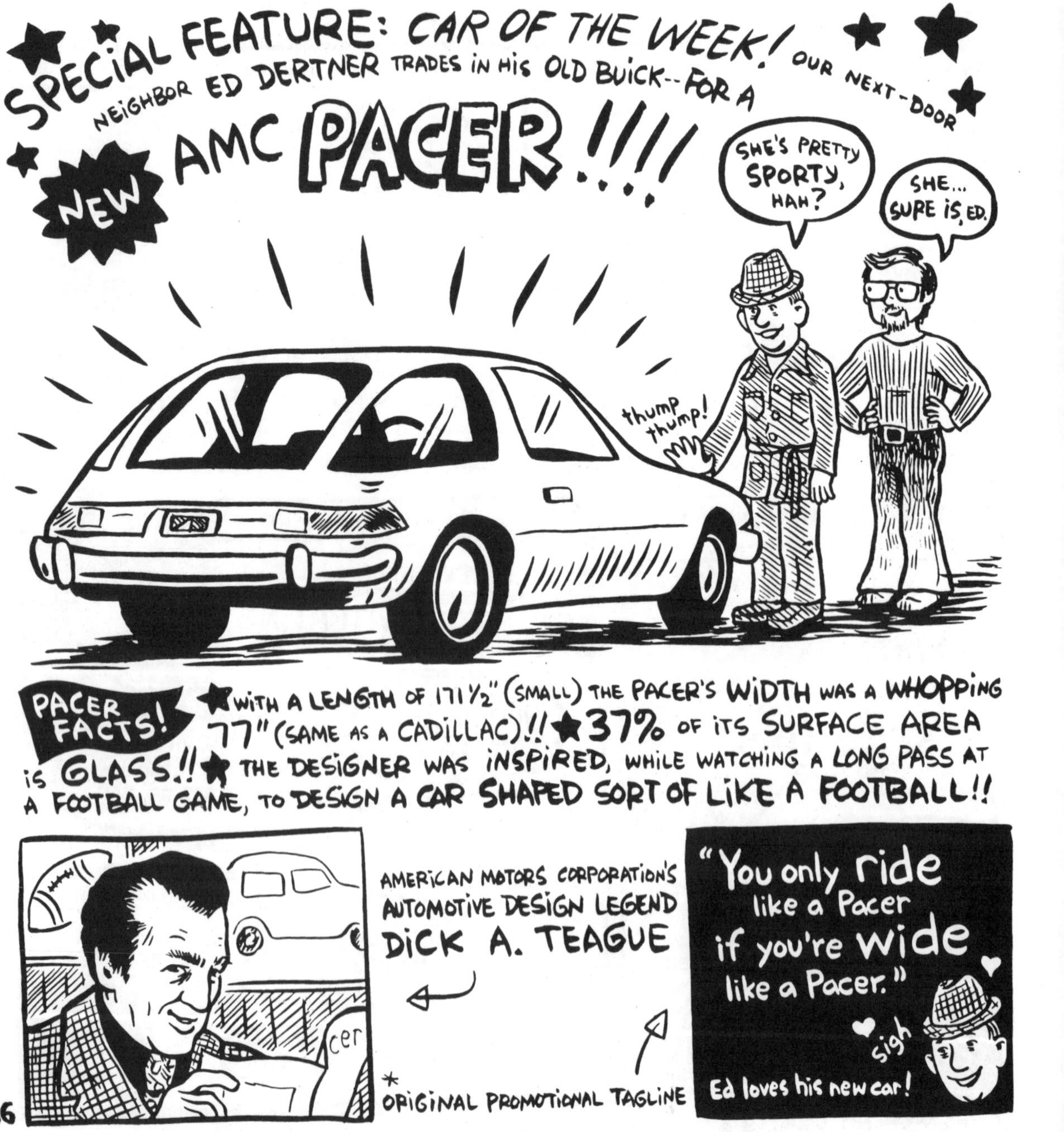
SPECIAL FEATURE: CAR OF THE WEEK! OUR NEXT-DOOR NEIGHBOR ED DERTNER TRADES IN HIS OLD BUICK--FOR A
NEW AMC PACER!!!!
SHE'S PRETTY SPORTY, HAH?
SHE... SURE IS, ED.
thump thump!
PACER FACTS!
WITH A LENGTH OF 171½" (SMALL) THE PACER'S WIDTH WAS A WHOPPING 77" (SAME AS A CADILLAC)!! 37% OF ITS SURFACE AREA IS GLASS!! THE DESIGNER WAS INSPIRED, WHILE WATCHING A LONG PASS AT A FOOTBALL GAME, TO DESIGN A CAR SHAPED SORT OF LIKE A FOOTBALL!!
cer
AMERICAN MOTORS CORPORATION'S AUTOMOTIVE DESIGN LEGEND DICK A. TEAGUE
* ORIGINAL PROMOTIONAL TAGLINE
"You only ride like a Pacer if you're wide like a Pacer."
sigh
Ed loves his new car!

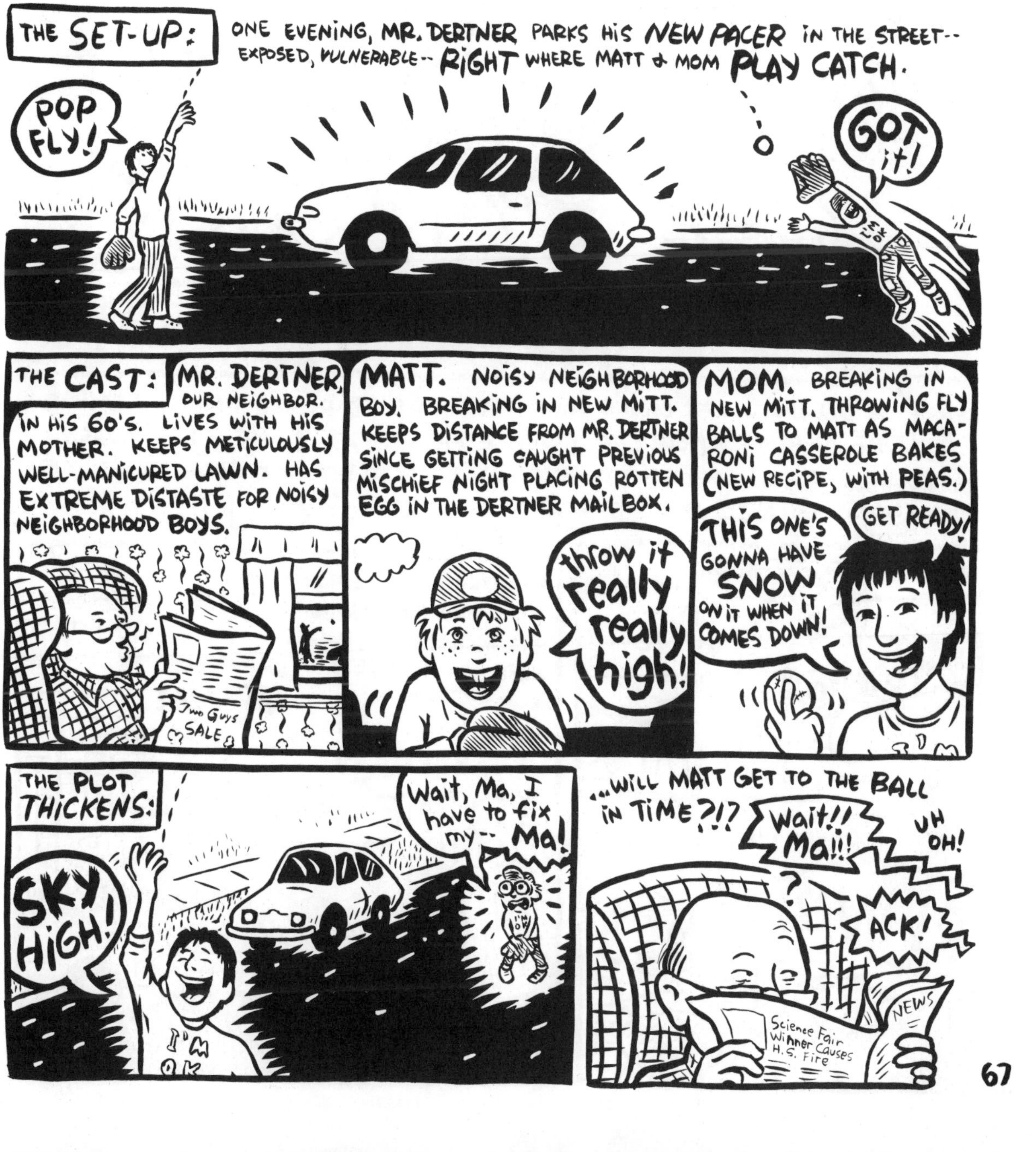
THE SET-UP:
ONE EVENING, MR. DERTNER PARKS HIS NEW PACER IN THE STREET-- EXPOSED, VULNERABLE-- RIGHT WHERE MATT & MOM PLAY CATCH.
POP FLY!
GOT it!
I'M OK
THE CAST:
MR. DERTNER, OUR NEIGHBOR. IN HIS 60'S. LIVES WITH HIS MOTHER. KEEPS METICULOUSLY WELL-MANICURED LAWN. HAS EXTREME DISTASTE FOR NOISY NEIGHBORHOOD BOYS.
Two Guys SALE
MATT. NOISY NEIGHBORHOOD BOY. BREAKING IN NEW MITT. KEEPS DISTANCE FROM MR. DERTNER SINCE GETTING CAUGHT PREVIOUS MISCHIEF NIGHT PLACING ROTTEN EGG IN THE DERTNER MAILBOX.
throw it really really high!
MOM. BREAKING IN NEW MITT. THROWING FLY BALLS TO MATT AS MACARONI CASSEROLE BAKES (NEW RECIPE, WITH PEAS.)
GET READY!
THIS ONE'S GONNA HAVE SNOW ON IT WHEN IT COMES DOWN!
THE PLOT THICKENS:
SKY HIGH!
Wait, Ma, I have to fix my-- Ma!
I'M OK
...WILL MATT GET TO THE BALL IN TIME?!?
Wait!! Ma!!
UH OH!
?
ACK!
NEWS
Science Fair Winner Causes H.S. Fire

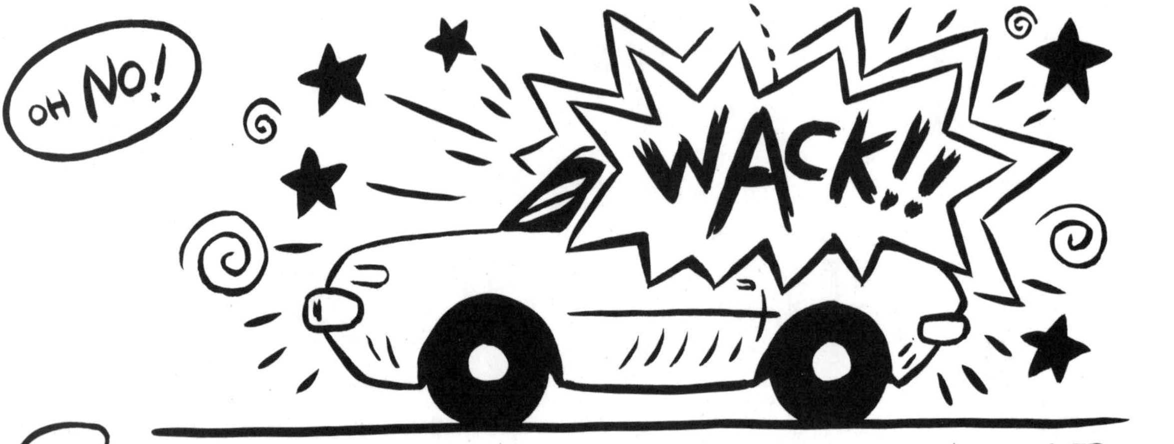
OH NO!
WACK!!

THE BASEBALL WAS COMING DOWN FAST AND HARD BY THE TIME IT REACHED MR. DERTNER'S NEW CAR. (SURFACE AREA = 37% GLASS..!) IT WASN'T IMMEDIATELY OBVIOUS WHETHER THE BALL HAD SMACKED INTO THE ROOF, OR INTO THE HATCHBACK WINDOW... IT WAS JUST VERY LOUD.

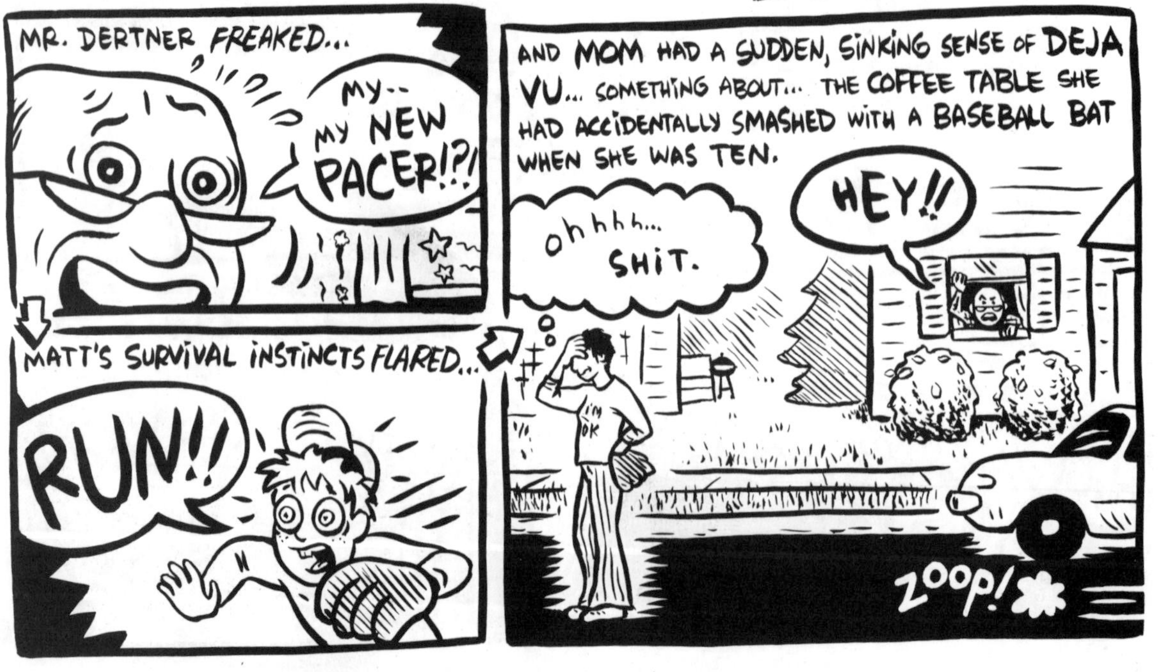
MR. DERTNER FREAKED...
MY-- MY NEW PACER!?!
MATT'S SURVIVAL INSTINCTS FLARED...
RUN!!
AND MOM HAD A SUDDEN, SINKING SENSE OF DEJA VU... SOMETHING ABOUT... THE COFFEE TABLE SHE HAD ACCIDENTALLY SMASHED WITH A BASEBALL BAT WHEN SHE WAS TEN.
HEY!!
OHHHH... SHIT.
I'M OK
ZOOP!

MR. DERTNER BARELY HAD TIME TO SLAP HIS TOUPEE ON HIS HEAD BEFORE HE WAS OUT THE DOOR AND YELLING. MOM'S MITT SOMEHOW ESCAPED HIS NOTICE.

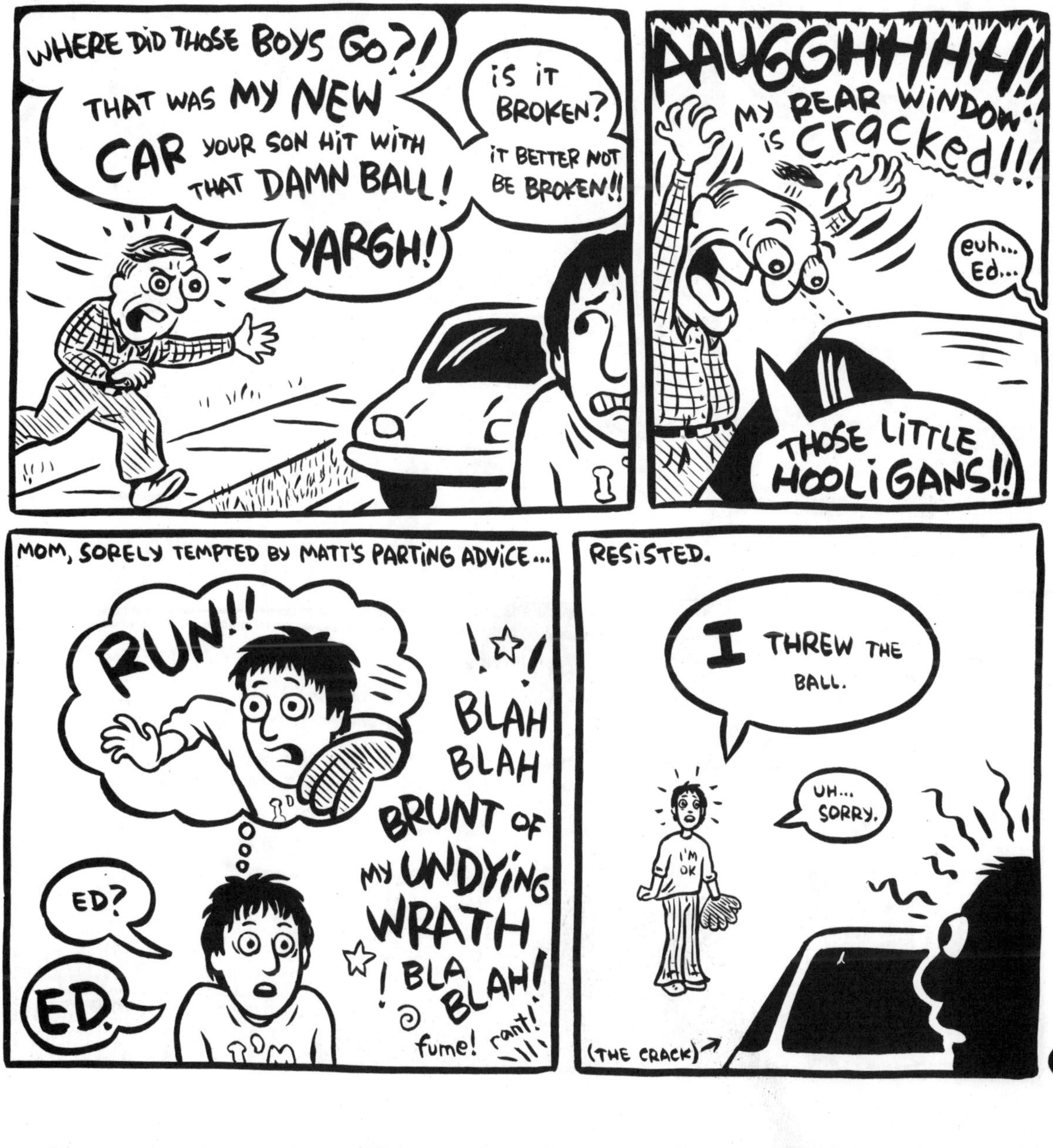

WHERE DID THOSE BOYS GO?!
THAT WAS MY NEW CAR YOUR SON HIT WITH THAT DAMN BALL!
YARGH!
IS IT BROKEN?
IT BETTER NOT BE BROKEN!!
AAUGGHHHHH!!
MY REAR WINDOW IS CRACKED!!!
euh... Ed...
THOSE LITTLE HOOLIGANS!!
MOM, SORELY TEMPTED BY MATT'S PARTING ADVICE...
RUN!!
BLAH BLAH
BRUNT OF MY UNDYING WRATH
BLA BLAH!
fume! rant!
ED?
ED.
RESISTED.
I THREW THE BALL.
UH... SORRY.
I'M OK
(THE CRACK)

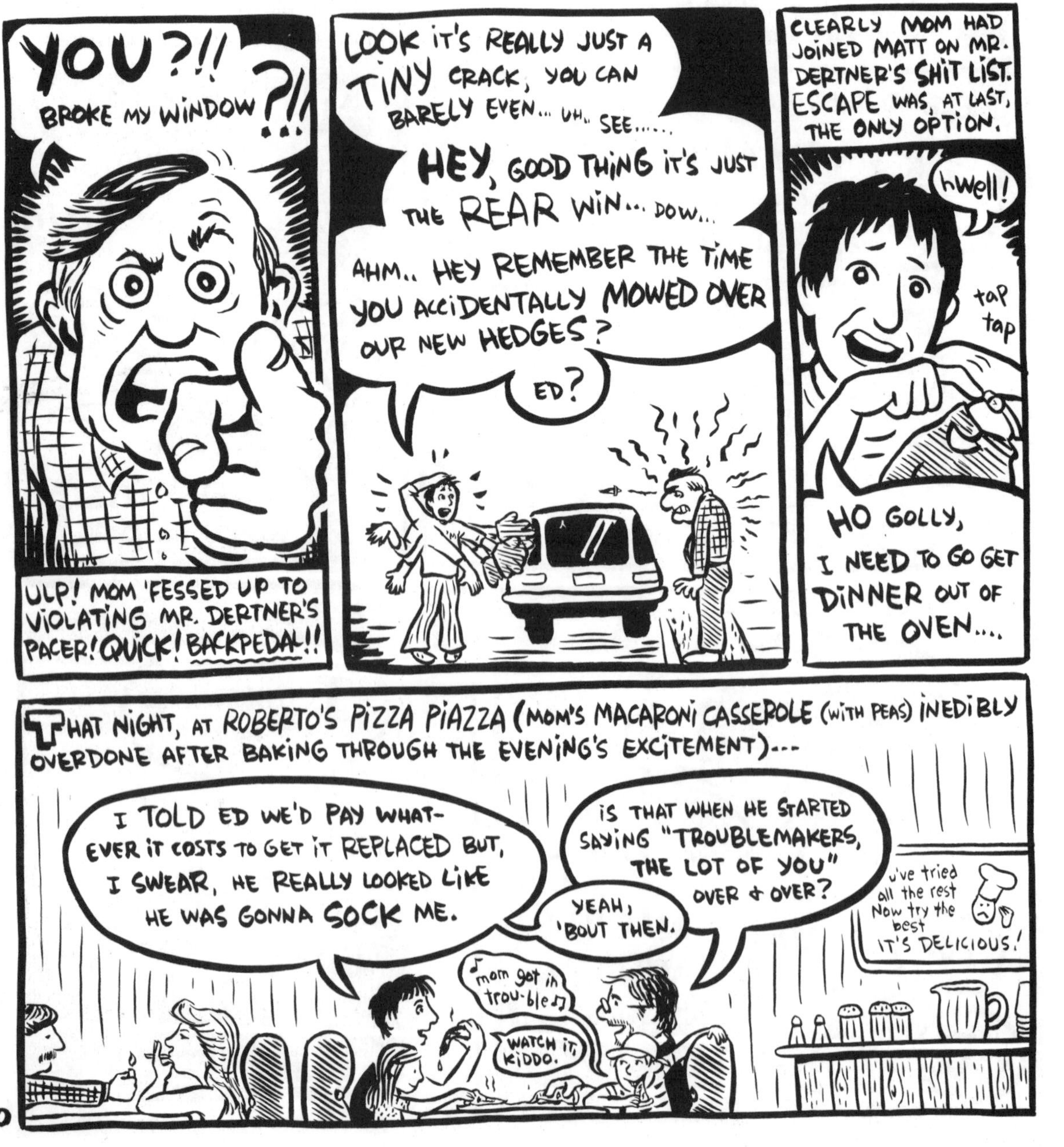
YOU?!! BROKE MY WINDOW?!!
ULP! MOM 'FESSED UP TO VIOLATING MR. DERTNER'S PACER! QUICK! BACKPEDAL!!
LOOK IT'S REALLY JUST A TINY CRACK, YOU CAN BARELY EVEN... UH.. SEE.....
HEY, GOOD THING IT'S JUST THE REAR WIN... DOW...
AHM.. HEY REMEMBER THE TIME YOU ACCIDENTALLY MOWED OVER OUR NEW HEDGES?
ED?
CLEARLY MOM HAD JOINED MATT ON MR. DERTNER'S SHIT LIST. ESCAPE WAS, AT LAST, THE ONLY OPTION.
hwell!
tap tap
HO GOLLY, I NEED TO GO GET DINNER OUT OF THE OVEN....
THAT NIGHT, AT ROBERTO'S PIZZA PIAZZA (MOM'S MACARONI CASSEROLE (WITH PEAS) INEDIBLY OVERDONE AFTER BAKING THROUGH THE EVENING'S EXCITEMENT)...
I TOLD ED WE'D PAY WHATEVER IT COSTS TO GET IT REPLACED BUT, I SWEAR, HE REALLY LOOKED LIKE HE WAS GONNA SOCK ME.
IS THAT WHEN HE STARTED SAYING "TROUBLEMAKERS, THE LOT OF YOU" OVER & OVER?
YEAH, 'BOUT THEN.
mom got in trou-ble
WATCH IT, KIDDO.
u've tried all the rest Now try the best IT'S DELICIOUS!

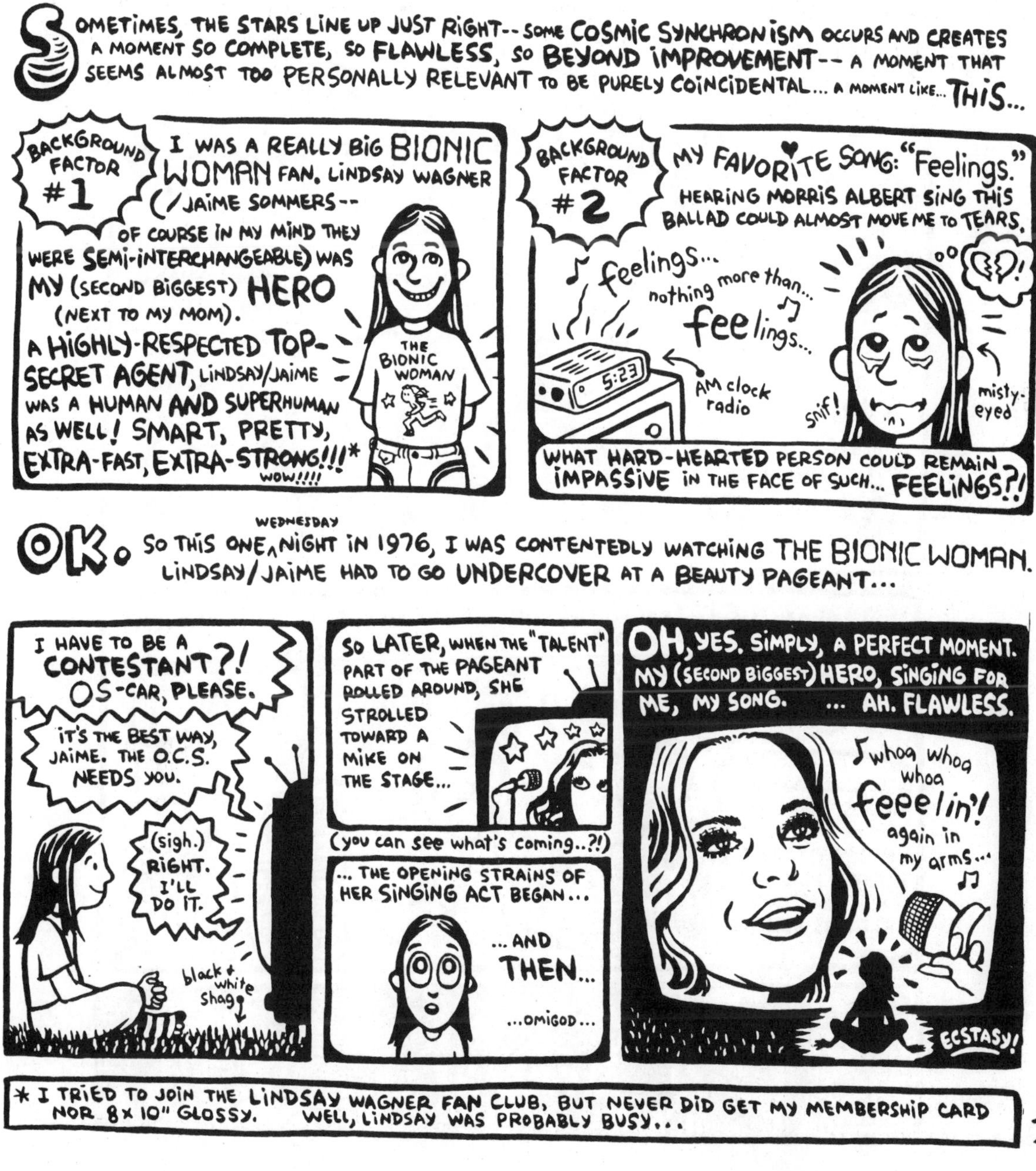
SOMETIMES, THE STARS LINE UP JUST RIGHT-- SOME COSMIC SYNCHRONISM OCCURS AND CREATES A MOMENT SO COMPLETE, SO FLAWLESS, SO BEYOND IMPROVEMENT-- A MOMENT THAT SEEMS ALMOST TOO PERSONALLY RELEVANT TO BE PURELY COINCIDENTAL... A MOMENT LIKE... THIS...
BACKGROUND FACTOR #1
I WAS A REALLY BIG BIONIC WOMAN FAN. LINDSAY WAGNER (/JAIME SOMMERS-- OF COURSE IN MY MIND THEY WERE SEMI-INTERCHANGEABLE) WAS MY (SECOND BIGGEST) HERO (NEXT TO MY MOM).
A HIGHLY-RESPECTED TOP-SECRET AGENT, LINDSAY/JAIME WAS A HUMAN AND SUPERHUMAN AS WELL! SMART, PRETTY, EXTRA-FAST, EXTRA-STRONG!!!*
WOW!!!!
THE BIONIC WOMAN
BACKGROUND FACTOR #2
MY FAVORITE SONG: "Feelings."
HEARING MORRIS ALBERT SING THIS BALLAD COULD ALMOST MOVE ME TO TEARS.
feelings... nothing more than... feelings...
5:23
AM clock radio
snif!
misty-eyed
WHAT HARD-HEARTED PERSON COULD REMAIN IMPASSIVE IN THE FACE OF SUCH... FEELINGS?!
OK. SO THIS ONE WEDNESDAY NIGHT IN 1976, I WAS CONTENTEDLY WATCHING THE BIONIC WOMAN. LINDSAY/JAIME HAD TO GO UNDERCOVER AT A BEAUTY PAGEANT...
I HAVE TO BE A CONTESTANT?! OS-CAR, PLEASE.
IT'S THE BEST WAY, JAIME. THE O.C.S. NEEDS YOU.
(sigh.) RIGHT. I'LL DO IT.
black & white shag
SO LATER, WHEN THE "TALENT" PART OF THE PAGEANT ROLLED AROUND, SHE STROLLED TOWARD A MIKE ON THE STAGE...
(you can see what's coming..?!)
... THE OPENING STRAINS OF HER SINGING ACT BEGAN...
... AND THEN...
...OMIGOD...
OH, YES. SIMPLY, A PERFECT MOMENT. MY (SECOND BIGGEST) HERO, SINGING FOR ME, MY SONG. ... AH. FLAWLESS.
whoa whoa whoa feeelin'! again in my arms...
ECSTASY!
* I TRIED TO JOIN THE LINDSAY WAGNER FAN CLUB, BUT NEVER DID GET MY MEMBERSHIP CARD NOR 8 x 10" GLOSSY. WELL, LINDSAY WAS PROBABLY BUSY...

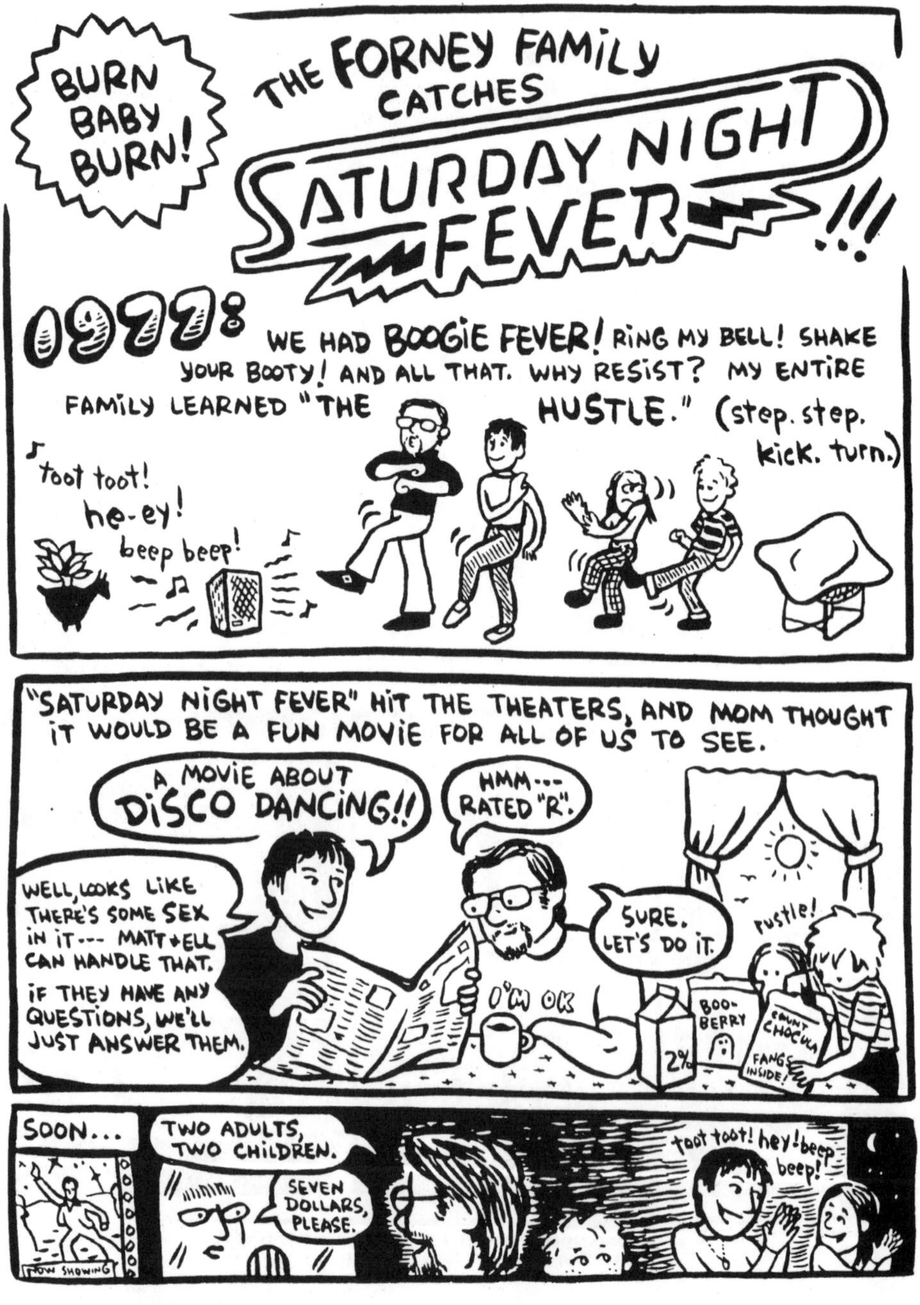
BURN BABY BURN!
THE FORNEY FAMILY CATCHES SATURDAY NIGHT FEVER!!!
1977:
WE HAD BOOGIE FEVER! RING MY BELL! SHAKE YOUR BOOTY! AND ALL THAT. WHY RESIST? MY ENTIRE FAMILY LEARNED "THE HUSTLE." (step. step. kick. turn.)
toot toot!
he-ey!
beep beep!
"SATURDAY NIGHT FEVER" HIT THE THEATERS, AND MOM THOUGHT IT WOULD BE A FUN MOVIE FOR ALL OF US TO SEE.
A MOVIE ABOUT DISCO DANCING!!
HMM... RATED "R".
WELL, LOOKS LIKE THERE'S SOME SEX IN IT--- MATT+ELL CAN HANDLE THAT.
IF THEY HAVE ANY QUESTIONS, WE'LL JUST ANSWER THEM.
SURE. LET'S DO IT.
rustle!
I'M OK
BOO-BERRY
COUNT CHOCULA
FANGS INSIDE!
2%
SOON...
NOW SHOWING
TWO ADULTS, TWO CHILDREN.
SEVEN DOLLARS, PLEASE.
toot toot! hey! beep beep!

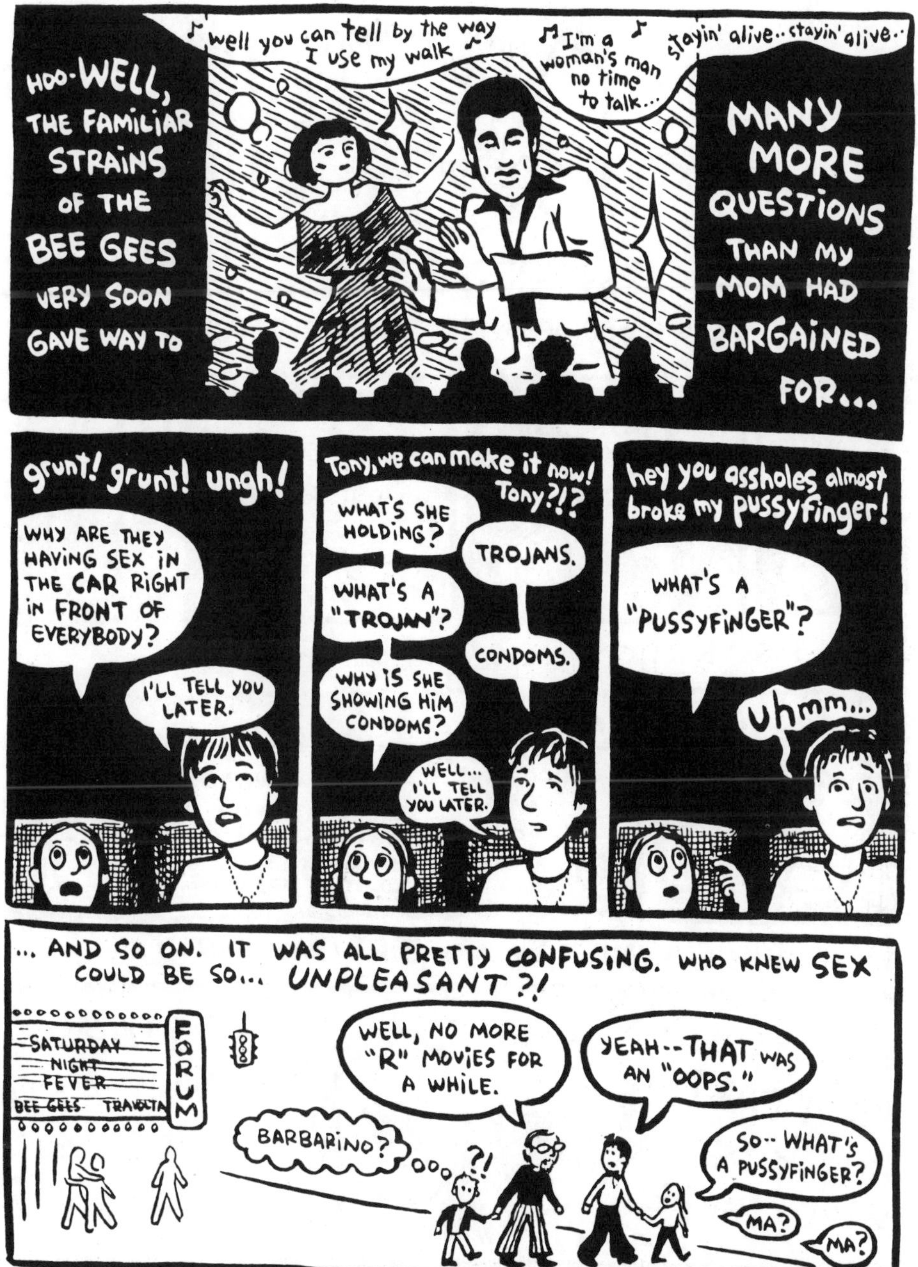

HOO-WELL, THE FAMILIAR STRAINS OF THE BEE GEES VERY SOON GAVE WAY TO
♪ well you can tell by the way I use my walk ♪
♪ I'm a ♪ woman's man no time to talk...
stayin' alive.. stayin' alive..
MANY MORE QUESTIONS THAN MY MOM HAD BARGAINED FOR...
grunt! grunt! ungh!
WHY ARE THEY HAVING SEX IN THE CAR RIGHT IN FRONT OF EVERYBODY?
I'LL TELL YOU LATER.
Tony, we can make it now! Tony?!?
WHAT'S SHE HOLDING?
TROJANS.
WHAT'S A "TROJAN"?
CONDOMS.
WHY IS SHE SHOWING HIM CONDOMS?
WELL... I'LL TELL YOU LATER.
hey you assholes almost broke my pussyfinger!
WHAT'S A "PUSSYFINGER"?
Uhmm...
... AND SO ON. IT WAS ALL PRETTY CONFUSING. WHO KNEW SEX COULD BE SO... UNPLEASANT?!
SATURDAY NIGHT FEVER
BEE GEES TRAVOLTA
FORUM
WELL, NO MORE "R" MOVIES FOR A WHILE.
YEAH--THAT WAS AN "OOPS."
BARBARINO?
?!
SO-- WHAT'S A PUSSYFINGER?
MA?
MA?

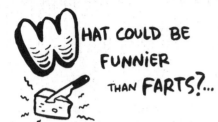

WHAT COULD BE FUNNIER THAN FARTS?...

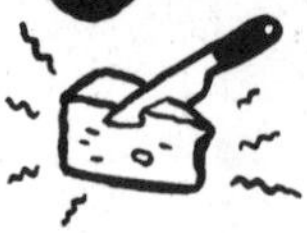

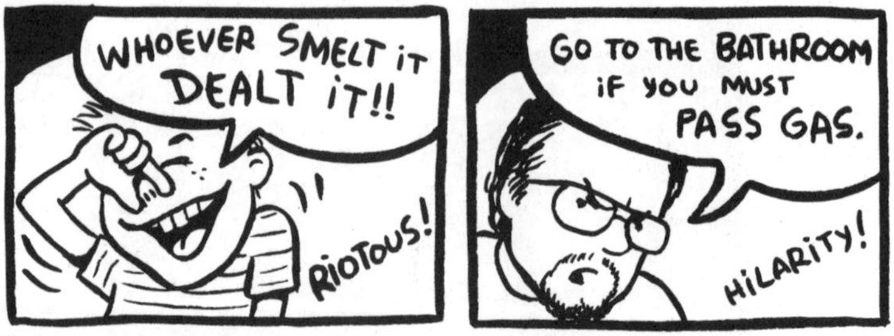
WHOEVER SMELT IT DEALT IT!!
RIOTOUS!
GO TO THE BATHROOM IF YOU MUST PASS GAS.
HILARITY!

AH, THE ROLLICKING FART GAMES OF YOUTH, HOW WE REMEMBER THEM FONDLY. HERE'S ONE OF MY BROTHER'S OLD FAVORITES:

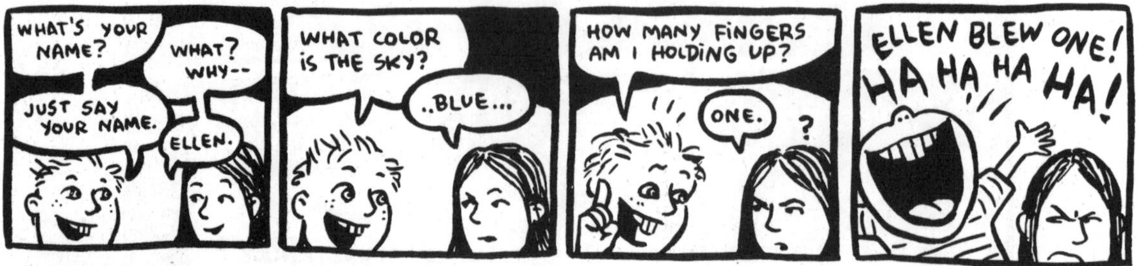
WHAT'S YOUR NAME?
WHAT? WHY--
JUST SAY YOUR NAME.
ELLEN.
WHAT COLOR IS THE SKY?
..BLUE...
HOW MANY FINGERS AM I HOLDING UP?
ONE.
?
ELLEN BLEW ONE!
HA HA HA HA!

HERE'S ONE FOR PRACTICING MUSCULAR CONTROL:

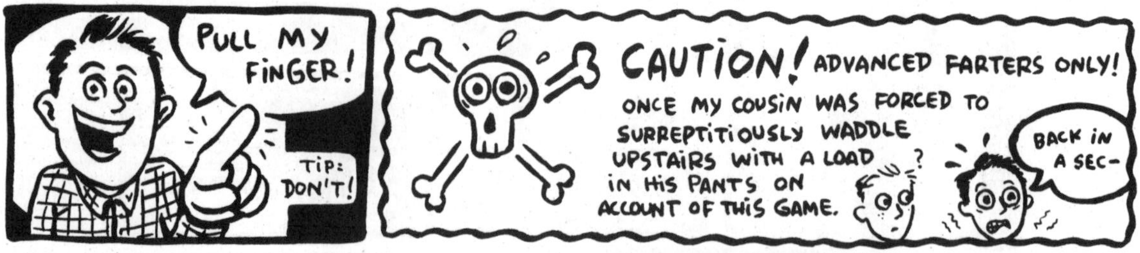
PULL MY FINGER!
TIP: DON'T!
CAUTION! ADVANCED FARTERS ONLY!
ONCE MY COUSIN WAS FORCED TO SURREPTITIOUSLY WADDLE UPSTAIRS WITH A LOAD IN HIS PANTS ON ACCOUNT OF THIS GAME.
?
BACK IN A SEC-

AND THIS RHYME'S A MUST AT ANY BIRTHDAY PARTY:

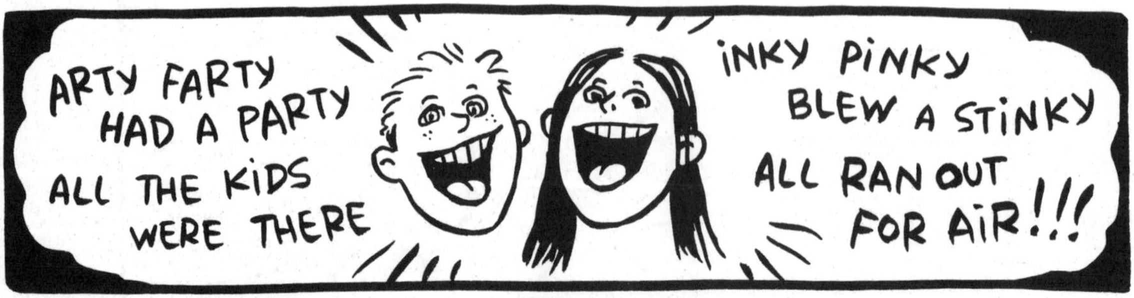
ARTY FARTY HAD A PARTY
ALL THE KIDS WERE THERE
INKY PINKY BLEW A STINKY
ALL RAN OUT FOR AIR!!!

me & Matt with pumpkins, 1973.

(photo taken by Dad)

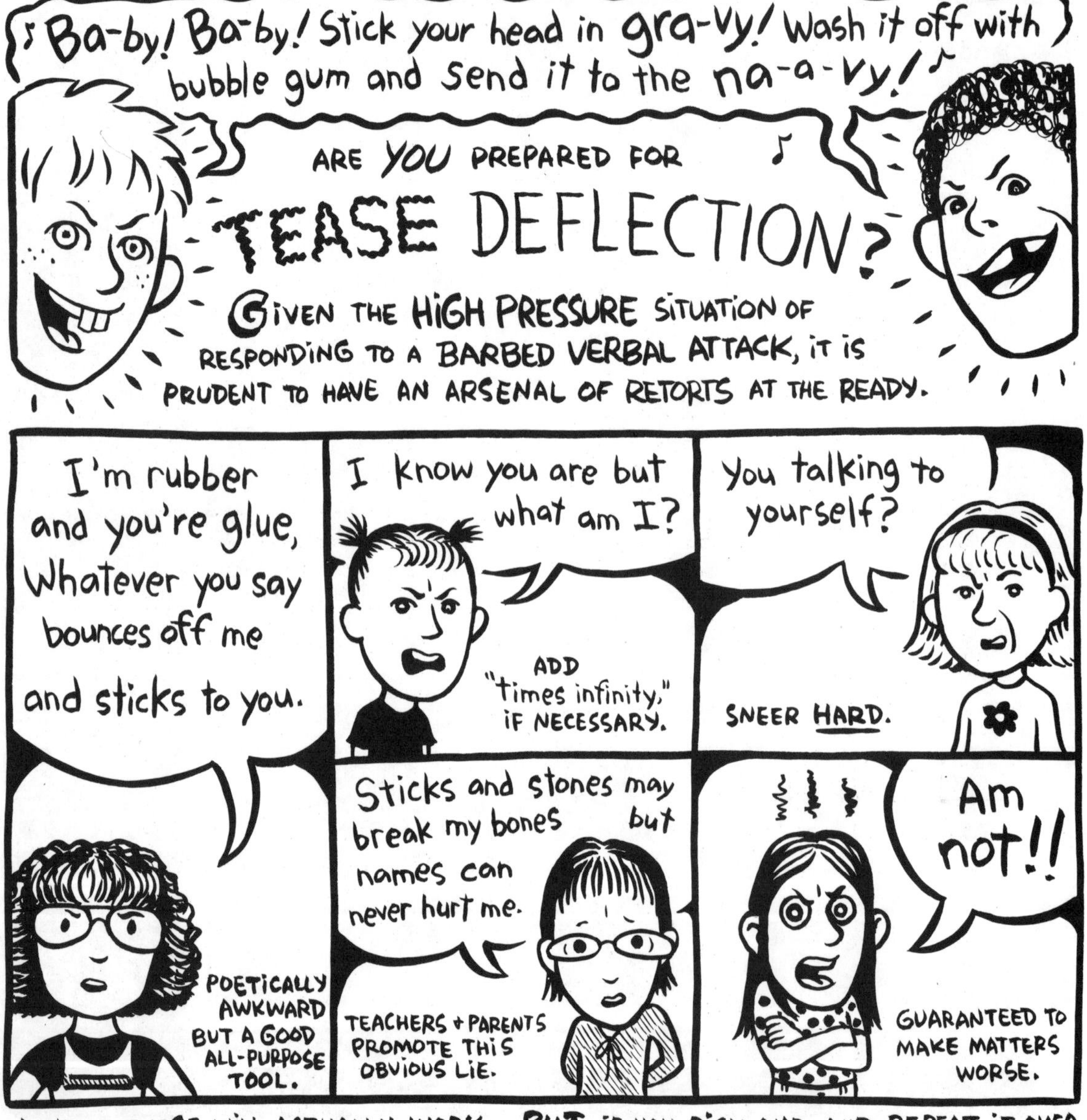
Ba-by! Ba-by! Stick your head in gra-vy! Wash it off with bubble gum and send it to the na-a-vy!
ARE YOU PREPARED FOR
TEASE DEFLECTION?
GIVEN THE HIGH PRESSURE SITUATION OF RESPONDING TO A BARBED VERBAL ATTACK, IT IS PRUDENT TO HAVE AN ARSENAL OF RETORTS AT THE READY.
I'm rubber and you're glue, Whatever you say bounces off me and sticks to you.
POETICALLY AWKWARD BUT A GOOD ALL-PURPOSE TOOL.
I know you are but what am I?
ADD "times infinity," IF NECESSARY.
You talking to yourself?
SNEER HARD.
Sticks and stones may break my bones but names can never hurt me.
TEACHERS + PARENTS PROMOTE THIS OBVIOUS LIE.
Am not!!
GUARANTEED TO MAKE MATTERS WORSE.

NONE OF THESE WILL ACTUALLY WORK. BUT, IF YOU PICK ONE AND REPEAT IT OVER AND OVER AT TOP VOLUME, AT LEAST YOU WON'T BE ABLE TO HEAR YOUR TEASER ANYMORE.

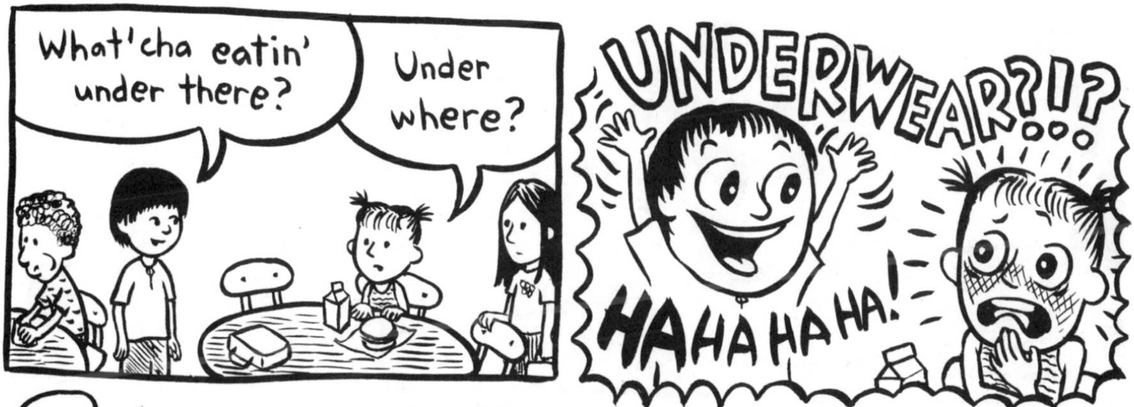
What'cha eatin' under there?
Under where?
UNDERWEAR?!?
HAHAHAHAHA!

THIS DECEPTIVELY SIMPLE TEASE CAN BRING DOWN THE MIGHTIEST OF FIRST-GRADERS. (WHAT COULD BE MORE MORTIFYING THAN INFORMING A SMIRKING CLASSMATE THAT YOU'RE EATING UNDERWEAR?!) I WAS VERY PROUD WHEN I THOUGHT OF A WAY AROUND THIS TRICK. I HAD MATT TEST ME:

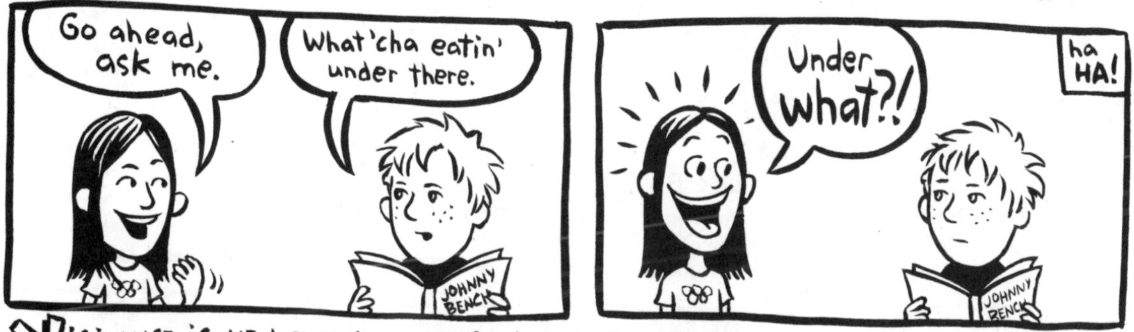
Go ahead, ask me.
What'cha eatin' under there.
JOHNNY BENCH
Under what?!
ha HA!
JOHNNY BENCH

VIGILANCE IS KEY, THOUGH... VARIATIONS ABOUND.

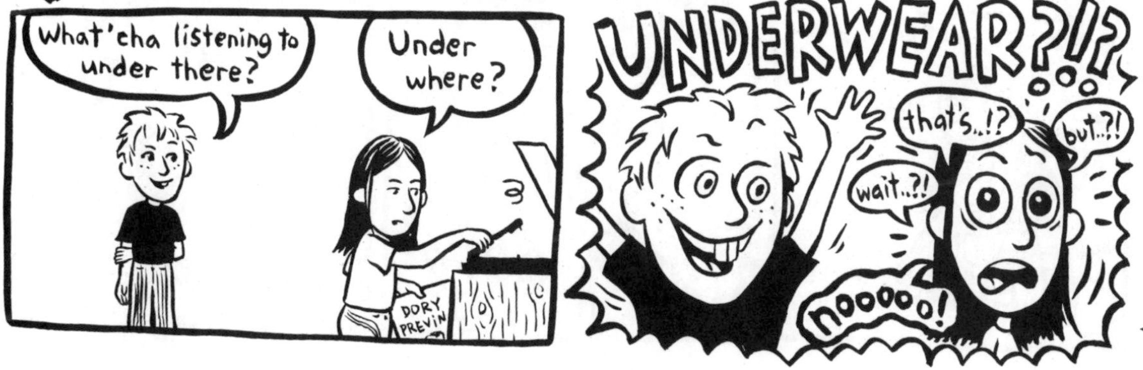
What'cha listening to under there?
Under where?
DORY PREVIN
UNDERWEAR?!?
that's..!?
but..?!
wait..?!
nooooo!

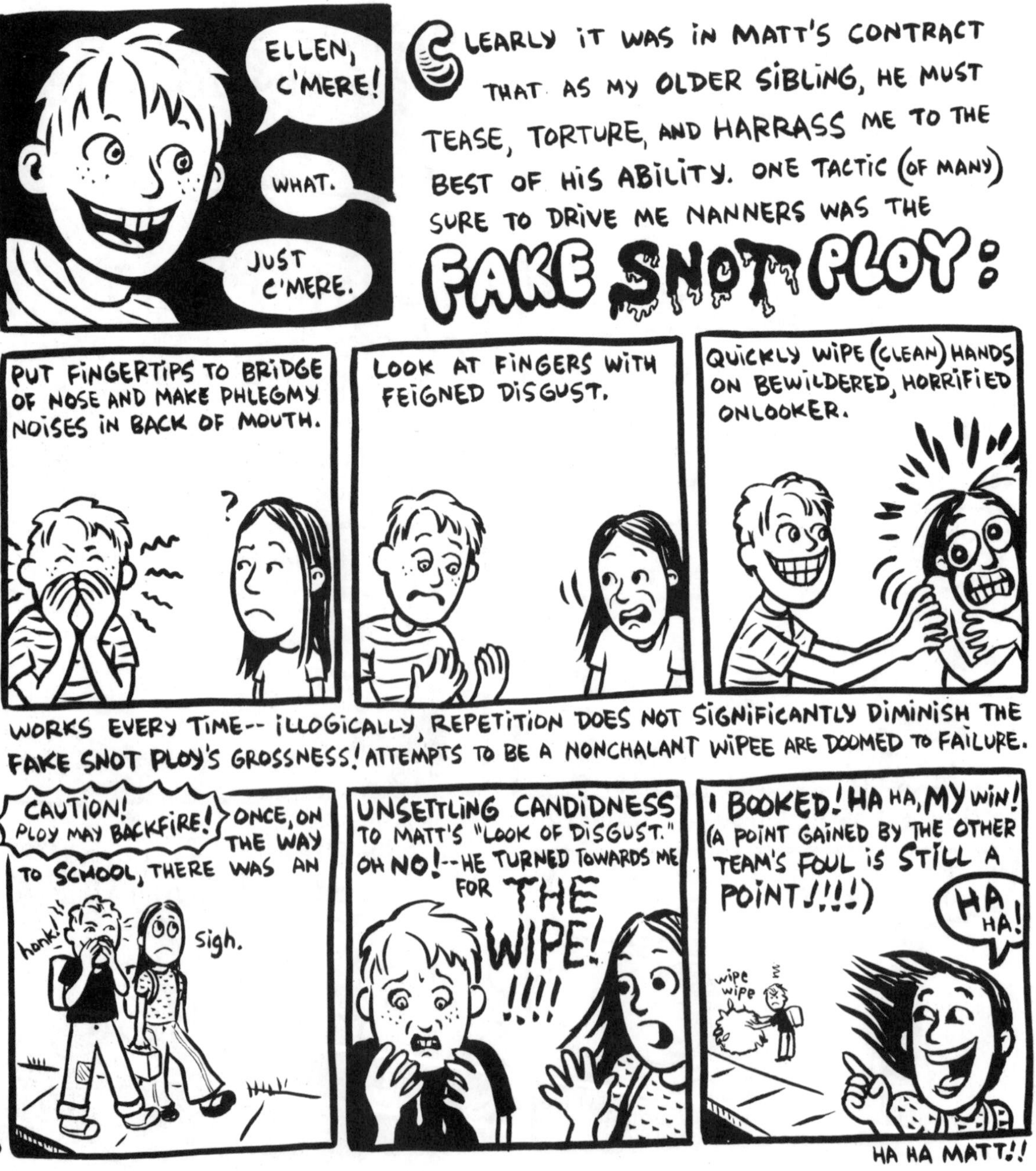

ELLEN, C'MERE!
WHAT.
JUST C'MERE.
CLEARLY IT WAS IN MATT'S CONTRACT THAT AS MY OLDER SIBLING, HE MUST TEASE, TORTURE, AND HARRASS ME TO THE BEST OF HIS ABILITY. ONE TACTIC (OF MANY) SURE TO DRIVE ME NANNERS WAS THE
FAKE SNOT PLOY:
PUT FINGERTIPS TO BRIDGE OF NOSE AND MAKE PHLEGMY NOISES IN BACK OF MOUTH.
?
LOOK AT FINGERS WITH FEIGNED DISGUST.
QUICKLY WIPE (CLEAN) HANDS ON BEWILDERED, HORRIFIED ONLOOKER.
WORKS EVERY TIME-- ILLOGICALLY, REPETITION DOES NOT SIGNIFICANTLY DIMINISH THE FAKE SNOT PLOY'S GROSSNESS! ATTEMPTS TO BE A NONCHALANT WIPEE ARE DOOMED TO FAILURE.
CAUTION! PLOY MAY BACKFIRE!
ONCE, ON THE WAY TO SCHOOL, THERE WAS AN
honk!
sigh.
UNSETTLING CANDIDNESS TO MATT'S "LOOK OF DISGUST." OH NO!--HE TURNED TOWARDS ME FOR THE WIPE! !!!!
I BOOKED! HA HA, MY WIN! (A POINT GAINED BY THE OTHER TEAM'S FOUL IS STILL A POINT!!!!)
HA HA!
wipe wipe
HA HA MATT!!

THOUGH I CERTAINLY HAD AMPLE OPPORTUNITY TO TRY, I NEVER DID LEARN TO PARRY MY BIG BROTHER'S GOADING. (WELL, EXCEPT FOR THE ONE TIME I PITCHED A GLOPPY TUNA FISH SANDWICH AT HIS HEAD.) EVER CREATIVE IN HIS METHODS, MATT WAS QUICK TO DISCOVER THAT A "SOFT RESPONSE" WAS AN EASY WAY TO MAKE MY HEAD EXPLODE.

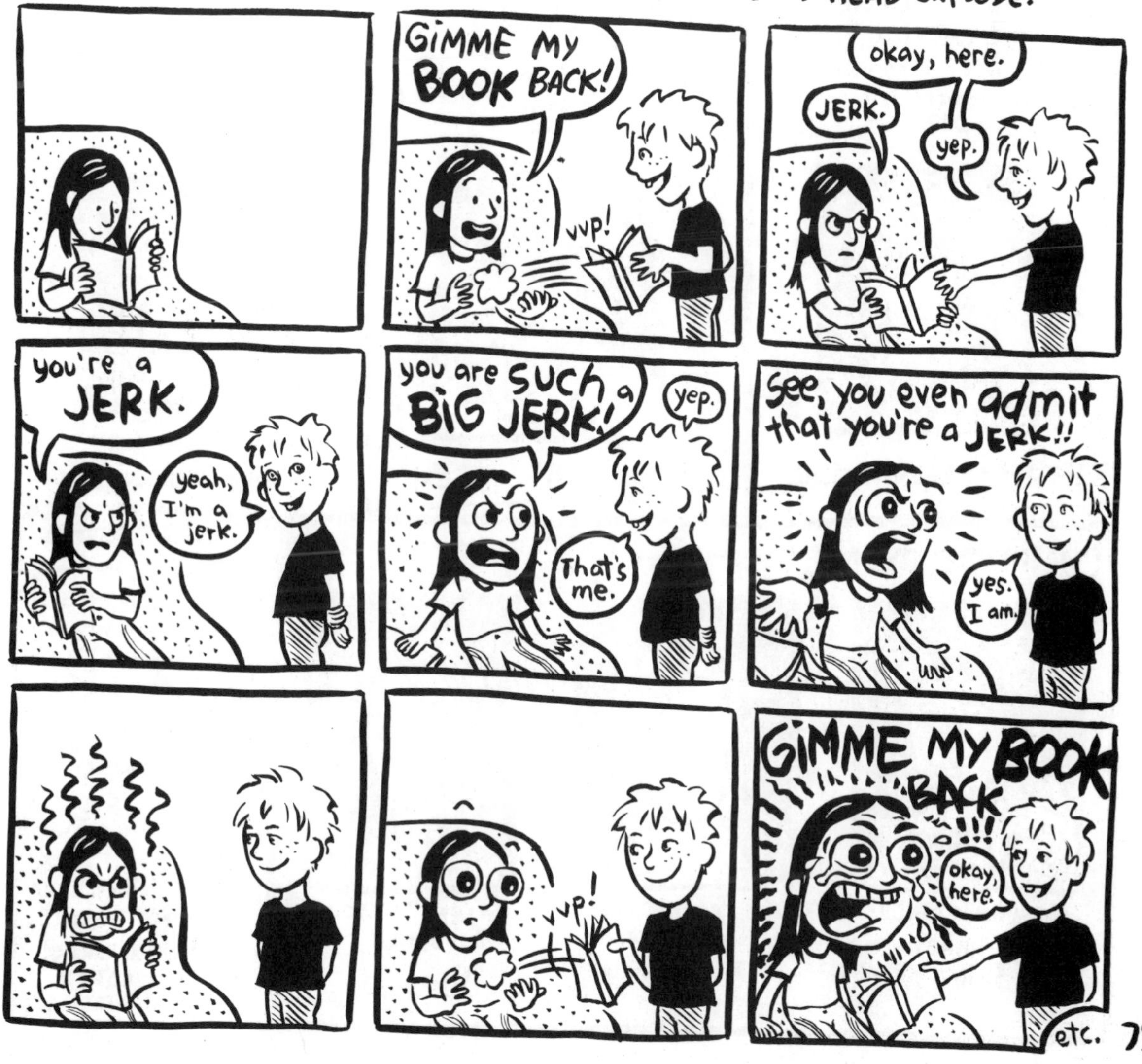
GIMME MY BOOK BACK!
vvp!
okay, here.
JERK.
yep.
you're a JERK.
yeah, I'm a jerk.
you are such a BIG JERK!
yep.
That's me.
See, you even admit that you're a JERK!!
yes. I am.
vvp!
GIMME MY BOOK BACK!!!
okay, here.
etc.

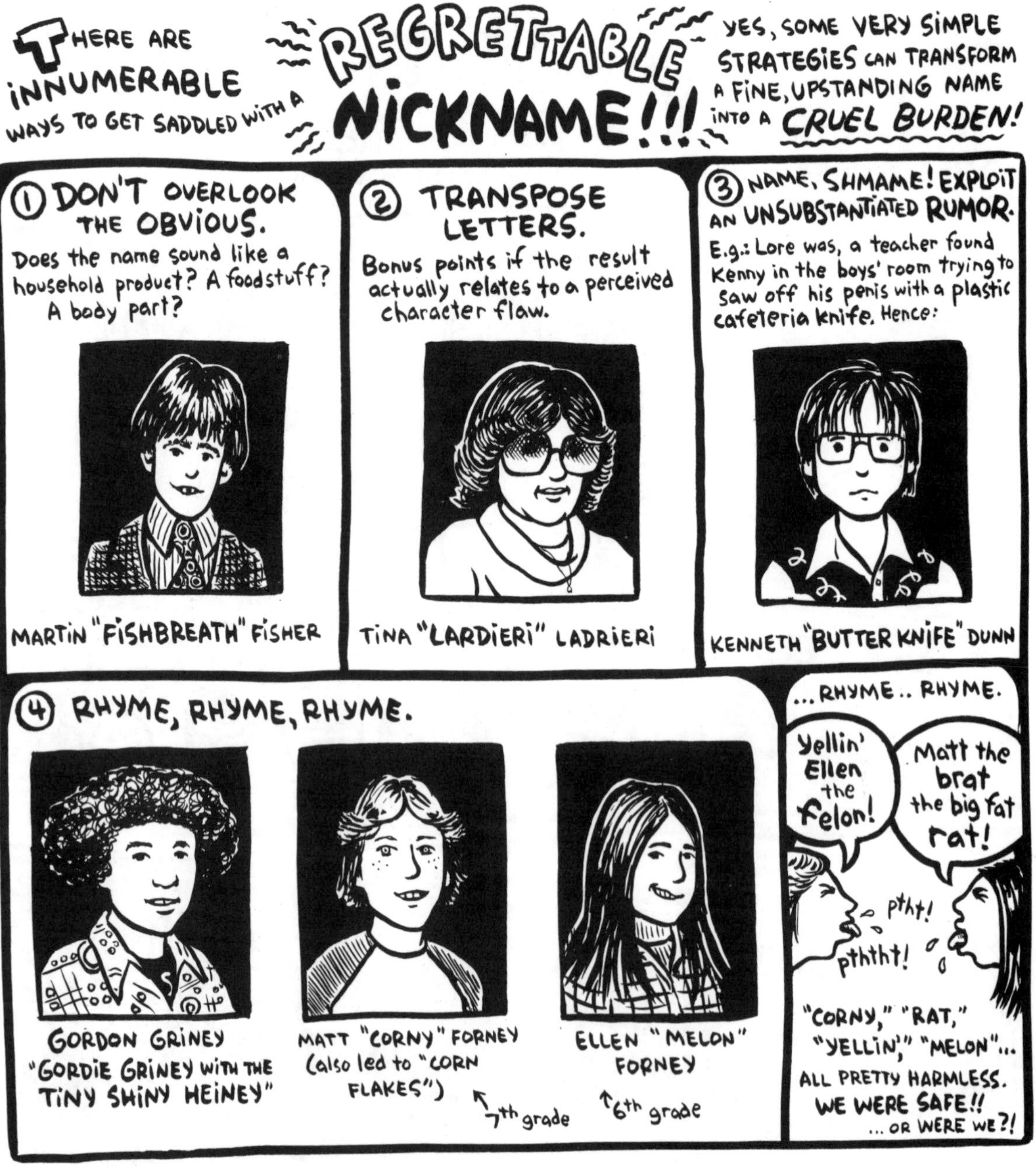
THERE ARE INNUMERABLE WAYS TO GET SADDLED WITH A REGRETTABLE NICKNAME!!!
YES, SOME VERY SIMPLE STRATEGIES CAN TRANSFORM A FINE, UPSTANDING NAME INTO A CRUEL BURDEN!
① DON'T OVERLOOK THE OBVIOUS.
Does the name sound like a household product? A foodstuff? A body part?
MARTIN "FISHBREATH" FISHER
② TRANSPOSE LETTERS.
Bonus points if the result actually relates to a perceived character flaw.
TINA "LARDIERI" LADRIERI
③ NAME, SHMAME! EXPLOIT AN UNSUBSTANTIATED RUMOR.
E.g.: Lore was, a teacher found Kenny in the boys' room trying to saw off his penis with a plastic cafeteria knife. Hence:
KENNETH "BUTTER KNIFE" DUNN
④ RHYME, RHYME, RHYME.
GORDON GRINEY "GORDIE GRINEY WITH THE TINY SHINY HEINEY"
MATT "CORNY" FORNEY (also led to "CORN FLAKES")
ELLEN "MELON" FORNEY
↑ 7th grade
↑ 6th grade
...RHYME.. RHYME.
Yellin' Ellen the felon!
Matt the brat the big fat rat!
ptht!
pththt!
"CORNY," "RAT," "YELLIN'," "MELON"... ALL PRETTY HARMLESS. WE WERE SAFE!!
...OR WERE WE?!

WHEN I WAS IN THIRD GRADE, I LEARNED A WORD THAT WOULD HAUNT ME FOR YEARS. PROVOCATIVE, DANGEROUS, A VERBAL LANDMINE, IT WAS BURIED IN A LONG, LONG JOKE MY DAD INFLICTED ON MY MOM DURING A CAR TRIP.

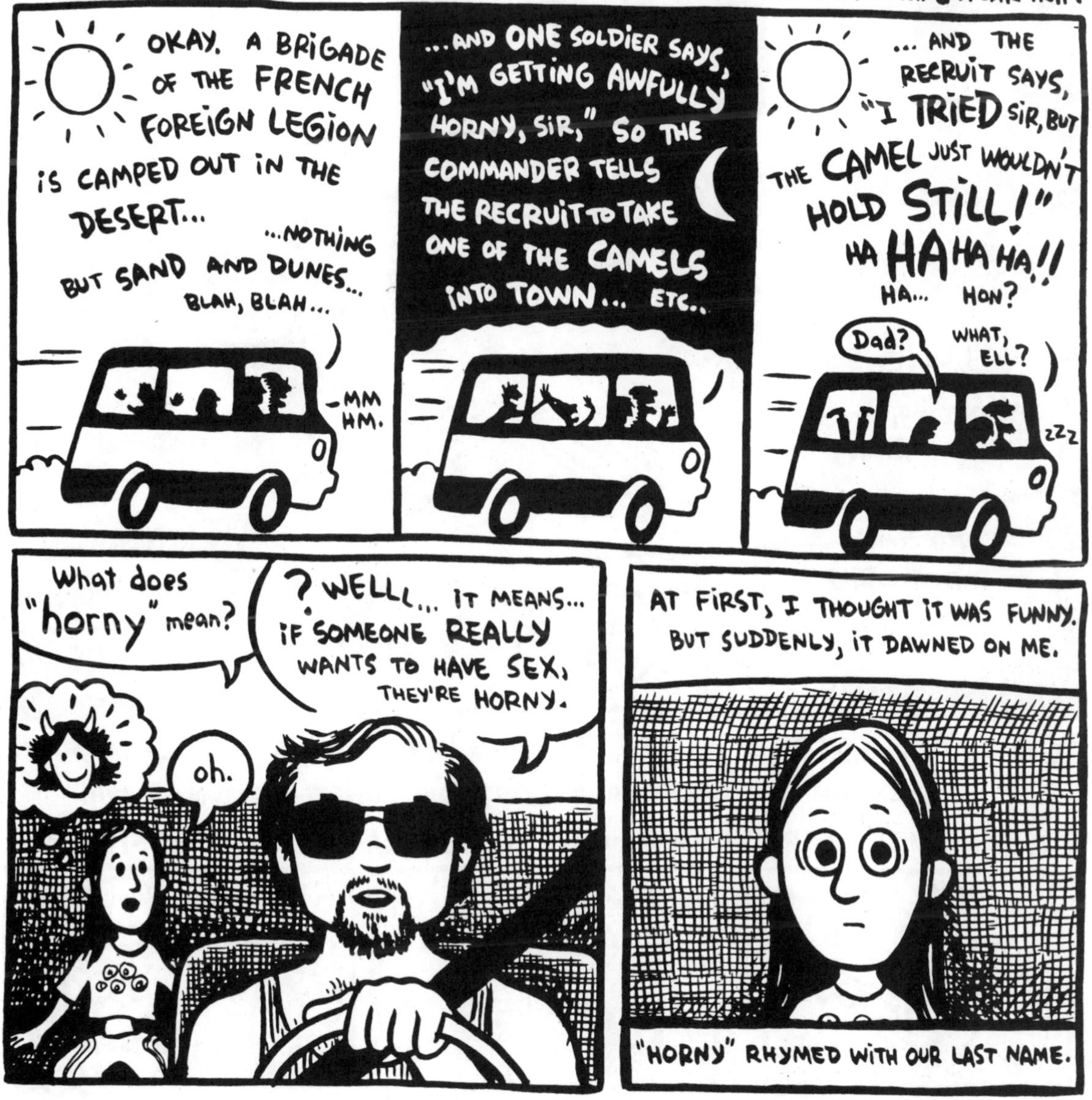

OKAY. A BRIGADE OF THE FRENCH FOREIGN LEGION IS CAMPED OUT IN THE DESERT...
...NOTHING BUT SAND AND DUNES...
BLAH, BLAH...
-MM HM.
...AND ONE SOLDIER SAYS, "I'M GETTING AWFULLY HORNY, SIR," SO THE COMMANDER TELLS THE RECRUIT TO TAKE ONE OF THE CAMELS INTO TOWN... ETC..
... AND THE RECRUIT SAYS, "I TRIED SIR, BUT THE CAMEL JUST WOULDN'T HOLD STILL!"
HA HA HA HA HA!!
HA... HON?
Dad?
WHAT, ELL?
ZZZ
What does "horny" mean?
? WELLL... IT MEANS... IF SOMEONE REALLY WANTS TO HAVE SEX, THEY'RE HORNY.
oh.
AT FIRST, I THOUGHT IT WAS FUNNY. BUT SUDDENLY, IT DAWNED ON ME.
"HORNY" RHYMED WITH OUR LAST NAME.

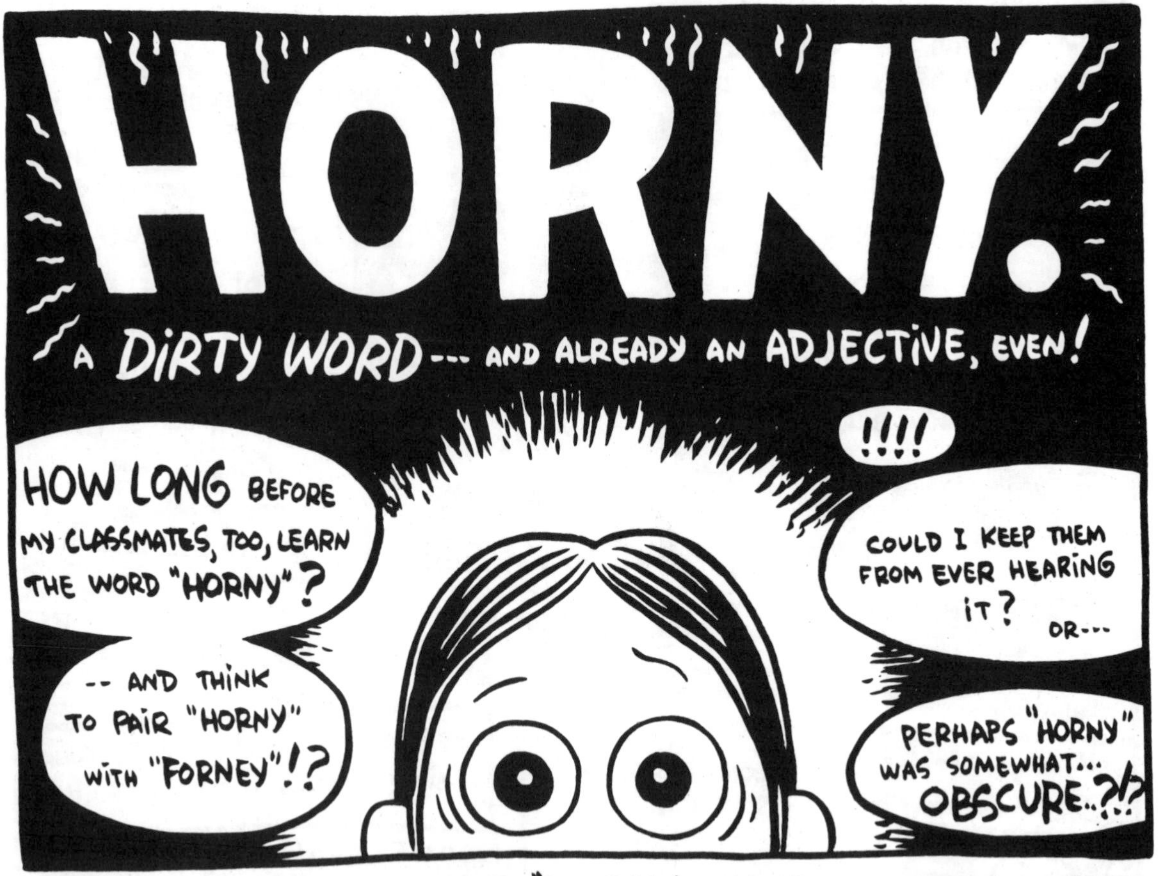
HORNY.
A DIRTY WORD--- AND ALREADY AN ADJECTIVE, EVEN!
HOW LONG BEFORE MY CLASSMATES, TOO, LEARN THE WORD "HORNY"?
-- AND THINK TO PAIR "HORNY" WITH "FORNEY"!?
!!!!
COULD I KEEP THEM FROM EVER HEARING IT? OR---
PERHAPS "HORNY" WAS SOMEWHAT... OBSCURE..?!?

I HAD TO PREPARE MYSELF. "PLAYING IT COOL" WAS HARDLY MY FORTE. SHORT ON COMEBACKS AND LONG ON CONSTERNATION, I WAS DISMAYINGLY FERTILE GROUND FOR A TRAUMA-INDUCING NICKNAME.

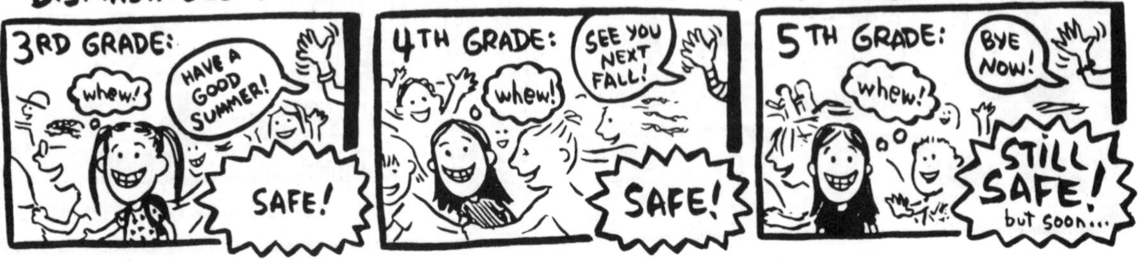
3RD GRADE:
whew!
HAVE A GOOD SUMMER!
SAFE!
4TH GRADE:
whew!
SEE YOU NEXT FALL!
SAFE!
5TH GRADE:
whew!
BYE NOW!
STILL SAFE!
but soon...

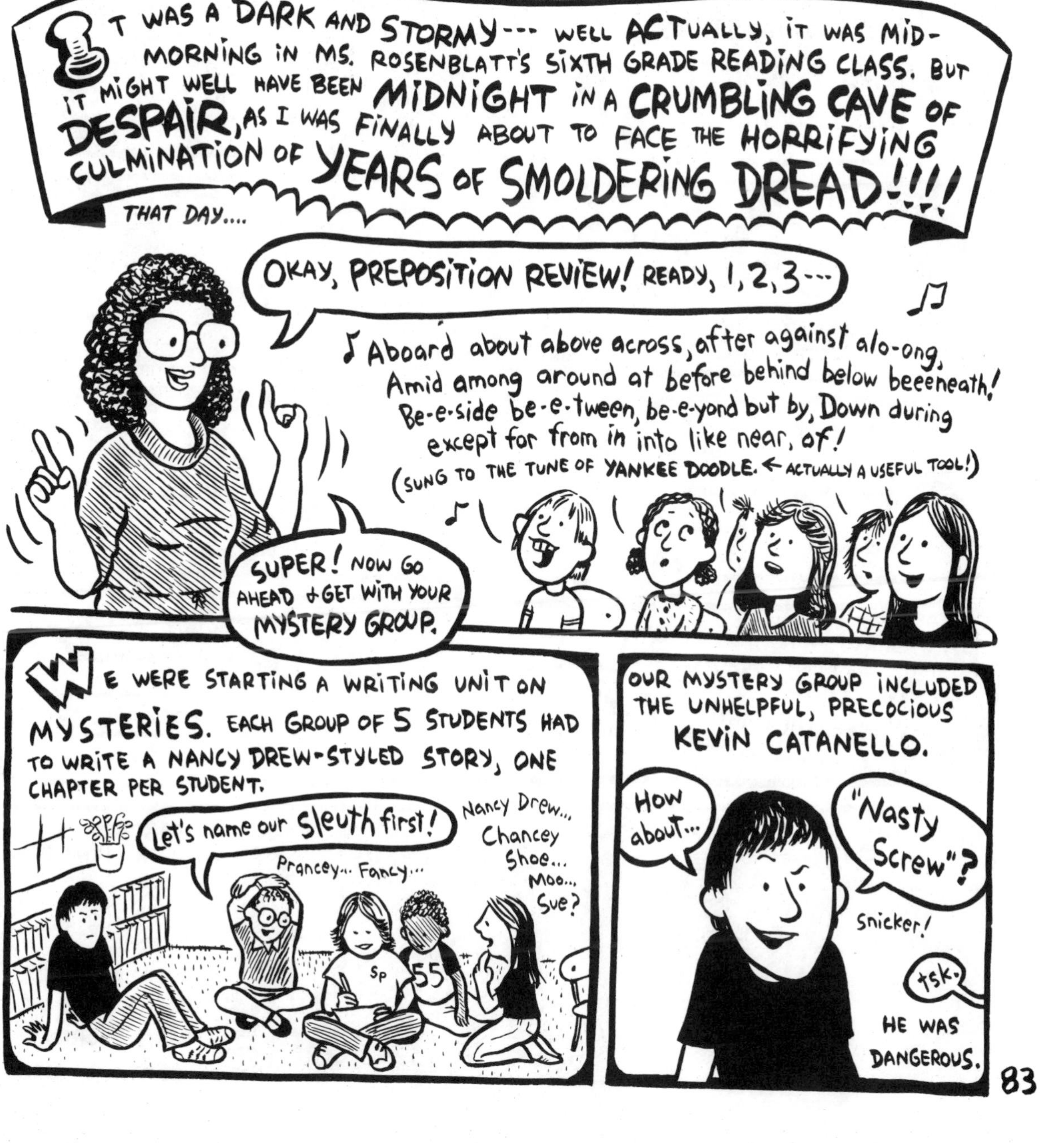
IT WAS A DARK AND STORMY--- WELL ACTUALLY, IT WAS MID-MORNING IN MS. ROSENBLATT'S SIXTH GRADE READING CLASS. BUT IT MIGHT WELL HAVE BEEN MIDNIGHT IN A CRUMBLING CAVE OF DESPAIR, AS I WAS FINALLY ABOUT TO FACE THE HORRIFYING CULMINATION OF YEARS OF SMOLDERING DREAD!!!!
THAT DAY....
OKAY, PREPOSITION REVIEW! READY, 1,2,3---
Aboard about above across, after against alo-ong, Amid among around at before behind below beeeneath! Be-e-side be-e-tween, be-e-yond but by, Down during except for from in into like near, of!
(SUNG TO THE TUNE OF YANKEE DOODLE. ← ACTUALLY A USEFUL TOOL!)
SUPER! NOW GO AHEAD & GET WITH YOUR MYSTERY GROUP.
WE WERE STARTING A WRITING UNIT ON MYSTERIES. EACH GROUP OF 5 STUDENTS HAD TO WRITE A NANCY DREW-STYLED STORY, ONE CHAPTER PER STUDENT.
Let's name our sleuth first!
Nancy Drew... Chancey Shoe... Moo... Sue?
Prancey... Fancy...
OUR MYSTERY GROUP INCLUDED THE UNHELPFUL, PRECOCIOUS KEVIN CATANELLO.
How about...
"Nasty Screw"?
Snicker!
tsk.
HE WAS DANGEROUS.

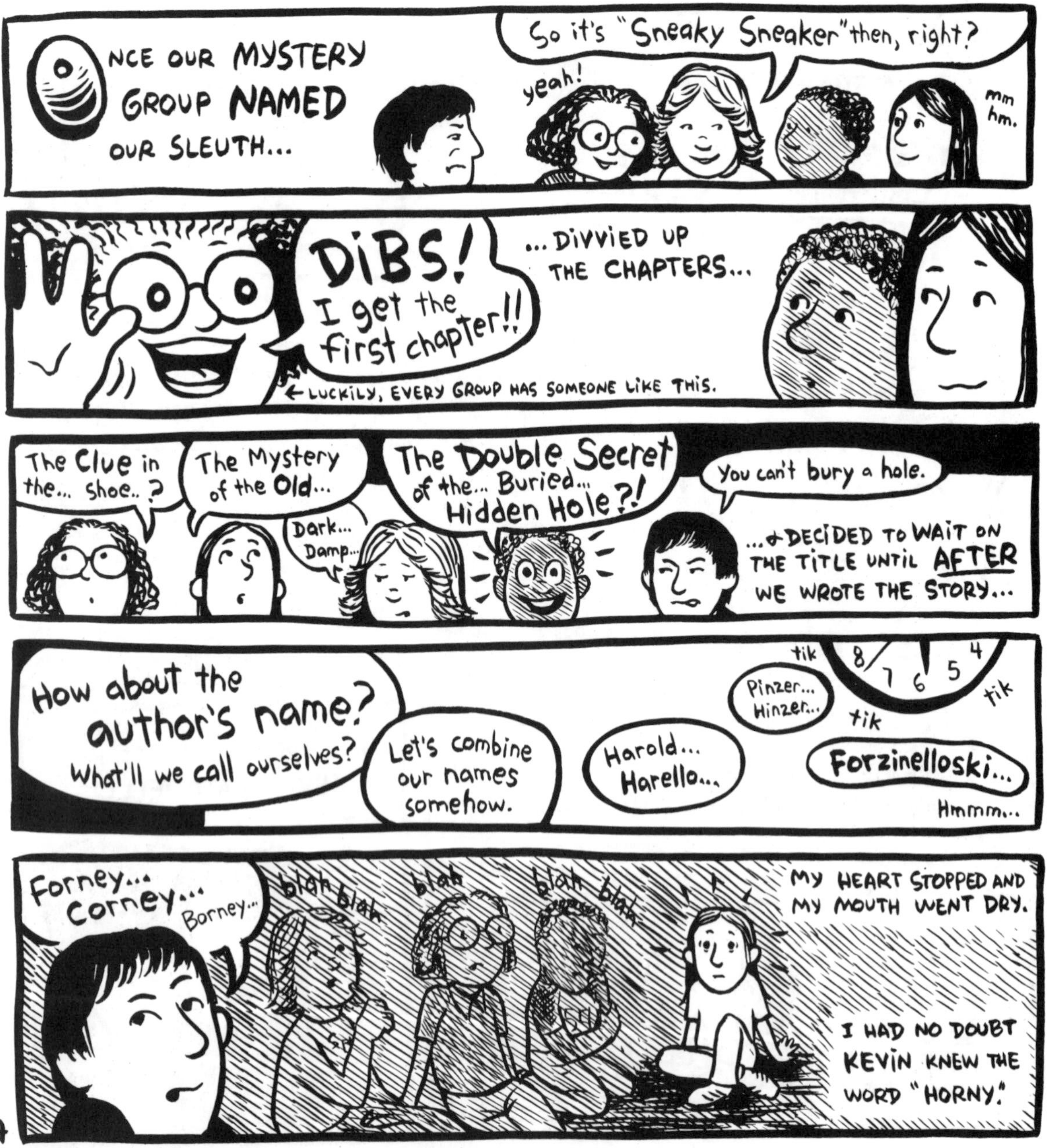
ONCE OUR MYSTERY GROUP NAMED OUR SLEUTH...
So it's "Sneaky Sneaker" then, right?
yeah!
mm hm.
DiBS! I get the first chapter!!
...DIVVIED UP THE CHAPTERS...
← LUCKILY, EVERY GROUP HAS SOMEONE LIKE THIS.
The Clue in the... Shoe..?
The Mystery of the Old...
Dark... Damp...
The Double Secret of the... Buried... Hidden Hole?!
You can't bury a hole.
...& DECIDED TO WAIT ON THE TITLE UNTIL AFTER WE WROTE THE STORY...
How about the author's name? What'll we call ourselves?
Let's combine our names somehow.
Harold... Harello...
Pinzer... Hinzer...
tik
tik
tik
Forzinelloski...
Hmmm...
Forney... Corney... Borney...
blah blah
blah
blah blah
MY HEART STOPPED AND MY MOUTH WENT DRY.
I HAD NO DOUBT KEVIN KNEW THE WORD "HORNY."

THE HUMAN BRAIN HAS A STRANGE ABILITY TO TAKE MOMENTS OF GREAT CALAMITY, AND PLAY THEM OUT IN VERY **SLOW MOTION.**
I DON'T KNOW WHY THIS IS... TO BETTER SAVOR OUR DISASTERS?

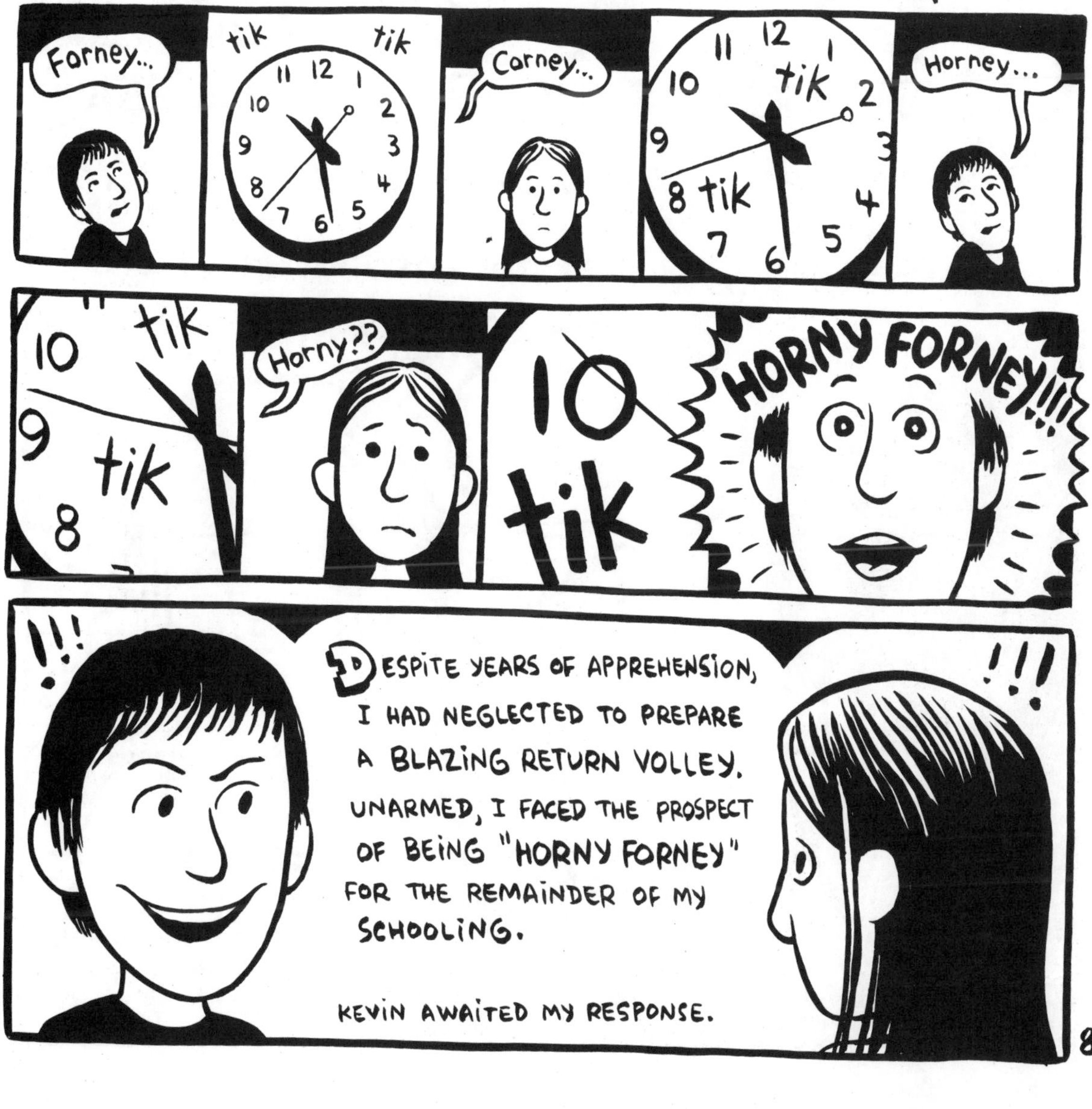

Forney...
tik
tik
Carney...
tik
tik
Horney...
tik
tik
Horny??
tik
HORNY FORNEY!!!
!!!
DESPITE YEARS OF APPREHENSION, I HAD NEGLECTED TO PREPARE A BLAZING RETURN VOLLEY. UNARMED, I FACED THE PROSPECT OF BEING "HORNY FORNEY" FOR THE REMAINDER OF MY SCHOOLING.
KEVIN AWAITED MY RESPONSE.
!!!

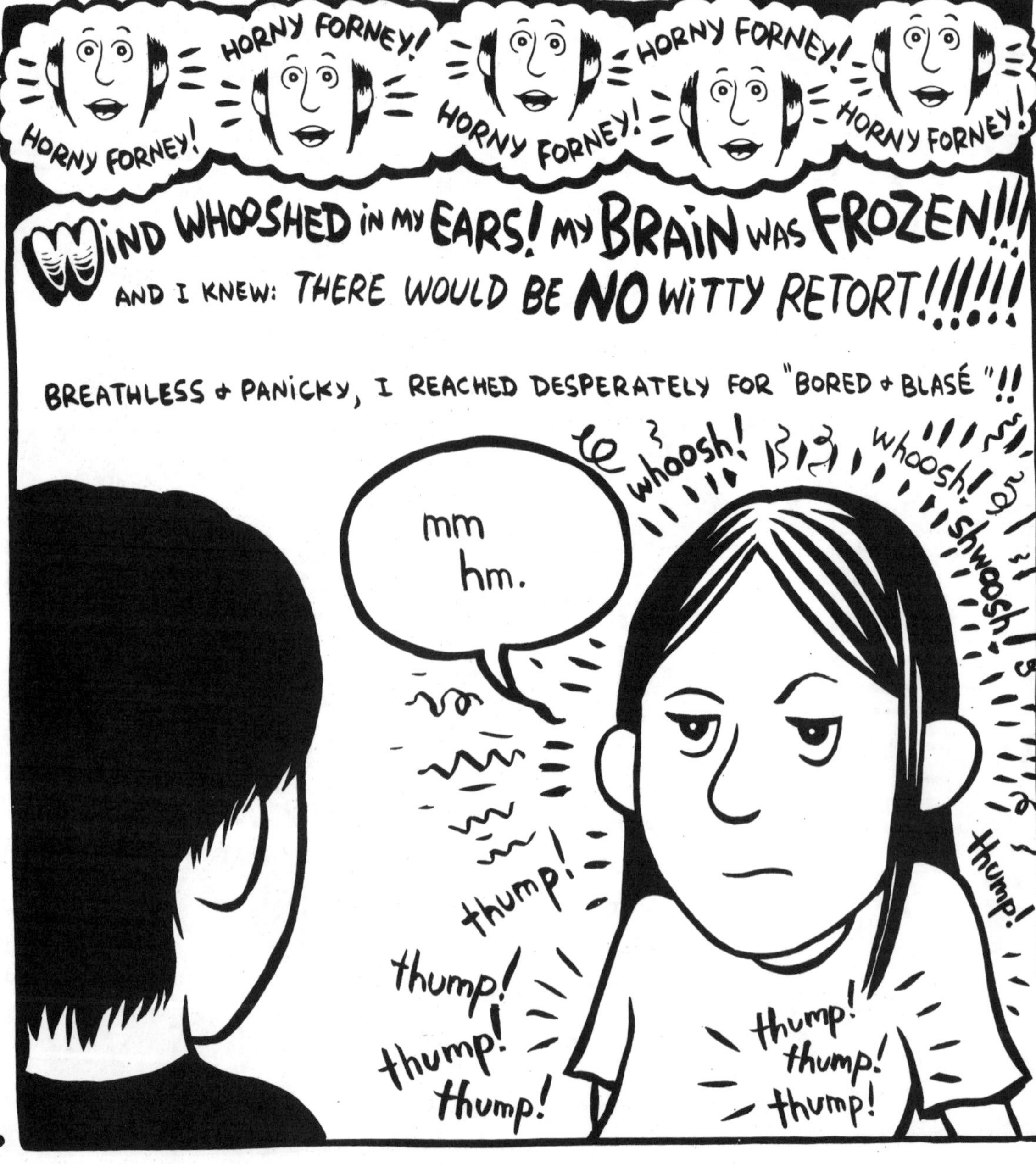
HORNY FORNEY!
HORNY FORNEY!
HORNY FORNEY!
HORNY FORNEY!
HORNY FORNEY!
WIND WHOOSHED IN MY EARS! MY BRAIN WAS FROZEN!!!
AND I KNEW: THERE WOULD BE NO WITTY RETORT!!!!!!!
BREATHLESS & PANICKY, I REACHED DESPERATELY FOR "BORED & BLASÉ"!!
whoosh!
whoosh!
shwoosh!
mm hm.
thump!
thump!
thump! thump! thump!
thump! thump! thump!

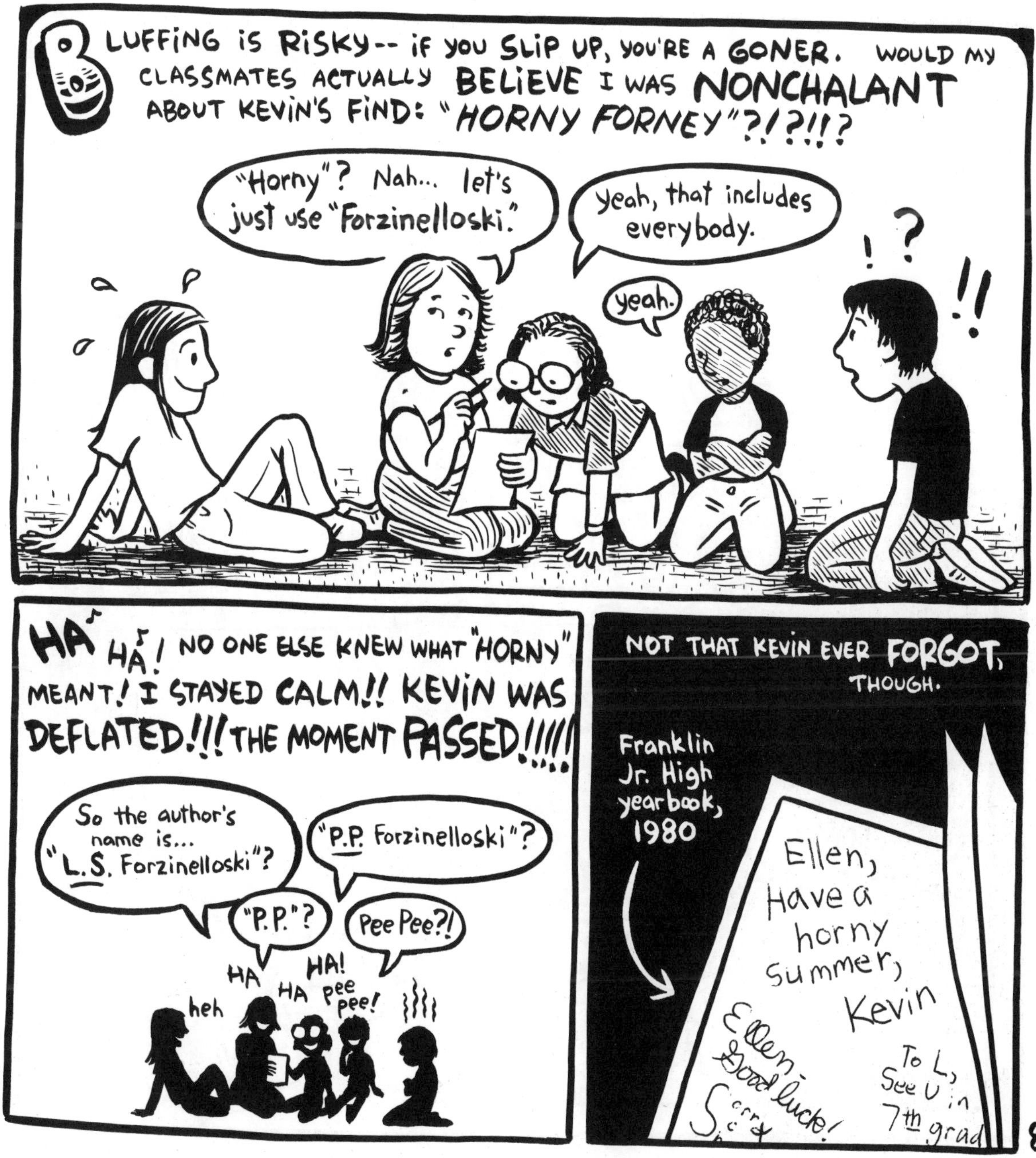
BLUFFING IS RISKY-- IF YOU SLIP UP, YOU'RE A GONER. WOULD MY CLASSMATES ACTUALLY BELIEVE I WAS NONCHALANT ABOUT KEVIN'S FIND: "HORNY FORNEY"?!?!!?
"Horny"? Nah... let's just use "Forzinelloski."
Yeah, that includes everybody.
yeah.
!?
!!
HA HA! NO ONE ELSE KNEW WHAT "HORNY" MEANT! I STAYED CALM!! KEVIN WAS DEFLATED!!! THE MOMENT PASSED!!!!!
So the author's name is... "L.S. Forzinelloski"?
"P.P. Forzinelloski"?
"P.P."?
Pee Pee?!
heh
HA
HA
HA!
pee pee!
NOT THAT KEVIN EVER FORGOT, THOUGH.
Franklin Jr. High yearbook, 1980
Ellen, Have a horny summer, Kevin
Ellen, Good luck!
To L, See U in 7th grad

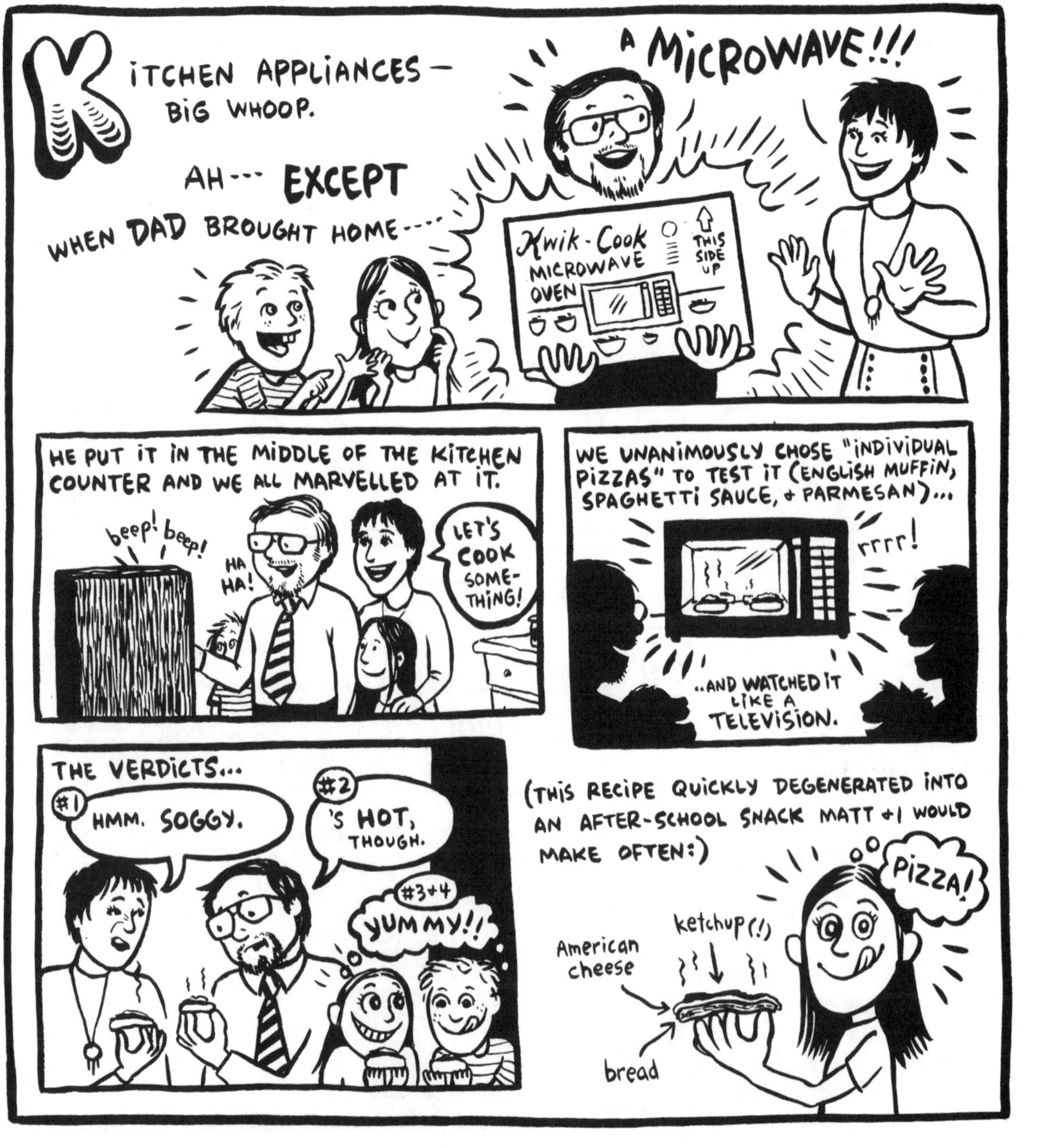
KITCHEN APPLIANCES — BIG WHOOP.
AH--- EXCEPT WHEN DAD BROUGHT HOME----
A MICROWAVE!!!
Kwik-Cook MICROWAVE OVEN
THIS SIDE UP
HE PUT IT IN THE MIDDLE OF THE KITCHEN COUNTER AND WE ALL MARVELLED AT IT.
beep! beep!
HA HA!
LET'S COOK SOME-THING!
WE UNANIMOUSLY CHOSE "INDIVIDUAL PIZZAS" TO TEST IT (ENGLISH MUFFIN, SPAGHETTI SAUCE, + PARMESAN)...
rrrr!
..AND WATCHED IT LIKE A TELEVISION.
THE VERDICTS...
#1 HMM. SOGGY.
#2 'S HOT, THOUGH.
#3+4 YUMMY!!
(THIS RECIPE QUICKLY DEGENERATED INTO AN AFTER-SCHOOL SNACK MATT +I WOULD MAKE OFTEN:)
PIZZA!
American cheese
ketchup (!)
bread

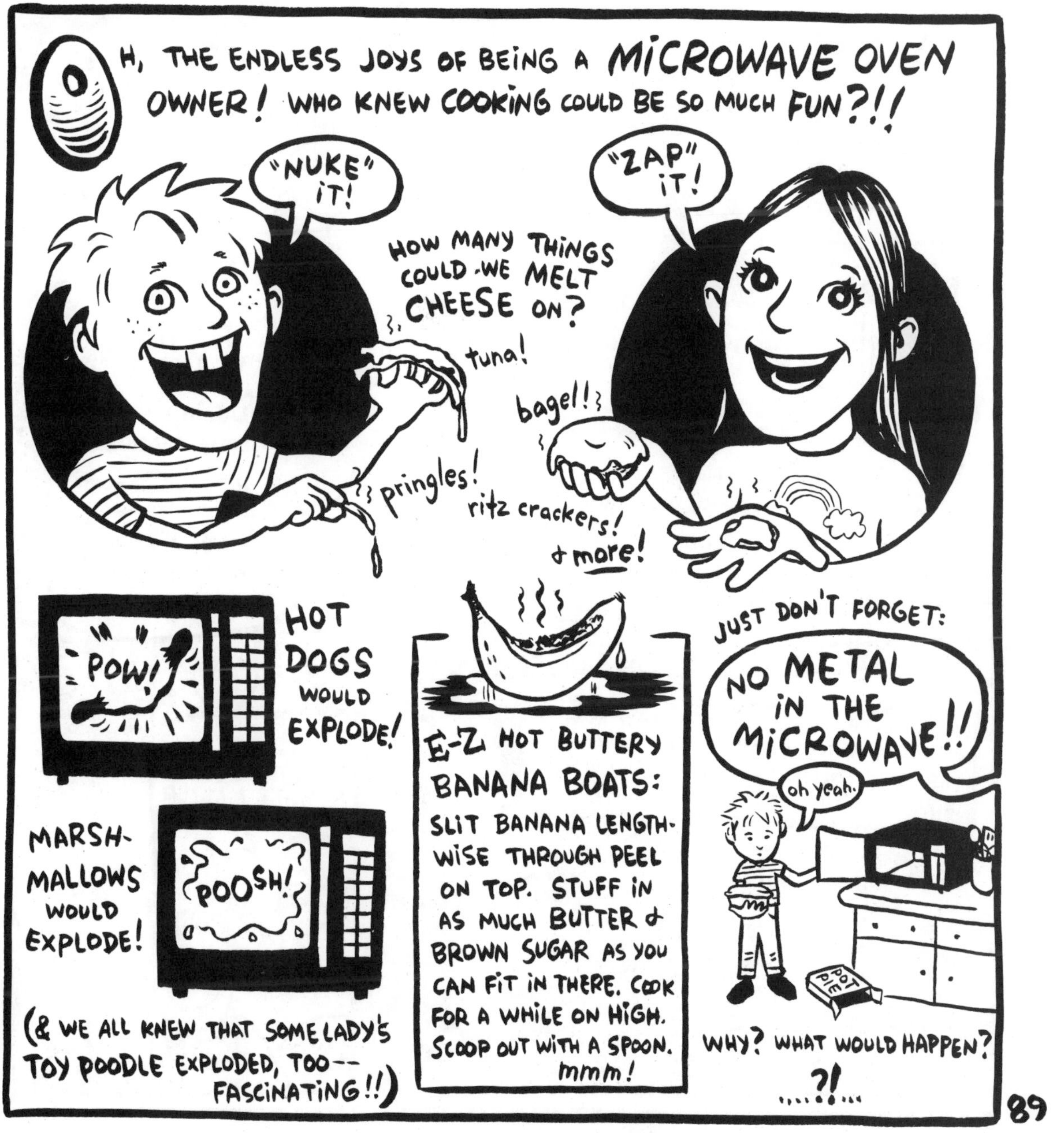
OH, THE ENDLESS JOYS OF BEING A MICROWAVE OVEN OWNER! WHO KNEW COOKING COULD BE SO MUCH FUN?!!
"NUKE" IT!
"ZAP" IT!
HOW MANY THINGS COULD WE MELT CHEESE ON?
tuna!
bagel!!
pringles!
ritz crackers!
& more!
HOT DOGS WOULD EXPLODE!
POW!
MARSH-MALLOWS WOULD EXPLODE!
POOSH!
(& WE ALL KNEW THAT SOME LADY'S TOY POODLE EXPLODED, TOO-- FASCINATING!!)
E-Z HOT BUTTERY BANANA BOATS:
SLIT BANANA LENGTH-WISE THROUGH PEEL ON TOP. STUFF IN AS MUCH BUTTER & BROWN SUGAR AS YOU CAN FIT IN THERE. COOK FOR A WHILE ON HIGH. SCOOP OUT WITH A SPOON.
mmm!
JUST DON'T FORGET:
NO METAL IN THE MICROWAVE!!
oh yeah.
POT PIE
WHY? WHAT WOULD HAPPEN?
.....?!....

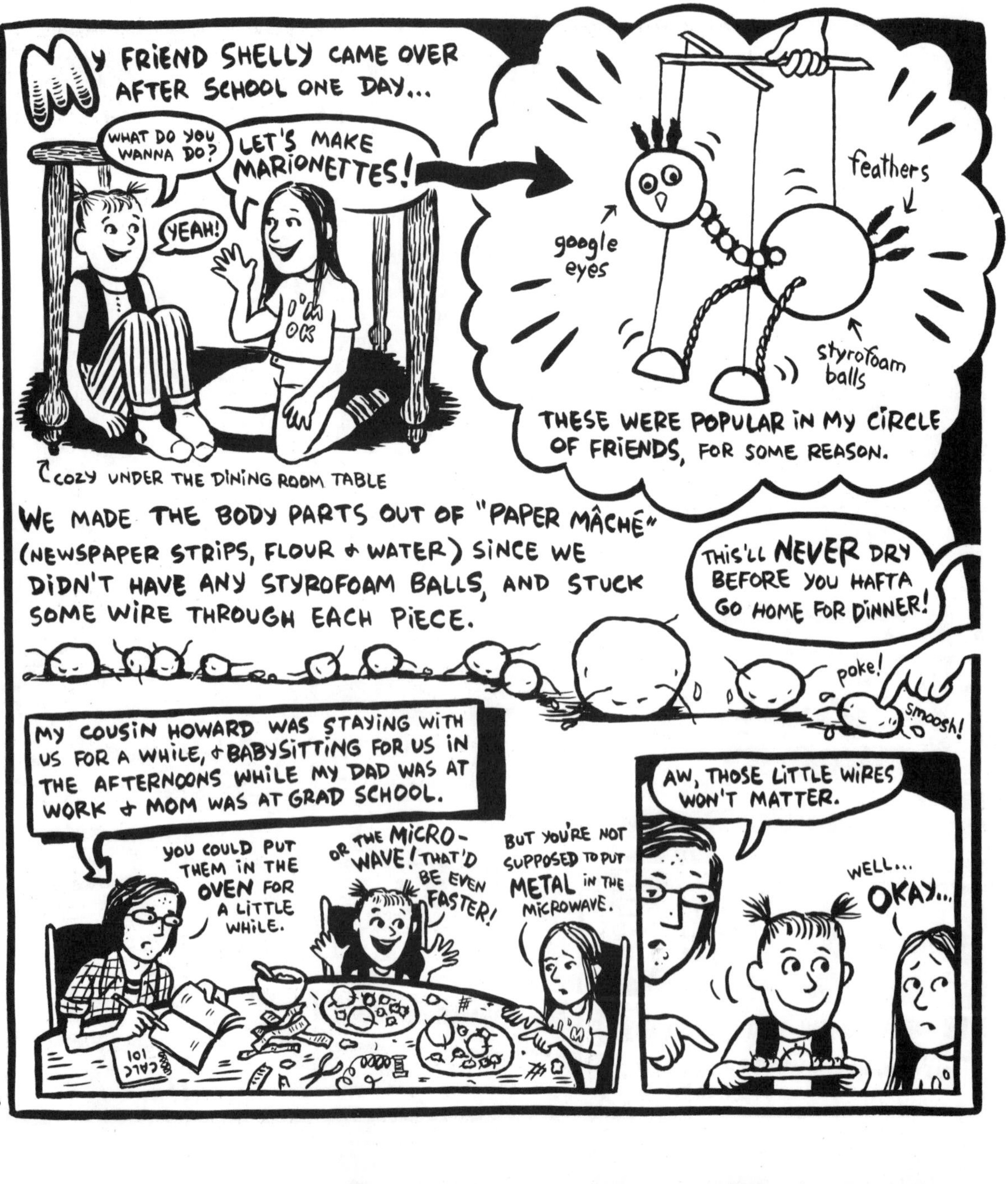
My friend Shelly came over after school one day...
What do you wanna do?
Let's make marionettes!
Yeah!
I'm OK
cozy under the dining room table
feathers
google eyes
styrofoam balls
These were popular in my circle of friends, for some reason.
We made the body parts out of "paper mâché" (newspaper strips, flour + water) since we didn't have any styrofoam balls, and stuck some wire through each piece.
This'll NEVER dry before you hafta go home for dinner!
poke!
smoosh!
My cousin Howard was staying with us for a while, + babysitting for us in the afternoons while my dad was at work + mom was at grad school.
You could put them in the oven for a little while.
Or the micro-wave! That'd be even faster!
But you're not supposed to put metal in the microwave.
Calc 101
Aw, those little wires won't matter.
Well... okay...

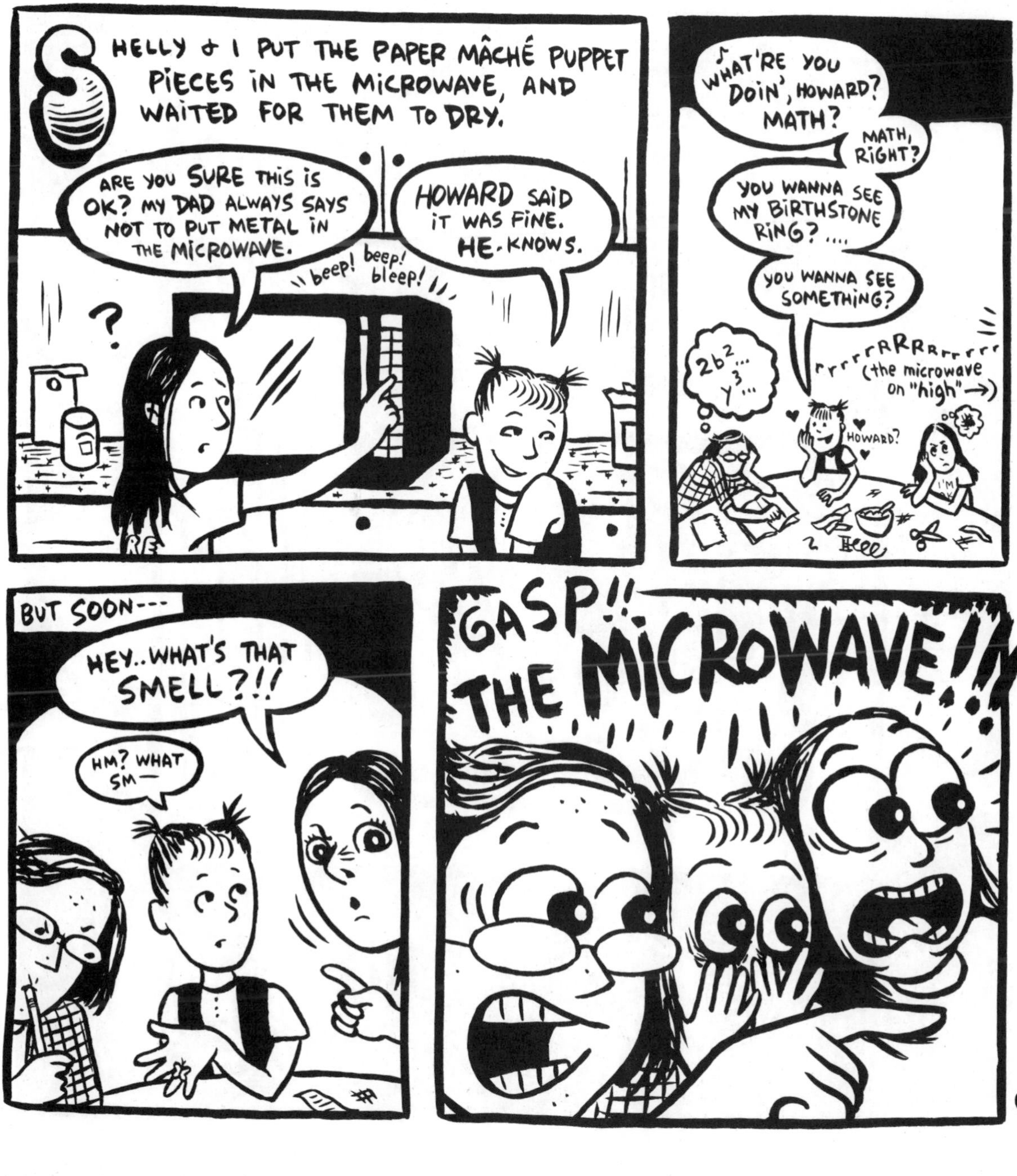
SHELLY & I PUT THE PAPER MÂCHÉ PUPPET PIECES IN THE MICROWAVE, AND WAITED FOR THEM TO DRY.
ARE YOU SURE THIS IS OK? MY DAD ALWAYS SAYS NOT TO PUT METAL IN THE MICROWAVE.
HOWARD SAID IT WAS FINE. HE KNOWS.
beep! beep! bleep!
?
WHAT'RE YOU DOIN', HOWARD? MATH?
MATH, RIGHT?
YOU WANNA SEE MY BIRTHSTONE RING? ....
YOU WANNA SEE SOMETHING?
2b²... y³...
rrrrrRRRrrrrrr (the microwave on "high" →)
HOWARD?
BUT SOON---
HEY.. WHAT'S THAT SMELL?!!
HM? WHAT SM—
GASP!!
THE MICROWAVE!!

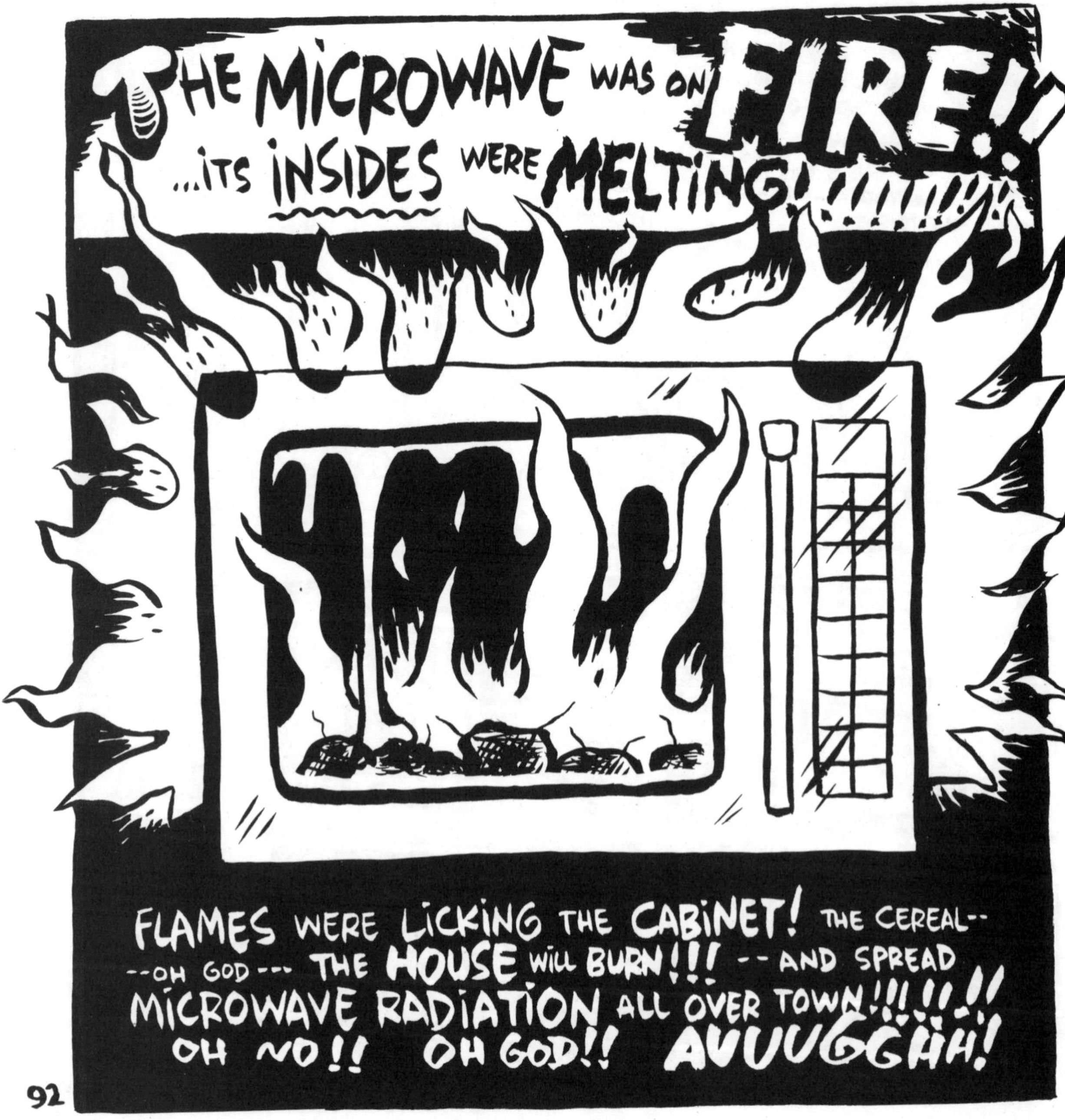
THE MICROWAVE WAS ON FIRE!!
...its INSIDES WERE MELTING!!!!!!!!!
FLAMES WERE LICKING THE CABINET! THE CEREAL--
--OH GOD--- THE HOUSE WILL BURN!!! --AND SPREAD
MICROWAVE RADIATION ALL OVER TOWN!!!!!!!
OH NO!! OH GOD!! AUUUGGHH!

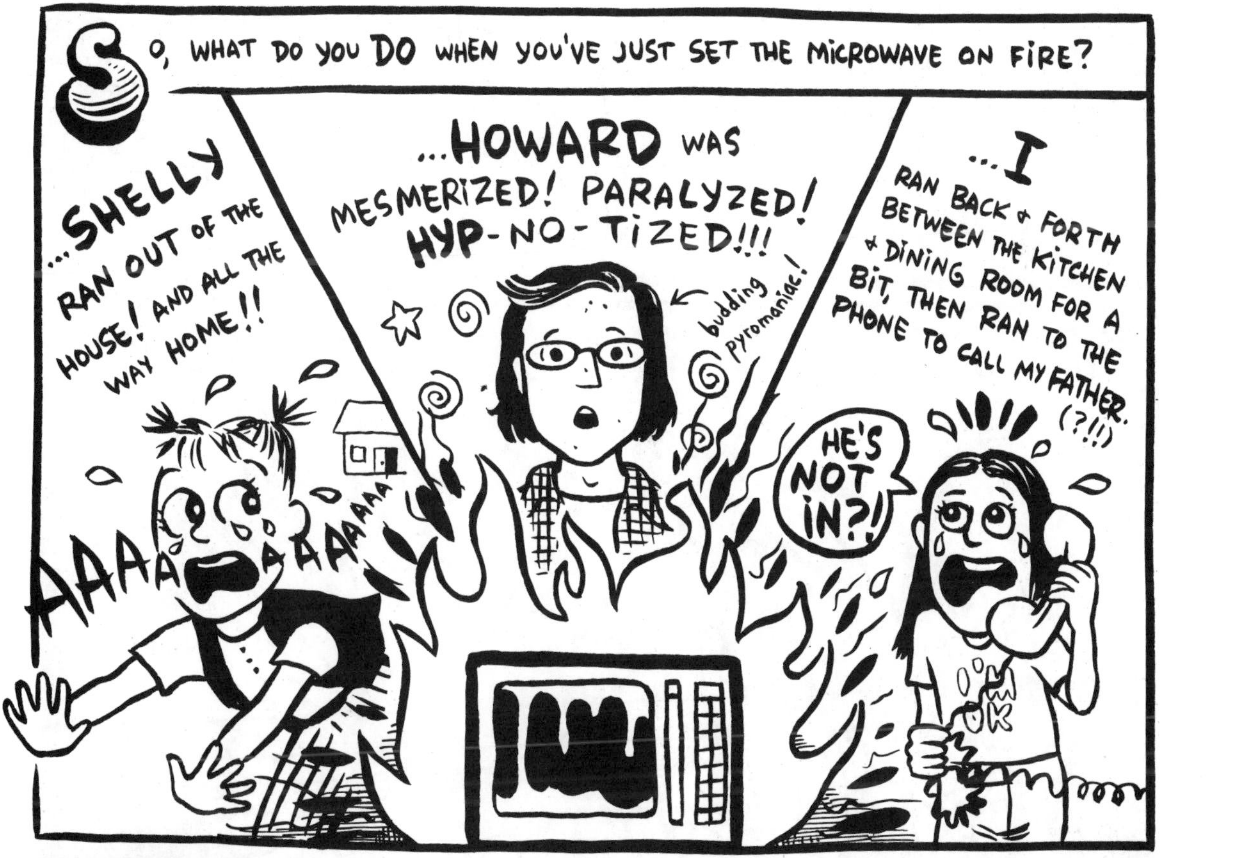
SO, WHAT DO YOU DO WHEN YOU'VE JUST SET THE MICROWAVE ON FIRE?
...SHELLY RAN OUT OF THE HOUSE! AND ALL THE WAY HOME!!
AAAAAAAAAAAAA
...HOWARD WAS MESMERIZED! PARALYZED! HYP-NO-TIZED!!!
budding pyromaniac!
...I RAN BACK & FORTH BETWEEN THE KITCHEN & DINING ROOM FOR A BIT, THEN RAN TO THE PHONE TO CALL MY FATHER. (?!!)
HE'S NOT IN?!

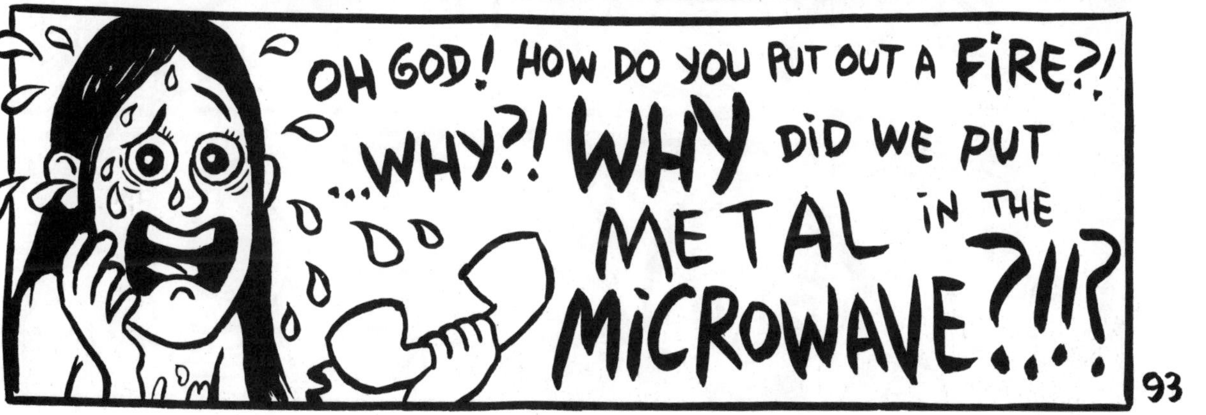
OH GOD! HOW DO YOU PUT OUT A FIRE?!
...WHY?! WHY DID WE PUT METAL IN THE MICROWAVE?!!?

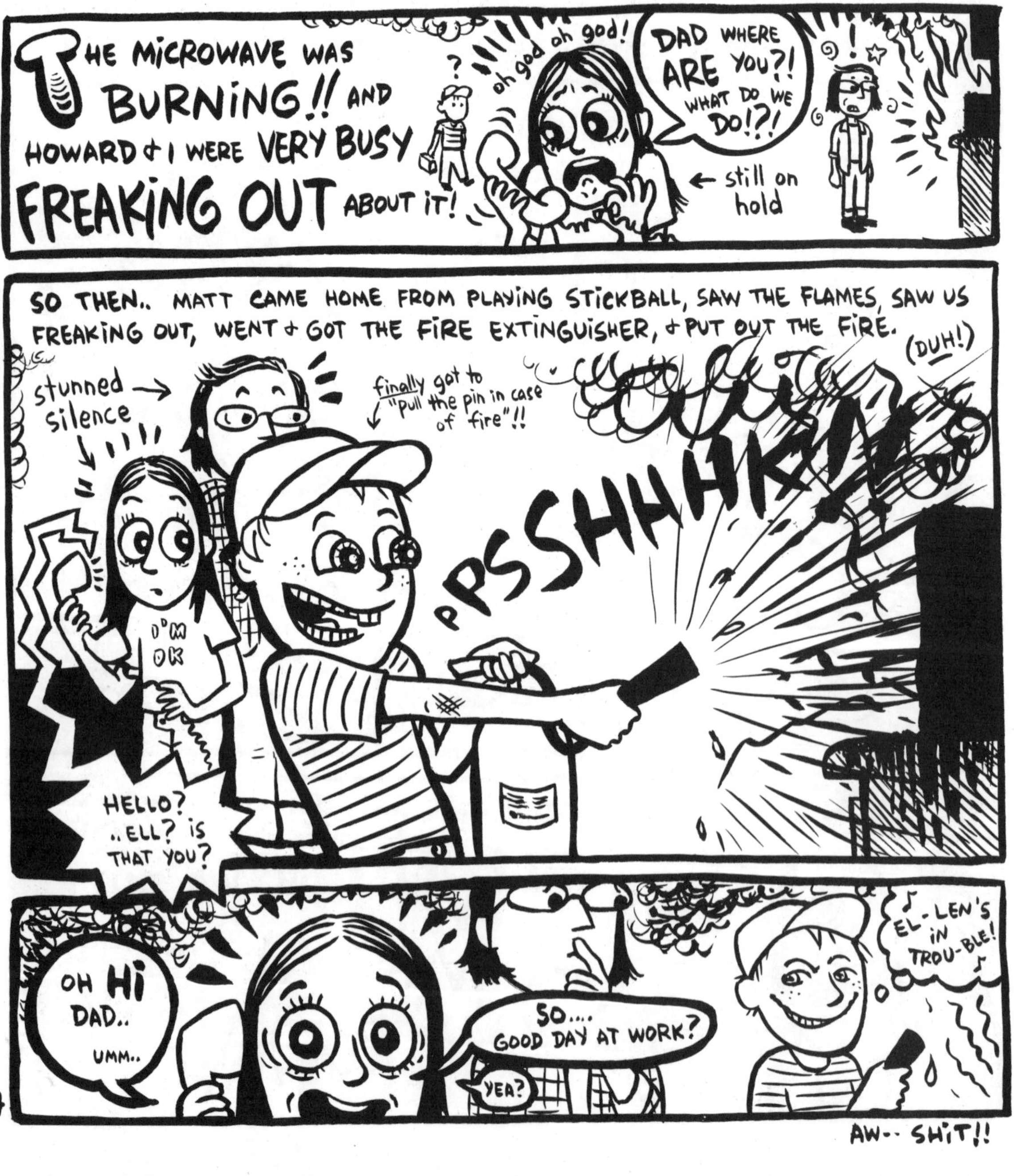
THE MICROWAVE WAS BURNING!! AND HOWARD & I WERE VERY BUSY FREAKING OUT ABOUT IT!
oh god oh god oh god!
DAD WHERE ARE YOU?! WHAT DO WE DO!?!
← still on hold
SO THEN.. MATT CAME HOME FROM PLAYING STICKBALL, SAW THE FLAMES, SAW US FREAKING OUT, WENT & GOT THE FIRE EXTINGUISHER, & PUT OUT THE FIRE.
(DUH!)
stunned silence
finally got to "pull the pin in case of fire"!!
PPSSHHHKKK!
I'M OK
HELLO? ..ELL? IS THAT YOU?
OH HI DAD.. UMM..
SO.... GOOD DAY AT WORK?
YEA?
EL-LEN'S IN TROU-BLE!
AW-- SHIT!!

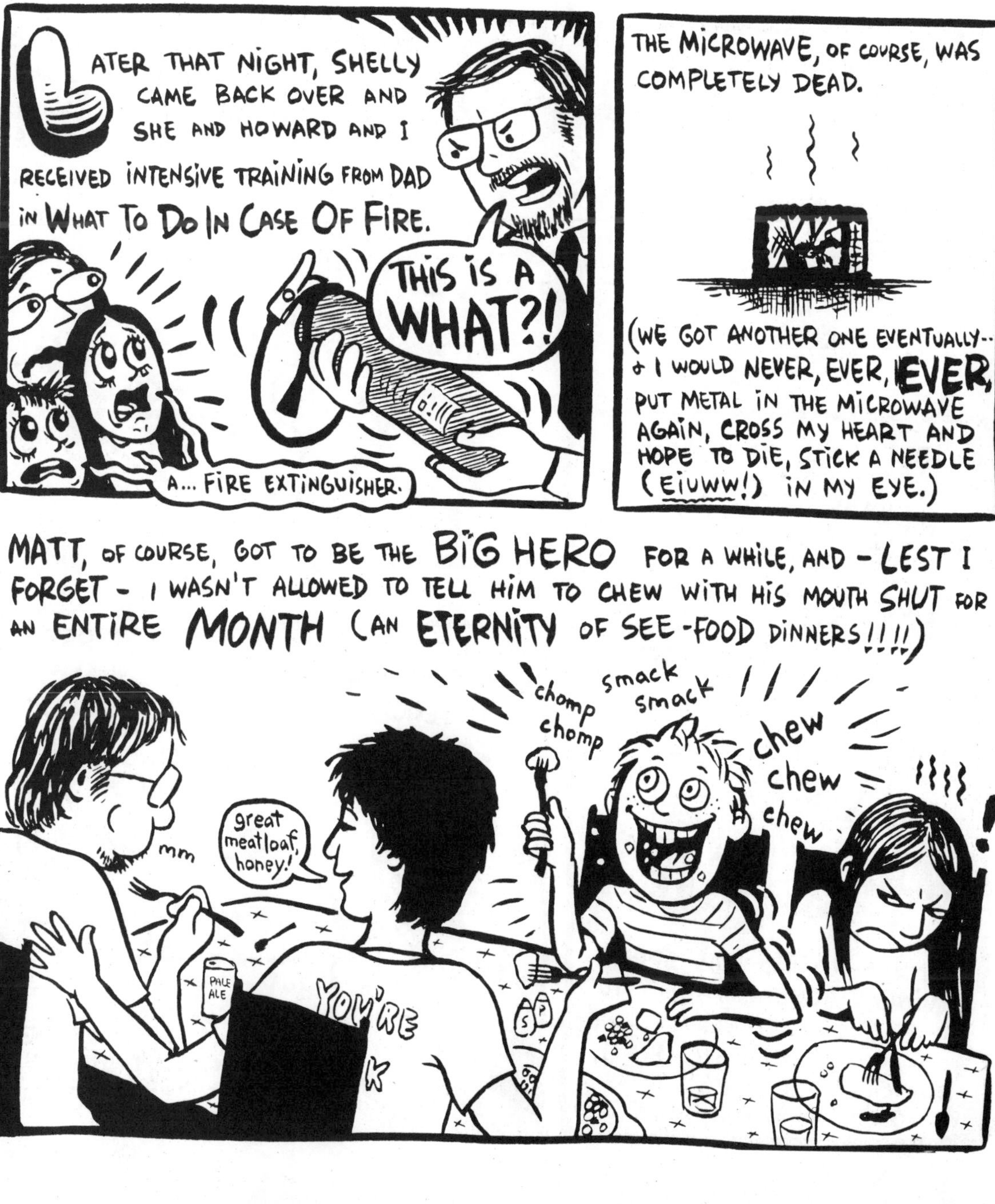
LATER THAT NIGHT, SHELLY CAME BACK OVER AND SHE AND HOWARD AND I RECEIVED INTENSIVE TRAINING FROM DAD IN WHAT TO DO IN CASE OF FIRE.
THIS IS A WHAT?!
A... FIRE EXTINGUISHER.
THE MICROWAVE, OF COURSE, WAS COMPLETELY DEAD.
(WE GOT ANOTHER ONE EVENTUALLY-- & I WOULD NEVER, EVER, EVER, PUT METAL IN THE MICROWAVE AGAIN, CROSS MY HEART AND HOPE TO DIE, STICK A NEEDLE (EIUWW!) IN MY EYE.)
MATT, OF COURSE, GOT TO BE THE BIG HERO FOR A WHILE, AND - LEST I FORGET - I WASN'T ALLOWED TO TELL HIM TO CHEW WITH HIS MOUTH SHUT FOR AN ENTIRE MONTH (AN ETERNITY OF SEE-FOOD DINNERS!!!!)
chomp chomp
smack smack
chew chew chew
mm
great meatloaf, honey!
PALE ALE
YOU'RE

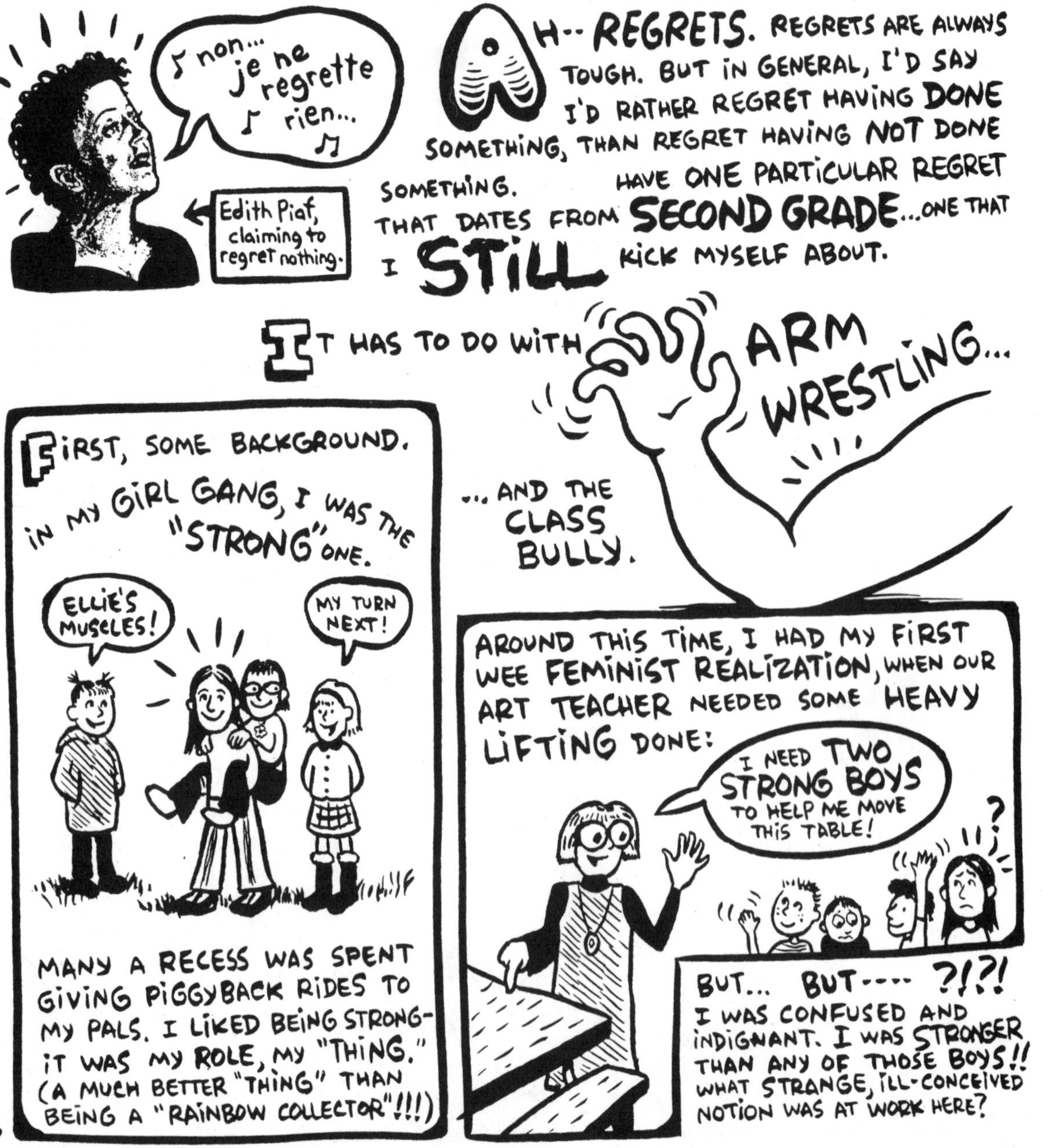
non... je ne regrette rien...
Edith Piaf, claiming to regret nothing.
AH-- REGRETS. REGRETS ARE ALWAYS TOUGH. BUT IN GENERAL, I'D SAY I'D RATHER REGRET HAVING DONE SOMETHING, THAN REGRET HAVING NOT DONE SOMETHING. I HAVE ONE PARTICULAR REGRET THAT DATES FROM SECOND GRADE...ONE THAT I STILL KICK MYSELF ABOUT.
IT HAS TO DO WITH ARM WRESTLING...
...AND THE CLASS BULLY.
FIRST, SOME BACKGROUND.
IN MY GIRL GANG, I WAS THE "STRONG" ONE.
ELLIE'S MUSCLES!
MY TURN NEXT!
MANY A RECESS WAS SPENT GIVING PIGGYBACK RIDES TO MY PALS. I LIKED BEING STRONG-IT WAS MY ROLE, MY "THING." (A MUCH BETTER "THING" THAN BEING A "RAINBOW COLLECTOR"!!!)
AROUND THIS TIME, I HAD MY FIRST WEE FEMINIST REALIZATION, WHEN OUR ART TEACHER NEEDED SOME HEAVY LIFTING DONE:
I NEED TWO STRONG BOYS TO HELP ME MOVE THIS TABLE!
?
BUT... BUT---- ?!?!
I WAS CONFUSED AND INDIGNANT. I WAS STRONGER THAN ANY OF THOSE BOYS!! WHAT STRANGE, ILL-CONCEIVED NOTION WAS AT WORK HERE?

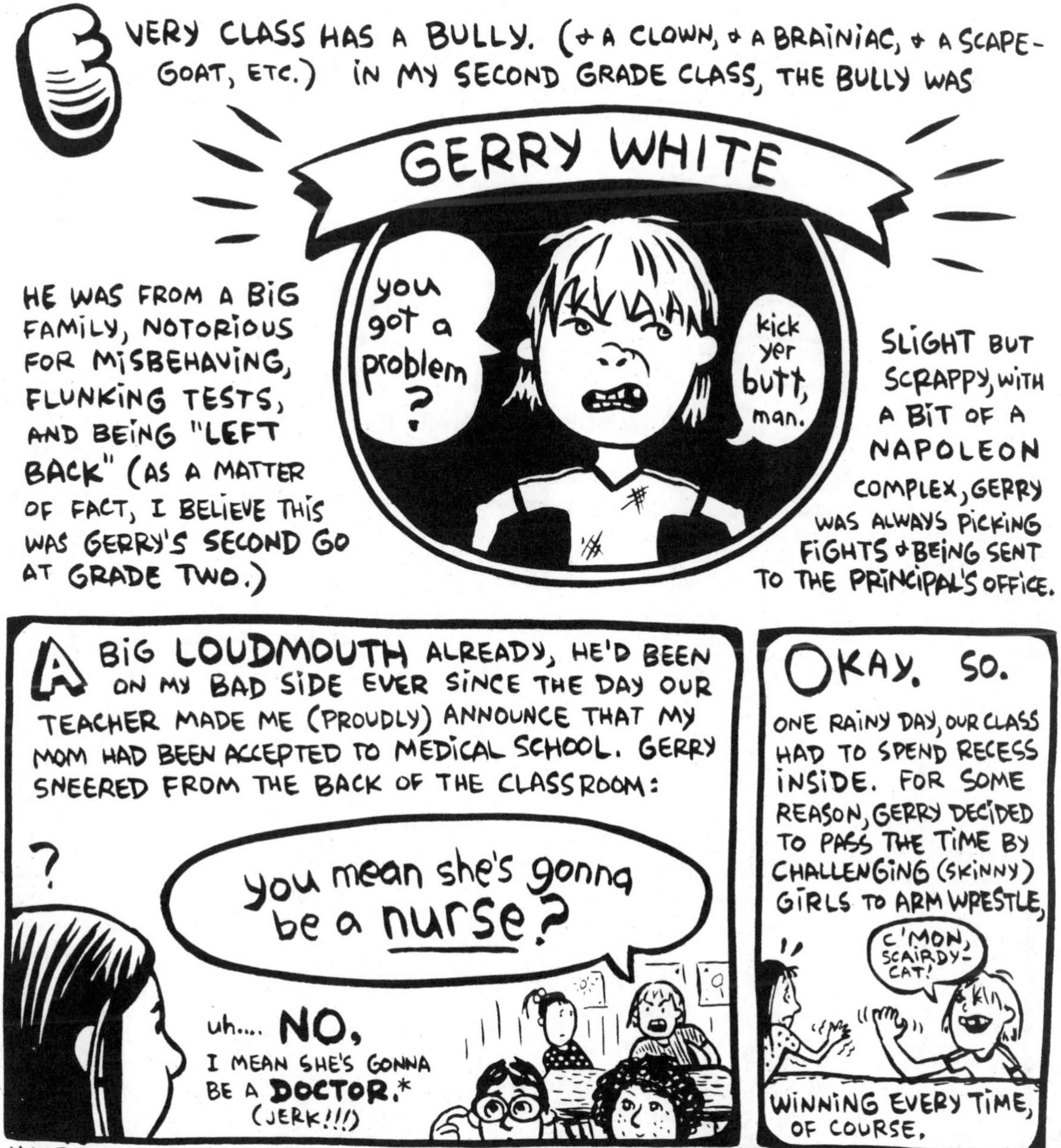
EVERY CLASS HAS A BULLY. (& A CLOWN, & A BRAINIAC, & A SCAPE-GOAT, ETC.) IN MY SECOND GRADE CLASS, THE BULLY WAS
GERRY WHITE
HE WAS FROM A BIG FAMILY, NOTORIOUS FOR MISBEHAVING, FLUNKING TESTS, AND BEING "LEFT BACK" (AS A MATTER OF FACT, I BELIEVE THIS WAS GERRY'S SECOND GO AT GRADE TWO.)
you got a problem?
kick yer butt, man.
SLIGHT BUT SCRAPPY, WITH A BIT OF A NAPOLEON COMPLEX, GERRY WAS ALWAYS PICKING FIGHTS & BEING SENT TO THE PRINCIPAL'S OFFICE.
A BIG LOUDMOUTH ALREADY, HE'D BEEN ON MY BAD SIDE EVER SINCE THE DAY OUR TEACHER MADE ME (PROUDLY) ANNOUNCE THAT MY MOM HAD BEEN ACCEPTED TO MEDICAL SCHOOL. GERRY SNEERED FROM THE BACK OF THE CLASSROOM:
?
you mean she's gonna be a nurse?
uh.... NO, I MEAN SHE'S GONNA BE A DOCTOR.* (JERK!!!)
OKAY. SO.
ONE RAINY DAY, OUR CLASS HAD TO SPEND RECESS INSIDE. FOR SOME REASON, GERRY DECIDED TO PASS THE TIME BY CHALLENGING (SKINNY) GIRLS TO ARM WRESTLE,
C'MON, SCAIRDY-CAT!
WINNING EVERY TIME, OF COURSE.

*NOT THAT THERE'S ANYTHING WRONG WITH BEING A NURSE, MIND YOU.

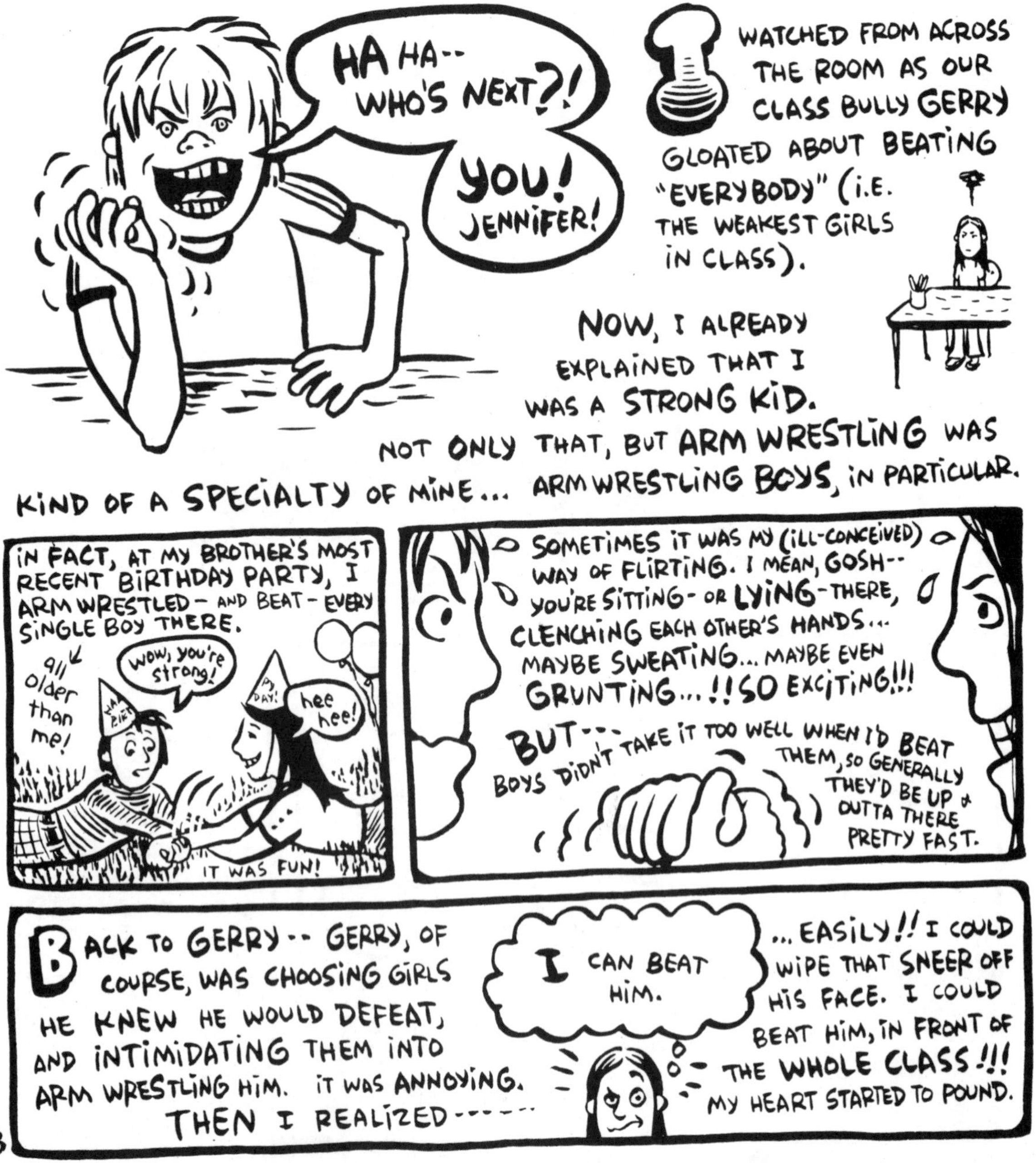

HA HA-- WHO'S NEXT?!
YOU! JENNIFER!
I WATCHED FROM ACROSS THE ROOM AS OUR CLASS BULLY GERRY GLOATED ABOUT BEATING "EVERYBODY" (i.e. THE WEAKEST GIRLS IN CLASS).
NOW, I ALREADY EXPLAINED THAT I WAS A STRONG KID.
NOT ONLY THAT, BUT ARM WRESTLING WAS KIND OF A SPECIALTY OF MINE... ARM WRESTLING BOYS, IN PARTICULAR.
IN FACT, AT MY BROTHER'S MOST RECENT BIRTHDAY PARTY, I ARM WRESTLED - AND BEAT - EVERY SINGLE BOY THERE.
all older than me!
WOW, you're strong!
hee hee!
IT WAS FUN!
SOMETIMES IT WAS MY (ILL-CONCEIVED) WAY OF FLIRTING. I MEAN, GOSH-- YOU'RE SITTING- OR LYING-THERE, CLENCHING EACH OTHER'S HANDS... MAYBE SWEATING... MAYBE EVEN GRUNTING...!! SO EXCITING!!!
BUT--- BOYS DIDN'T TAKE IT TOO WELL WHEN I'D BEAT THEM, SO GENERALLY THEY'D BE UP & OUTTA THERE PRETTY FAST.
BACK TO GERRY -- GERRY, OF COURSE, WAS CHOOSING GIRLS HE KNEW HE WOULD DEFEAT, AND INTIMIDATING THEM INTO ARM WRESTLING HIM. IT WAS ANNOYING. THEN I REALIZED------
I CAN BEAT HIM.
...EASILY!! I COULD WIPE THAT SNEER OFF HIS FACE. I COULD BEAT HIM, IN FRONT OF THE WHOLE CLASS!!! MY HEART STARTED TO POUND.

WELL.... THIS MAY COME AS SOMETHING OF A SURPRISE TO THOSE OF YOU WHO KNOW ME NOW, BUT I WAS ACTUALLY A PRETTY SHY KID.

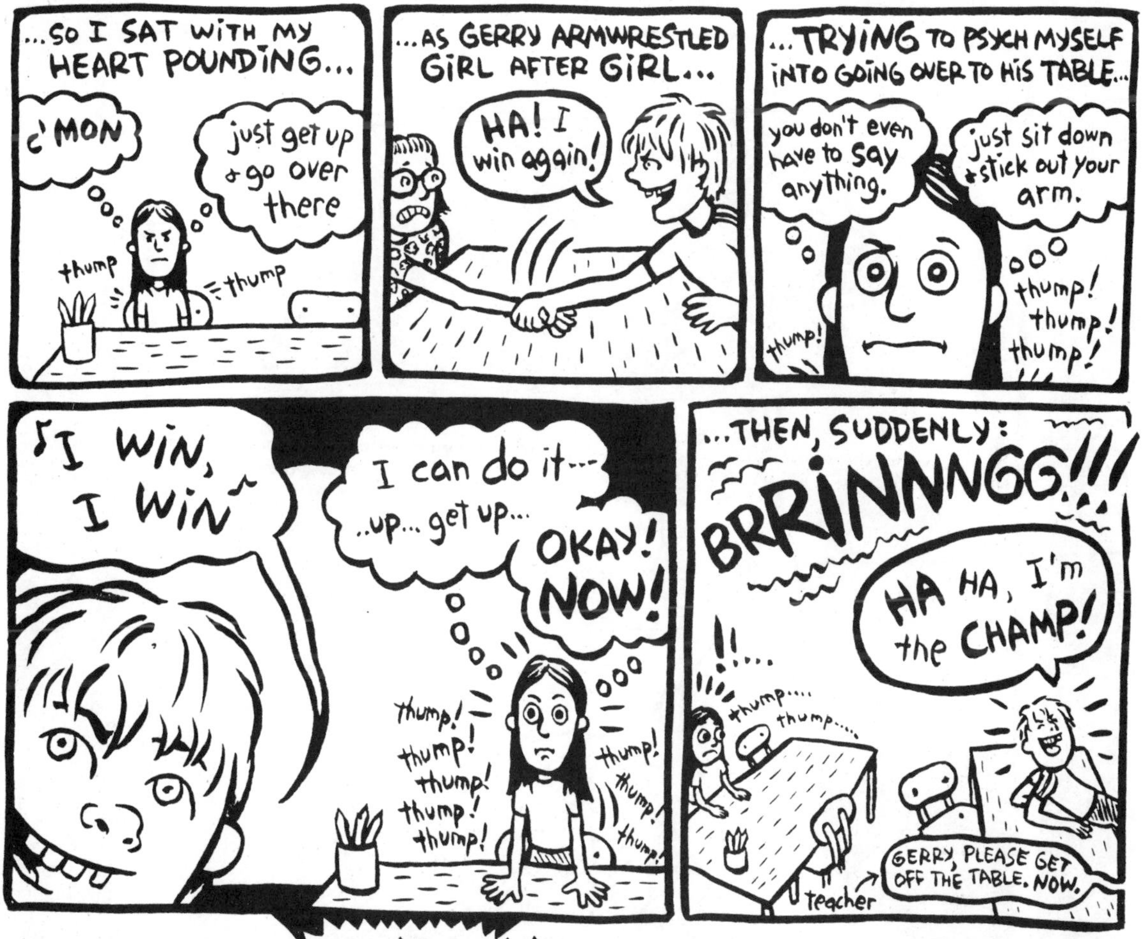
...SO I SAT WITH MY HEART POUNDING...
¿'MON
just get up & go over there
thump
thump
...AS GERRY ARMWRESTLED GIRL AFTER GIRL...
HA! I win again!
...TRYING TO PSYCH MYSELF INTO GOING OVER TO HIS TABLE...
you don't even have to say anything.
just sit down & stick out your arm.
thump!
thump! thump! thump!
I WIN, I WIN
I can do it--- ...up... get up...
OKAY! NOW!
thump! thump! thump! thump! thump!
thump! thump! thump!
...THEN, SUDDENLY:
BRRINNNGG!!!
HA HA, I'm the CHAMP!
!!...
thump.... thump....
GERRY, PLEASE GET OFF THE TABLE. NOW.
teacher

RECESS WAS OVER!! I'D MISSED MY CHANCE!!!!

GERRY HAD WON EVERY MATCH. Ohhhhh..........

SO...THAT'S MY BIG REGRET FROM SECOND GRADE. YEP, STILL KICK MYSELF ABOUT IT. (sigh.)

Well. (Anyone wanna armwrestle?!)

Mom's new perm, 1980

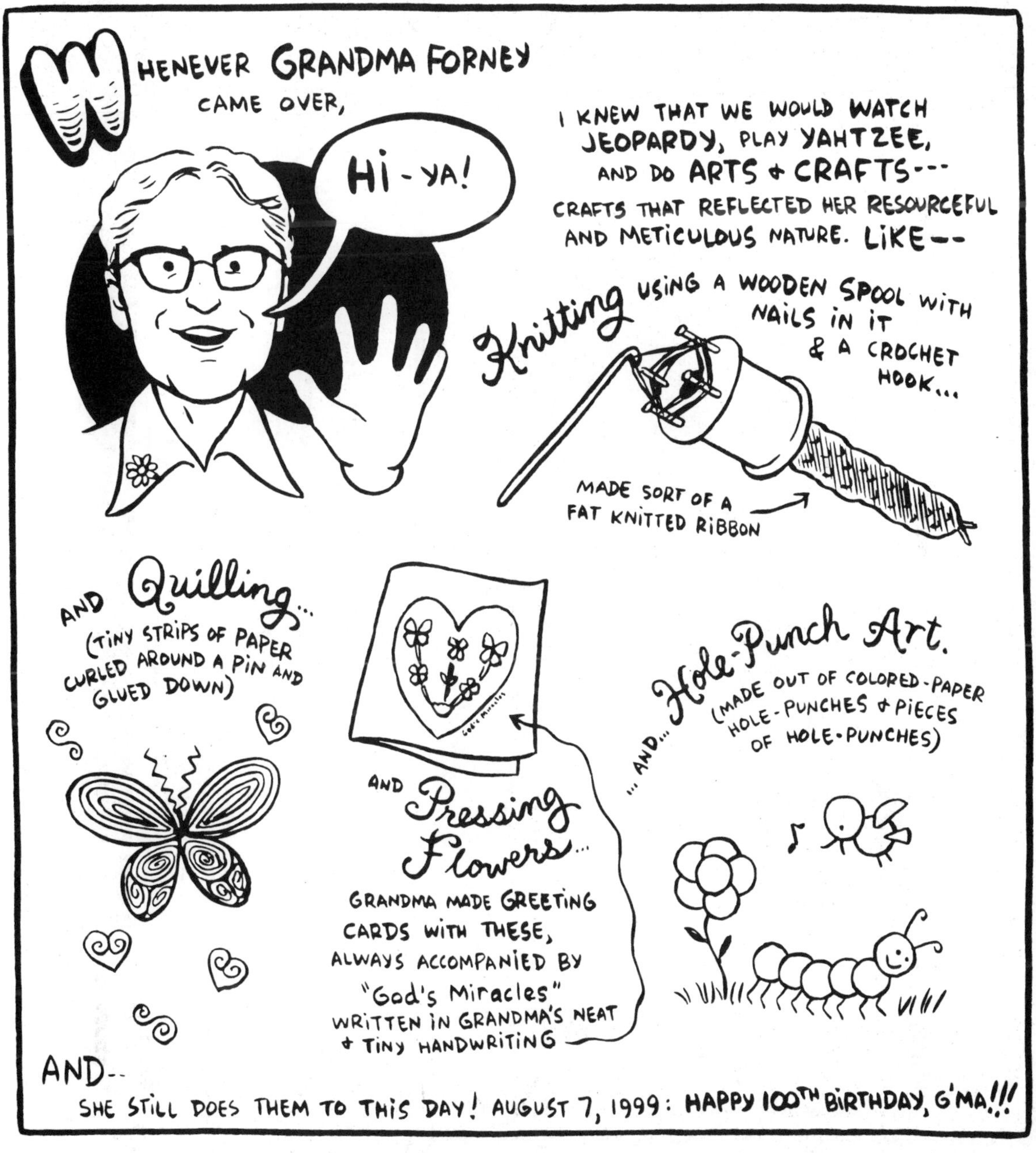
WHENEVER GRANDMA FORNEY CAME OVER,
HI-YA!
I KNEW THAT WE WOULD WATCH JEOPARDY, PLAY YAHTZEE, AND DO ARTS & CRAFTS--- CRAFTS THAT REFLECTED HER RESOURCEFUL AND METICULOUS NATURE. LIKE--
Knitting USING A WOODEN SPOOL WITH NAILS IN IT & A CROCHET HOOK...
MADE SORT OF A FAT KNITTED RIBBON
AND Quilling...
(TINY STRIPS OF PAPER CURLED AROUND A PIN AND GLUED DOWN)
AND Pressing Flowers...
GRANDMA MADE GREETING CARDS WITH THESE, ALWAYS ACCOMPANIED BY "God's Miracles" WRITTEN IN GRANDMA'S NEAT & TINY HANDWRITING
...AND... Hole-Punch Art.
(MADE OUT OF COLORED-PAPER HOLE-PUNCHES & PIECES OF HOLE-PUNCHES)
AND--
SHE STILL DOES THEM TO THIS DAY! AUGUST 7, 1999: HAPPY 100TH BIRTHDAY, G'MA!!!

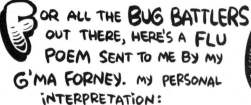 OR ALL THE **BUG BATTLERS** OUT THERE, HERE'S A **FLU** POEM SENT TO ME BY MY **G'MA FORNEY**. MY PERSONAL INTERPRETATION:

 A FLEA AND A FLY IN A FLUE

 WERE IMPRISONED, SO WHAT COULD THEY DO?

 SAID THE FLY, *Let us flee!*

 SAID THE FLEA, *Let us fly!*

 SO THEY **FLEW** THROUGH A **FLAW** IN THE **FLUE**!

free bug!

 G'MA FORNEY WOULD SOMETIMES TUCK SUCH A POEM, NEATLY TYPED ON A SMALL SCRAP OF PAPER, →

A flea and a fly in a flue are imprisoned y do?

God's Miracles

INTO A DAINTILY HANDWRITTEN LETTER SCRIPTED ON ONE OF HER METICULOUSLY HANDCRAFTED GREETING CARDS. (NOTE CARD'S DECORATIVE PRESSED PANSIES & LEAF, ACCOMPANIED BY BIRDS MADE FROM HOLE PUNCHES, UNDER CLEAR CONTACT PAPER. WOW!)

HERE'S ANOTHER POEM, A PUZZLE-Y ONE: →

Y Y U R,
Y Y U B,
I C U R,
Y Y 4 Me.

(No Peekin'!)
Too wise you are,
Too wise you be,
I see you are
Too wise for me.

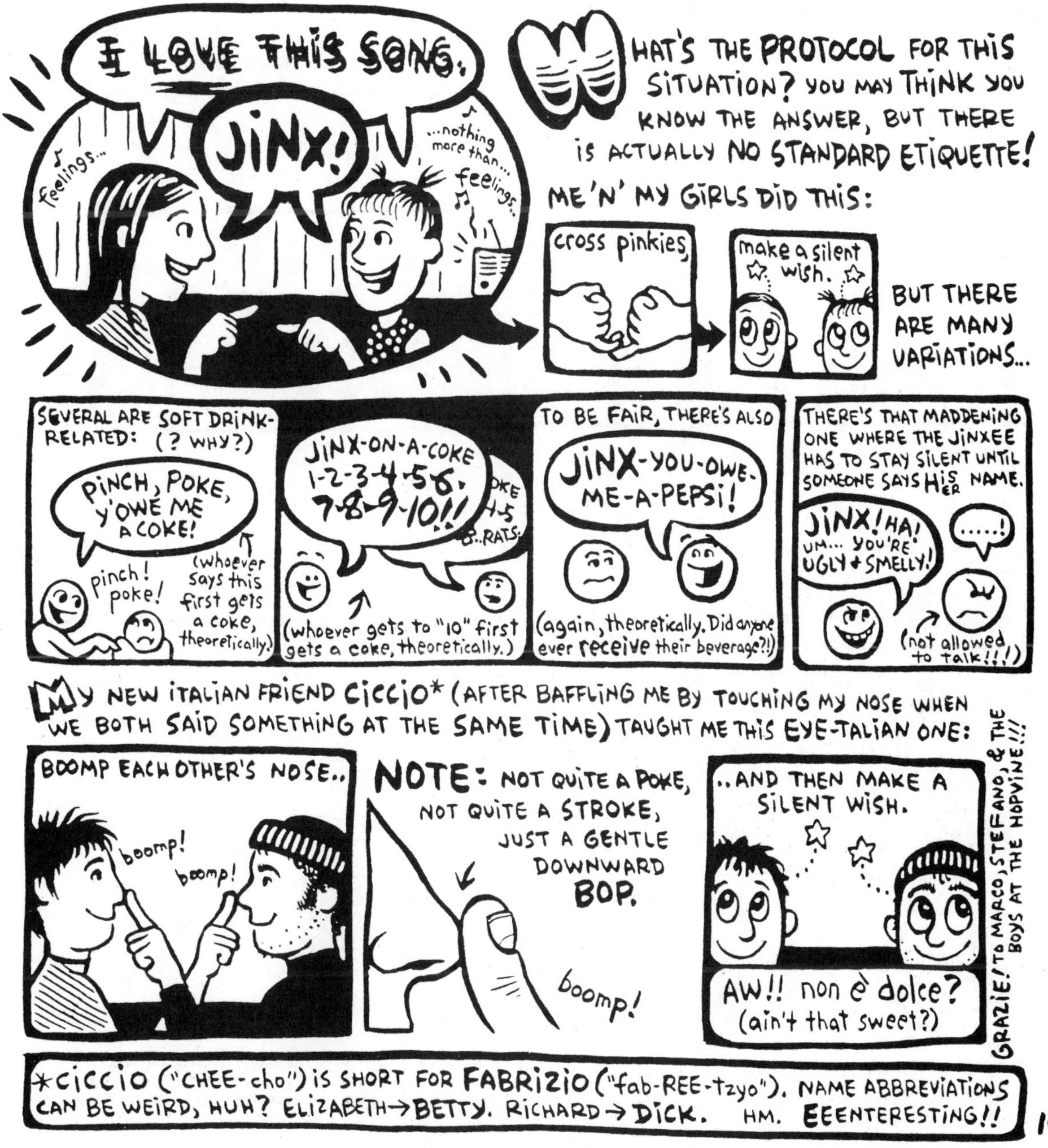
I LOVE THIS SONG.
JINX!
♪ feelings...
...nothing more than... feelings... ♪
WHAT'S THE PROTOCOL FOR THIS SITUATION? YOU MAY THINK YOU KNOW THE ANSWER, BUT THERE IS ACTUALLY NO STANDARD ETIQUETTE!
ME 'N' MY GIRLS DID THIS:
cross pinkies,
make a silent wish.
BUT THERE ARE MANY VARIATIONS...
SEVERAL ARE SOFT DRINK-RELATED: (? WHY?)
PINCH, POKE, Y'OWE ME A COKE!
pinch! poke!
(whoever says this first gets a coke, theoretically.)
JINX-ON-A-COKE 1-2-3-4-5-6, 7-8-9-10!!
...OKE ...4-5 ...8..RATS.
(whoever gets to "10" first gets a coke, theoretically.)
TO BE FAIR, THERE'S ALSO
JINX-YOU-OWE-ME-A-PEPSI!
(again, theoretically. Did anyone ever receive their beverage?!)
THERE'S THAT MADDENING ONE WHERE THE JINXEE HAS TO STAY SILENT UNTIL SOMEONE SAYS HIS/HER NAME.
JINX! HA! UM... YOU'RE UGLY & SMELLY!
.....!
(not allowed to talk!!!)
MY NEW ITALIAN FRIEND CICCIO* (AFTER BAFFLING ME BY TOUCHING MY NOSE WHEN WE BOTH SAID SOMETHING AT THE SAME TIME) TAUGHT ME THIS EYE-TALIAN ONE:
BOOMP EACH OTHER'S NOSE..
boomp! boomp!
NOTE: NOT QUITE A POKE, NOT QUITE A STROKE, JUST A GENTLE DOWNWARD BOP.
boomp!
..AND THEN MAKE A SILENT WISH.
AW!! non è dolce? (ain't that sweet?)
GRAZIE! TO MARCO, STEFANO, & THE BOYS AT THE HOPVINE!!!
*CICCIO ("CHEE-cho") IS SHORT FOR FABRIZIO ("fab-REE-tzyo"). NAME ABBREVIATIONS CAN BE WEIRD, HUH? ELIZABETH→BETTY. RICHARD→DICK. HM. EEENTERESTING!!

WHERE DID THIS MYSTERIOUS LITTLE CHANT COME FROM? WHAT DOES IT MEAN? WELL, WHO KNOWS. BUT AS A LI'L GIRL, WHEN ONE HAD A HANKERING TO LIFT UP ONE'S SHIRT, THIS BORDERLINE ETHNIC SLUR POEM WAS THE ONLY CORRECT WAY:

HOW TO EXPOSE THOSE WEE BOOBIES!

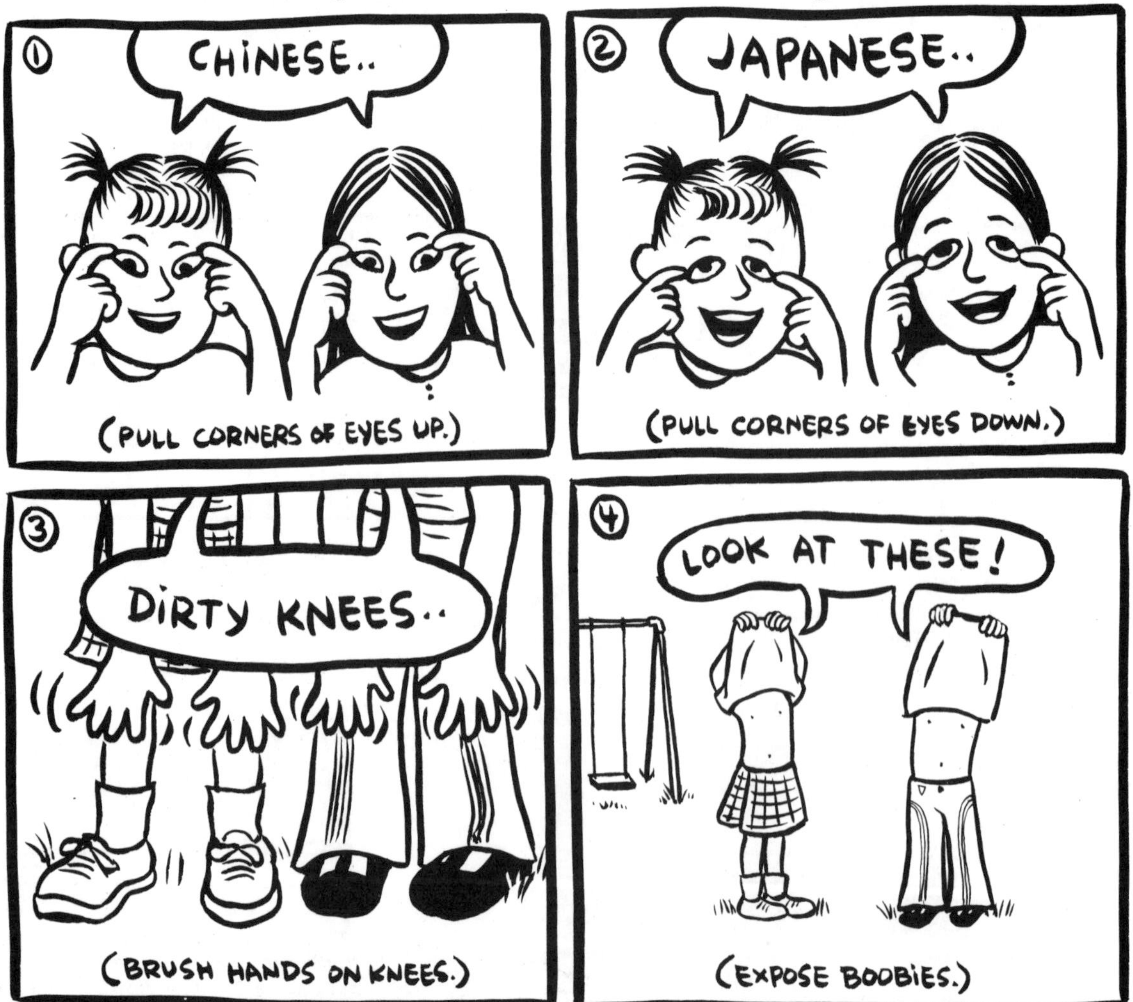

①
CHINESE..
(PULL CORNERS OF EYES UP.)
②
JAPANESE..
(PULL CORNERS OF EYES DOWN.)
③
DIRTY KNEES..
(BRUSH HANDS ON KNEES.)
④
LOOK AT THESE!
(EXPOSE BOOBIES.)

A GOOD WAY TO EMBARRASS SKITTISH BOYS!! USE SELECTIVELY AND WITH CAUTION.

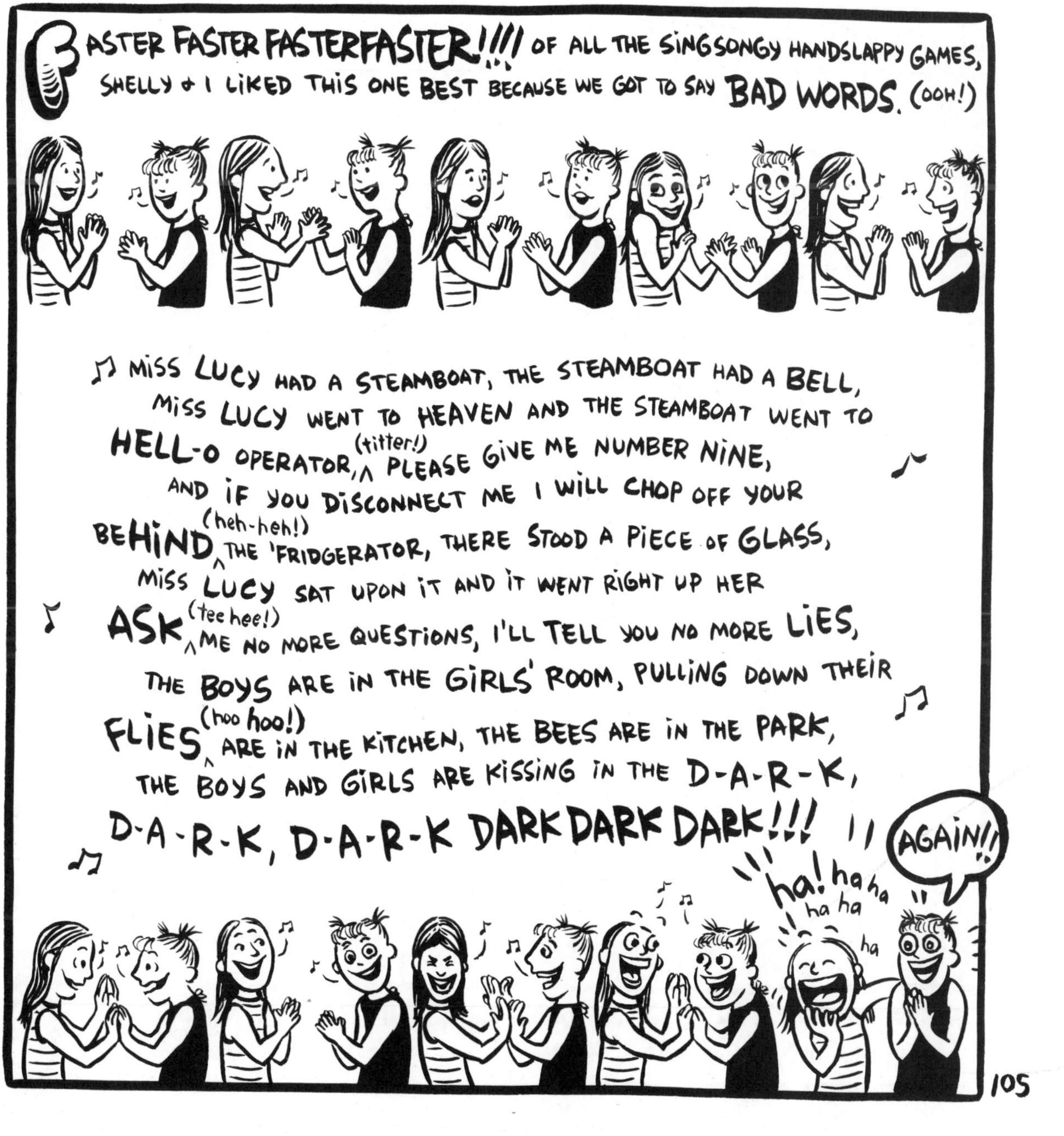
FASTER FASTER FASTERFASTER!!!! OF ALL THE SINGSONGY HANDSLAPPY GAMES, SHELLY & I LIKED THIS ONE BEST BECAUSE WE GOT TO SAY BAD WORDS. (OOH!)
MISS LUCY HAD A STEAMBOAT, THE STEAMBOAT HAD A BELL,
MISS LUCY WENT TO HEAVEN AND THE STEAMBOAT WENT TO
HELL-O OPERATOR, (titter!) PLEASE GIVE ME NUMBER NINE,
AND IF YOU DISCONNECT ME I WILL CHOP OFF YOUR
BEHIND (heh-heh!) THE 'FRIDGERATOR, THERE STOOD A PIECE OF GLASS,
MISS LUCY SAT UPON IT AND IT WENT RIGHT UP HER
ASK (tee hee!) ME NO MORE QUESTIONS, I'LL TELL YOU NO MORE LIES,
THE BOYS ARE IN THE GIRLS' ROOM, PULLING DOWN THEIR
FLIES (hoo hoo!) ARE IN THE KITCHEN, THE BEES ARE IN THE PARK,
THE BOYS AND GIRLS ARE KISSING IN THE D-A-R-K,
D-A-R-K, D-A-R-K DARK DARK DARK!!!
ha! ha ha ha ha ha
AGAIN!!

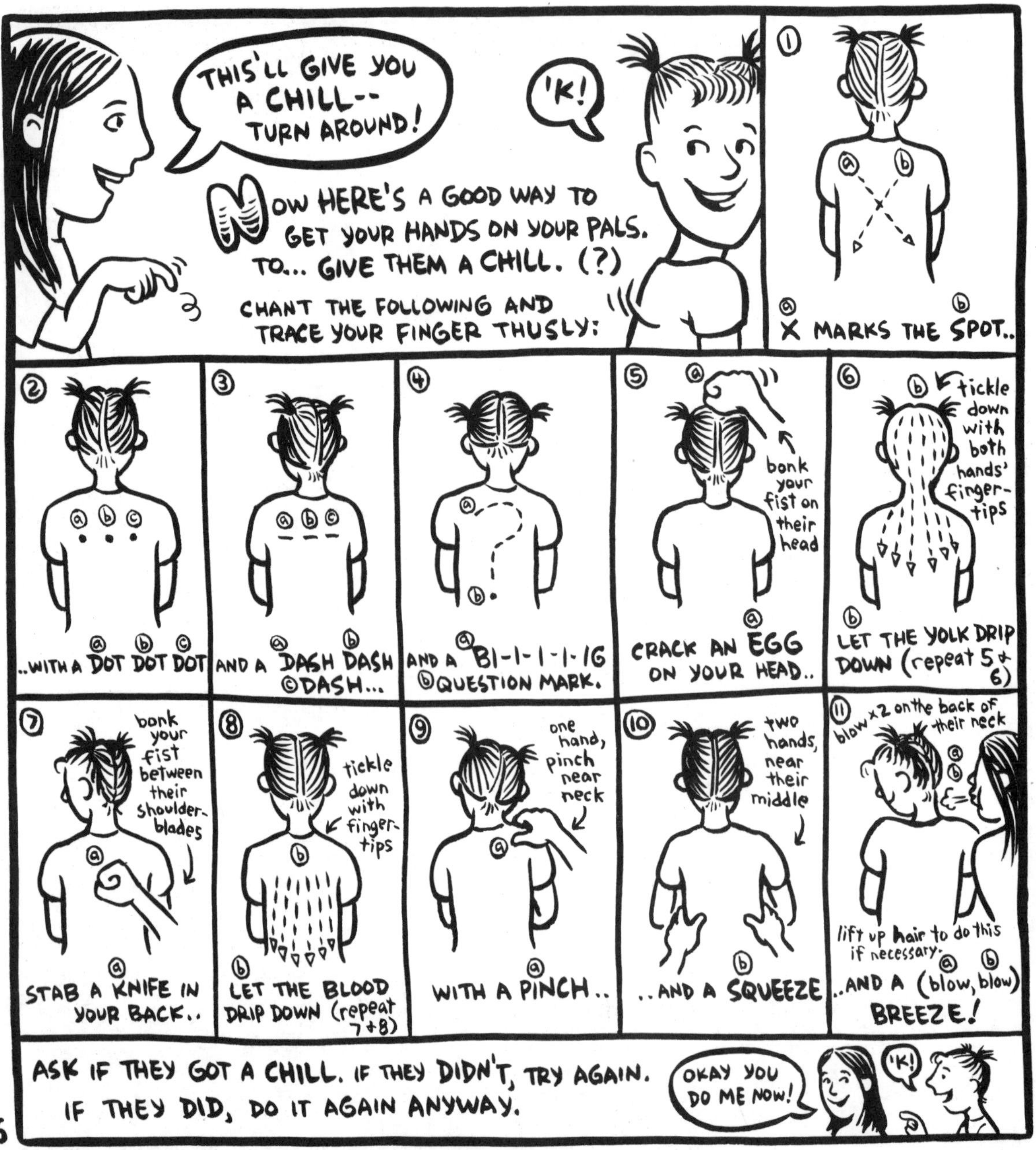
THIS'LL GIVE YOU A CHILL-- TURN AROUND!
'K!
NOW HERE'S A GOOD WAY TO GET YOUR HANDS ON YOUR PALS. TO... GIVE THEM A CHILL. (?)
CHANT THE FOLLOWING AND TRACE YOUR FINGER THUSLY:
1 X MARKS THE SPOT..
2 ..WITH A DOT DOT DOT
3 AND A DASH DASH DASH...
4 AND A BI-I-I-I-IG QUESTION MARK.
5 bonk your fist on their head
CRACK AN EGG ON YOUR HEAD..
6 tickle down with both hands' finger-tips
LET THE YOLK DRIP DOWN (repeat 5 & 6)
7 bonk your fist between their shoulder-blades
STAB A KNIFE IN YOUR BACK..
8 tickle down with finger-tips
LET THE BLOOD DRIP DOWN (repeat 7 + 8)
9 one hand, pinch near neck
WITH A PINCH..
10 two hands, near their middle
..AND A SQUEEZE
11 blow x2 on the back of their neck
lift up hair to do this if necessary.
..AND A (blow, blow) BREEZE!
ASK IF THEY GOT A CHILL. IF THEY DIDN'T, TRY AGAIN. IF THEY DID, DO IT AGAIN ANYWAY.
OKAY YOU DO ME NOW!
'K!

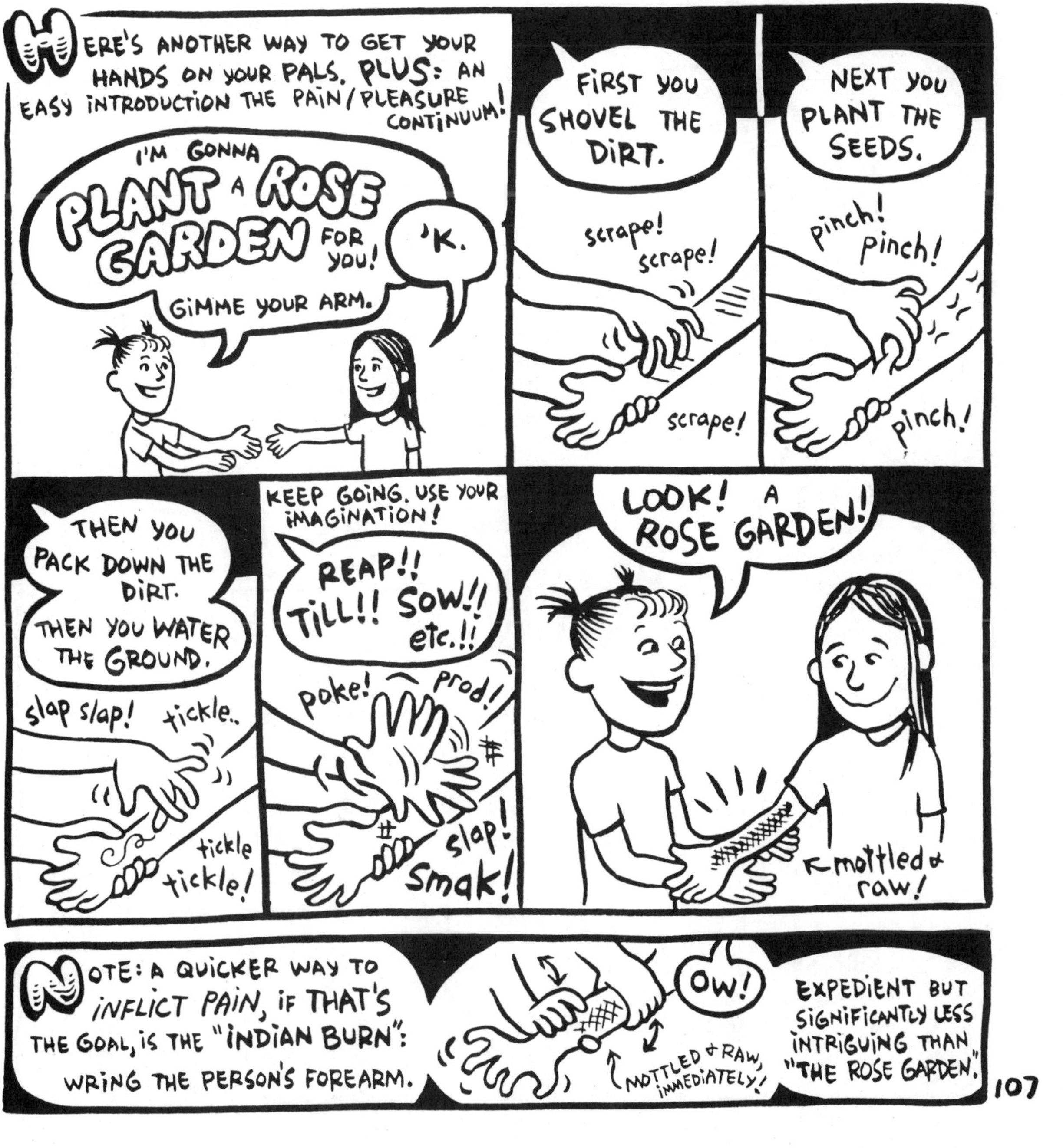
HERE'S ANOTHER WAY TO GET YOUR HANDS ON YOUR PALS. PLUS: AN EASY INTRODUCTION THE PAIN/PLEASURE CONTINUUM!
I'M GONNA PLANT A ROSE GARDEN FOR YOU!
GIMME YOUR ARM.
'K.
FIRST YOU SHOVEL THE DIRT.
scrape! scrape!
scrape!
NEXT YOU PLANT THE SEEDS.
pinch! pinch!
pinch!
THEN YOU PACK DOWN THE DIRT.
THEN YOU WATER THE GROUND.
slap slap! tickle..
tickle tickle!
KEEP GOING. USE YOUR IMAGINATION!
REAP!! TILL!! SOW!! etc.!!
poke! prod!
slap! smak!
LOOK! A ROSE GARDEN!
← mottled & raw!
NOTE: A QUICKER WAY TO INFLICT PAIN, IF THAT'S THE GOAL, IS THE "INDIAN BURN": WRING THE PERSON'S FOREARM.
OW!
MOTTLED & RAW, IMMEDIATELY!
EXPEDIENT BUT SIGNIFICANTLY LESS INTRIGUING THAN "THE ROSE GARDEN".

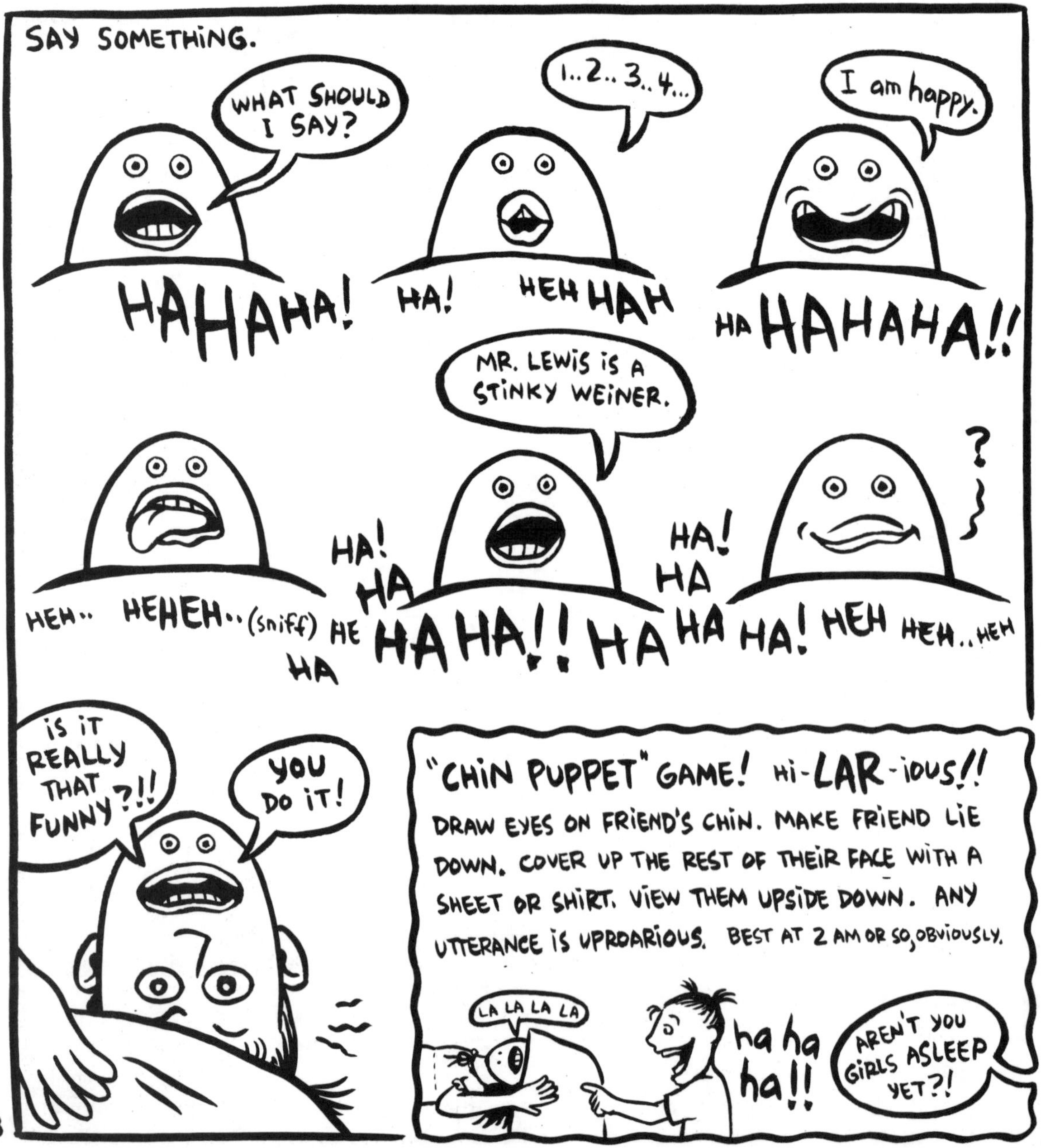
SAY SOMETHING.
WHAT SHOULD I SAY?
HAHAHA!
1..2..3..4...
HA! HEH HAH
I am happy.
HA HAHAHA!!
HEH.. HEHEH..(sniff)
MR. LEWIS IS A STINKY WEINER.
HA! HA HE HA HAHA!! HA
HA! HA HA
HA! HEH HEH..HEH
?
IS IT REALLY THAT FUNNY?!!
YOU DO IT!
"CHIN PUPPET" GAME! HI-LAR-IOUS!!
DRAW EYES ON FRIEND'S CHIN. MAKE FRIEND LIE DOWN. COVER UP THE REST OF THEIR FACE WITH A SHEET OR SHIRT. VIEW THEM UPSIDE DOWN. ANY UTTERANCE IS UPROARIOUS. BEST AT 2 AM OR SO, OBVIOUSLY.
LA LA LA LA
ha ha ha!!
AREN'T YOU GIRLS ASLEEP YET?!

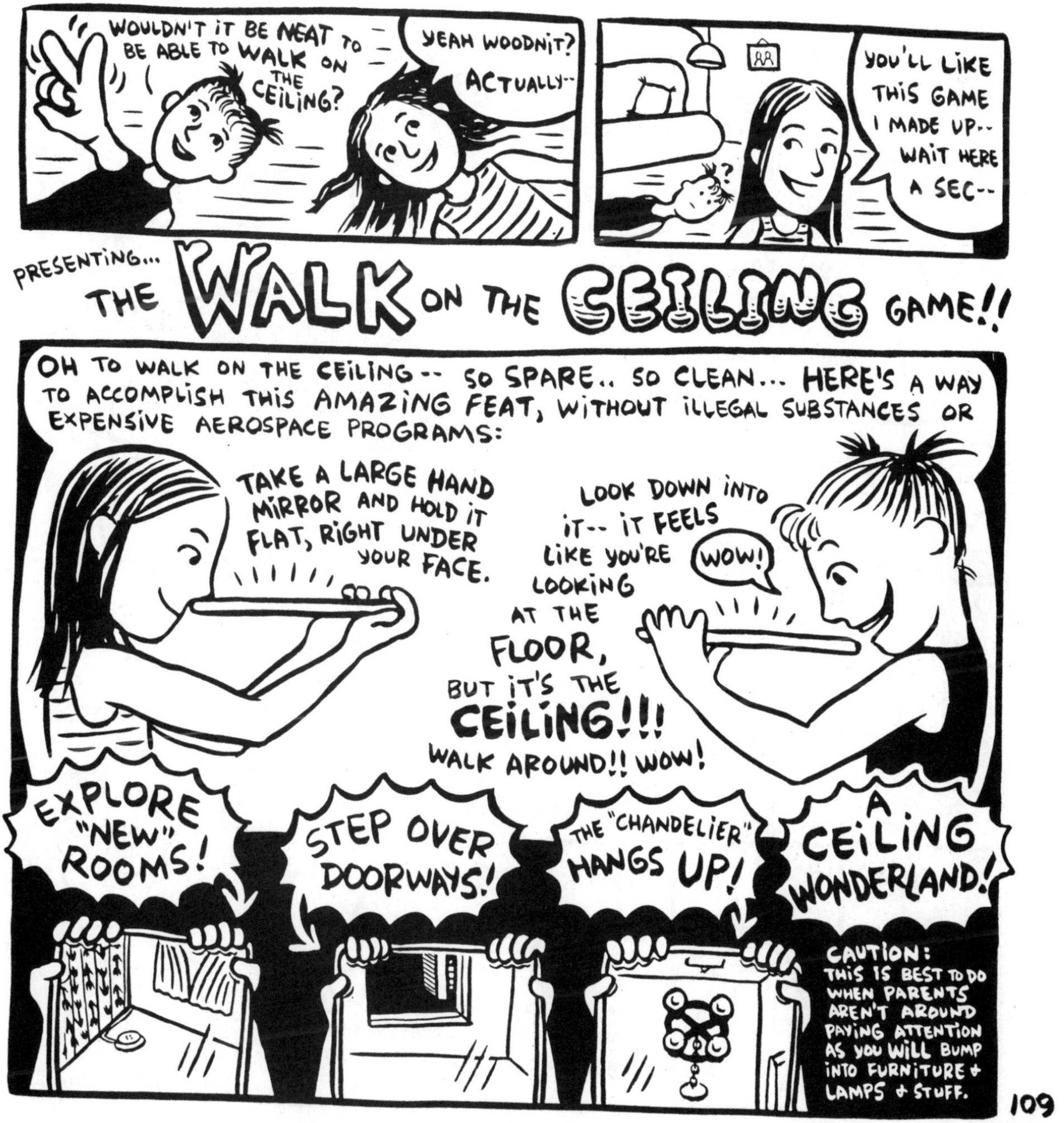

WOULDN'T IT BE NEAT TO BE ABLE TO WALK ON THE CEILING?
YEAH WOODNIT?
ACTUALLY--
YOU'LL LIKE THIS GAME I MADE UP-- WAIT HERE A SEC--
?
PRESENTING... THE WALK ON THE CEILING GAME!!
OH TO WALK ON THE CEILING-- SO SPARE.. SO CLEAN... HERE'S A WAY TO ACCOMPLISH THIS AMAZING FEAT, WITHOUT ILLEGAL SUBSTANCES OR EXPENSIVE AEROSPACE PROGRAMS:
TAKE A LARGE HAND MIRROR AND HOLD IT FLAT, RIGHT UNDER YOUR FACE.
LOOK DOWN INTO IT-- IT FEELS LIKE YOU'RE LOOKING AT THE FLOOR, BUT IT'S THE CEILING!!!
WOW!
WALK AROUND!! WOW!
EXPLORE "NEW" ROOMS!
STEP OVER DOORWAYS!
THE "CHANDELIER" HANGS UP!
A CEILING WONDERLAND!
CAUTION: THIS IS BEST TO DO WHEN PARENTS AREN'T AROUND PAYING ATTENTION AS YOU WILL BUMP INTO FURNITURE & LAMPS & STUFF.

ON HAPPY DAYS, PINKY TUSCADERO HAD A PRETTY COOL "WAITING AROUND" THING SHE DID WITH HER HANDS → ("NERVOUS HABIT"? WHO YOU CALLIN' NERVOUS!?) ...WORTH TRYING...

..BUT FOR MOST GIRLS, THE COOLEST WAITING-AROUND THING WAS

snap snap clop

① snap ② snap ③ clop

DO 1-3 VERY QUICKLY, AS ONE MOTION: SNAPSNAPCLOP. REPEAT, REPEAT, REPEAT.

GHOST ARMS

IF YOU DO THIS RIGHT, IT LOOKS LIKE YOUR ARMS PASS RIGHT THROUGH EACH OTHER AT THE ELBOWS!

ENTIRE MOVEMENT SHOULD SWING SMOOTHLY AND RAPIDLY.

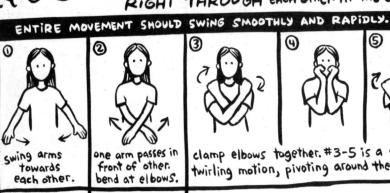

① swing arms towards each other.

② one arm passes in front of other. bend at elbows.

③ ④ ⑤ clamp elbows together. #3-5 is a quick twirling motion, pivoting around the elbows.

⑥ swing arms back down

⑦ and out.

REPEAT, REPEAT, REPEAT, REPEAT,

USE THIS WHEN STANDING IN LINE, ANYWHERE.

REMEMBER TO LOOK BORED. (GHOST ARMS SHOULD LOOK VERY NONCHALANT. PRACTICE YOUR "TEEN ENNUI" FACE & POSTURE.)

COOL!

twirl!

me & Mom, 1975. "Say cheese!"

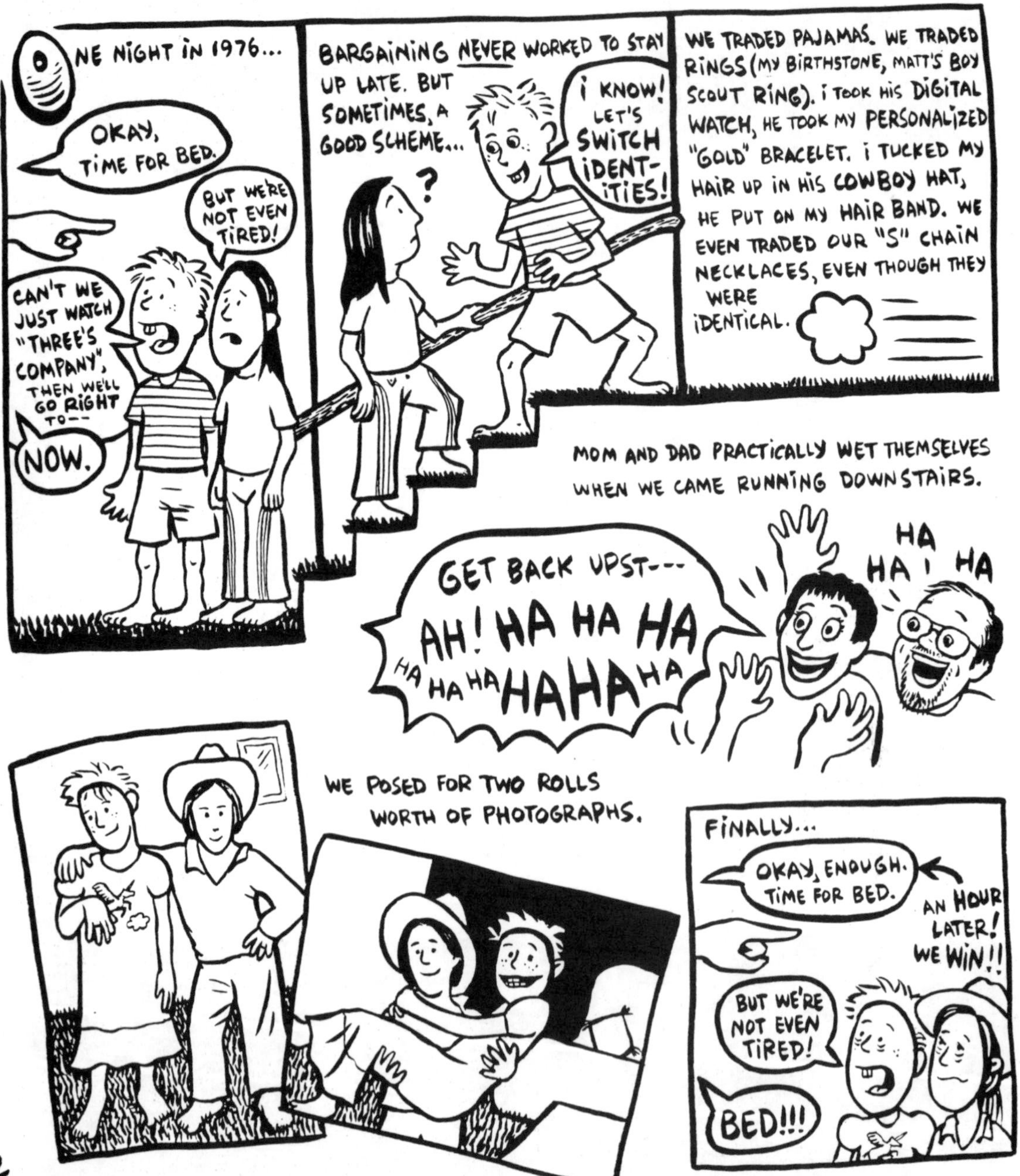
ONE NIGHT IN 1976...
OKAY, TIME FOR BED.
BUT WE'RE NOT EVEN TIRED!
CAN'T WE JUST WATCH "THREE'S COMPANY", THEN WE'LL GO RIGHT TO--
NOW.
BARGAINING NEVER WORKED TO STAY UP LATE. BUT SOMETIMES, A GOOD SCHEME...
?
I KNOW! LET'S SWITCH IDENTITIES!
WE TRADED PAJAMAS. WE TRADED RINGS (MY BIRTHSTONE, MATT'S BOY SCOUT RING). I TOOK HIS DIGITAL WATCH, HE TOOK MY PERSONALIZED "GOLD" BRACELET. I TUCKED MY HAIR UP IN HIS COWBOY HAT, HE PUT ON MY HAIR BAND. WE EVEN TRADED OUR "S" CHAIN NECKLACES, EVEN THOUGH THEY WERE IDENTICAL.
MOM AND DAD PRACTICALLY WET THEMSELVES WHEN WE CAME RUNNING DOWNSTAIRS.
GET BACK UPST--- AH! HA HA HA HA HA HA HAHAHA HA
HA HA HA
WE POSED FOR TWO ROLLS WORTH OF PHOTOGRAPHS.
FINALLY...
OKAY, ENOUGH. TIME FOR BED.
AN HOUR LATER! WE WIN!!
BUT WE'RE NOT EVEN TIRED!
BED!!!

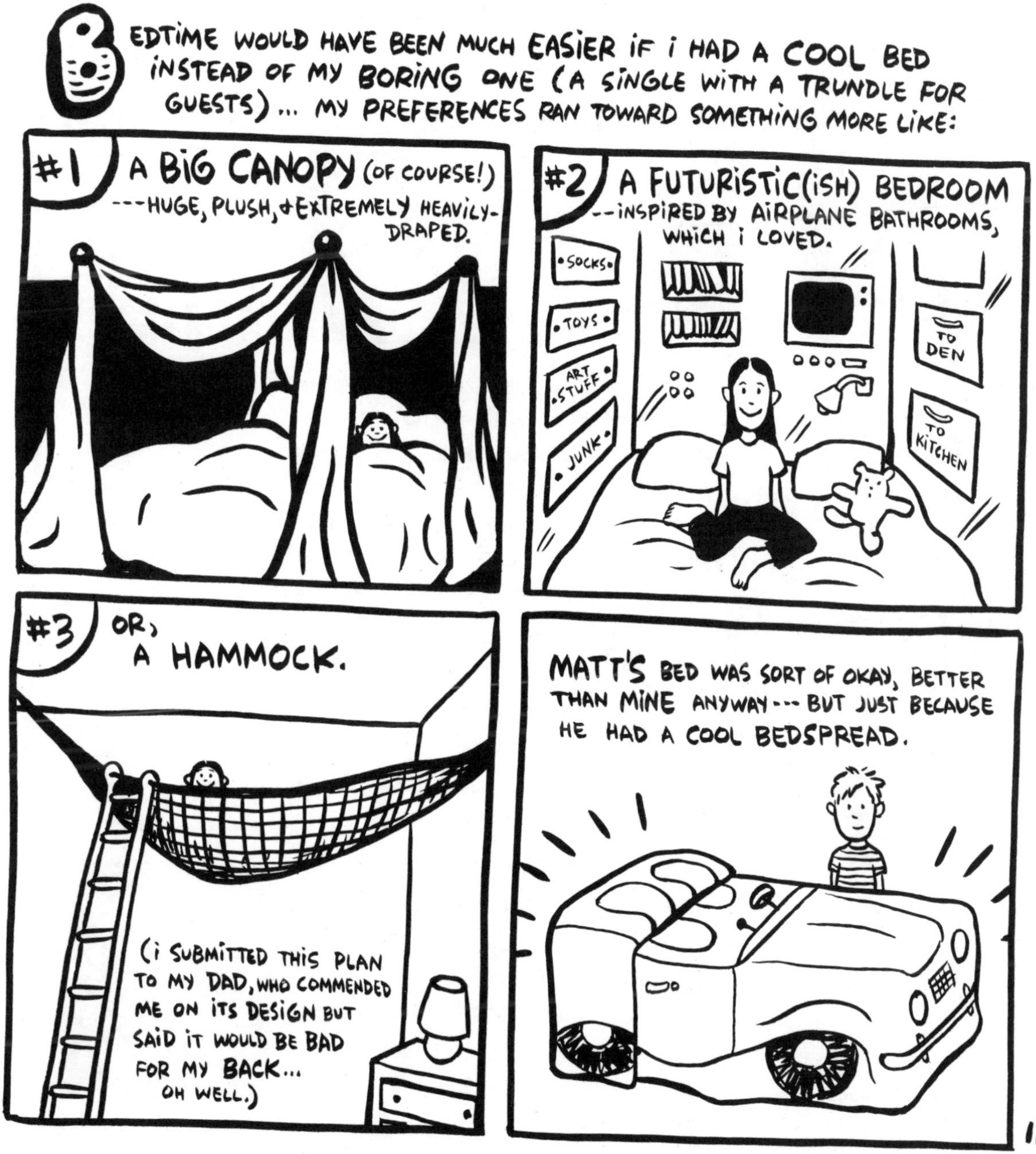
BEDTIME WOULD HAVE BEEN MUCH EASIER IF I HAD A COOL BED INSTEAD OF MY BORING ONE (A SINGLE WITH A TRUNDLE FOR GUESTS)... MY PREFERENCES RAN TOWARD SOMETHING MORE LIKE:
#1
A BIG CANOPY (OF COURSE!) ---HUGE, PLUSH, & EXTREMELY HEAVILY-DRAPED.
#2
A FUTURISTIC(ISH) BEDROOM --INSPIRED BY AIRPLANE BATHROOMS, WHICH I LOVED.
SOCKS
TOYS
ART STUFF
JUNK
TO DEN
TO KITCHEN
#3
OR, A HAMMOCK.
(I SUBMITTED THIS PLAN TO MY DAD, WHO COMMENDED ME ON ITS DESIGN BUT SAID IT WOULD BE BAD FOR MY BACK... OH WELL.)
MATT'S BED WAS SORT OF OKAY, BETTER THAN MINE ANYWAY--- BUT JUST BECAUSE HE HAD A COOL BEDSPREAD.

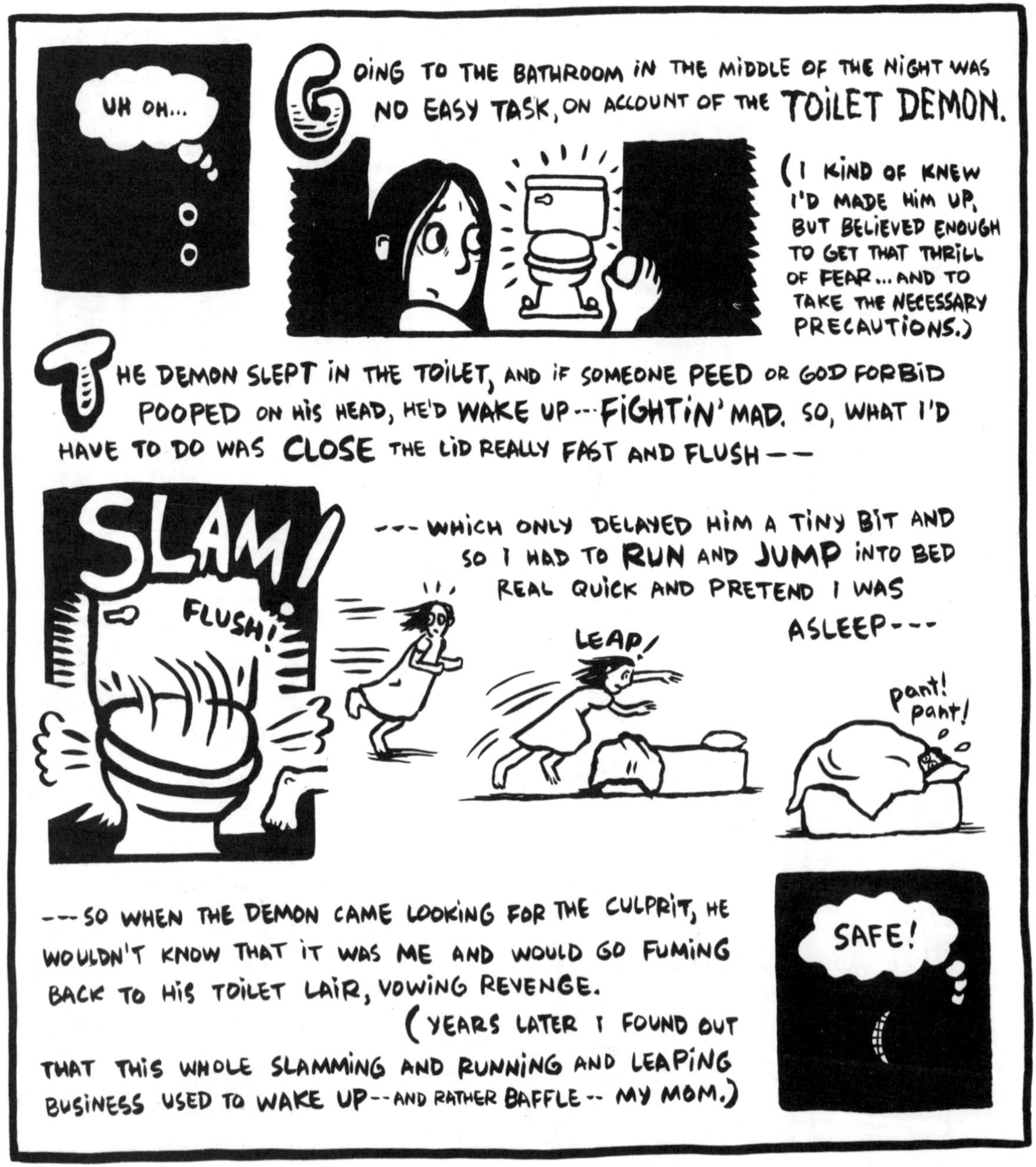
UH OH...
GOING TO THE BATHROOM IN THE MIDDLE OF THE NIGHT WAS NO EASY TASK, ON ACCOUNT OF THE TOILET DEMON.
(I KIND OF KNEW I'D MADE HIM UP, BUT BELIEVED ENOUGH TO GET THAT THRILL OF FEAR... AND TO TAKE THE NECESSARY PRECAUTIONS.)
THE DEMON SLEPT IN THE TOILET, AND IF SOMEONE PEED OR GOD FORBID POOPED ON HIS HEAD, HE'D WAKE UP--- FIGHTIN' MAD. SO, WHAT I'D HAVE TO DO WAS CLOSE THE LID REALLY FAST AND FLUSH --
SLAM!
FLUSH!
--- WHICH ONLY DELAYED HIM A TINY BIT AND SO I HAD TO RUN AND JUMP INTO BED REAL QUICK AND PRETEND I WAS ASLEEP---
LEAP!
pant! pant!
--- SO WHEN THE DEMON CAME LOOKING FOR THE CULPRIT, HE WOULDN'T KNOW THAT IT WAS ME AND WOULD GO FUMING BACK TO HIS TOILET LAIR, VOWING REVENGE.
(YEARS LATER I FOUND OUT THAT THIS WHOLE SLAMMING AND RUNNING AND LEAPING BUSINESS USED TO WAKE UP -- AND RATHER BAFFLE -- MY MOM.)
SAFE!

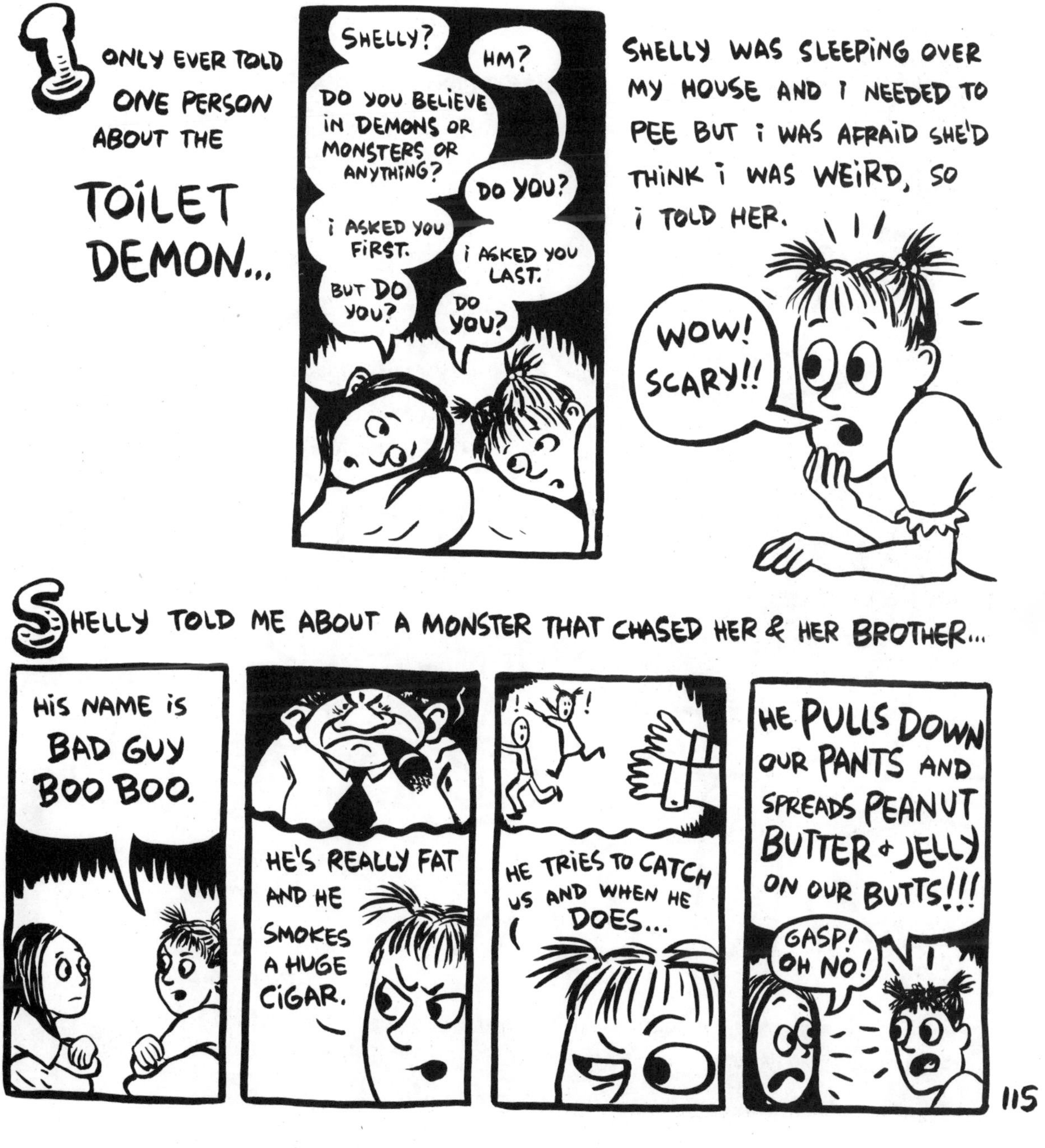
I ONLY EVER TOLD ONE PERSON ABOUT THE
TOILET DEMON...
SHELLY?
HM?
DO YOU BELIEVE IN DEMONS OR MONSTERS OR ANYTHING?
DO YOU?
I ASKED YOU FIRST.
I ASKED YOU LAST.
BUT DO YOU?
DO YOU?
SHELLY WAS SLEEPING OVER MY HOUSE AND I NEEDED TO PEE BUT I WAS AFRAID SHE'D THINK I WAS WEIRD, SO I TOLD HER.
WOW! SCARY!!
SHELLY TOLD ME ABOUT A MONSTER THAT CHASED HER & HER BROTHER...
HIS NAME IS BAD GUY BOO BOO.
HE'S REALLY FAT AND HE SMOKES A HUGE CIGAR.
HE TRIES TO CATCH US AND WHEN HE DOES...
HE PULLS DOWN OUR PANTS AND SPREADS PEANUT BUTTER & JELLY ON OUR BUTTS!!!
GASP! OH NO!

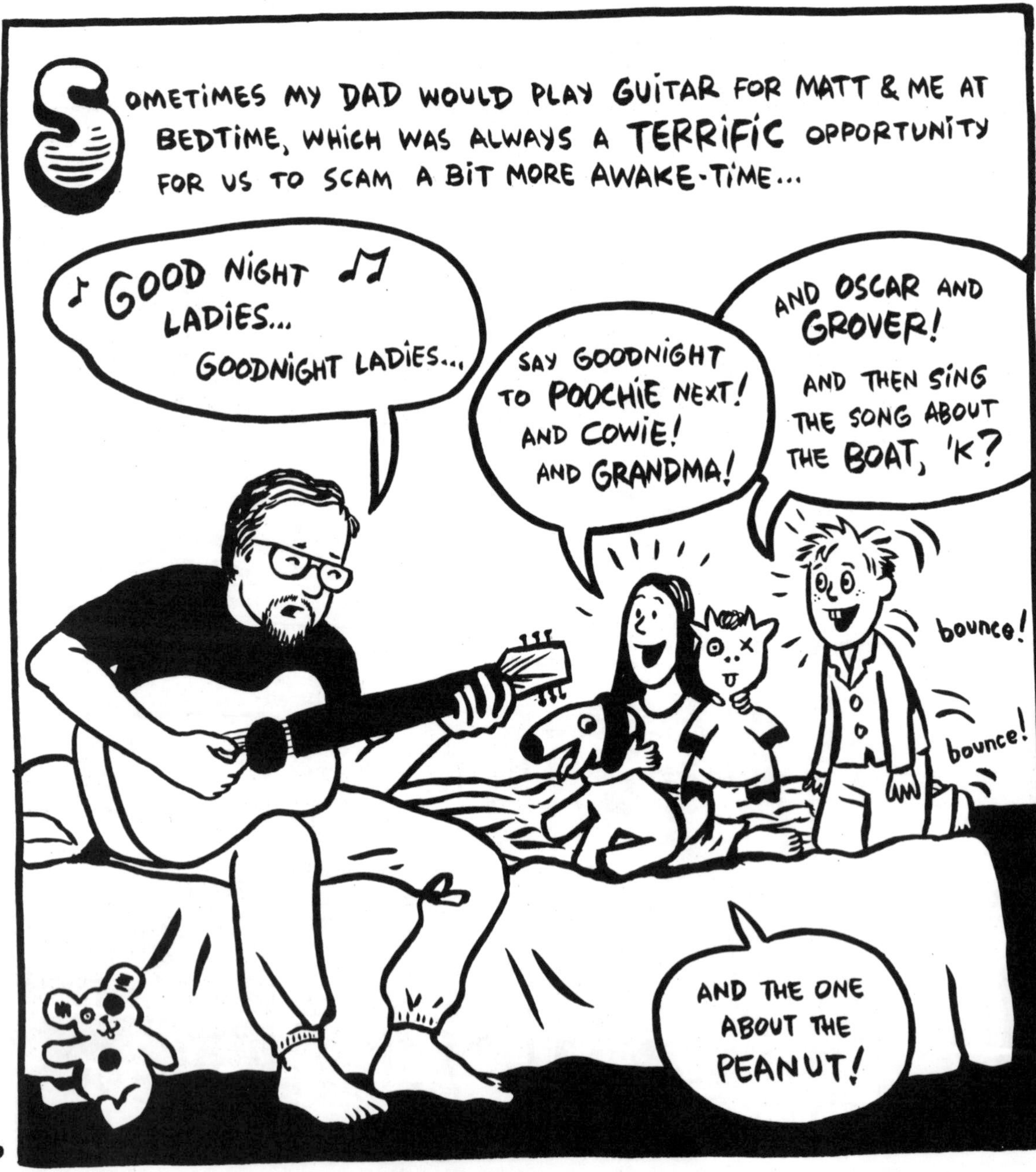
SOMETIMES MY DAD WOULD PLAY GUITAR FOR MATT & ME AT BEDTIME, WHICH WAS ALWAYS A TERRIFIC OPPORTUNITY FOR US TO SCAM A BIT MORE AWAKE-TIME...
♪ GOOD NIGHT ♫ LADIES... GOODNIGHT LADIES...
SAY GOODNIGHT TO POOCHIE NEXT! AND COWIE! AND GRANDMA!
AND OSCAR AND GROVER! AND THEN SING THE SONG ABOUT THE BOAT, 'K?
bounce!
bounce!
AND THE ONE ABOUT THE PEANUT!

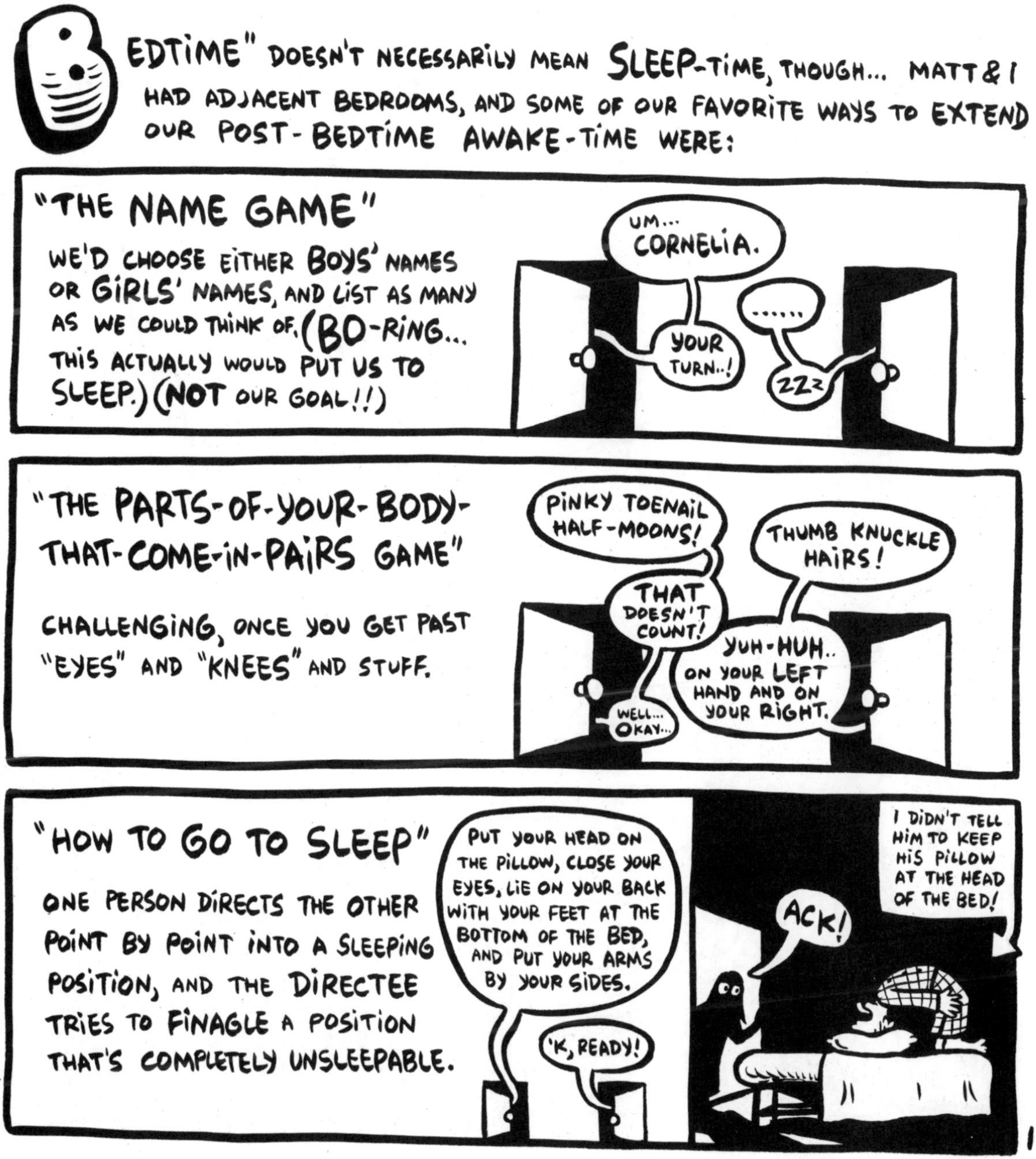
"BEDTIME" DOESN'T NECESSARILY MEAN SLEEP-TIME, THOUGH... MATT & I HAD ADJACENT BEDROOMS, AND SOME OF OUR FAVORITE WAYS TO EXTEND OUR POST-BEDTIME AWAKE-TIME WERE:
"THE NAME GAME"
WE'D CHOOSE EITHER BOYS' NAMES OR GIRLS' NAMES, AND LIST AS MANY AS WE COULD THINK OF. (BO-RING... THIS ACTUALLY WOULD PUT US TO SLEEP.) (NOT OUR GOAL!!)
UM... CORNELIA.
YOUR TURN..!
......
ZZZ
"THE PARTS-OF-YOUR-BODY-THAT-COME-IN-PAIRS GAME"
CHALLENGING, ONCE YOU GET PAST "EYES" AND "KNEES" AND STUFF.
PINKY TOENAIL HALF-MOONS!
THUMB KNUCKLE HAIRS!
THAT DOESN'T COUNT!
YUH-HUH.. ON YOUR LEFT HAND AND ON YOUR RIGHT.
WELL... OKAY...
"HOW TO GO TO SLEEP"
ONE PERSON DIRECTS THE OTHER POINT BY POINT INTO A SLEEPING POSITION, AND THE DIRECTEE TRIES TO FINAGLE A POSITION THAT'S COMPLETELY UNSLEEPABLE.
PUT YOUR HEAD ON THE PILLOW, CLOSE YOUR EYES, LIE ON YOUR BACK WITH YOUR FEET AT THE BOTTOM OF THE BED, AND PUT YOUR ARMS BY YOUR SIDES.
'K, READY!
ACK!
I DIDN'T TELL HIM TO KEEP HIS PILLOW AT THE HEAD OF THE BED!

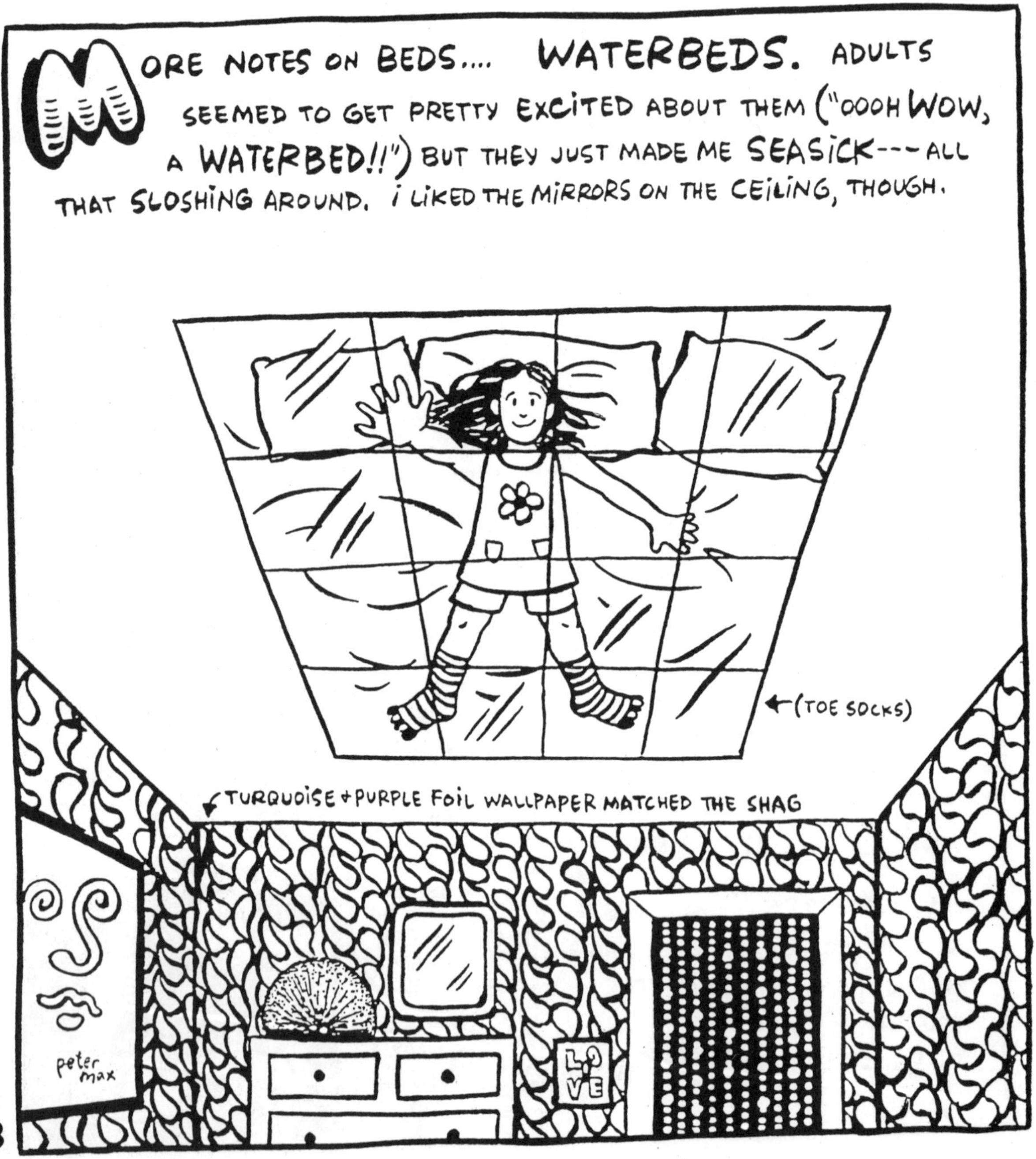
MORE NOTES ON BEDS.... WATERBEDS. ADULTS SEEMED TO GET PRETTY EXCITED ABOUT THEM ("OOOH WOW, A WATERBED!!") BUT THEY JUST MADE ME SEASICK---ALL THAT SLOSHING AROUND. I LIKED THE MIRRORS ON THE CEILING, THOUGH.
(TOE SOCKS)
TURQUOISE + PURPLE FOIL WALLPAPER MATCHED THE SHAG
peter max
LOVE

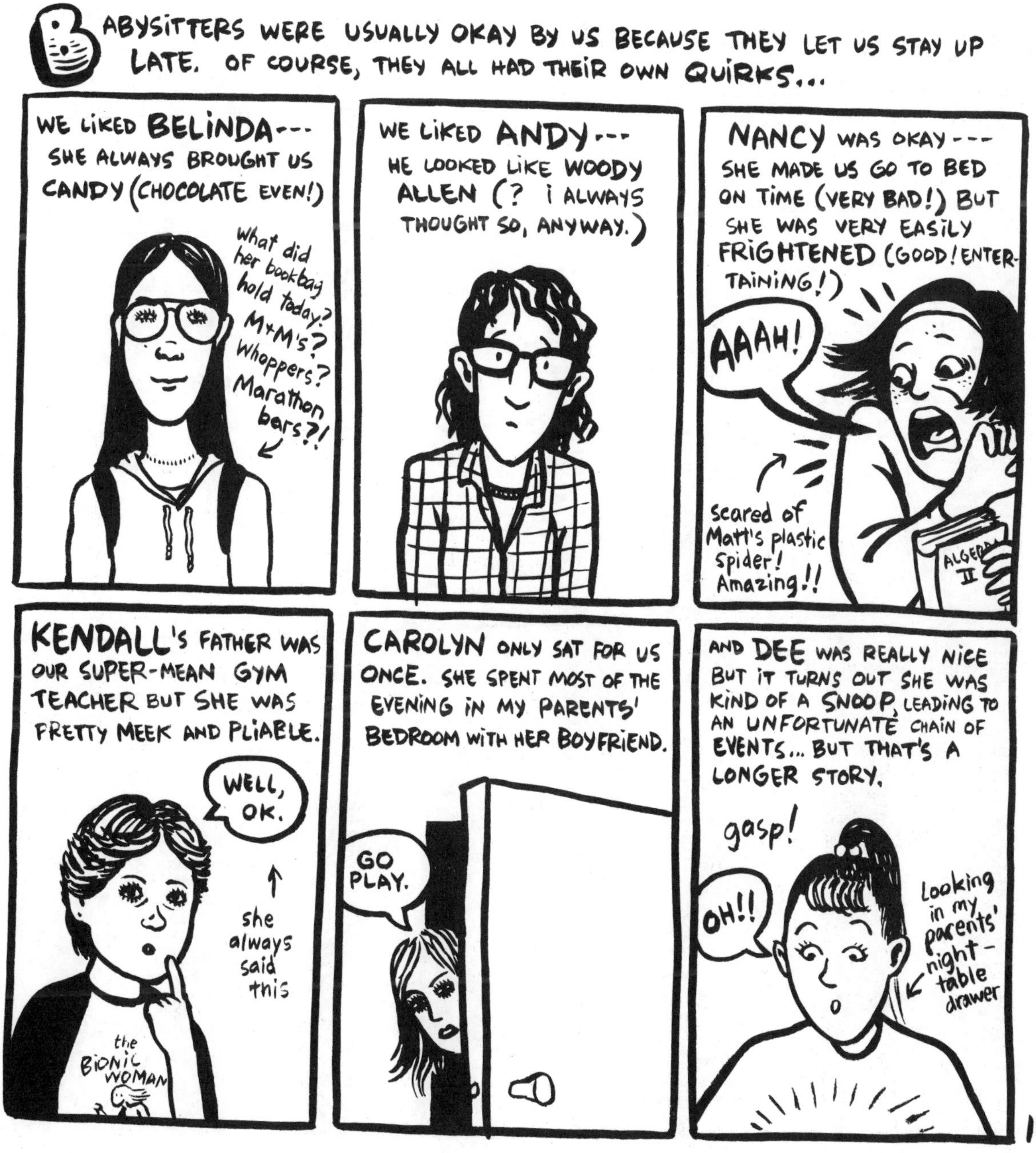
BABYSITTERS WERE USUALLY OKAY BY US BECAUSE THEY LET US STAY UP LATE. OF COURSE, THEY ALL HAD THEIR OWN QUIRKS...
WE LIKED BELINDA--- SHE ALWAYS BROUGHT US CANDY (CHOCOLATE EVEN!)
What did her bookbag hold today? M+M's? Whoppers? Marathon bars?!
WE LIKED ANDY--- HE LOOKED LIKE WOODY ALLEN (? I ALWAYS THOUGHT SO, ANYWAY.)
NANCY WAS OKAY--- SHE MADE US GO TO BED ON TIME (VERY BAD!) BUT SHE WAS VERY EASILY FRIGHTENED (GOOD! ENTERTAINING!)
AAAH!
scared of Matt's plastic spider! Amazing!!
KENDALL'S FATHER WAS OUR SUPER-MEAN GYM TEACHER BUT SHE WAS PRETTY MEEK AND PLIABLE.
WELL, OK.
she always said this
the BIONIC WOMAN
CAROLYN ONLY SAT FOR US ONCE. SHE SPENT MOST OF THE EVENING IN MY PARENTS' BEDROOM WITH HER BOYFRIEND.
GO PLAY.
AND DEE WAS REALLY NICE BUT IT TURNS OUT SHE WAS KIND OF A SNOOP, LEADING TO AN UNFORTUNATE CHAIN OF EVENTS... BUT THAT'S A LONGER STORY.
gasp!
OH!!
Looking in my parents' night-table drawer

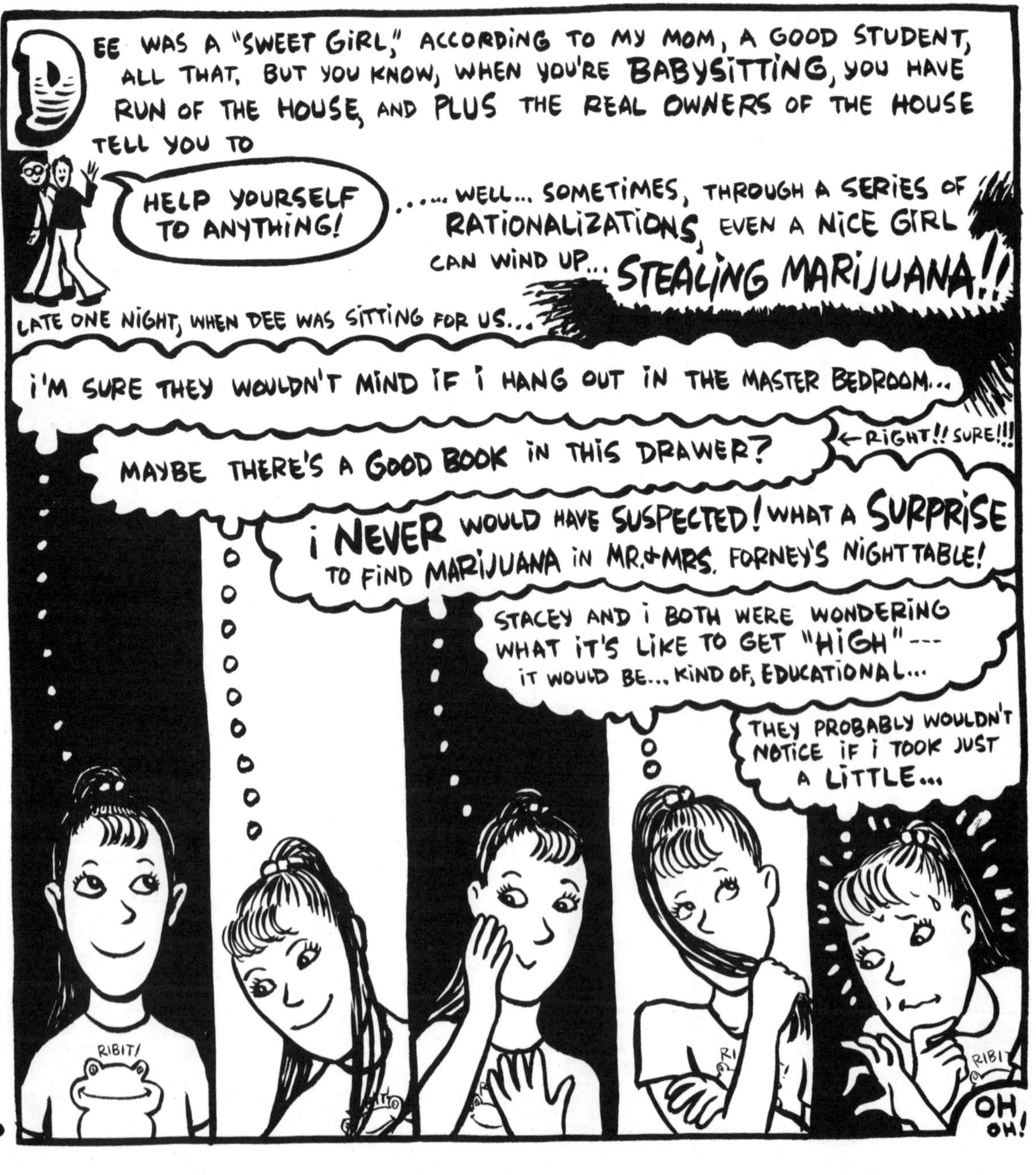
DEE WAS A "SWEET GIRL," ACCORDING TO MY MOM, A GOOD STUDENT, ALL THAT. BUT YOU KNOW, WHEN YOU'RE BABYSITTING, YOU HAVE RUN OF THE HOUSE, AND PLUS THE REAL OWNERS OF THE HOUSE TELL YOU TO
HELP YOURSELF TO ANYTHING!
..... WELL... SOMETIMES, THROUGH A SERIES OF RATIONALIZATIONS, EVEN A NICE GIRL CAN WIND UP... STEALING MARIJUANA!!
LATE ONE NIGHT, WHEN DEE WAS SITTING FOR US...
I'M SURE THEY WOULDN'T MIND IF I HANG OUT IN THE MASTER BEDROOM...
MAYBE THERE'S A GOOD BOOK IN THIS DRAWER?
← RIGHT!! SURE!!!
I NEVER WOULD HAVE SUSPECTED! WHAT A SURPRISE TO FIND MARIJUANA IN MR.&MRS. FORNEY'S NIGHTTABLE!
STACEY AND I BOTH WERE WONDERING WHAT IT'S LIKE TO GET "HIGH"--- IT WOULD BE... KIND OF, EDUCATIONAL...
THEY PROBABLY WOULDN'T NOTICE IF I TOOK JUST A LITTLE...
RIBIT!
OH, OH!

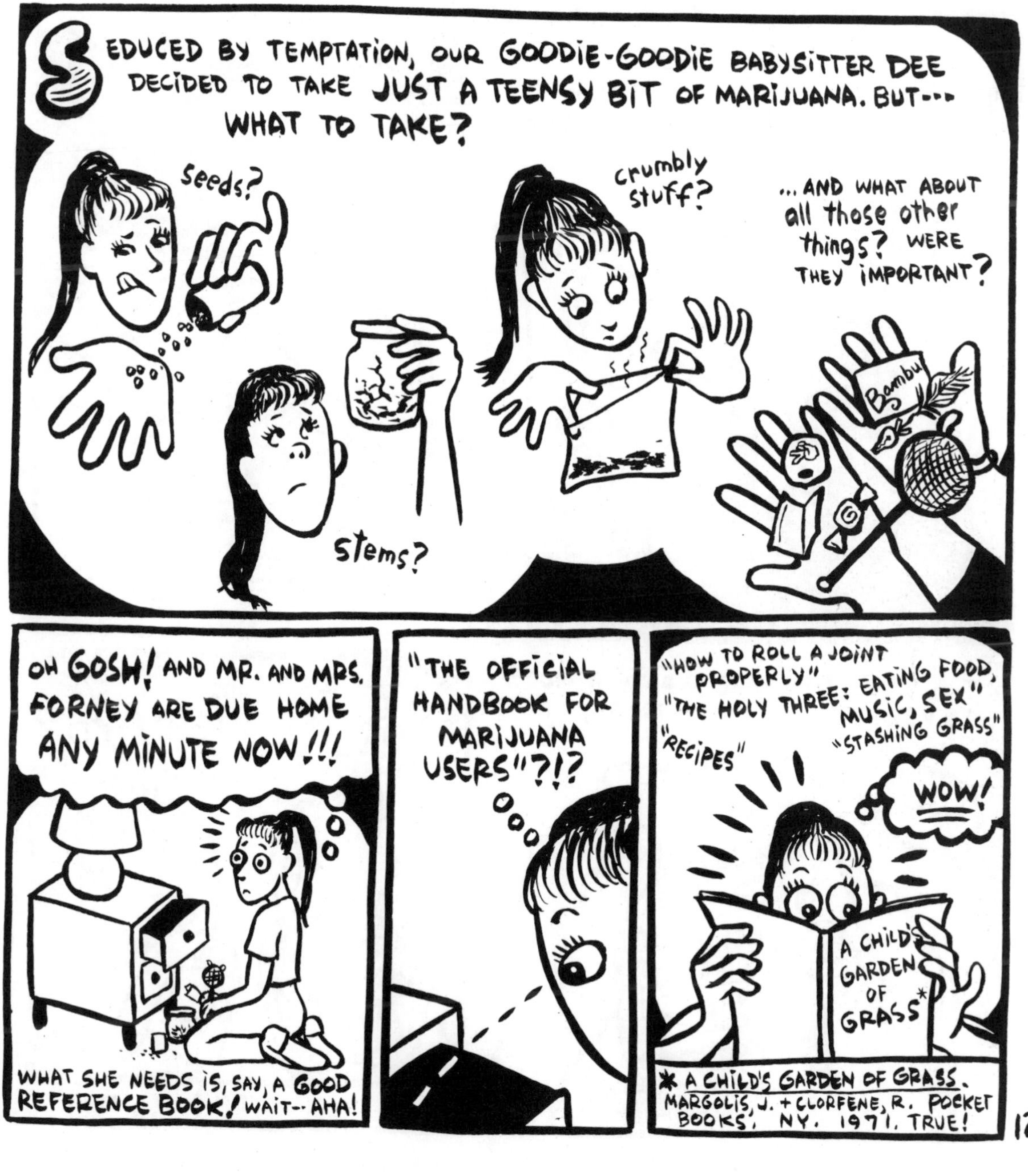
SEDUCED BY TEMPTATION, OUR GOODIE-GOODIE BABYSITTER DEE DECIDED TO TAKE JUST A TEENSY BIT OF MARIJUANA. BUT... WHAT TO TAKE?
seeds?
stems?
crumbly stuff?
...AND WHAT ABOUT all those other things? WERE THEY IMPORTANT?
Bambu
OH GOSH! AND MR. AND MRS. FORNEY ARE DUE HOME ANY MINUTE NOW!!!
WHAT SHE NEEDS IS, SAY, A GOOD REFERENCE BOOK! WAIT--AHA!
"THE OFFICIAL HANDBOOK FOR MARIJUANA USERS"?!?
"HOW TO ROLL A JOINT PROPERLY"
"THE HOLY THREE: EATING FOOD, MUSIC, SEX"
"STASHING GRASS"
"RECIPES"
WOW!
A CHILD'S GARDEN OF GRASS*
* A CHILD'S GARDEN OF GRASS. MARGOLIS, J. + CLORFENE, R. POCKET BOOKS, NY. 1971. TRUE!

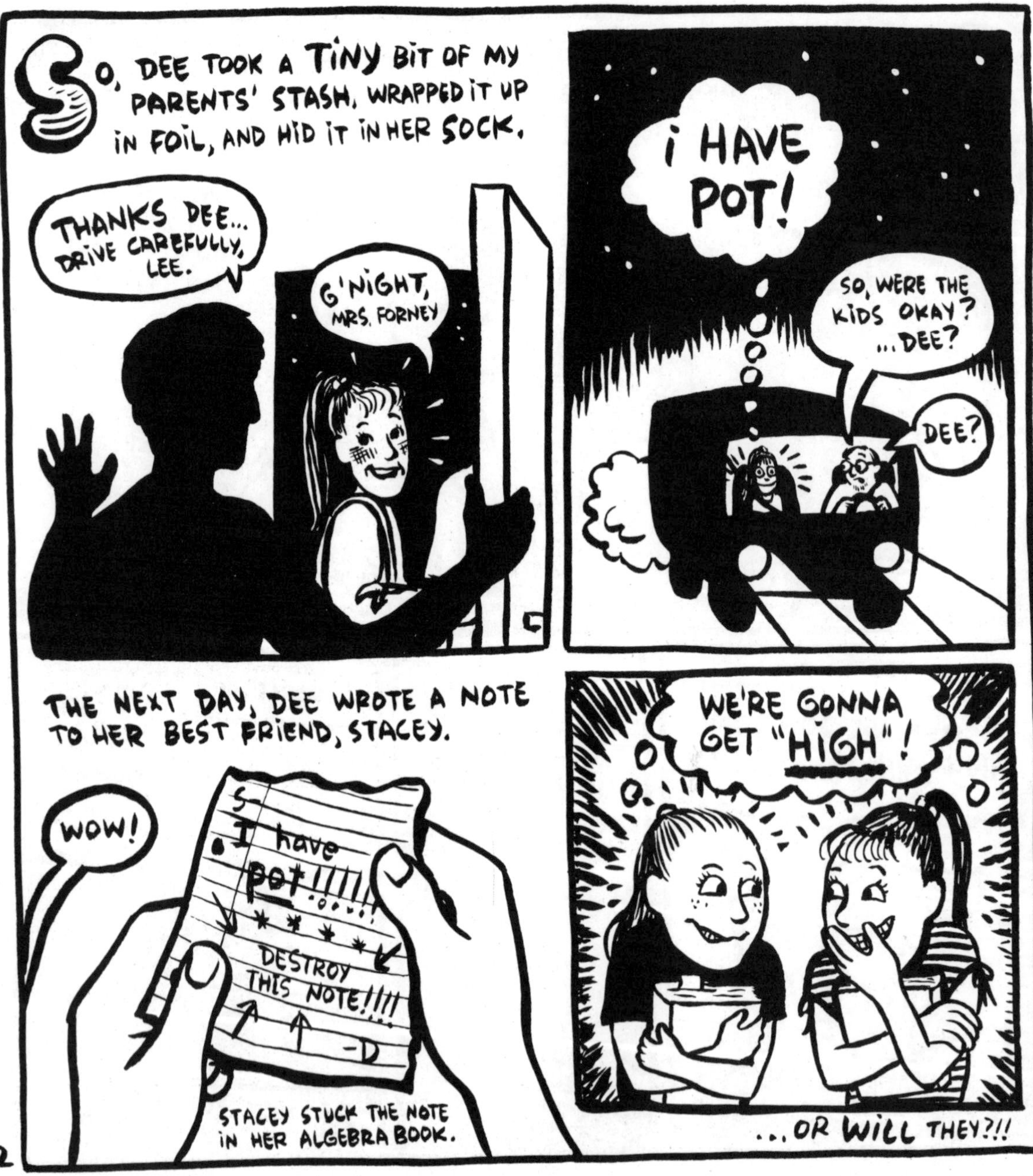
SO, DEE TOOK A TINY BIT OF MY PARENTS' STASH, WRAPPED IT UP IN FOIL, AND HID IT IN HER SOCK.
THANKS DEE... DRIVE CAREFULLY, LEE.
G'NIGHT, MRS. FORNEY
I HAVE POT!
SO, WERE THE KIDS OKAY? ...DEE?
DEE?
THE NEXT DAY, DEE WROTE A NOTE TO HER BEST FRIEND, STACEY.
WOW!
S- I have pot!!!!!
DESTROY THIS NOTE!!!!
-D
STACEY STUCK THE NOTE IN HER ALGEBRA BOOK.
WE'RE GONNA GET "HIGH"!
...OR WILL THEY?!!

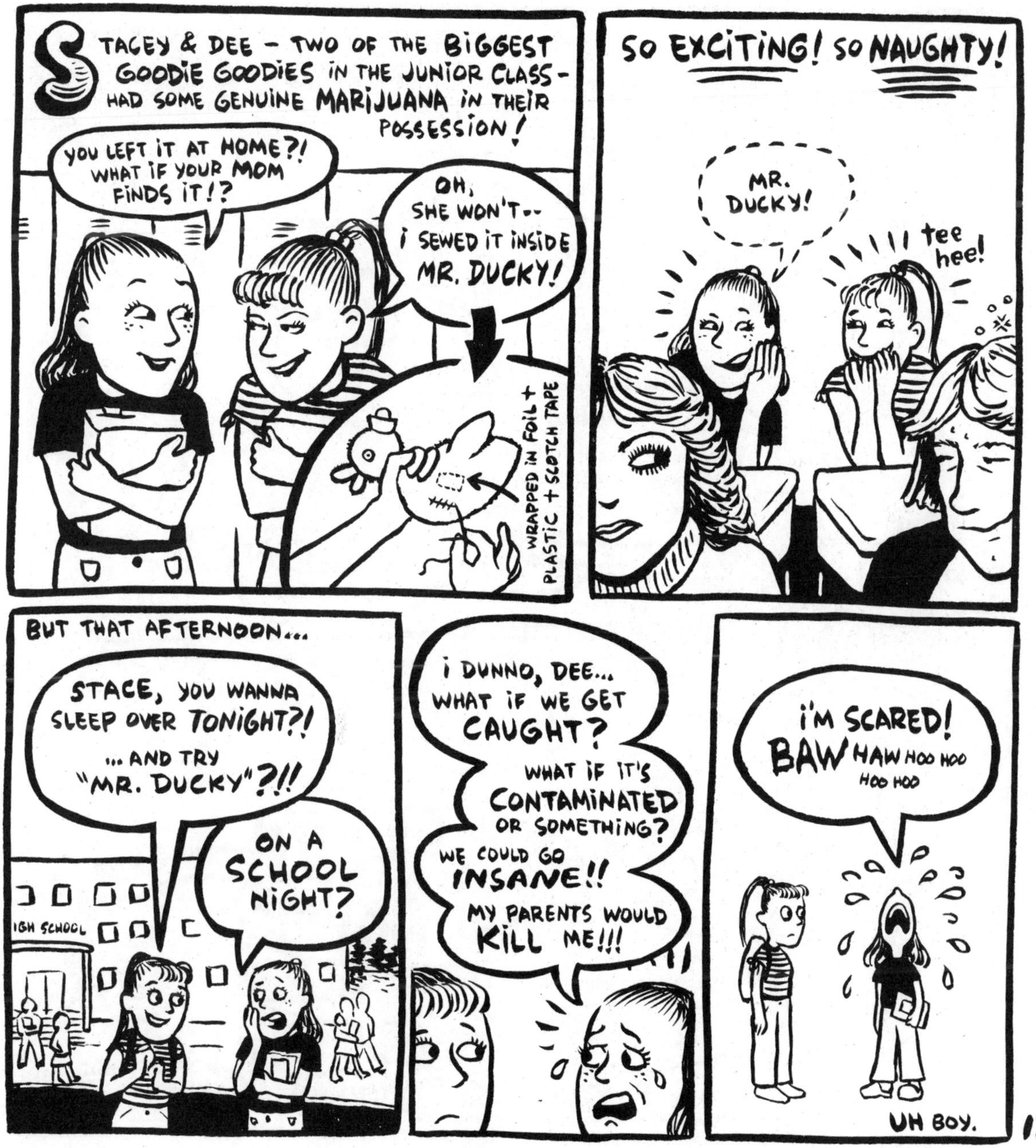
STACEY & DEE - TWO OF THE BIGGEST GOODIE GOODIES IN THE JUNIOR CLASS - HAD SOME GENUINE MARIJUANA IN THEIR POSSESSION!
YOU LEFT IT AT HOME?! WHAT IF YOUR MOM FINDS IT!?
OH, SHE WON'T.. I SEWED IT INSIDE MR. DUCKY!
WRAPPED IN FOIL + PLASTIC + SCOTCH TAPE
SO EXCITING! SO NAUGHTY!
MR. DUCKY!
tee hee!
BUT THAT AFTERNOON...
STACE, YOU WANNA SLEEP OVER TONIGHT?! ... AND TRY "MR. DUCKY"?!!
ON A SCHOOL NIGHT?
IGH SCHOOL
I DUNNO, DEE... WHAT IF WE GET CAUGHT?
WHAT IF IT'S CONTAMINATED OR SOMETHING?
WE COULD GO INSANE!!
MY PARENTS WOULD KILL ME!!!
I'M SCARED! BAW HAW HOO HOO HOO HOO
UH BOY.

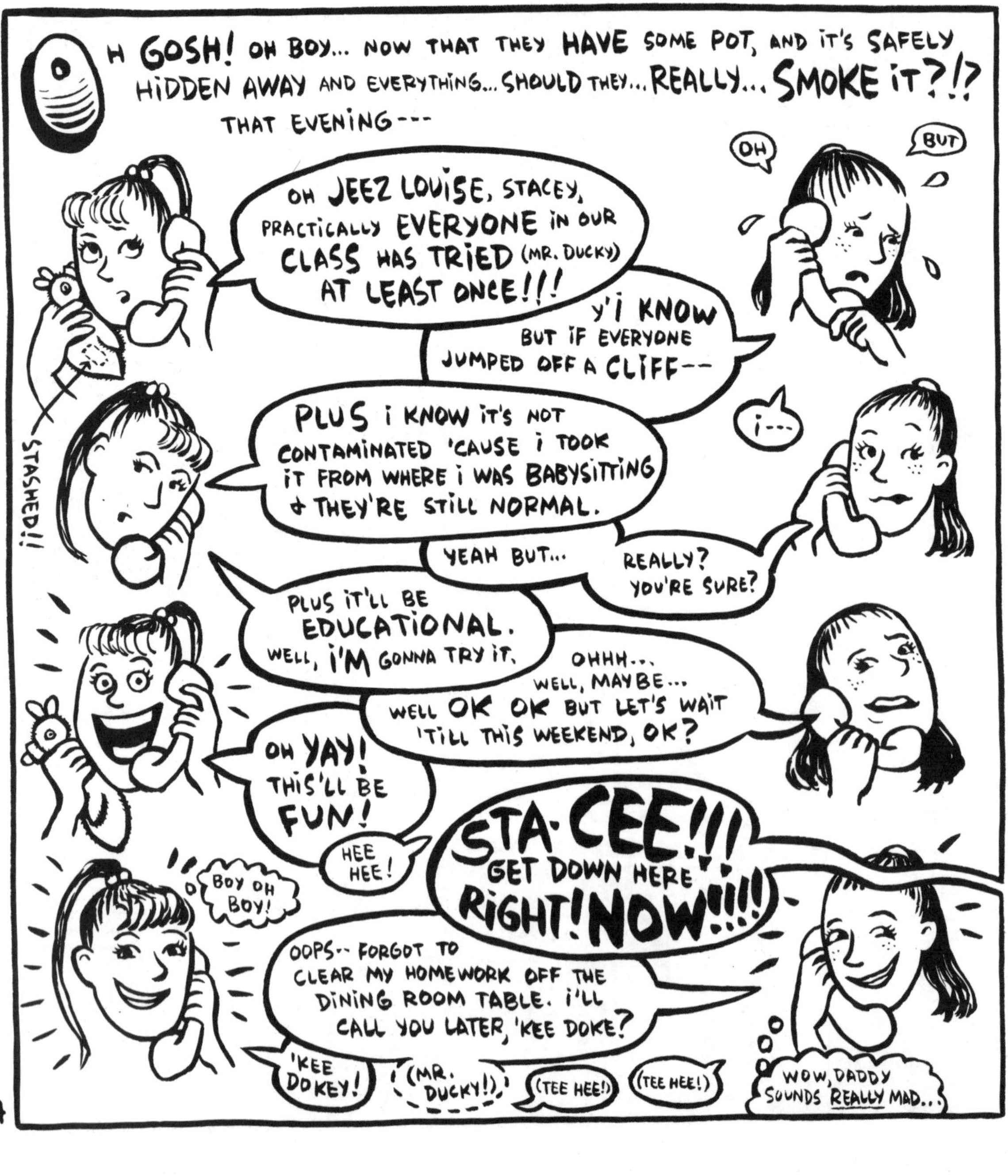
OH GOSH! OH BOY... NOW THAT THEY HAVE SOME POT, AND IT'S SAFELY HIDDEN AWAY AND EVERYTHING... SHOULD THEY... REALLY... SMOKE IT?!?
THAT EVENING---
OH
BUT
OH JEEZ LOUISE, STACEY, PRACTICALLY EVERYONE IN OUR CLASS HAS TRIED (MR. DUCKY) AT LEAST ONCE!!!
Y'I KNOW BUT IF EVERYONE JUMPED OFF A CLIFF--
STASHED!!
I---
PLUS I KNOW IT'S NOT CONTAMINATED 'CAUSE I TOOK IT FROM WHERE I WAS BABYSITTING & THEY'RE STILL NORMAL.
YEAH BUT...
REALLY? YOU'RE SURE?
PLUS IT'LL BE EDUCATIONAL. WELL, I'M GONNA TRY IT.
OHHH... WELL, MAYBE... WELL OK OK BUT LET'S WAIT 'TILL THIS WEEKEND, OK?
OH YAY! THIS'LL BE FUN!
HEE HEE!
STA-CEE!!! GET DOWN HERE RIGHT! NOW!!!!
BOY OH BOY!
OOPS-- FORGOT TO CLEAR MY HOMEWORK OFF THE DINING ROOM TABLE. I'LL CALL YOU LATER, 'KEE DOKE?
'KEE DOKEY!
(MR. DUCKY!)
(TEE HEE!)
(TEE HEE!)
WOW, DADDY SOUNDS REALLY MAD...

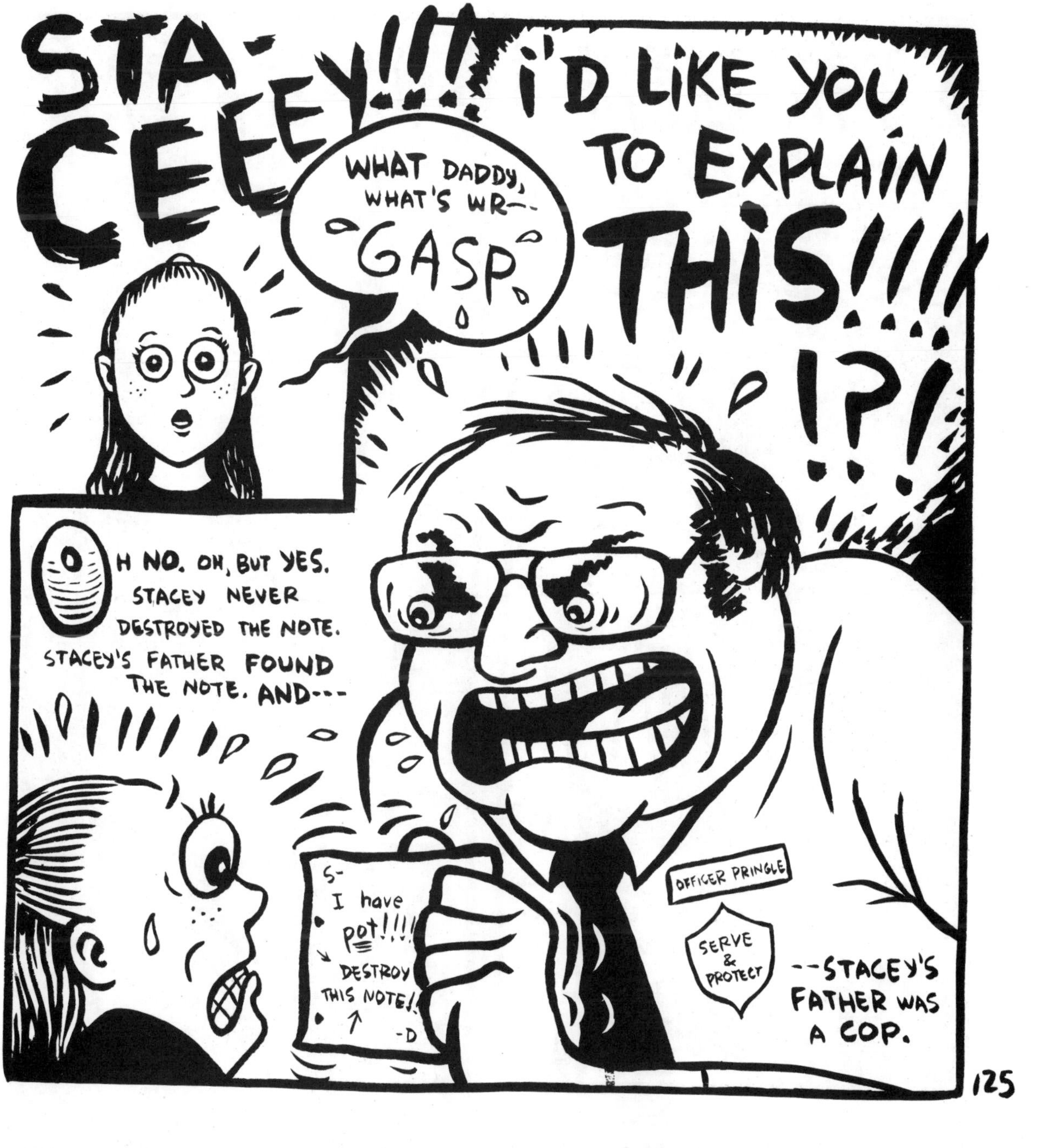
STA-CEEEY!!!!
I'D LIKE YOU TO EXPLAIN THIS!!!! !?!
WHAT DADDY, WHAT'S WR--- GASP
OH NO. OH, BUT YES. STACEY NEVER DESTROYED THE NOTE. STACEY'S FATHER FOUND THE NOTE. AND---
S- I have pot!!!! DESTROY THIS NOTE!! -D
OFFICER PRINGLE
SERVE & PROTECT
--STACEY'S FATHER WAS A COP.

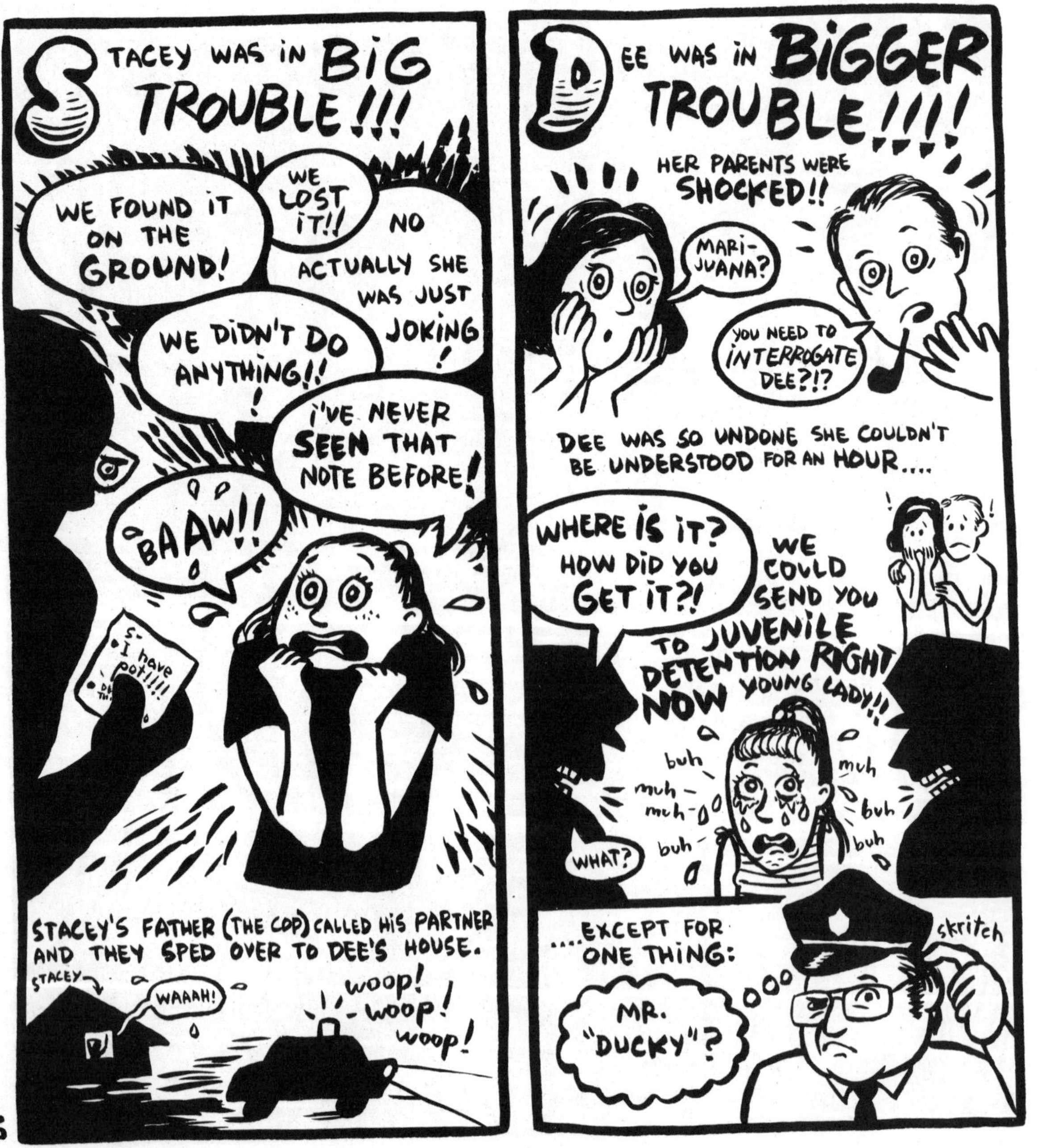
STACEY WAS IN BIG TROUBLE!!!
WE FOUND IT ON THE GROUND!
WE LOST IT!!
NO ACTUALLY SHE WAS JUST JOKING!
WE DIDN'T DO ANYTHING!!!
I'VE NEVER SEEN THAT NOTE BEFORE!
BAAW!!
S- I have pot!!!!
STACEY'S FATHER (THE COP) CALLED HIS PARTNER AND THEY SPED OVER TO DEE'S HOUSE.
STACEY
WAAAH!
woop! woop! woop!
DEE WAS IN BIGGER TROUBLE!!!!
HER PARENTS WERE SHOCKED!!
MARI-JUANA?
YOU NEED TO INTERROGATE DEE?!?
DEE WAS SO UNDONE SHE COULDN'T BE UNDERSTOOD FOR AN HOUR....
WHERE IS IT? HOW DID YOU GET IT?!
WE COULD SEND YOU TO JUVENILE DETENTION RIGHT NOW YOUNG LADY!!
buh muh muh buh
muh buh buh
WHAT?
....EXCEPT FOR ONE THING:
skritch
MR. "DUCKY"?

"NAUGHTY" WAS UNFAMILIAR ENOUGH FOR STACEY AND DEE; "POSSESSION OF AN ILLEGAL SUBSTANCE", THOUGH-- THAT WAS OFF THE CHARTS!! (INVOLVING, LIKE, POLICE INTERROGATION + STUFF!)

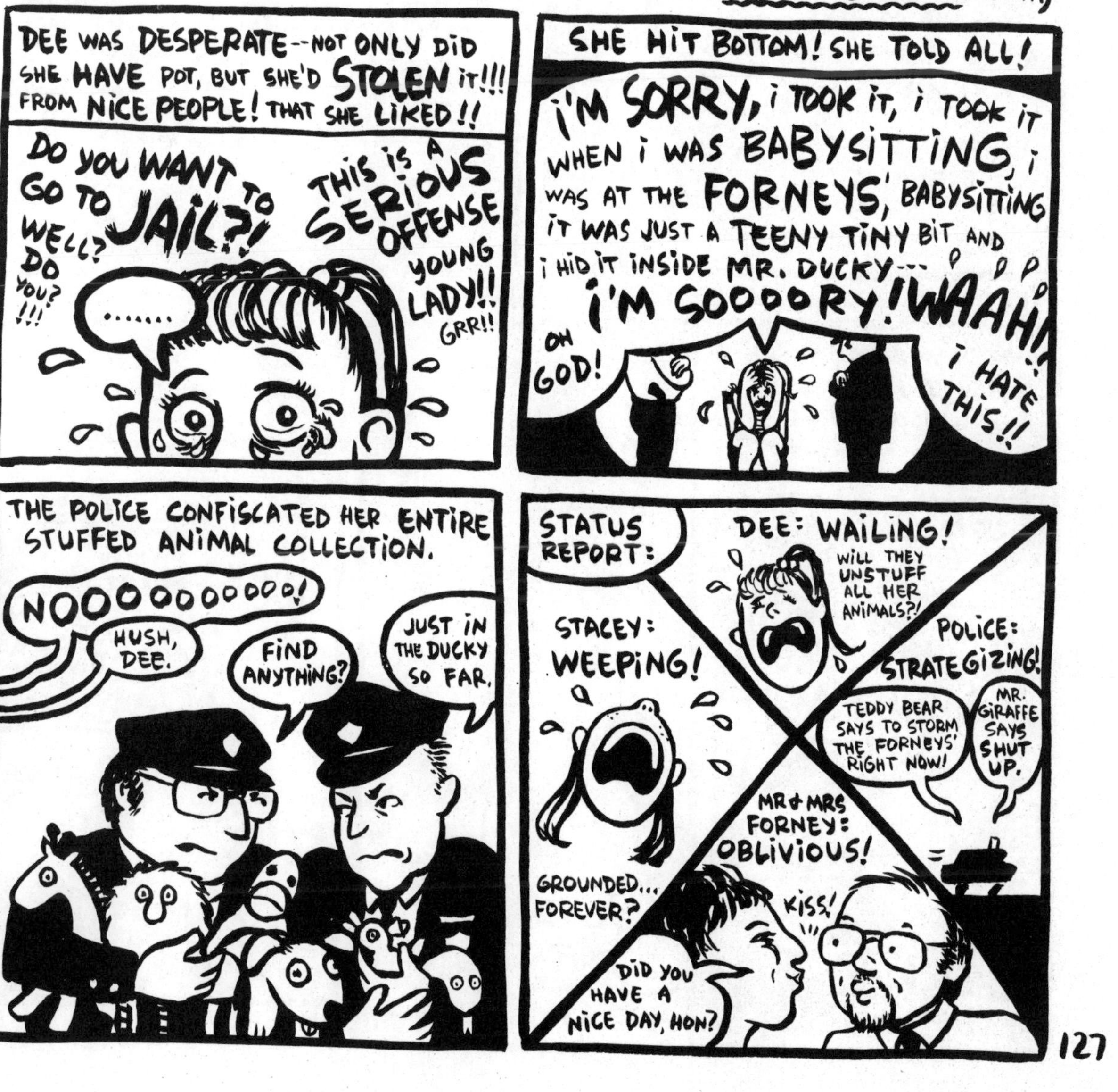

DEE WAS DESPERATE--NOT ONLY DID SHE HAVE POT, BUT SHE'D STOLEN IT!!! FROM NICE PEOPLE! THAT SHE LIKED!!
DO YOU WANT TO GO TO JAIL?!
WELL? DO YOU? !!!
....
THIS IS A SERIOUS OFFENSE YOUNG LADY!! GRR!!
SHE HIT BOTTOM! SHE TOLD ALL!
I'M SORRY, I TOOK IT, I TOOK IT WHEN I WAS BABYSITTING, I WAS AT THE FORNEYS', BABYSITTING IT WAS JUST A TEENY TINY BIT AND I HID IT INSIDE MR. DUCKY--- I'M SOOOORY! WAAH!!
OH GOD!
I HATE THIS!!
THE POLICE CONFISCATED HER ENTIRE STUFFED ANIMAL COLLECTION.
NOOOOOOOOOOO!
HUSH, DEE.
FIND ANYTHING?
JUST IN THE DUCKY SO FAR.
STATUS REPORT:
DEE: WAILING!
WILL THEY UNSTUFF ALL HER ANIMALS?!
STACEY: WEEPING!
POLICE: STRATEGIZING!
TEDDY BEAR SAYS TO STORM THE FORNEYS' RIGHT NOW!
MR. GIRAFFE SAYS SHUT UP.
GROUNDED... FOREVER?
MR & MRS FORNEY: OBLIVIOUS!
KISS!
DID YOU HAVE A NICE DAY, HON?

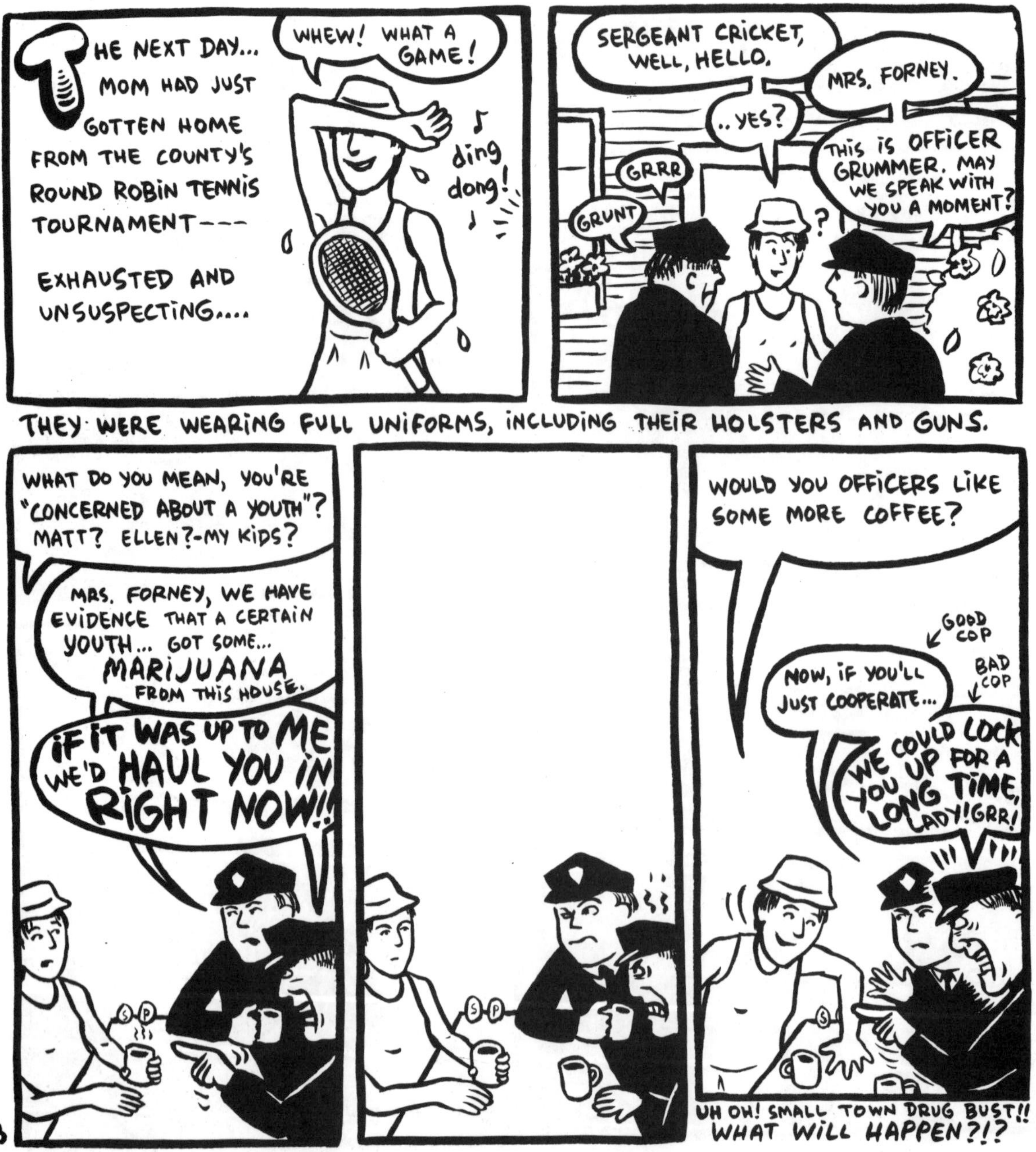
THE NEXT DAY... MOM HAD JUST GOTTEN HOME FROM THE COUNTY'S ROUND ROBIN TENNIS TOURNAMENT---
EXHAUSTED AND UNSUSPECTING....
WHEW! WHAT A GAME!
ding dong!
SERGEANT CRICKET, WELL, HELLO.
MRS. FORNEY.
..YES?
GRRR
GRUNT
THIS IS OFFICER GRUMMER. MAY WE SPEAK WITH YOU A MOMENT?
?
THEY WERE WEARING FULL UNIFORMS, INCLUDING THEIR HOLSTERS AND GUNS.
WHAT DO YOU MEAN, YOU'RE "CONCERNED ABOUT A YOUTH"? MATT? ELLEN?-MY KIDS?
MRS. FORNEY, WE HAVE EVIDENCE THAT A CERTAIN YOUTH... GOT SOME... MARIJUANA FROM THIS HOUSE.
IF IT WAS UP TO ME WE'D HAUL YOU IN RIGHT NOW!!
S P
WOULD YOU OFFICERS LIKE SOME MORE COFFEE?
GOOD COP
BAD COP
NOW, IF YOU'LL JUST COOPERATE...
WE COULD LOCK YOU UP FOR A LONG TIME, LADY! GRR!
UH OH! SMALL TOWN DRUG BUST!! WHAT WILL HAPPEN?!?

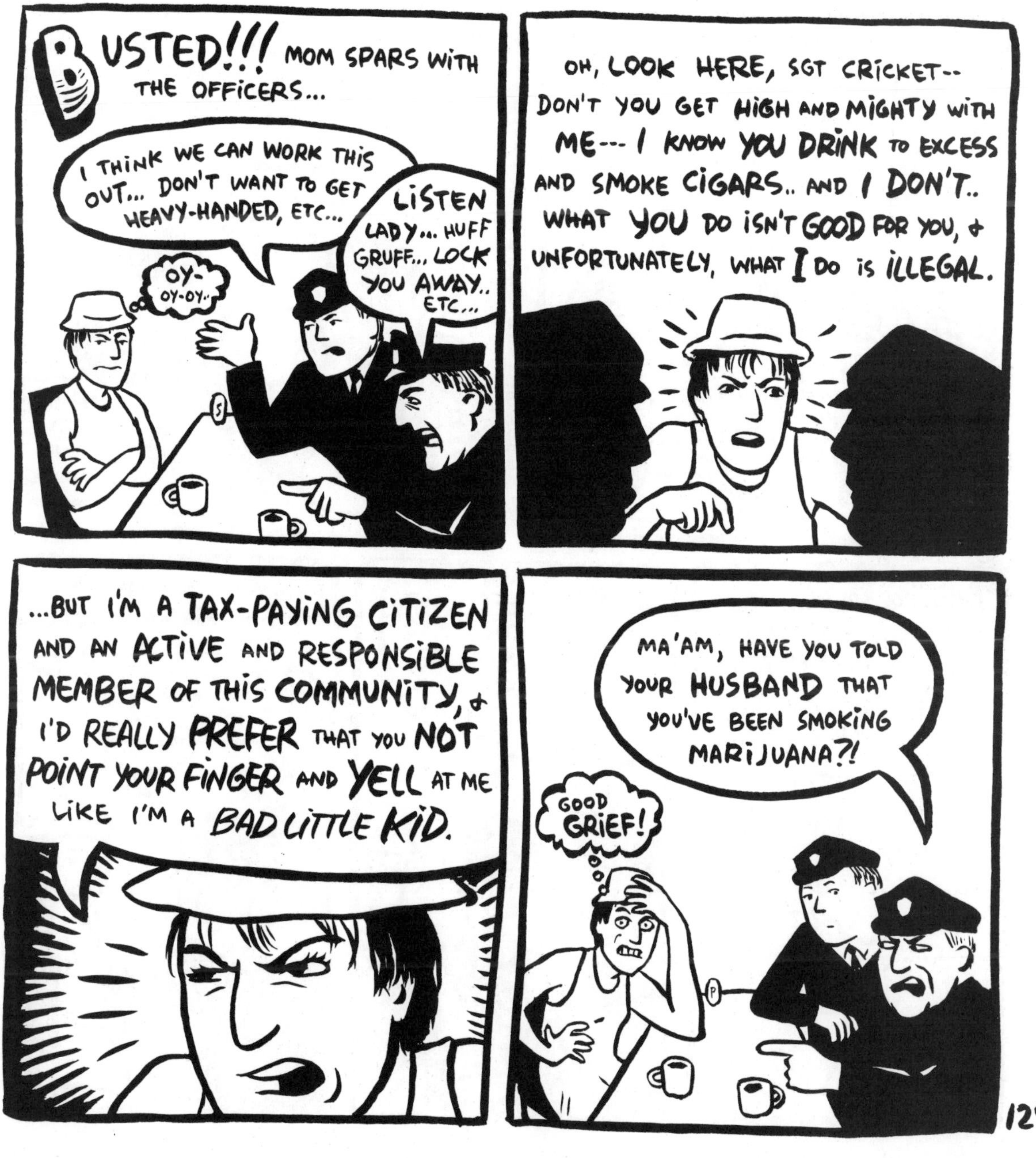
BUSTED!!! MOM SPARS WITH THE OFFICERS...
I THINK WE CAN WORK THIS OUT... DON'T WANT TO GET HEAVY-HANDED, ETC...
LISTEN LADY... HUFF GRUFF... LOCK YOU AWAY.. ETC...
OY-OY-OY..
S
OH, LOOK HERE, SGT CRICKET-- DON'T YOU GET HIGH AND MIGHTY WITH ME--- I KNOW YOU DRINK TO EXCESS AND SMOKE CIGARS.. AND I DON'T.. WHAT YOU DO ISN'T GOOD FOR YOU, & UNFORTUNATELY, WHAT I DO IS ILLEGAL.
...BUT I'M A TAX-PAYING CITIZEN AND AN ACTIVE AND RESPONSIBLE MEMBER OF THIS COMMUNITY, & I'D REALLY PREFER THAT YOU NOT POINT YOUR FINGER AND YELL AT ME LIKE I'M A BAD LITTLE KID.
MA'AM, HAVE YOU TOLD YOUR HUSBAND THAT YOU'VE BEEN SMOKING MARIJUANA?!
GOOD GRIEF!
P

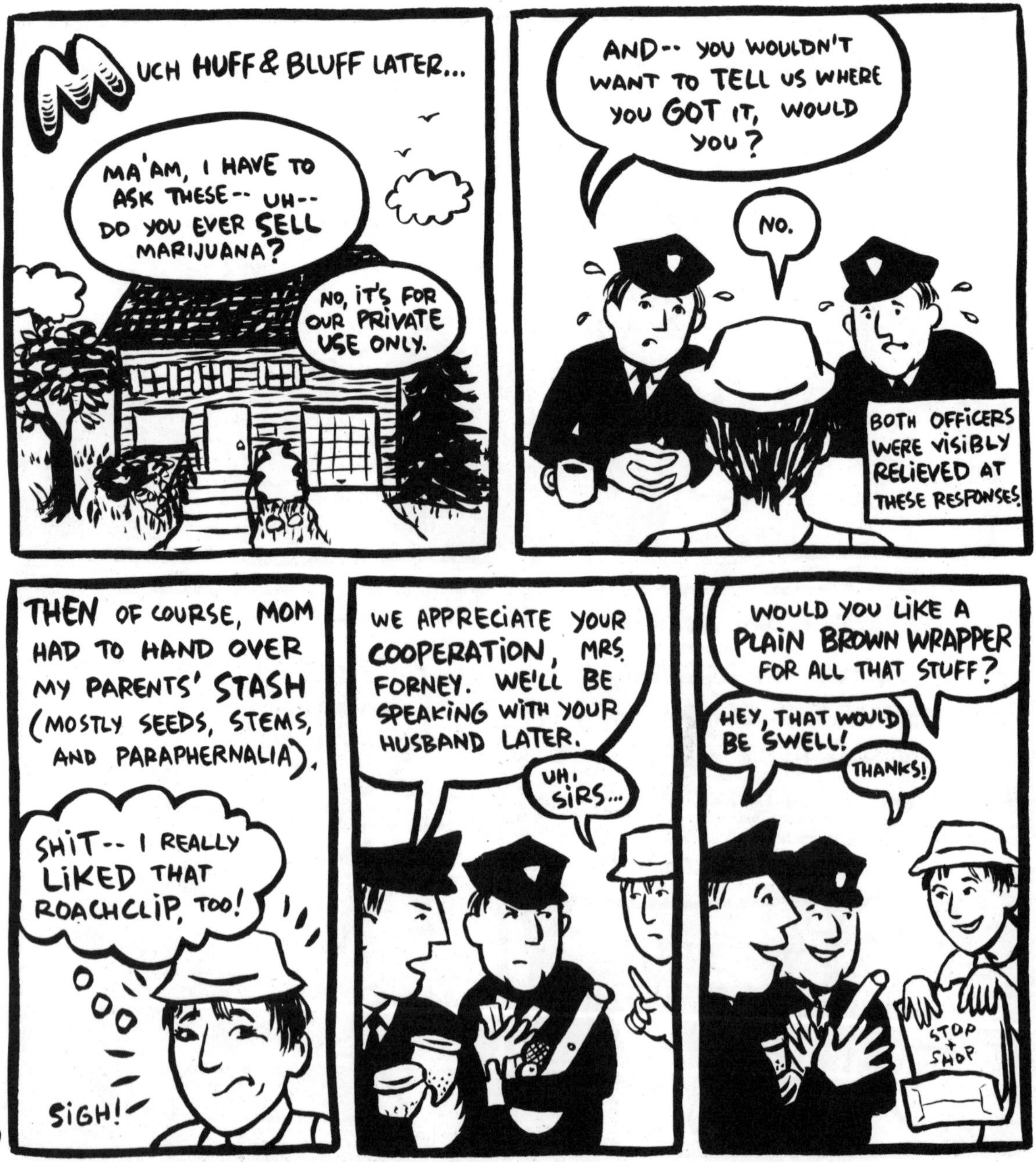
MUCH HUFF & BLUFF LATER...
MA'AM, I HAVE TO ASK THESE-- UH-- DO YOU EVER SELL MARIJUANA?
NO, IT'S FOR OUR PRIVATE USE ONLY.
AND-- YOU WOULDN'T WANT TO TELL US WHERE YOU GOT IT, WOULD YOU?
NO.
BOTH OFFICERS WERE VISIBLY RELIEVED AT THESE RESPONSES.
THEN OF COURSE, MOM HAD TO HAND OVER MY PARENTS' STASH (MOSTLY SEEDS, STEMS, AND PARAPHERNALIA).
SHIT-- I REALLY LIKED THAT ROACHCLIP, TOO!
SIGH!
WE APPRECIATE YOUR COOPERATION, MRS. FORNEY. WE'LL BE SPEAKING WITH YOUR HUSBAND LATER.
UH, SIRS...
WOULD YOU LIKE A PLAIN BROWN WRAPPER FOR ALL THAT STUFF?
HEY, THAT WOULD BE SWELL!
THANKS!
STOP + SHOP

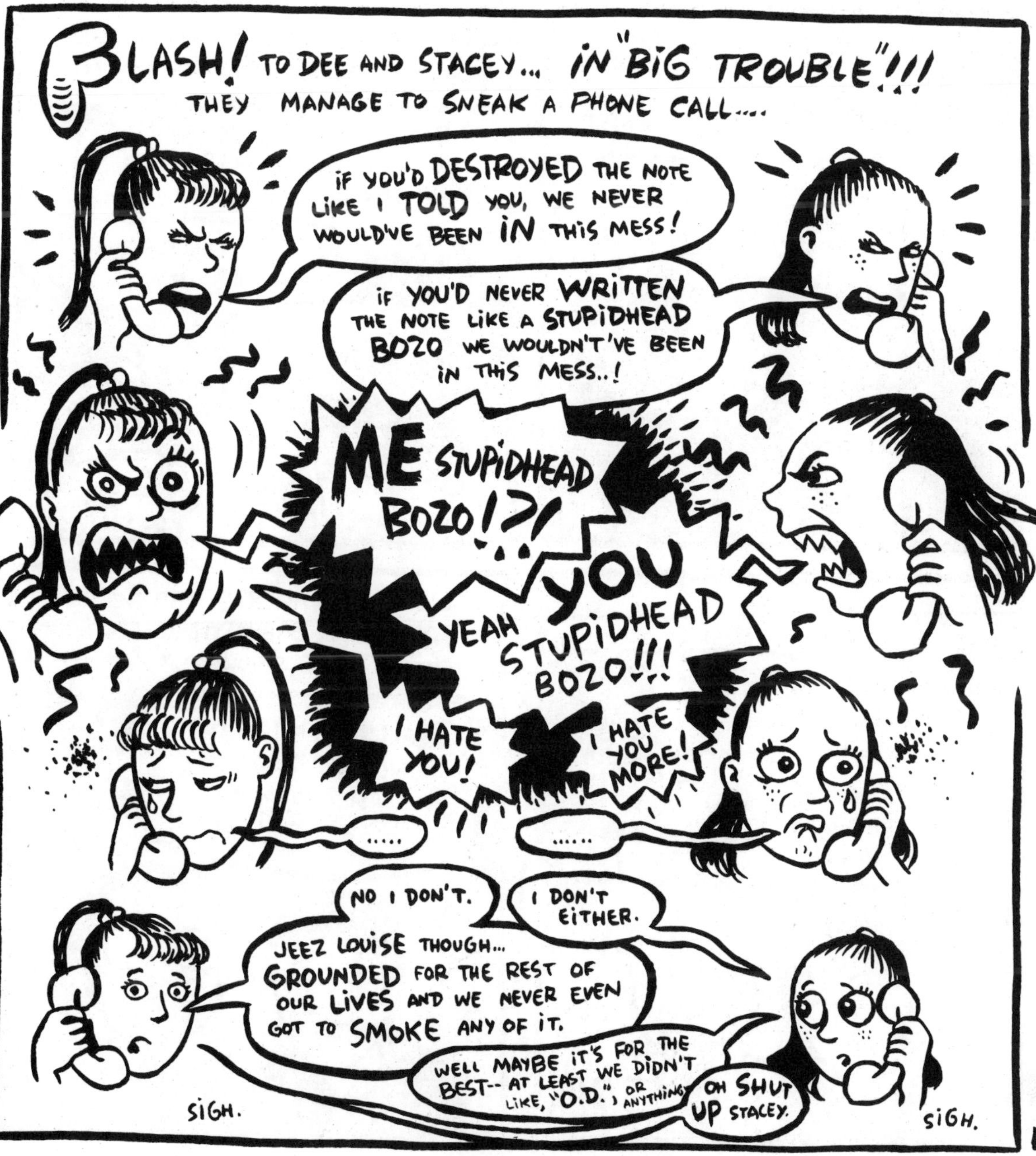
BLASH! TO DEE AND STACEY... IN "BIG TROUBLE"!!! THEY MANAGE TO SNEAK A PHONE CALL....
IF YOU'D DESTROYED THE NOTE LIKE I TOLD YOU, WE NEVER WOULD'VE BEEN IN THIS MESS!
IF YOU'D NEVER WRITTEN THE NOTE LIKE A STUPIDHEAD BOZO WE WOULDN'T'VE BEEN IN THIS MESS..!
ME STUPIDHEAD BOZO!?!...
YEAH YOU STUPIDHEAD BOZO!!!
I HATE YOU!
I HATE YOU MORE!
.....
......
NO I DON'T.
I DON'T EITHER.
JEEZ LOUISE THOUGH... GROUNDED FOR THE REST OF OUR LIVES AND WE NEVER EVEN GOT TO SMOKE ANY OF IT.
WELL MAYBE IT'S FOR THE BEST-- AT LEAST WE DIDN'T LIKE, "O.D." OR ANYTHING
OH SHUT UP STACEY.
SIGH.
SIGH.

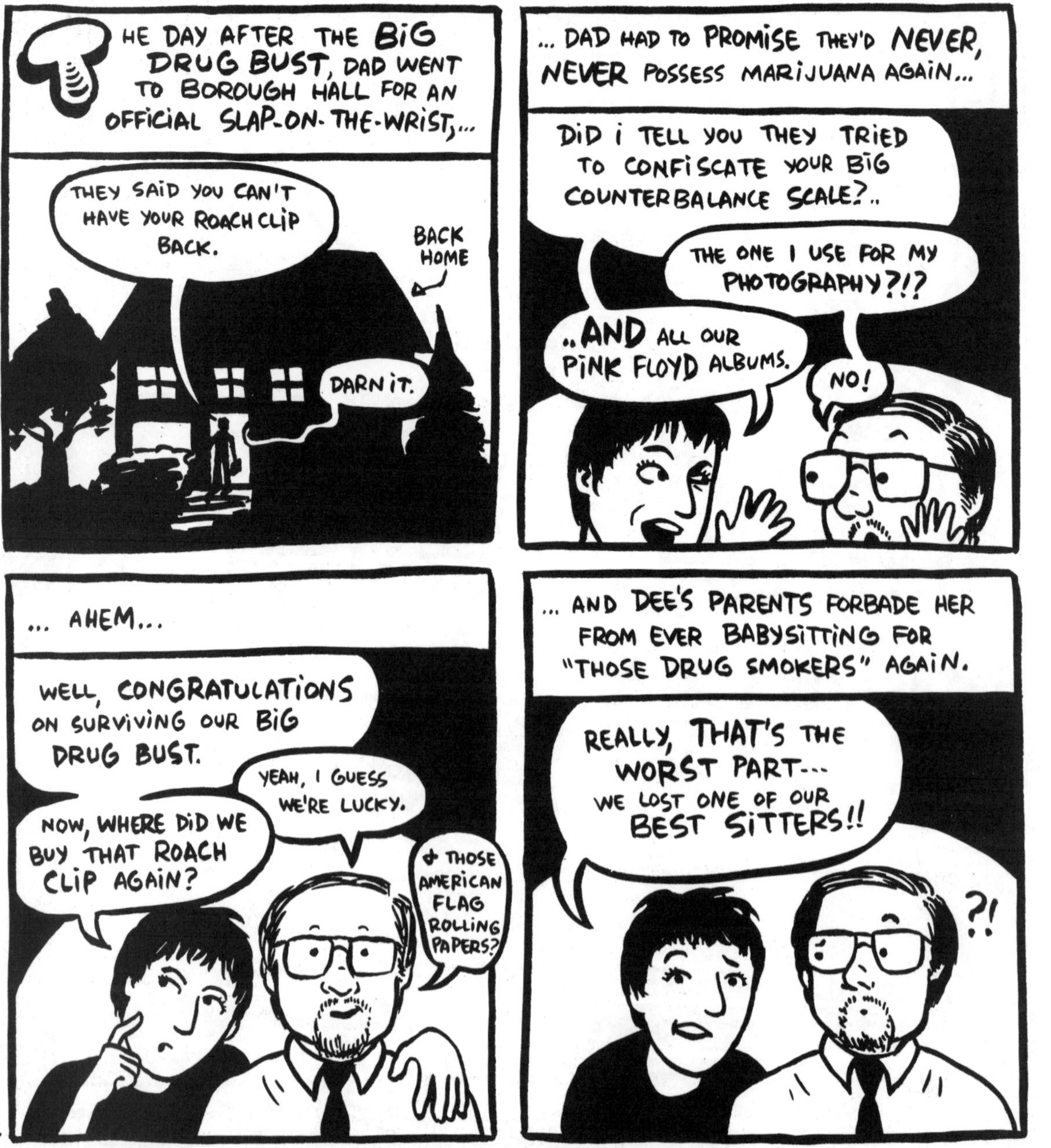
THE DAY AFTER THE BIG DRUG BUST, DAD WENT TO BOROUGH HALL FOR AN OFFICIAL SLAP-ON-THE-WRIST,...
THEY SAID YOU CAN'T HAVE YOUR ROACH CLIP BACK.
BACK HOME
DARN IT.
... DAD HAD TO PROMISE THEY'D NEVER, NEVER POSSESS MARIJUANA AGAIN...
DID I TELL YOU THEY TRIED TO CONFISCATE YOUR BIG COUNTERBALANCE SCALE?..
THE ONE I USE FOR MY PHOTOGRAPHY?!?
..AND ALL OUR PINK FLOYD ALBUMS.
NO!
... AHEM...
WELL, CONGRATULATIONS ON SURVIVING OUR BIG DRUG BUST.
YEAH, I GUESS WE'RE LUCKY.
NOW, WHERE DID WE BUY THAT ROACH CLIP AGAIN?
& THOSE AMERICAN FLAG ROLLING PAPERS?
... AND DEE'S PARENTS FORBADE HER FROM EVER BABYSITTING FOR "THOSE DRUG SMOKERS" AGAIN.
REALLY, THAT'S THE WORST PART... WE LOST ONE OF OUR BEST SITTERS!!
?!

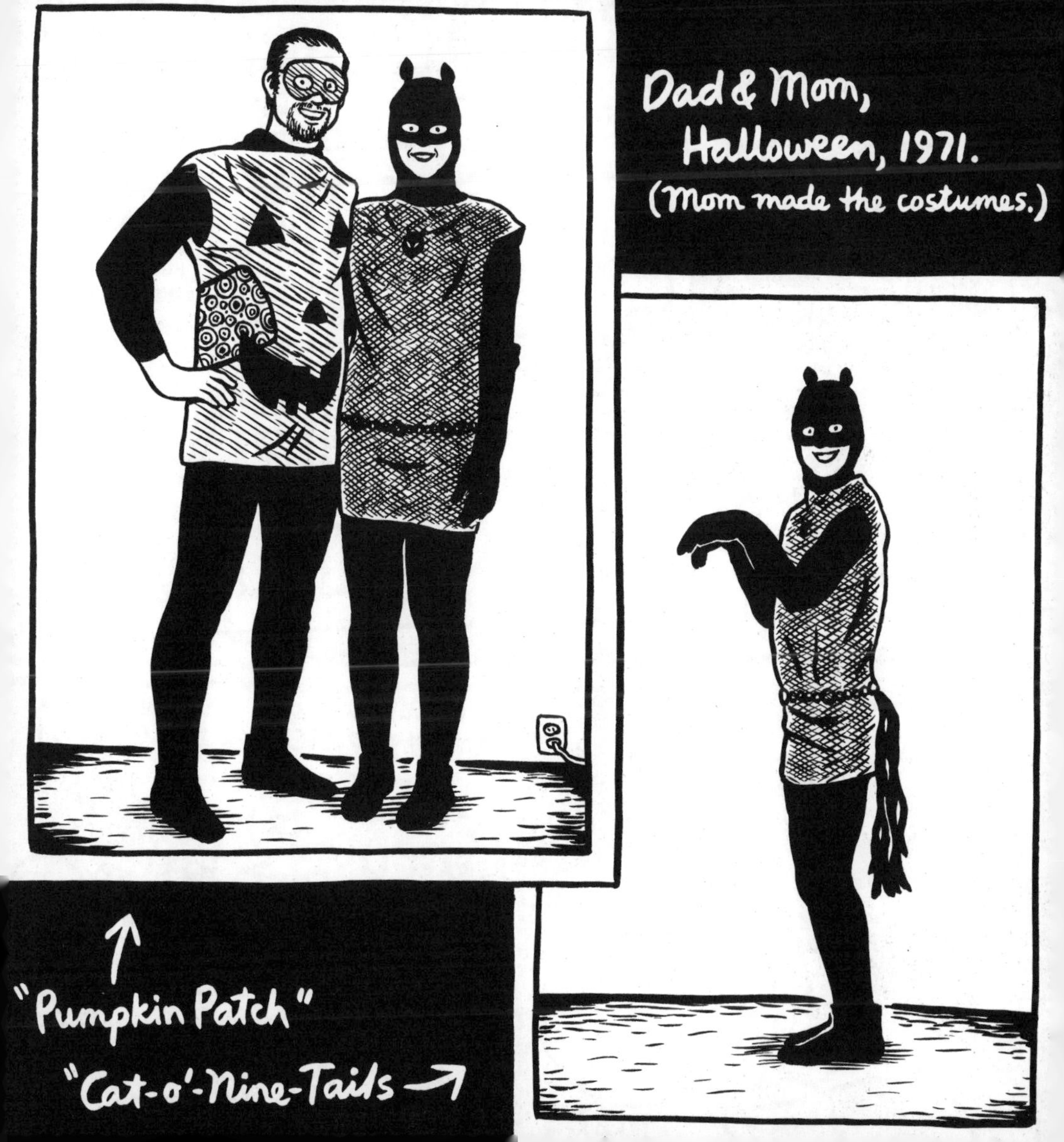
Dad & Mom,
Halloween, 1971.
(Mom made the costumes.)
"Pumpkin Patch"
"Cat-o'-Nine-Tails

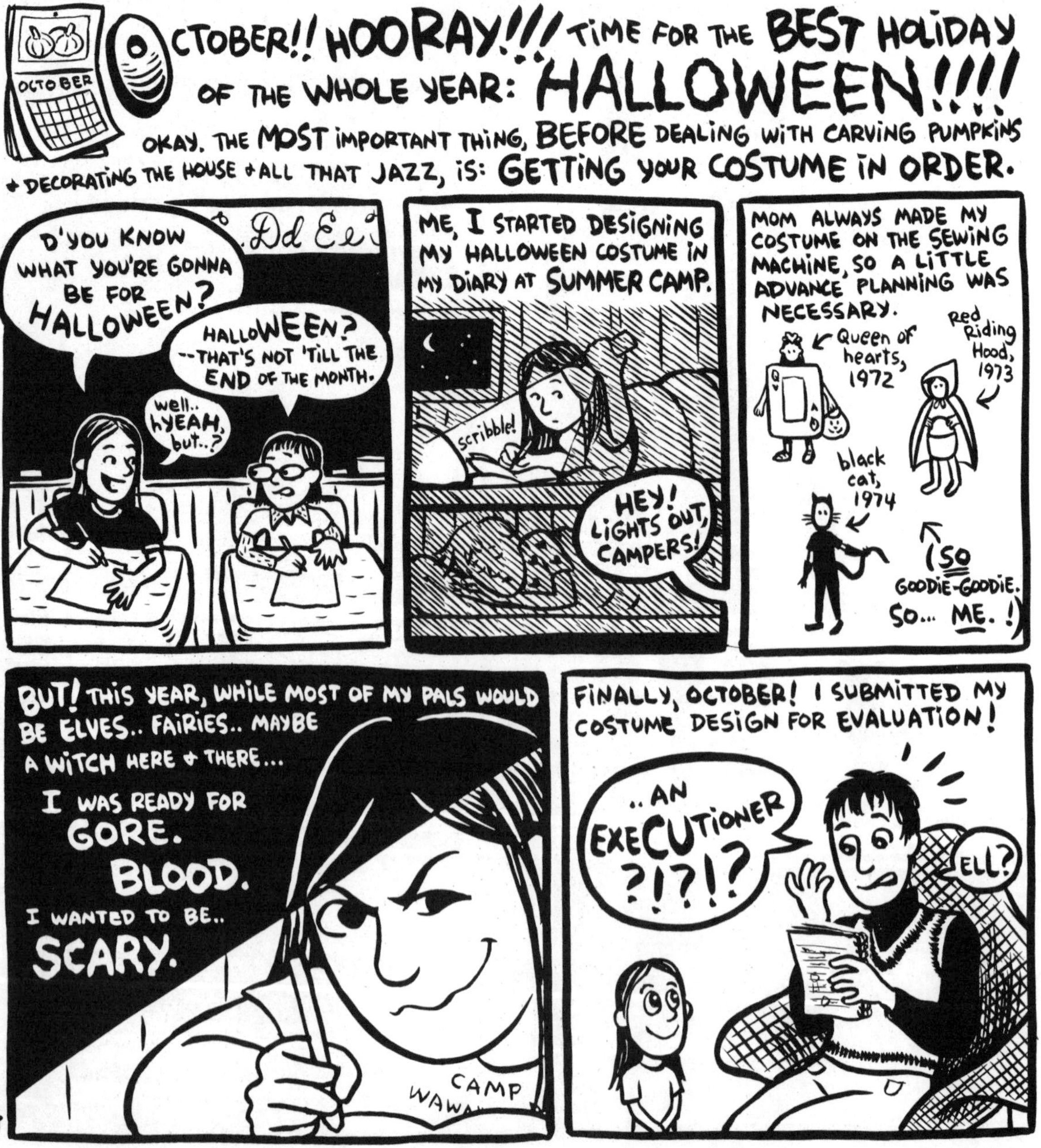

OCTOBER
OCTOBER!! HOORAY!!!! TIME FOR THE BEST HOLIDAY OF THE WHOLE YEAR: HALLOWEEN!!!!
OKAY. THE MOST IMPORTANT THING, BEFORE DEALING WITH CARVING PUMPKINS & DECORATING THE HOUSE & ALL THAT JAZZ, IS: GETTING YOUR COSTUME IN ORDER.
D'YOU KNOW WHAT YOU'RE GONNA BE FOR HALLOWEEN?
HALLOWEEN? --THAT'S NOT 'TILL THE END OF THE MONTH.
well.. hYEAH, but..?
ME, I STARTED DESIGNING MY HALLOWEEN COSTUME IN MY DIARY AT SUMMER CAMP.
scribble!
HEY! LIGHTS OUT, CAMPERS!
MOM ALWAYS MADE MY COSTUME ON THE SEWING MACHINE, SO A LITTLE ADVANCE PLANNING WAS NECESSARY.
Queen of hearts, 1972
Red Riding Hood, 1973
black cat, 1974
(SO GOODIE-GOODIE. SO... ME.!)
BUT! THIS YEAR, WHILE MOST OF MY PALS WOULD BE ELVES.. FAIRIES.. MAYBE A WITCH HERE & THERE...
I WAS READY FOR GORE.
BLOOD.
I WANTED TO BE.. SCARY.
CAMP WAWA
FINALLY, OCTOBER! I SUBMITTED MY COSTUME DESIGN FOR EVALUATION!
.. AN EXECUTIONER ?!?!?
ELL?

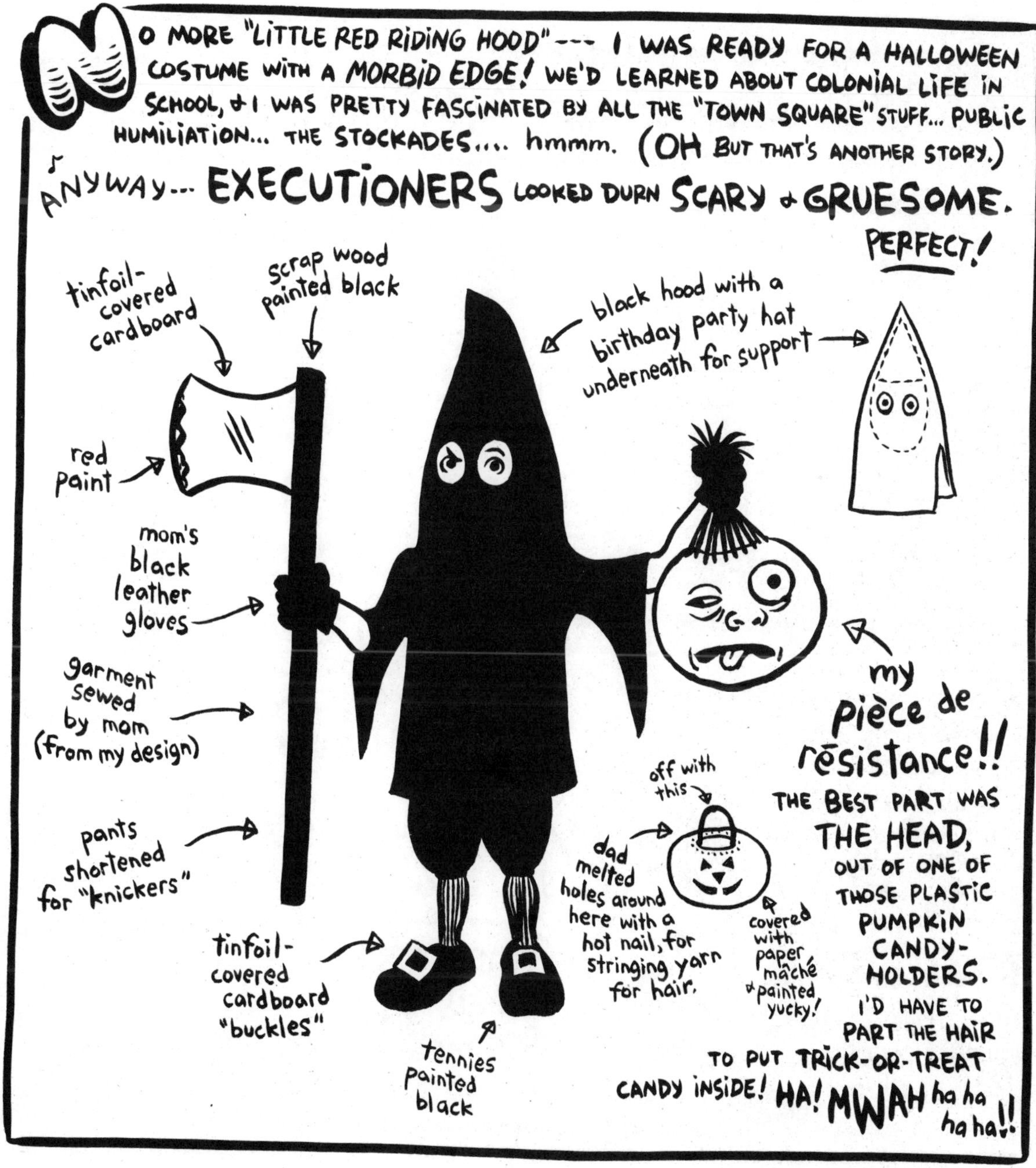
NO MORE "LITTLE RED RIDING HOOD"--- I WAS READY FOR A HALLOWEEN COSTUME WITH A MORBID EDGE! WE'D LEARNED ABOUT COLONIAL LIFE IN SCHOOL, & I WAS PRETTY FASCINATED BY ALL THE "TOWN SQUARE" STUFF... PUBLIC HUMILIATION... THE STOCKADES.... hmmm. (OH BUT THAT'S ANOTHER STORY.)
ANYWAY... EXECUTIONERS LOOKED DURN SCARY & GRUESOME.
PERFECT!
tinfoil-covered cardboard
scrap wood painted black
black hood with a birthday party hat underneath for support
red paint
mom's black leather gloves
garment sewed by mom (from my design)
pants shortened for "knickers"
tinfoil-covered cardboard "buckles"
tennies painted black
my pièce de résistance!!
off with this
dad melted holes around here with a hot nail, for stringing yarn for hair.
covered with paper mâché & painted yucky!
THE BEST PART WAS THE HEAD, OUT OF ONE OF THOSE PLASTIC PUMPKIN CANDY-HOLDERS. I'D HAVE TO PART THE HAIR TO PUT TRICK-OR-TREAT CANDY INSIDE! HA! MWAH ha ha ha ha!!

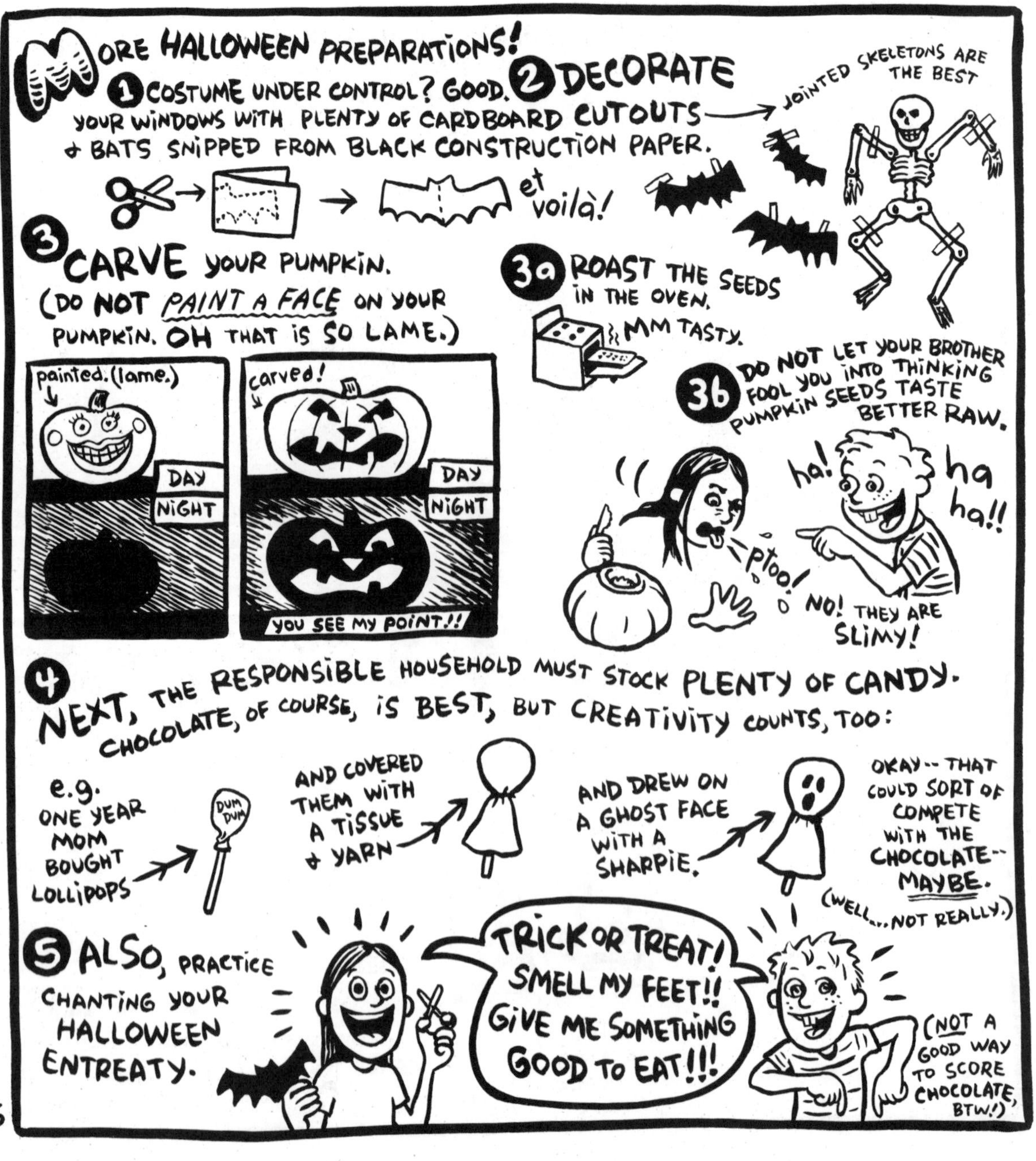
MORE HALLOWEEN PREPARATIONS!
1 COSTUME UNDER CONTROL? GOOD. 2 DECORATE
YOUR WINDOWS WITH PLENTY OF CARDBOARD CUTOUTS
& BATS SNIPPED FROM BLACK CONSTRUCTION PAPER.
JOINTED SKELETONS ARE THE BEST
et voilà!
3 CARVE YOUR PUMPKIN.
(DO NOT PAINT A FACE ON YOUR PUMPKIN. OH THAT IS SO LAME.)
3a ROAST THE SEEDS IN THE OVEN.
MM TASTY.
painted. (lame.)
DAY
NIGHT
carved!
DAY
NIGHT
YOU SEE MY POINT!!
3b DO NOT LET YOUR BROTHER FOOL YOU INTO THINKING PUMPKIN SEEDS TASTE BETTER RAW.
ha!
ha ha!!
ptoo!
NO! THEY ARE SLIMY!
4 NEXT, THE RESPONSIBLE HOUSEHOLD MUST STOCK PLENTY OF CANDY.
CHOCOLATE, OF COURSE, IS BEST, BUT CREATIVITY COUNTS, TOO:
e.g. ONE YEAR MOM BOUGHT LOLLIPOPS
DUM DUM
AND COVERED THEM WITH A TISSUE & YARN
AND DREW ON A GHOST FACE WITH A SHARPIE.
OKAY -- THAT COULD SORT OF COMPETE WITH THE CHOCOLATE -- MAYBE.
(WELL... NOT REALLY.)
5 ALSO, PRACTICE CHANTING YOUR HALLOWEEN ENTREATY.
TRICK OR TREAT! SMELL MY FEET!! GIVE ME SOMETHING GOOD TO EAT!!!
(NOT A GOOD WAY TO SCORE CHOCOLATE, BTW!)

DAD WAS REALLY INTO **PHOTOGRAPHY** IN THE EARLY SEVENTIES, SO WE HAVE LOTS OF PICTURES OF MOM & MATT & ME, BUT NOT SO MANY OF MY DAD. ONCE A YEAR OR SO, THOUGH, DAD WOULD SET UP HIS TRIPOD & TAKE A **FAMILY PORTRAIT.** THIS IS ONE HE TOOK IN 1971:

WHILE HE TOOK LIGHT READINGS & STUFF, WE'D POSE, LEAVING AN EMPTY SPACE FOR HIM TO JUMP INTO THE PICTURE WHILE THE LITTLE RED LIGHT WAS STILL FLASHING. (MADE ME NERVOUS! -- WOULD HE MAKE IT IN TIME?!!)

THE BLACK BLOB IN MATT'S ARMS IS OUR GUINEA PIG, LADY.*

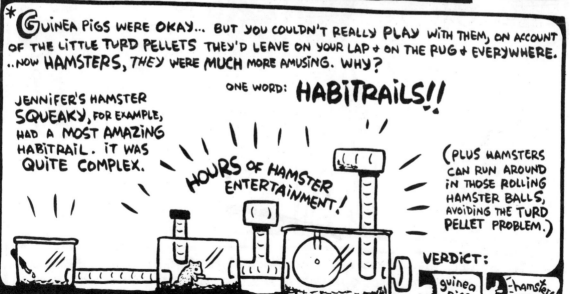

*GUINEA PIGS WERE OKAY... BUT YOU COULDN'T REALLY **PLAY** WITH THEM, ON ACCOUNT OF THE LITTLE TURD PELLETS THEY'D LEAVE ON YOUR LAP & ON THE RUG & EVERYWHERE. ..NOW HAMSTERS, *THEY* WERE **MUCH** MORE AMUSING. WHY?

ONE WORD: **HABITRAILS!!**

JENNIFER'S HAMSTER **SQUEAKY,** FOR EXAMPLE, HAD A MOST AMAZING HABITRAIL. IT WAS **QUITE COMPLEX.**

HOURS OF HAMSTER ENTERTAINMENT!

(PLUS HAMSTERS CAN RUN AROUND IN THOSE ROLLING HAMSTER BALLS, AVOIDING THE TURD PELLET PROBLEM.)

VERDICT:

guinea pigs.

hamsters!

137

"SINCE I MAKE MOST OF MY MONEY BY LOOKING MY WORST WHEN PLAYING VARIOUS CHARACTERS, I TAKE GREAT PRIDE IN HOW I LOOK AS **RUTH BUZZI**," ADMITS THE WELL-LOVED CHARACTER ACTRESS/COMEDIENNE. "I HAVE A VERY STRANGE FACE, SO I HAVE TO MAKE THE MOST OF IT."

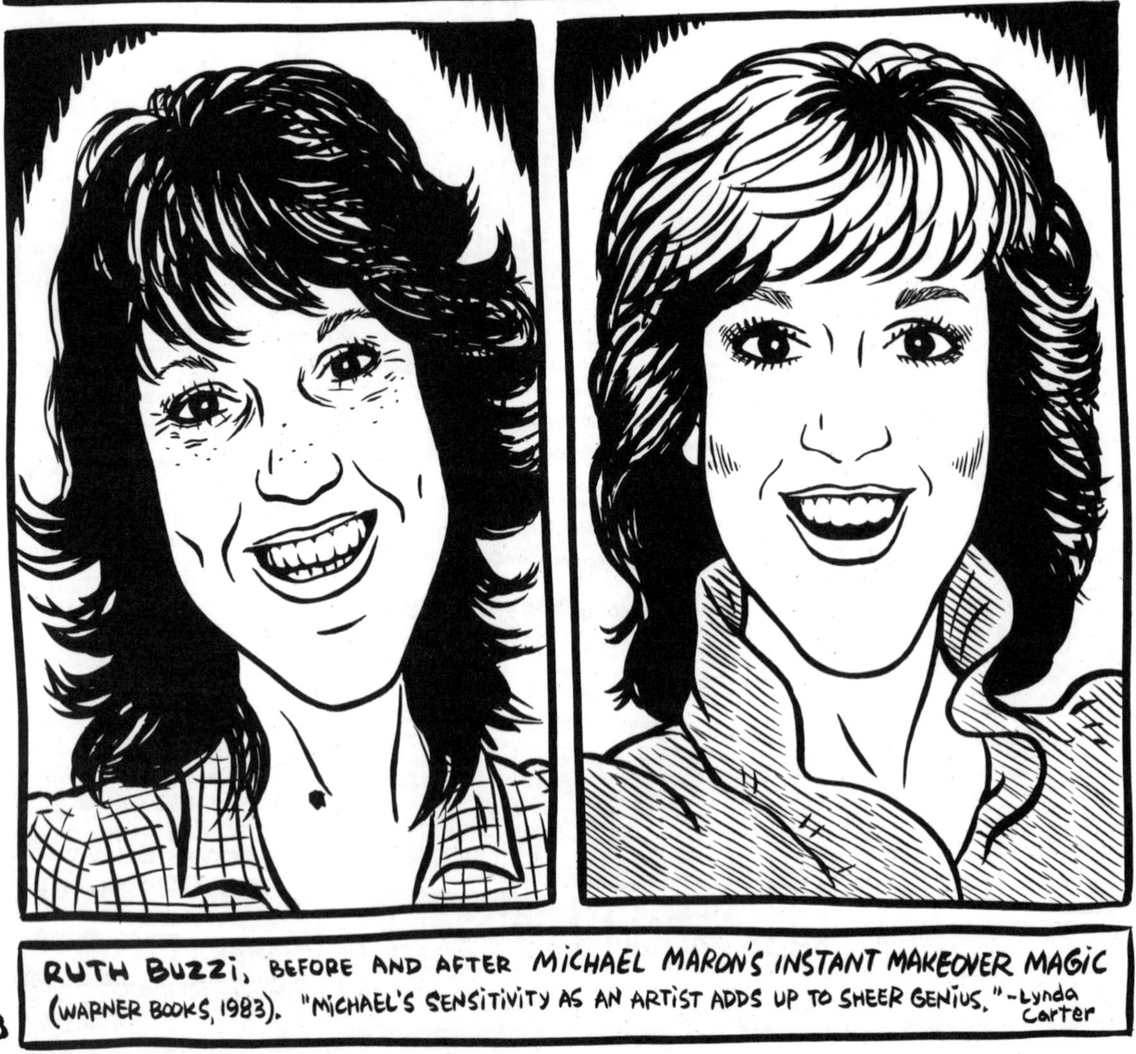

RUTH BUZZI, BEFORE AND AFTER *MICHAEL MARON'S INSTANT MAKEOVER MAGIC* (WARNER BOOKS, 1983). "MICHAEL'S SENSITIVITY AS AN ARTIST ADDS UP TO SHEER GENIUS." –Lynda Carter

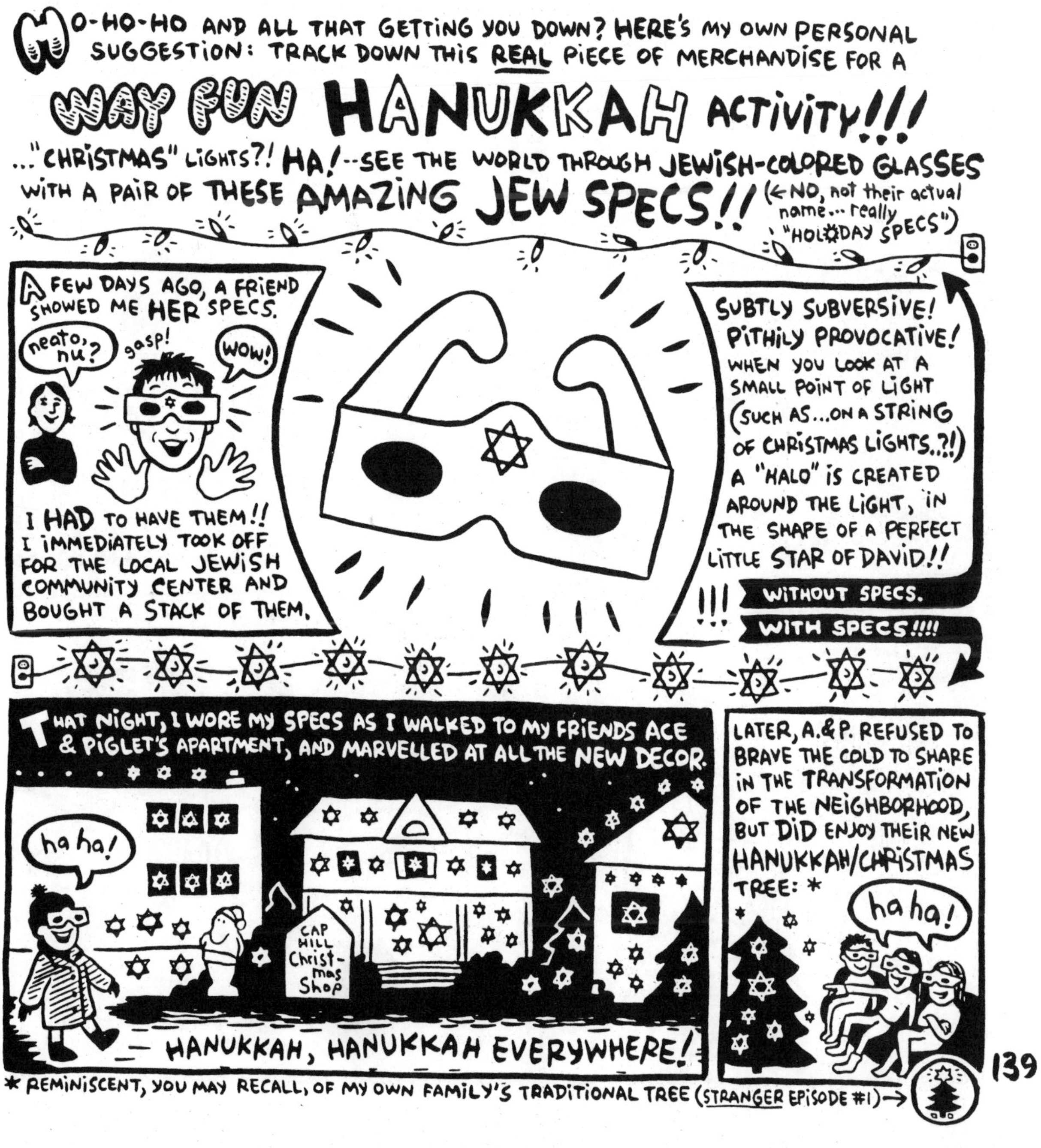
HO-HO-HO AND ALL THAT GETTING YOU DOWN? HERE'S MY OWN PERSONAL SUGGESTION: TRACK DOWN THIS REAL PIECE OF MERCHANDISE FOR A
WAY FUN HANUKKAH ACTIVITY!!!
..."CHRISTMAS" LIGHTS?! HA! --SEE THE WORLD THROUGH JEWISH-COLORED GLASSES WITH A PAIR OF THESE AMAZING JEW SPECS!!
(← NO, not their actual name... really "HOLIDAY SPECS")
A FEW DAYS AGO, A FRIEND SHOWED ME HER SPECS.
neato, nu?
gasp!
WOW!
I HAD TO HAVE THEM!! I IMMEDIATELY TOOK OFF FOR THE LOCAL JEWISH COMMUNITY CENTER AND BOUGHT A STACK OF THEM.
SUBTLY SUBVERSIVE! PITHILY PROVOCATIVE! WHEN YOU LOOK AT A SMALL POINT OF LIGHT (SUCH AS...ON A STRING OF CHRISTMAS LIGHTS..?!) A "HALO" IS CREATED AROUND THE LIGHT, IN THE SHAPE OF A PERFECT LITTLE STAR OF DAVID!!
!!!
WITHOUT SPECS.
WITH SPECS!!!!
THAT NIGHT, I WORE MY SPECS AS I WALKED TO MY FRIENDS ACE & PIGLET'S APARTMENT, AND MARVELLED AT ALL THE NEW DECOR.
ha ha!
CAP HILL Christmas Shop
HANUKKAH, HANUKKAH EVERYWHERE!
LATER, A.&P. REFUSED TO BRAVE THE COLD TO SHARE IN THE TRANSFORMATION OF THE NEIGHBORHOOD, BUT DID ENJOY THEIR NEW HANUKKAH/CHRISTMAS TREE: *
ha ha!
* REMINISCENT, YOU MAY RECALL, OF MY OWN FAMILY'S TRADITIONAL TREE (STRANGER EPISODE #1) →

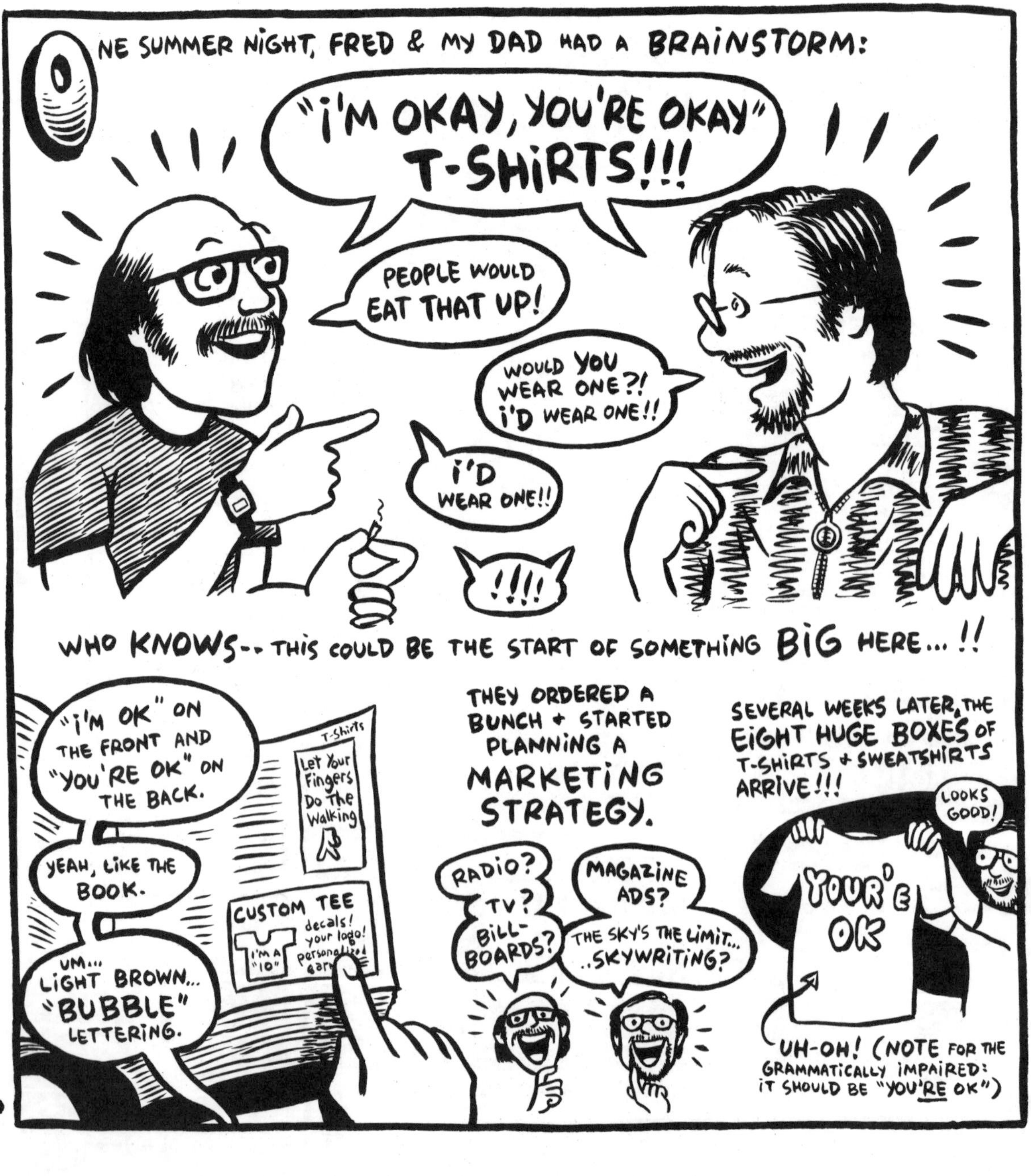
ONE SUMMER NIGHT, FRED & MY DAD HAD A BRAINSTORM:
"I'M OKAY, YOU'RE OKAY" T-SHIRTS!!!
PEOPLE WOULD EAT THAT UP!
WOULD YOU WEAR ONE?! I'D WEAR ONE!!
I'D WEAR ONE!!
!!!!
WHO KNOWS -- THIS COULD BE THE START OF SOMETHING BIG HERE... !!
"I'M OK" ON THE FRONT AND "YOU'RE OK" ON THE BACK.
YEAH, LIKE THE BOOK.
UM... LIGHT BROWN... "BUBBLE" LETTERING.
T-Shirts
Let Your Fingers Do The Walking
CUSTOM TEE
decals! your logo! personalized
I'M A "10"
THEY ORDERED A BUNCH + STARTED PLANNING A MARKETING STRATEGY.
RADIO? TV? BILL-BOARDS?
MAGAZINE ADS?
THE SKY'S THE LIMIT... ..SKYWRITING?
SEVERAL WEEKS LATER, THE EIGHT HUGE BOXES OF T-SHIRTS + SWEATSHIRTS ARRIVE!!!
LOOKS GOOD!
YOUR'E OK
UH-OH! (NOTE FOR THE GRAMMATICALLY IMPAIRED: IT SHOULD BE "YOU'RE OK")

After wrangling with the T-shirt people about whose fault the misspelling was, Dad & Fred got a new, correctly-spelled batch of shirts. Phil & Alona from the Unitarian Society posed for the ads:

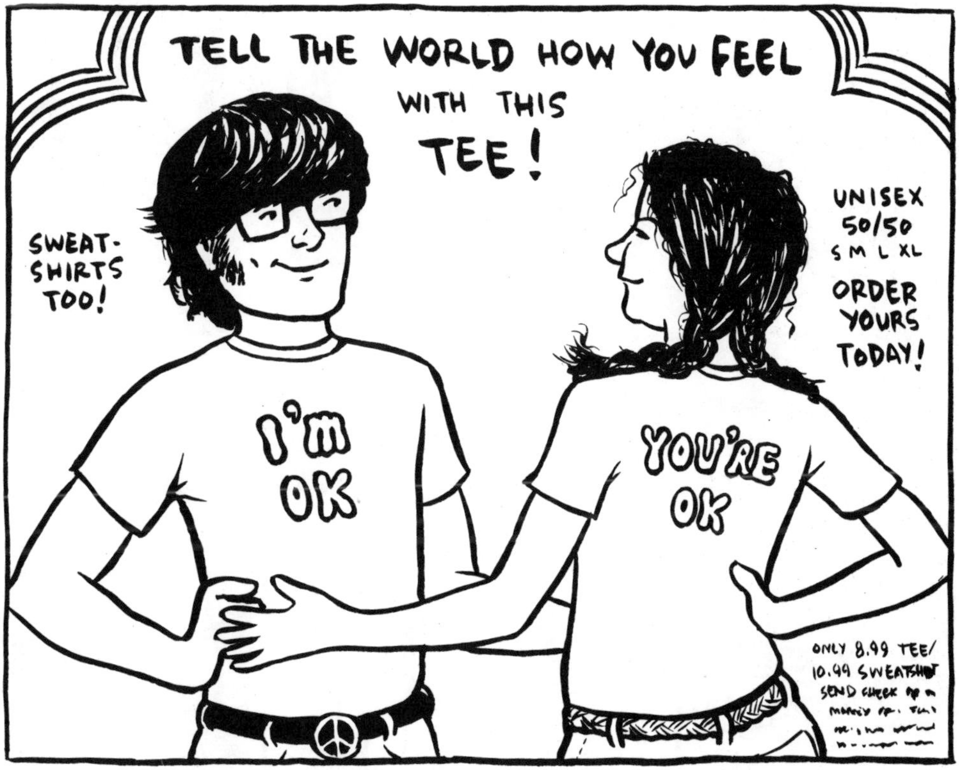
TELL THE WORLD HOW YOU FEEL
WITH THIS
TEE!
SWEAT-SHIRTS TOO!
UNISEX
50/50
S M L XL
ORDER YOURS TODAY!
I'M OK
YOU'RE OK
ONLY 8.99 TEE/

Surely all those readers the book had "helped to help themselves" would want to sport one of these..?

... Dad & Fred waited for the orders to pour in!!

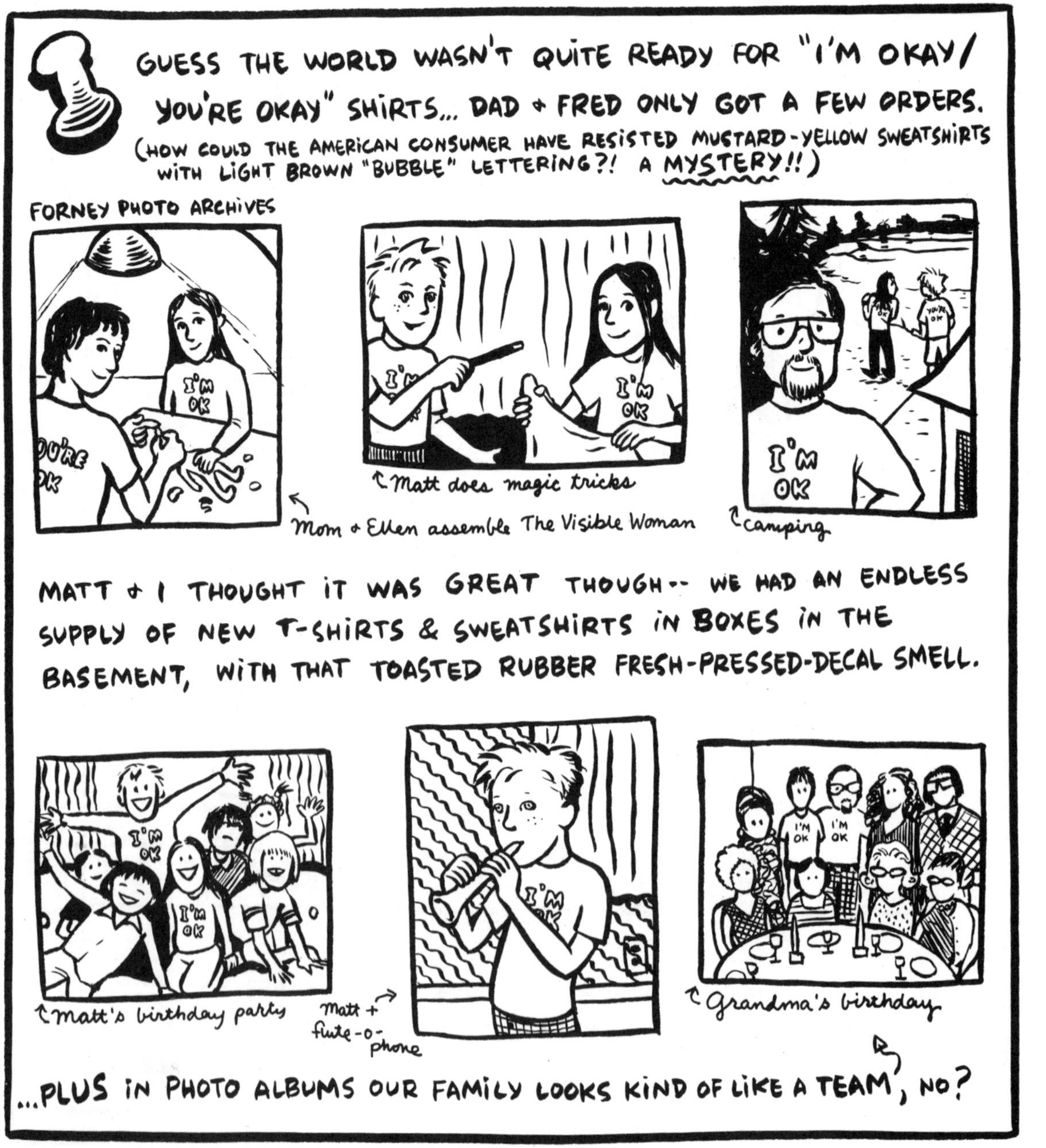
GUESS THE WORLD WASN'T QUITE READY FOR "I'M OKAY/ YOU'RE OKAY" SHIRTS... DAD & FRED ONLY GOT A FEW ORDERS.
(HOW COULD THE AMERICAN CONSUMER HAVE RESISTED MUSTARD-YELLOW SWEATSHIRTS WITH LIGHT BROWN "BUBBLE" LETTERING?! A MYSTERY!!)
FORNEY PHOTO ARCHIVES
YOU'RE OK
I'M OK
Mom & Ellen assemble The Visible Woman
I'M OK
I'M OK
Matt does magic tricks
YOU'RE OK
I'M OK
camping
MATT & I THOUGHT IT WAS GREAT THOUGH-- WE HAD AN ENDLESS SUPPLY OF NEW T-SHIRTS & SWEATSHIRTS IN BOXES IN THE BASEMENT, WITH THAT TOASTED RUBBER FRESH-PRESSED-DECAL SMELL.
I'M OK
I'M OK
Matt's birthday party
Matt + flute-o-phone
I'M OK
I'M OK
Grandma's birthday
...PLUS IN PHOTO ALBUMS OUR FAMILY LOOKS KIND OF LIKE A TEAM, NO?

THE
END!

www.ellenforney.com